AMERICAN FURNITURE

Queen Anne

and Chippendale Periods

AMERICAN FURNITURE

Queen Anne
and Chippendale Periods

IN THE HENRY FRANCIS DU PONT WINTERTHUR MUSEUM

A Winterthur Book by
JOSEPH DOWNS

Foreword by Henry Francis du Pont

BONANZA BOOKS
NEW YORK

FOREWORD

Joseph Downs, who has written this study of the Queen Anne and Chippendale furniture at Winterthur, has asked me to tell a little about how I started the collection. I am happy to contribute my word to this important book.

A philosophy of collecting is of necessity highly subjective. Each individual who collects anything of a serious nature thinks in increasingly creative terms, almost as if his growing collection were a kind of artistic medium. This is true, I think, because a foremost drive for the collector is a love of his materials. To him these are of such beauty or importance as to cause him to preserve them, by no means for himself alone, but in order to share his discoveries. Because he believes in what he collects, he wants others to do so, too.

These factors, I realize, were basic to the making of my collection. It seemed to me that early-American arts and crafts had not been given the recognition they deserved. Serious collectors had for too long focused their attention on Europe and the East, to the exclusion of this country. I hoped, therefore, that, by preserving under one roof examples of architecture, furniture, and widely divergent early-American materials of all kinds, interest in this field would be stimulated and that the magnificent contribution of our past would be helped to come into its own.

My background knowledge of my subject was, at the outset, very limited. All my life, however, the actual process of collecting had attracted me. Minerals, birds' eggs, and stamps were among my earliest hobbies; and later on, during visits to Europe, I began to gather furniture, porcelain, and textiles. Repeated trips to many museums gave me endless pleasure as well as training in colors and proportion, and seeing many French and English houses was a liberal education in period interiors.

A visit to Mrs. Watson Webb's house in Shelburne, Vermont, in 1923 gave me, however, my first introduction to an early-American interior. Among other things, I was fascinated by the colors of a pine dresser filled with pink Staffordshire plates. Seeing Harry Sleeper's house in Gloucester, Massachusetts, a few days later made me decide to build an American house at Southhampton.

One day that autumn I bought a dated chest of drawers and some Philadelphia woodwork in Pennsylvania — my first American antiques. At about the same time I was shown several houses in and near Chestertown, Maryland, where I bought paneled rooms. I also found some simpler rooms with paneled fireplace ends in Massachusetts.

When I had got these different rooms together, I asked an architect, the late John W. Cross, to draw me plans for a house to incorporate them, keeping the original sizes and placing of windows and doors of the rooms.

When Chestertown House, as I called it, was finished, I equipped it with early furniture, some much earlier than the house, which was in the style of about 1770. As my only acquaintance with American mahogany was with the Empire veneered variety which had been in the home of my family and which I heartily disliked, I decided we would not have a piece of it in Southampton; my furniture there was pine, walnut, fruit, and other native woods. These early pieces are all now at Winterthur.

The first auction I attended was in June, 1924, in Connecticut. There I bought my first iron floor lights and a slant-top desk with manifold later embellishments which by now have turned a completely different color. Luckily I was not the successful bidder on a straight-leg wing chair with curly maple wings, which at the time I thought was the ultimate!

When Chestertown House was almost finished I had occasion to buy another paneled room from Chestertown. I realized it was too sophisticated for the other rooms in the Southampton house; so for the time being I stored it in my barn in Delaware. As time went on, I developed the plan of adding this and other rooms to Winterthur, my family home near Wilmington, in order to create a wing that would show America as it had been. Through friends I learned of Belle Isle house at Boer, Virginia; the Port Royal house near Frankford Junction, Pennsylvania; Readbourne in Maryland; and other eighteenth-century houses from which I was able to acquire much of the original woodwork.

With all of this woodwork on hand, I asked the architect, Albert Ely Ives, to draw plans; as the rooms were to be kept in their original height and width, with the windows and doors as they had been in the old houses, it was quite an undertaking. The rooms were all of the Chippendale period, and I had some Chinese wallpaper of the same date for the entrance hall and the sitting room, which was to be the transition between the old house and the new. Therefore I began collecting Chippendale furniture. This appealed to me for various reasons. It was sturdy, and suitable for practical use. Also, I was interested in its many variations, not only within one type, such as Philadelphia chairs, but among the widely differing products of regions showing different influences — Boston, Newport, New York, and Philadelphia.

After a very short time I felt I must Americanize the rest of the house. Mr. Ives had moved to Honolulu, and I was fortunate in meeting the late Thomas T. Waterman, who helped me install seventeenth-century and early and late eighteenth-century rooms, the court, and Shop Lane.

During the years that I have collected, I have had many satisfactions and only one regret. The latter is for the things I might have acquired, but allowed to escape me. My satisfactions are in the contacts I have made with a great number of interesting people, in my greater consciousness of the development of our country, and in my immensely increased appreciation of the generations that have preceded us.

Looking back on it now, I also am glad that I have been able to preserve in some degree the evidences of early life in America, and I am gratified to feel that others too may find my collection a source of knowledge and inspiration.

H. F. du Pont

ACKNOWLEDGMENTS

Many individuals and institutions have given helpful advice and assistance in one way or another for the completion of this book. For permission to use original documents, the author is indebted to Herbert O. Brigham, librarian of the Newport Historical Society; Stephen T. Riley, librarian of the Massachusetts Historical Society, Bart Anderson, of the Chester County Historical Society; the Staffs of the Library Company of Philadelphia; the Historical Society of Pennsylvania; the New Hampshire Historical Society; the Cooper Museum in New York; the New York Genealogical and Biographical Society; the New York State Library at Albany; the Hall of Records in Manhattan; the Print Department of the Metropolitan Museum of Art; the Widener Library of Harvard University; and the Connecticut State Library at Hartford. Special thanks are due to Mrs. Alfred Coxe Prime for the privilege of having access to transcripts of newspaper advertisements in her possession and the unrestricted use of them; and to Arthur K. McComb for his persistent efforts in securing copies of original documents. Charles A. MacLellan gave valuable assistance in the identification of southern woods.

Many members of the Museum Staff have been ready to cooperate at all times. To my colleague, Charles F. Montgomery, for his suggestions, constant interest, and enthusiasm in the progress of the book, I am especially grateful, and to Miss M. Elinor Betts for her careful attention to detail in the final stages of its preparation. To Gilbert Ask for his skill and painstaking care in photographing the furniture, grateful acknowledgment is also made. In the repair and restoration of the furniture before photography, the fine craftsmanship of Arthur Van Reeth and of Park J. McCann was appreciated.

Cecil Scott, associate editor of The Macmillan Company, was helpful at all times with advice and constructive criticism for the completion of the book.

To Henry Francis du Pont my sincere thanks are given for the opportunity of studying and interpreting this superb collection, and to the Directors of the Henry Francis du Pont Winterthur Museum for undertaking its publication.

All of the colored photographs were made by Gottscho-Schleisner except Plate I, which was made by James Ricau.

J. D.

CONTENTS

FOREWORD   V

ACKNOWLEDGMENTS   VII

INTRODUCTION   XI

NOTES TO THE INTRODUCTION   XXXIX

A GROUP OF QUEEN ANNE AND CHIPPENDALE INTERIORS   I-X

ILLUSTRATIONS FROM THE WINTERTHUR COLLECTION

     BEDS   FIGURES 1-10

     CHAIRS   11-164

     CHESTS   165-201

     CLOCKS   202-209

     COUCHES   210-212

     DESKS AND BOOKCASES   213-233

     FIRE SCREENS   234-241

     LOOKING GLASSES   242-268

     SOFAS   269-276

     STANDS   277-290

     STOOLS   291-298

     TABLES   299-388

     LABELS AND INSCRIPTIONS   389-401

NOTES TO THE PLATES AND ILLUSTRATIONS

INDEX

INTRODUCTION

The superb collection of Queen Anne and Chippendale furniture at Winterthur provides an opportunity without parallel to observe the finest expression of eighteenth-century craftsmanship as it developed in the northern, middle, and southern colonies. The range is wide, beginning with the simple curvilinear style as it emerged from the ponderous weight of seventeenth-century forms, and growing luxuriant with carved ornament, gilding, and veneers until its culmination in the phenomenal richness of the rococo style just before the Revolution.

The names *Queen Anne* and *Chippendale* have come to describe two of the principal styles of American furniture, although none of it was made during the reign of Queen Anne or by Thomas Chippendale. As the names imply, the structural lines and ornamental detail found their roots in English furniture, from which they flourished independent of the parent stock.

In the late seventeenth century the form of English furniture developed from royal alliances with Holland and with the influx of Huguenot craftsmen expelled from France, when Europe had grown rich from the East Indian trade and her farspread colonies. As the new century began, the influences of the Far East mingled with those of Europe. Queen Anne chairs, for example, echo the shape of Chinese porcelains in their splats; the origin of their claw-and-ball feet may be the dragon's claw grasping a pearl, the ancient Oriental symbol of evil in the world.

The design of furniture as a whole assumed a fresh aspect in this age of walnut. It attained new standards of human comfort by the invention of a greater variety of forms, in the coordinated curves of its structural lines, and in its reduced scale from a monumental palace style to one suited to domestic use. This was an age of able craftsmen trained by the companies or guilds through long apprenticeship and strict standards of performance. In the era of expanding prosperity following Marlborough's victories, great houses were built and furnished — Blenheim, Castle Howard, Houghton Hall, and smaller manor houses without number. The eighteenth century was the golden age of living, of leisure, taste, intellectual curiosity, and culture matched by the extremes of poverty, ignorance, and indifference to human suffering. Hogarth could lampoon them in his *Marriage à la Mode* and *Gin Lane*. In the last years of George II the architectural fantasy at Badminton with its Chinese pagoda interiors or of Strawberry Hill lathed in Gothic fan vaulting found ready interpreters to furnish them. Chippendale was among the first who combined and adapted the genius of others to create a style and cap it with his name. The Chinese, French, and Gothic ornaments were grafted to the Anglo-Saxon stock as a proof of the sophisticated taste of gentlemen returned from the grand tour.

Cabinetmakers — Their Work and Their Times

Colonial cabinetmakers, chairmakers, upholsterers, gilders, japanners, and other artisans whose crafts contributed to the completion of furniture were loosely organized, dependent on the apprentice system of shop training youths and "finding" them for a period of years. Runaway apprentices were frequently advertised in newspapers from the earliest issues in 1705. In the Boston *Gazette*, May 10, 1756, there was this notice:

> "Ran-away from his Master Robert Macintire of Salem, on Monday the 3d Instant, an apprentice lad, named Benjamin Orne, jr, (who was lately impressed into Colonel Plaistead's Regiment) about 18 & ½ old, about 5 Foot high, a well sett, sturdy fellow; Had on, either a blue Serge Suit, lin'd with black, or a gray Jacket with a spotted Flannel one under it, wears a cap, and had Pewter Buckles on his Shoes . . ."

Newspapers in all colonial cities carried advice of newly arrived craftsmen, conversant with the newest fashions from London. With craftsmen moving from one city to another to escape competition or to find wider markets, the unstable character of the industry was constant. During the Revolution the occupation by the British of the most flourishing centers of furniture making, the blockading of the ports of trade, and the seizure of merchant ships, together with the departure of thousands of Loyalists from the colonies, saw almost the end of the Chippendale era of furniture. When trade and prosperity revived after the Peace, the artistic mood had shifted to the classical taste, although here and there the style persisted until after 1800.

Eighteenth-century colonial furniture at its best is recognized for the soundness of its conception, its appropriate ornament subservient to form, and its functional purpose. In general it is more sober in design than its English contemporaries with an ever-new interpretation of pattern. Even in simple furniture a rhythmic line and a balance of the salient elements of the composition are achieved.

Prosperity came to the American colonies early in the eighteenth century as their natural resources were developed for trade among themselves and with England and the West Indies. By and large the early settlers had come from the middle and lower classes — merchants, artisans, and servants, with a sprinkling of ne'er-do-wells and adventurers — but all had the desire to better themselves by economic security, freedom of worship, or easier living. Boston, the principal city of New England, had lost many in the early years by its narrow theocracy of clergy who exercised the leadership of Church and State. The Puritan John Cotton said, and Governor John Winthrop agreed, "Democracy I do not conceive that God ever did ordain as a fit government either for Church or Commonwealth."[1] Then by the renewal of its charter in 1688, the Province of Massachusetts Bay was governed by royal appointment, and religious dissenters were given the right of protection.

Although the Puritan influence long remained evident in customs and tradition, a taste for worldly things made steady headway, and commerce gained supremacy over religion as the dominant force in Massachusetts. At the end of the seventeenth century the population of Boston had risen to 7000 and had more than doubled by 1750. Thriving trade was the

The Notes to the Introduction are to be found on page XXXIX.

basis of prosperity; by 1740 there were 160 warehouses along the Boston waterfront. Fish, lumber, furniture, rum, whale oil, and shoes were important outgoing cargoes; sugar, molasses, mahogany, and slaves from the West Indies, and woolens, silks, wines, and other manufactured luxuries came by way of England. Fortunes were made, too, in privateering until it was outlawed in 1856, and traffic with pirates was not always scorned when the rewards were great.

As the capital of the Province, Boston became the seat of a miniature court patterned on English social life around which the more worldly element gathered. John Adams, on his way from Boston to the first Continental Congress in 1774, wrote from New York: "I have not seen one real gentleman, one well bred man, since I came to town." Further proof of the Bostonian's superiority came when he reached Philadelphia: "The morals of our people are much better; their manners are more polite and agreeable; they are purer English, our language is better, our taste is better, our persons are handsomer, our spirit is greater, our laws are wiser, our religion is superior, our education is better."[2]

The taste in living and the demand for the best in workmanship and design by the leaders in New England were recorded in their houses. Seldom are their furnishings now intact; but from contemporary examples of first-rate furniture, their pristine appearance may be visualized. In this period of American Queen Anne and Chippendale furniture commercial prosperity increased the demand for elegance and comfort and the innovations of new forms to satisfy it.

Sir William Pepperell, created a baronet by George II following the Siege of Louisburg, built at Kittery, Maine, a four-story gambrel-roofed mansion, paneled in the heavy molded style of the William and Mary period. Across the Piscataqua River in nearby Portsmouth, Archibald Macphaedris' brick house, buttressed with tall end chimneys, shows painted stair walls from Verelst's portraits of Indian sachems, and rich graining of exotic figure on the dining room paneled wainscot. At Portsmouth, too, Lieutenant Governor John Wentworth's house combined stained paneling with the great beams of the previous century. In Massachusetts comfortable middle-class houses were scattered well inland from the seaports, whence came the principal wealth of the colonists. In Deerfield, then a far outpost, the Reverend Jonathan Ashley was established in 1733 in a commodious dwelling, neatly wainscoted to match its neighbors, the John Williams and Sheldon houses, with scrolled-top Palladian doorways — all built since the fire and Massacre of 1704.[3] At Marblehead and Salem the four-square wooden mansions of Jeremiah Lee, "King" Hooper, and Jerathmeel Peirce preceded the prolific merchants' brick mansions on Chestnut Street. In Boston the house of the royal Governor Thomas Hutchinson, sacked at the beginning of the Revolution, was famous for its library, its furniture, and its handsome paneled rooms. Thomas Hancock, whose fortune from the usual privateering and commerce in slaves and other trading ventures was bequeathed to his nephew, John Hancock, lived in regal splendor overlooking Boston Common; the house, demolished nearly a century ago, contained both fine English and American furniture. Henry Vassall's house in Cambridge, remembered now as the home of Henry Wadsworth Longfellow, stands as the typical expression in wood of the New England Georgian style, its quoining grooved to imitate masonry, its interior carved in rococo detail, its fireplaces framed with Liverpool transfer-printed tiles. Isaac Royall and his family, shown in Smibert's famous portrait, lived in adjacent Medford; his commodious dwelling has deep, arched bays of great ingenuity and beauty flanking the parlor fireplace.

Well over 150 cabinetmakers, chairmakers, and carvers were active in Boston prior to the Revolution, but relatively little identified work of theirs is known.[4] John Pimm, a cabinetmaker, signed a handsome japanned highboy in the Queen Anne style; Thomas Johnston, a japanner and engraver active in 1732 and until 1767, may have decorated it; his son Thomas and son-in-law Daniel Rea painted clock dials, furniture, and floor cloths "in cubes, yellow & black diamonds, and turkey Fatchion." Benjamin Frothingham, who served as a major in the Revolution, gave a distinctive elegance to the block-front and reverse-serpentine-shaped desks and chests that he labeled with the trade cards neatly engraved by Nathaniel Hurd.[5] John Cogswell can now be credited with the finest known bombé-shaped chests and bookcases in the rocaille manner — one of them signed and dated as late as 1782. Simeon Skillin and his sons carved allegorical figures for ships and furniture and a plain, claw-foot merchant's desk for John Hancock. John Skillin, born in 1746, signed a serpentine-front chest with widespread claw feet. In Boston, too, Stone and Alexander made plain serpentine-front desks of fine simplicity, a type repeated in Salem and Newburyport by Abner Toppan, Joseph Short, and Elijah Sanderson, as well as by Daniel Clay in Greenfield well after the end of the colonial period. The last-named cabinetmaker was born in 1770, the son of a successful rum merchant who left a sizable fortune to the Episcopal Church. In Northampton Abner Barnard's cherry furniture, made for his daughter's marriage in 1774, has unusual grace in the plain Chippendale manner of the period and is carved with fine bird's-claw feet. Joseph Hosmer, in Concord, was exceptionally able and followed the same tradition as Frothingham in his block-front and serpentine-shaped cabinetwork of cherry and maple.[6]

Newport, founded nine years after Boston, was a flourishing and cosmopolitan seaport long in control of the Friends, although Portuguese Jews, West Indian planters, and Huguenots from the southern colonies were numerous there. After 1730 great fortunes were made in the triangular trade with Africa and the West Indies; rum from Newport was exchanged for slaves in Africa, who were exchanged for sugar and molasses in the Barbadoes, which were brought back to Newport for more rum. In 1770 Newport's foreign trade was greater than that of New York, but it was entirely destroyed while the British occupied the city from 1776 to 1779. French troops were quartered there after the British evacuation. Two famous houses of worship, the Synagogue and Trinity Church, as well as the Old State House, Deputy-Governor Nichols' mansion, the Redwood Library, and the Vernon House, with its chinoiserie frescoes admired by Rochambeau in 1780 carry the influence of Newport's inspired architect, Peter Harrison, or its able house carpenter, Richard Munday.

In Newport a group of cabinetmakers unique in the history of American craftsmanship were the Townsends and Goddards, twenty in all, of three generations, closely allied by their Quaker faith, their family loyalties and intermarriage, and their standards of excellence in furniture making.[7] Their superb performance has long been recognized in the unique block-front and shell-carved desks and bookcases, and chests of drawers, as well as in many distinctive patterns of chairs, tables, urn stands, and clock cases. Of those who were active during the Queen Anne and Chippendale periods, Christopher Townsend and his son John, and Job Townsend and his sons Job, Jr., and Edmund, and John Goddard are best known by the records of their work. The labeled desk and bookcase by Job Townsend and the dressing table he made in 1746 for Samuel Ward, later the governor of Rhode Island, gave only a promise of the burgeoning of the Newport school in the next generation. It was then that the genius of Edmund and John Townsend and the latter's brother-in-law John Goddard had full play. The shaped tea table made for Jabez Bowen and the desk and bookcase made for Joseph Brown by Goddard, the kneehole desk labeled by Edmund Townsend, and the chest of drawers nearly matching it signed by his cousin John Townsend in 1765 are among the choicest flowers in any field of cabinetmaking. In 1767 the combined efforts of the brothers Job and Edmund Townsend produced "a Large Mahogany Desk, at £330.0.0" for Nicholas Anderese, now unknown.[8]

Before the War disrupted all commerce, dispersed the merchants, and destroyed many of the wharves and houses of Newport, over fifty joiners, cabinetmakers, and carvers were active there. Adam Coe, although born in 1770, continued to work in the Chippendale style, as is proved by his signature on a fine sofa distinguished by its bold lines.

The coast of New Hampshire was explored by Captain John Smith, and his report in 1614 to Prince Charles first gave currency to the name *New England;* but it was Captain John Mason, a merchant from London, whose name of *New Hampshire* recalled his old home in Hampshire, England. The first settlement at Portsmouth was made for the profitable commerce of fishing, lumber, and shipbuilding; much later, John Paul Jones' famous *Ranger* was built there. The province grew slowly; by 1732 it had only 12,500 population, and until 1741 New Hampshire shared its governors with Massachusetts.

Among the joiners in New Hampshire John Gaines and Samuel Dunlap II are recognized for their individuality. Gaines went to Portsmouth from Ipswich in 1724 and worked there until his death in 1743. Gaines' son, George, a Major in the Revolution was active as a cabinetmaker until his death in 1809.[9] Dunlap, born in 1751 and apprenticed as a carpenter, worked at Henniker, Chester, and Salisbury and created a style of maple high chests, chairs, and desks unique in their combination of carved intaglio fans, scrolls, and open, interlaced pediments. The woodwork of his own house now moved to New Boston from Salisbury is carved with the same detail as his furniture. A curly-maple desk and bookcase signed by Walter Edge in Gilmanton and dated 1799 has a serpentine-curved base and corkscrew finials of Salem design.[10]

Connecticut, settled in the early 1630's by disaffected Puritans from the Massachusetts Bay Colony, was largely agricultural, although its manufactures developed at an early date. The country peddler and his wooden nutmeg eventually embodied Yankee ingenuity there.

The Commissioners for Trade and Plantations laid before Parliament on January 23, 1733, a report from the Governors of the colonies. Of Connecticut the report said: "Productions of this colony are Timber, Boards, all Sorts of English Grain, Hemp, Flax, Sheep, Cattle, Swine, Horses, Goats, and Tobacco, of which they export Horses and Lumber to the West Indies, and receive in return Sugar, Salt, Molasses, and Rum. We likewise find that their manufactures are very considerable, the people being generally employed in Tillage or

Building, and in Tanning, Shoemaking and other necessary Handycrafts, such as Taylors, Joiners, and Smiths work without which they could not subsist."[11]

Hartford was the earliest center of craftsmen; East Windsor, Middletown, Norwich, and Guilford developed schools of furniture. Among the early joiners of Connecticut, Benjamin Cheney was active in East Hartford before 1721, and his son Timothy was likewise a joiner. Another son Benjamin, Jr., made wooden clocks. Timothy Phelps, who died in 1756 in Hartford, and his son Timothy, Jr., were other early cabinetmakers; in 1784 the latter "Left New Unfinished desk, 3 Chairs Unfinished, 1 Unfinished Desk and Bookcase," and mahogany planks, brasses, and tools. His brother John, born in 1728, moved to Virginia and engaged in importing goods from New England for sale in the South.[12]

Benjamin Burnham was established by 1769 in Norwich after he had "sarved his time in Filadelphia"; his labeled work is a florid interpretation of block-front design flanked with stop-fluted pilasters highly ambitious in its conception. This was before the advent of John Townsend, the Quaker refugee from Newport who spent several war years (after his release from a British prison ship in 1777) in Norwich and Middletown and contributed to the development of the block-front style there.

Eliphalet (or Eliphelet) Chapin, born in East Windsor in 1741, also had a brief career in Philadelphia and was again established in East Windsor by 1771, where he worked until his death in 1807. His second cousin, Aaron Chapin, twelve years younger, spent nine years in East Windsor and probably learned furniture making in Eliphalet's shop.[13] He moved to Hartford in 1783. The cherrywood case furniture attributed to the Chapins has a peculiar grace lent to it by its narrow proportions, the occasional serpentine lines of its drawer fronts, and the delicate pedimented tops filled with pierced scrolls and surmounted by an airy "seahorse" cartouche. Fluted quarter columns often repeat a detail more prevalent on Philadelphia furniture. After Aaron Chapin died in 1838, he was mentioned as "a man of great piety, universally loved and respected. In early life he was a cabinetmaker, being quite a mechanical genius; later in life he cleaned and repaired watches." One of his engraved watch papers is in the Winterthur Collection. His son Laertes, born in 1778, was also a cabinetmaker in Hartford.

The signed double chest of Reuben Beman, of Kent, and the serpentine chest of drawers and the looking glass labeled by Kneeland and Adams, of Hartford, in the Winterthur Collection are excellent and hitherto unknown examples of Chippendale design by contemporaries of the better-known Chapins.

Aaron Roberts, in New Britain, has long been recognized as an able cabinetmaker of double chests and other case pieces in cherry; several with rope-twist columns at the corners may be from his hand. He lived from 1758 to 1830.[14]

When the English took over New York from the Dutch in 1664, a century of continuous struggle commenced between the local inhabitants and the royal agents. Trade with the Indians in furs for barter overseas was the mainspring of prosperity, together with rum and lumber, and was continued by smuggling when taxes and limitations became too oppressive. With a population of 8,622 in 1731, New York had only 12,000 inhabitants at the beginning of the Revolution, and many of them went into voluntary exile with the departure of the

British. The burning of Governor Tryon's house in 1770 by rebels indicated the temper of the city, conceded to be a focal point of resistance to royal authority. The price of war to New York was increased by the loss of all its commerce and a disastrous fire. After New York became the Federal Capital in 1784, with a new influx of population, wealth, and trade, it then had the aspect of a metropolis.

In Manhattan and the Hudson Valley, the old Dutch patroonships of vast acreage held together by the law of primogeniture until dissolved at President Jefferson's insistence, produced on the one hand the Van Rensselaer and Schuyler houses — Fort Crailo, the Pastures, the Manor House, and Cherry Hill — and also comfortable mansions along the East River in Manhattan on Pearl, Van Brugh, and Wall Streets for merchants whose names indicate their Dutch and Flemish ancestry — Nicholas Roosevelt, William Beekman, Abraham de Peyster, and Samuel Verplanck. The lavishness of William Walton's mansion in Pearl Street — of red brick and brownstone, three stories high, with a garden to the river — was cited in Parliament in 1759 as a reason to increase colonial taxes.[15] Mrs. James Alexander, mother of the unofficially titled Lord Sterling, bequeathed to her children in 1760 rooms hung in red, green, or blue damask with furniture en suite, together with comfortable fortunes in money, silverplate, and jewelry.

A Freeman took an oath of loyalty to Great Britain's king, paid fees and taxes to the city, and stood watch; these were requirements of all shop keepers and tradesmen in colonial New York. The lists of Freeman cabinetmakers, joiners, upholsterers, and carvers between 1701 and 1775 included the names of 109 craftsmen that are typical of the polyglot population in Manhattan to this day. A few of them were John Pelletreau and Thomas Gleaves in 1719; Peter Galatian and John Covenhoven in 1740; Samuel McGee and Moses Clement in 1757; Garrit Van Gelder and Marinus Willet in 1765; Jacob DeGroot and Richard Wenman in 1770. Samuel Prince, who left a sizable estate at his death in 1778, including "an outset of furniture on the day of their marriage" to his five children, turned out in his shop in Cart and Horse Street a pitch-pedimented mahogany desk and bookcase, embellished with Chinese frets, fluted chamfered corners, and boldly knuckled claw feet. A double chest of similar detail is featured on his engraved trade card. Another labeled piece by Prince is perhaps a "lady's dressing draws" or chest fitted with a looking glass and compartments in its upper drawer. Thomas Burling illustrated a "French" ribbon-back chair in his advertisements in the New York *Gazeteer* in 1774, and labeled a variety of desks and wardrobes made with straight bracket or claw feet and carved with gadrooned skirting; his engraved trade card sets forth a further variety of furniture. Daniel Ferguson's signed armchair made at 174 Fulton Street has a tall, pierced, simple back splat, and Chinese fret brackets below the seat. Among the earliest Chippendale chairs were those inscribed by Gilbert Ash in Wall Street, where he was established in 1756 and remained active for seven years; the latticed diamond chair back is repeated with variations in his work.

In Philadelphia Penn's "Holy Experiment" on the Delaware flourished from its beginning in 1683 as the grain and lumber mart of the Atlantic Coast. Industrially it led all other colonial towns in the crafts of weaving, woodworking, glass blowing, and iron, fostered by the activity of German, Quaker, Welsh, and English settlers. In 1735, 427 vessels arrived at or cleared the port of Philadelphia; at the beginning of the Revolution 35,000 inhabitants occupied 5743 houses within the city. Quakers and worldly folk saw their city surpass all others in size and population; it became likewise the leader in sophisticated living, a fact commented on repeatedly by visitors. Samuel Powel, home from the grand tour, in 1768 settled with his wife, Elizabeth Willing, at 244 South Third Street; their ballroom with stucco ceiling and rococo-carved paneling is among the handsomest rooms known of that period. Neighboring houses, like the Stamper house in nearby Pine Street, were equally ornate. Governor John Penn's country seat, Lansdowne, north of the city, was later occupied by the William Binghams, whose style of living was legendary. Earlier houses represented the conservative taste of an older generation. Graeme Park, built in 1718 by Governor Keith at Horsham, and Stenton, built ten years later for James Logan in Germantown to house his great library on the second floor, lack any frivolous note in their plain paneled walls. Cliveden is remarkable as one of the few colonial houses still occupied by the same family and furnished with much rare Philadelphia Chippendale furniture. John Adams wrote of it: "Dined with Mr. Chew, Chief Justice. We were shown into a grand entry and staircase, and into an elegant and most magnificent chamber until dinner. About four o'clock we were called down to dinner. The furniture was all rich."[16] Mount Pleasant, built on the banks of the Schuylkill by John Macpherson, whose fortune came from privateering, recalls by its site and flanking outbuildings the southern plantation houses; its interior woodwork is superbly carved.

Philadelphia was the undisputed center of furniture making before the Revolution, where the development of the Philadelphia Chippendale style reached the apogee of colonial achievement in its interpretation of the rococo. The numerous cabinetmakers whose names are identified with signed furniture give the Philadelphia school certain and undisputed supremacy. Many other examples, still unidentified with a specific shop or master, are no less important for their unmatched quality and genius of conception. The whole vocabulary of contemporary design, made familiar by imported pattern books, was explored and adapted to the high chests of drawers, the marble slab side tables, tea, breakfast, and card tables, screens, chairs, and sofas in endless profusion. Thomas Affleck, whose work for Governor John Penn at Lansdowne and his Sixth Street house brought an unparalleled urbanity of Chinese Chippendale pattern to Philadelphia furniture;[17] Jonathan Gostelowe, the originator of the imposing serpentine and fluted-corner chests of drawers; Thomas Tufft, whose chairs and carved high chests and matching dressing tables set a standard of exquisite detail; William Savery, whose gamut of work ranged from maple rush-bottom chairs to carved mahogany high chests of quiet elegance; Adam Hains, known for his shapely gadrooned breakfast tables; Benjamin Randolph, credited with the six famous *sample* chairs of incomparable richness; James Gillingham, remembered for his distinctive trefoil pattern of chair backs; and John Folwell, known for his interpretation from the London *Director* of the florid pediment of the famous Rittenhouse orrery case[18] — these are but a few of the known cabinetmakers and chairmakers. In Benjamin Randolph's receipt book for the years 1763 to 1777, now in the Winterthur Collection, other well-known craftsmen with whom he dealt are recorded, among them James Claypoole, William and Joseph Trumble, Edward Duffield, Ephraim Haines, Samuel Walton, John Elliott, Jr., Samuel Bagnall, and Thomas Shoemaker.

In Maryland, manor houses were scattered along both shores of the Chesapeake, isolated by spreading acres whence came their support in tobacco, wheat, and corn — Bohemia, Sotterley, and Readbourne, to name a few, whose grants often dated from Caroline kings. At Cloverfields the stucco-finished walls recall Franklin's letter from London to Mayor Samuel Rhoads in Philadelphia on June 26, 1770: "Of late indeed they begin here to leave off wainscoting their rooms and instead of it cover the walls with stucco, often formed into Pannels like wainscot, which being painted is very strong and warm." Annapolis, the metropolis of Maryland before Baltimore assumed its later leadership, could boast of the Brice house, its interior ornament in plaster and carved wood, and the Hammond-Harwood house designed by William Buckland, two of many handsome brick mansions of that city. Annapolis was Maryland's earliest center of colonial furniture making, but was limited to some eighteen craftsmen before the Revolution, and none of their work is identified by a signature. An early notice was published in the *Maryland Gazette* in 1746: "John Anderson . . . from Liverpool, makes chairs, tables, bureaus, dressing tables, clock cases, and all kinds of furniture."

In 1762 Baltimore had only 150 houses; and, when the War began, its population numbered 5,934. In that conflict Baltimore's major contribution was by sea, which earned it the British epithet of "a nest of pirates" because of the constant sea raiding by enemy ships. Baltimore's prosperity boomed when its rivals were crippled by British occupation; in 1776 and 1777 Congress met there, having fled from Philadelphia. A cabinetmaker advertised in the *Maryland Gazette* on April 9, 1767: "Gerrard Hopkins, son of Samuel, cabinet and chair maker from Philadelphia at the Sign of the Tea Table and Chair, in Gay Street Baltimore Town . . ." In the *Maryland Journal* for January 19, 1773, this notice appeared: "Gerrard Hopkins, son of Samuel, cabinet and chair maker, hath for sale in Gay Street Baltimore Town, mahogany boards, planks, also logs. He still continues business in its various branches as usual." As he claimed, he had worked in Philadelphia as early as 1760, with Robert Moore. His advertisements continued until 1787. Other pre-Revolutionary cabinetmakers of Baltimore were Robert, Thomas, and William Moore. At Hagerstown in 1783 George Wolz made clock cases and chests of drawers in walnut with fluted corners in the Philadelphia style. Only after the prosperity of the new Republic made Baltimore flourish did craftsmen multiply; over 200 were listed before 1820, and their work is unmistakable by its rich inlays, veneers, and painted glass panel inserts.

The same pattern of country houses was repeated in Tidewater Virginia on an even larger scale, where the manor houses — Stratford, the seat of the Lees; Westover, Upper and Lower Brandon of the Byrd families; Carters' Grove, Shirley, and Nomini Hall of the Carters — were only less important than Mount Vernon and the Governor's Palace at Williamsburg. Leisure, made possible by the slave labor of plantation economy, and isolation from town life bred a different plan of living from northern towns and cities, where dependence on trade and personal effort for survival were the rule. The diary of Philip Vickers Fithian, a tutor from Princeton in the household of Colonel Robert Carter at Nomini Hall in 1773 and 1774, often makes revealing observations of Virginia life.[19] Of a four-day Ball for seventy guests, given by Richard Lee, of Lee Hall, Westmoreland County, he records:

"The Ladies dined first, when some Good Order was preserved; when they rose, each nimblest Fellow dined first — The Dinner was as elegant as could be well expected when so great an Assembly were to be kept for so long a time. For Drink there was several sorts of Wine, a good Lemon Punch, Toddy, Cyder, Porter &c. About Seven the Ladies and Gentlemen begun to dance in the Ball-Room — first Minuets one Round; Second Giggs; third Reels; And last of All Country-Dances; tho' they struck several Marches occasionally — The Music was a French-Horn and two Violins — The Ladies were Dressed Gay, and Splendid, & when dancing, their Skirts & Brocades rustled and trailed behind them! But all did not join in the Dance for there were parties in Rooms made up, some at Cards; some drinking for Pleasure; some toasting the Sons of America; some singing 'Liberty Songs.'"

A visit to Mount Airy, the famous house of Colonel John Tayloe, is recorded:

"We set out about three; Mr. Carter travels in a small, neat *Chair*, with two waiting Men — We rode across the Country which is now in full Bloom; in every field we saw Negroes planting corn, or plowing, or hoeing; we arrived at the Colonels about five, Distance twelve miles. Here is an elegant Seat! The House is about the size of Mr. Carters, built of stone, & finished curiously, & ornamented with various paintings, & rich Pictures. This Gentleman owns *Yorick*, who won the prize of 500 £ last November, from Dr. Flood's horse *Gift* — In the Dining Room, besides many other fine Pieces, are twenty four of the most celebrated among the English Race-Horses, Drawn masterly, & set in elegant gilt Frames. He has near the Great House, two fine two Story stone Houses, the one is used as a Kitchen, & the other for a nursery, & Lodging Rooms — He has also a large, well formed, beautiful Garden, as fine in every Respect as any I have seen in Virginia. In it stand four large beautiful Marble Statues."

Virginia furniture even now is less often recognized because it has been so widely scattered or destroyed. The direct trade in tobacco and other crops of the Tidewater region with England was once presumed to have brought by exchange cargoes much English furniture for the planters' houses. Identification of the native woods such as tulip, cherry, and hard yellow pine as secondary woods in furniture proves many known examples to be native made. Virginia furniture was made in remote areas where groups of craftsmen were few and itinerant workmen and plantation slaves were employed. A principal center of activity was at Williamsburg, where notices in the *Virginia Gazette* before the Revolution offered the services of numerous cabinetmakers.

Among the colonies, the most flourishing province south of Philadelphia was Charles Town (named *Charleston* after the Revolution), whose cosmopolitan population included English, Irish, Dutch, and French Huguenots, among others; in 1773 more than half of the 12,000 people there were Negroes or mulattoes. Rice grown in flooded swamps by slave labor produced a valuable crop increasing from 18,000 barrels in 1724 to 120,000 barrels in 1770. Josiah Quincy, Jr., arriving in Charleston from Boston in 1773, wrote in his *Journal:* "The number of shipping far surpassed all I have seen in Boston . . . I was told that there were then not so many as common at this season, though about 350 sail lay off the town . . . In grandeur, splendor of buildings, decorations, equipages, numbers, commerce, shipping and indeed in almost everything it far surpasses all I ever saw, or ever expect to see in America."[20]

A large engraved view of Charles Town, published by B. Roberts in 1739, now at Winterthur, describes the city in its title: "It is ye fairest and most fruitfull Province belonging to Great Britain and by far ye most extensive, reaching several Degrees in breadth, in length, from ye Atlantick Ocean to ye South-Sea . . . it has adoriforous Woods green all ye Year, and produces such Fruit, that they who once tast of it, will dispise ye watry tast of that in England; Its Silk is preferable to any, and its Rice is ye best in ye World, provisions of all kinds are extreamly good, and very cheap, & ye Inhabitants are hurt by no particular distemper, except Such as proceed from Intemperance; So that it is no wonder if Charles Town, which a few years agoe was a Small and inconsiderable place, but now a very great and flourishing Town, adorned with handsome and commodious buildings, both private and Publick, amongst which ye Church of St. Philip, may instly be reckoned ye finest Structure in America."

Grown prosperous on the export of rice and indigo, the city, the first one to have a public theater, became famous for its cultivated taste, with numerous plantation and city houses. Built by William Drayton in 1740 on the Ashley River, Drayton Hall with its monumental double staircase, wainscoted rooms painted in three colors, and fireplaces of foreign marble; Miles Brewton's house in town, its carved and paneled ballroom lighted by a double-tiered cut-glass chandelier; St. James' Church at Goose Creek, lavishly finished in early Georgian detail of marbelized stucco — all of these suggest the richness witnessed by Josiah Quincy, Jr. The house of Thomas Heyward, the Signer, built in 1749, was a fine three-story brick house, leased for Washington's residence in 1791; perhaps unique is the mahogany pierced fret forming the overmantel of the second-floor drawing room, as an accent for the florid carving of the room.

Charleston furniture is eloquent of the sophisticated life of plantation owners along the Ashley and Cooper Rivers and in Charleston itself. Newspaper notices indicate the activity of many cabinetmakers, upholsterers, and allied craftsmen there during the eighteenth century. The well-known account book of Thomas Elfe, one of the most able and prosperous furniture makers, records during the years 1768 through 1775 the wide patronage he enjoyed from Charleston's first citizens, what he made for them, and the workmen he employed, including several handicraft slaves.[21] Some of the extant mahogany Chippendale furniture might well fit the descriptions listed in Elfe's book, although no labeled example of any Charleston cabinetmaker of the pre-Revolutionary period is known. As in Virginia, the furniture of Charleston has been much scattered; but it is possible to identify several important case pieces of Charleston origin because of the repetition of their design, their secondary woods, and their long family ownership.

Sixty-nine cabinetmakers, carvers, and chairmakers were occupied in Charleston before the Revolution — some from the North, like Charles Warham of Boston who offered besides a full line of furniture, coffins and funeral work.[22] Josiah Claypoole arrived from Philadelphia in 1740; and many came from London, including John Fisher and John Lord, the partners of Thomas Elfe. Elfe also employed John and William Crips and Adam Carne as carvers and

Richard Magrath and John Blott as upholsterers. William Luyten, another cabinetmaker employed by Elfe, is still remembered for the cypress headboard in St. Michael's graveyard, built and inscribed by him in 1770 to mark his young wife's grave.

Others were James Drummond and Abraham Pearce, and John Linton, who moved to Philadelphia in 1775 and established himself as an upholsterer; his name is chalked on the frame of John Dickinson's handsome sofa in the Winterthur Collection.

Thomas Elfe's account book not only indicates his wide activity and the impressive amount of fine cabinetwork produced in one shop, but also proves the "handycraft" slaves he owned: "four sawyers valued at £1400 and five joiners and cabinetmakers, £2250." It also shows the income he derived from their labor to other shops. In February, 1775, he recorded, "Handycraft Slaves for hire of Oxford the Carpenter £46.1.10 . . . for Liverpool's Work £15"; in November, 1770, "To Handycraft Slaves 28th Received for 2 months work of Oxford £30." His entries of work completed are often unusual:

For John Gaillard	
2 french elbow Chairs	£60
To a Chineas Teable [Tea Table] wᵗʰ a Stretcher	26
2 Commode Card Tables	70
For James Smith	
To a Tea Kettle Stand wᵗʰ a frett	£10
12 Mahoᵍ Chairs Carv'd Backs & 2 Elbo dᵒ	215
For Sommers Humphry	
To a double chest of drawers with a frett around	£80
For Thomas Phepo	
To a Mahogany book Case pediment head With a frett	£75
For John Barnwell	
A Mahogany Desk & Book Case Chinˢ Dores	£150
For Jane Simmons	
a Mahoᵍ Bedstead & Carved Cornish	£60

More modest were his charges to some of his customers:

To Chaˢ Cotes Pinckney, Octᵉʳ 5ᵗʰ 1774	
for 2 Cypress Stools	£ 5
2 Cypress Desks	13
For James Wakefield	
a case of draws of Cypress	£2.10
To the Widow Moultrie	
a black Cypress Coffin	£7

Some of Elfe's personal expenses in December of 1771 included:

Paid Willᵐ Oakes for a Satin Coat	£8.5
Paid Mrs. Hayland for my Daughters Scool	9.0
Gave away this Christmas	30.0

Terminology of Furniture

Contemporary descriptions of early furniture found in account books, inventories of houses, wills, and bills of sale not only reveal the cultural richness of colonial houses, but also bring to light a difference of terminology from that of the present day. The names are often illuminating and apt for the purposes of the furniture. There is little doubt of the uses of a *bottle board* or a *cheese stand* made in 1773.

Bed furniture referred particularly to the fabrics which draped the cornices and posts of a bed and was invariably given separate mention because of its especial value.

An *elbow chair* described an open armchair with a stuffed back and seat and was published as a *French Chair* in Chippendale's *Director*. An *easy chair* had a solidly upholstered frame with projecting wings for protection against drafts, and the current name of *wing chair* derives from that construction. A *corner chair* is recognized as the low, half-circular armchair to serve at a writing desk or to fill a corner; *roundabout* was a frequent name for it.

A *couch* was an early long chair or daybed made from the seventeenth century onward and furnished with squabs and cushions; it lost favor after the Queen Anne period, and a couch of the Chippendale style is rarely developed equally with contemporary chairs.

A *desk and bookcase* was the customary term for a two-part secretary with an upper section enclosed by doors. A *scrutoir* was a writing desk without the bookcase top.

No mention of a *highboy* or *lowboy* has been found in eighteenth-century records to describe a high chest of drawers fitting a separate base or its matching low chest or dressing table supported on legs; frequently a *high chest of drawers* and *low chest,* as well as a *high chest* and *half chest,* are listed together to suggest a matching pair.

A *double-chest* and more rarely a *chest-on-chest* were contemporary names for two sections of chests of drawers, one above the other. Rarely was a *triple chest* attempted, like that made for the Paschall family at Cedar Grove, in Philadelphia.

Long-case clock suggested the size of a tall clock, or the lately named *grandfather clock.*

For centuries *looking glass* meant a silvered plate of glass to mirror a reflection. When candle arms were fixed before the glass to give increased light, *girandole* and *sconce* were names applied to them. *Mirror* did not describe a looking glass in the eighteenth century.

A *pole screen* was a fire screen to distinguish it from a cheval, or horse, fire screen on four legs; from its tripod base a shaft supported the screen panel.

The terminology of tables was detailed, to describe their many forms. A *snap table* and *turn up table* referred to their tilting tops, for convenience when unneeded. *China table* indicated a raised edge to fence the display of china against damage. A *scallop tea table* likewise gave attention to the table top, curved in outline. A *slab table* and *slab frame for marble* offered an exact clue to the marble-topped tables of many sizes; some of the *sideboard-table* form served as pier tables in halls or dining rooms. A *table with a flap* indicated a drop-leaf shape; when it had a *fly foot,* its support was a swinging leg. A triangular drop-leaf suggests the current name of *handkerchief table.*

Gaming table and *card table* were names used for folding-top tables with a smooth top or with inset pockets to hold coins and counters. More exact names, as *backgammon table,* were less often mentioned.

Regional Characteristics

There were several schools of cabinetmaking in the Queen Anne and Chippendale period, created by isolated groups of workmen, in towns or cities different from one another in climate and economy. Variations within one style crystallized into regional expressions recognized by their repetition and special qualities. To explain the infinite changes of form and carving of American furniture, we are bound to acknowledge how versatile the craftsmen were, how well endowed with imagination and sympathy for the material at their command, and how independent in spirit of improvisation and exploration. It is a perennial cause for admiration and wonder that, in the confines of the small colonial towns and cities, the contributions in the limited realm of furniture should be so great; no other period of time in our history has matched the accomplishment in the decorative arts of the second and third quarters of the eighteenth century.

The English design books of Chippendale and the lesser ones that followed by Robert Manwaring, Ince and Mayhew, and Thomas Johnson were no less useful to American craftsmen than were the books of architecture by Batty Langley, Isaac Ware, William Salmon, Abraham Swan, and Robert Morris to carpenters and builders here. In several parts of New England, in New York, New Jersey, and Pennsylvania, as well as in the South, regional variations of the English patterns are widely different, given a distinction by local materials in the hands of workmen with various inherited traditions, who were guided by the economic factors and the demands of their patrons. The varied contributions of the Dutch, the Swiss, the French Huguenots, the Irish, and the Germans lent a regional aspect to colonial furniture; the basic character of the peoples of Europe had molded the original styles in much the same way. But the basic influence was from England.

In New Hampshire and Massachusetts the high chests of drawers, or highboys, are sparely built, their pediments roofed over from back to front; the carving of a fan or shell is confined to the center drawer in the upper and lower sections, and the supporting cabriole legs are a marvel of lightness. Carving may find expression in the flanking pilasters of the doors of a desk and bookcase and the streamers from the rosettes of the scrolled pediment. Case pieces of bombé, or kettle-shape, and serpentine-curved drawer fronts provide an inspired sweep of line that epitomizes the fine performance of the Massachusetts Bay group in Newburyport, Salem, Boston, and Roxbury. On the carved feet of furniture there, the bird's claws lightly grasp the ball feet, and the flanking claws curve backward in a sharply diagonal line. The work of Cogswell, Short, and Frothingham shows that shape of foot, carved in Boston, Newburyport, and Charlestown. Finials to mark the corners of pediments are almost invariably a neat corkscrew, rising from an urn; rarely is a pierced and carved flame used there. Chairs have a persistent lightness of proportion; their splats and undercut cabriole legs seem to challenge structural soundness; turned stretchers of the block-and-spindle shape or straight members reinforce the understructure. The shape of the inside-seat braces varies in regional practice; in Queen Anne chairs of New England the mortising of seat rails and the heavy block tops of the legs give ample strength; in Chippendale chairs, large rectangles of white pine or maple are nailed across the corners.

The sides of drawers in well-made Massachusetts pieces sometimes have a double molding along their top edges, cut in the soft pine. In rare instances mahogany was used for drawer linings, as in Peter Faneuil's needlework-top card table of Queen Anne design. Whatever the chosen wood, it is cut thin for ease of handling, and held by closely cut dovetails at the corners, rabbeted at the lower sides and nailed along the back to hold the edges firmly.

In Connecticut the cabinetmaker's hand, if heavier, shows originality and merit. The pediments of high chests are frequently pierced and finished with pinwheel volutes; rope-twist columns often flank double tiers of drawers, and wide ogee bracket feet are trimmed with scrolls and connected by a straight-ribbed, gadrooned molding. The thickness of the white pine drawer lining of Connecticut chests exceeds that of other regions, save in the work of Samuel Dunlap of New Hampshire. The dovetails are often heavy, as earlier practice dictated.

In Newport furniture the familiar raised blocking upon drawers and bookcase doors is carried up to fill the scrolled pediment of tall case furniture, punctuated by formally petaled volutes above it. The flamboyant shells, fixed to the solidly cut block-front chests are repeated with less conciseness on Connecticut cherry furniture; the tiny spiral curling down the bracket foot of Newport chests is a sure signature of its origin. Two antipodal details are equally revealing: the pediment finials carved not quite around with upstanding intaglio petals and topped by a corkscrew flame; and the open talons of the elongated, webless claws upon the ball foot. The undercut claws were not attempted outside of Newport, but do show on fine English furniture, on pieces of the George II period.

Newport Queen Anne chairs probably made by the first of the Townsend dynasty give a prophecy of the second generation's genius in their compact lines, shell-carved knees and top rails, and choice mahogany and walnut woods. Some high chests are made with detachable legs for ease and safety in moving, a feature unnoticed in other parts of the colonies.

In New York the Dutch character of a century earlier lingers in the broadly built wardrobes and desks, deeply curved gaming tables, and wide-seated chairs. Generously proportioned and carved with broad strokes and simple, undulating gadrooning, the typical aspect of New York furniture is that of comfort and hospitality, sometimes lacking the elegance of detail and graceful proportion found in Philadelphia and New England but strongly individual in style.

Peculiar to New York Queen Anne chairs are the emphatic curves of the broad splat to which the flanking stiles conform in line. A thickened, pointed foot terminating the cabriole leg of this period is distinctive, too, of New York. Chairmakers adopted generally the claw-and-ball feet for their Queen Anne designs rather than web, trifid, and slipper feet seen in the colonies to the north and south, although round pad feet were especially favored on stuffed-back armchairs. Medial stretchers were seldom added to New York chairs, and the rear legs, round in section, were tapered down to a squared or shod pad foot. Diagonal strips, similar to English construction, were frequently used in the underframing of chairs.

Few Chippendale high chests of drawers, or highboys, were made in New York, where a preference was shown for the double chest ornamented with a fretted cornice and broad, fluted, chamfered corners. The claw feet are most often blocked squarely in profile at the knuckles, although those on the signed chairs by Gilbert Ash are sinuously curved.

Philadelphia Queen Anne furniture gave promise early of the individual virtues it soon developed and of the unique flowering of the Chippendale style which followed it, combining Quaker stability with worldly elegance. Chairs well show the mastery of calculated curves wherein their ornaments of double scrolls and shells are closely integrated. Their out-curving arms supported on concaved posts are innovations here; the seat frames, horseshoe shaped, are cut to form an inside square and hold the doweled legs pinned from below. This construction is made further memorable by the side rails, mortised through the outside of the rear legs. The latter becomes a detail of Philadelphia construction by its prevalence on chairs of the Chippendale period. It appears, too, on Connecticut chairs, possibly by Eliphalet Chapin, and rarely in New York, but is omitted on some of Benjamin Randolph's labeled chairs in Philadelphia. Quarter-round blocks of white cedar and tulipwood hold innerseat frames. The shapes of chair feet are widely different in form — the slipper, the web, and the plain pad of Elliott's stools, as well as the trifid and bird's-claw-and-ball feet, all of which alternate on Queen Anne furniture. In the Chippendale period the repertory is enlarged to include the rare French or scroll shape, the hairy paw, the square Marlboro foot, and the ubiquitous bird's claw firmly grasping a ball. Rear legs of stump shape are customary.

The sophistication of design is a striking feature of Philadelphia furniture, owing to its derivation from contemporary London books, particularly Chippendale's *Director*. Although chair backs and scrolled pediments can be traced to engraved sources, the improvisation of them in Philadelphia created wholly new interpretations in colonial furniture, unparalleled elsewhere. The high chests of drawers and their matching dressing tables, the so-called highboy and lowboy, enriched with a galaxy of shells, streamers, and rococo curves at pediment and skirting, epitomize the quality of colonial furniture. Frequently the corners are inset with quarter columns, fluted or carved with vines, and the scrolled pediments carry a pierced cartouche flanked by tall, twisted-flame finials. Round tea tables on a tripod base, with a flattened ball pillar, first made in the mid-century with a plain dished top, and then elaborated with a piecrust edge in the flamboyant era of carving, are pre-eminent forms. The Gothic, Chinese, and French themes introduced into every variety of Philadelphia furniture are expressed structurally and, by means of pierced frets and carving in high relief and suave movement, are incomparably well executed.

Both New Jersey and Maryland furniture shares in part the character of Philadelphia cabinetwork. The flattened serpentine stretcher and the slipper foot are both encountered on the walnut chairs of Southern New Jersey. Tables often show a lightness of proportion and graceful line of cabriole support reminiscent of New England.

In Maryland the high chest of drawers, or highboy, is related in concept to its northern neighbor, although with a less florid display of ornament in the shells and streamers carved on center drawer fronts; the quarter-round fluted or carved corners are less in evidence than the broadly chamfered ones. Wide splats of Chippendale chairs which nearly fill the opening between the vertical stiles are other features which are repeated in Maryland.[28] Tulipwood is most often used in drawer linings. The seat rails of stuffed chairs were sometimes cut from mahogany, an unusual occurrence in the North. The inside corner blocks are yellow pine and quarter round, a shape favored by Philadelphia joiners. The side rails are usually tenoned through the back legs.

Virginia-made furniture reveals the isolation of craftsmen from the centers of current fashion in its naive interpretation of orthodox styles. In the Queen Anne period walnut was principally used and, less often, fruitwood, with southern yellow pine for secondary purposes. Chairs are compact and conservative in design, without carving, not unlike English provincial models. Tables show the use of straight, rounded legs ending in a slanting pad foot; and plain flat-topped desks and bookcases have paneled doors and simple bracket feet. Cellarettes of yellow pine or walnut stand on abruptly curving cabriole legs or square fluted supports. In the Chippendale period case pieces were embellished with interlaced frets, and several with leaf-covered knees and carved, scrolled backs. Simple pierced back-splats and straight legs seem more typical of Virginia chairs.[24]

Tall desks and bookcases have arched, paneled, or square-paned glazed doors; their cautiously scrolled or pitch pediments are topped by stiff, ball-turned or flame finials. Corner and china cupboards of walnut, cherry, and southern yellow pine show paneled fronts and bracket feet. Nowhere in Virginia furniture is there evidence of the heights scaled by carvers and cabinetmakers in the North.

North Carolina furniture was given its own character by the Germans, the Swiss, the Scotch, and the Irish who migrated down the Shenandoah Valley to the Piedmont, as well as by the English from the seacoast. Much of it has an element of rusticity. Scalloped, open-shelved dressers are familiar transplanted Pennsylvania forms there, and in Moravian furniture early turned elements combine with later features. More sophisticated is a fine walnut block-front desk lined with hard pine, and inscribed with three local Scotton family names; so far, it is a unique expression of the southern block-front style.[25] Several mahogany-and-marble side tables offer a new expression in the Chinese Chippendale style with their deep, fret-carved skirts and angular, blocked legs.

In Charleston mahogany early became the favored wood for cabinetwork; and walnut is rare in the handsome double chests, the four-part bookcases, or the wardrobes that are invariably carved with bands of fretwork along their cornices, and surmounted with domed or broken pediments, sometimes fancifully pierced after the engraved plates of Chippendale's *Director*. Broadly chamfered corners and ogee bracket feet are other accepted features of Charleston case furniture.[26] A prodigally ornate side chair, memorable for its hairy-paw feet and intricately carved and pierced back, and a fine marble-topped serpentine-shaped side table, its knees carved with rococo arabesques, both have been owned in South Carolina since 1865 or before and suggest new high lights on the quality of southern furniture. A carved candlestand with a piecrust top, more emphatic in its carving and pedestal turning than those familiar in the middle colonies, may be of Charleston origin. Any pedigreed prototype of the three foregoing pieces is lacking to support an exact attribution of their origin in Charleston. No high chests of drawers of the highboy form, well known in the North, are associated with either the Virginia or the Carolina school.

XXXIII

Furniture Exports and Imports

Considerable cargoes of colonial furniture were shipped from New England to the southern colonies and the West Indies. Reports of the record of clearances of the British Customs from Portsmouth, Salem, Boston, and Newport indicate the consignments to sea captains who acted as agents of the owners.[27] This venture trading became a profitable source of revenue over a long period and continued well into the nineteenth century. From the latter period a large four-part bookcase with the name of the Salem maker Nehemiah Adams was found in South Africa several decades ago and is now in the Winterthur Collection. Besides the triangular trade to Africa, the West Indies, and home ports, there was a coastwide trade between North and South for the exchange of cargoes. Furniture was sent in considerable quantities in return for food products, especially wheat and corn, and for tobacco, all more easily grown in the South. From Boston in 1744 the lists include among many items:

The Brig *Sarah* for West Indies — 4 desks, 11 tables, 2 dozen chairs

Sloop *Betty* to Philadelphia — 18 leather chairs

Sloop *Lydia* for New York — 12 dozen chairs, 1 Scrutoire & bookcase, 3 tables

Sloop *Willingmind* for Virginia — 1 dozen chairs, chest

From New England desks, tables and chairs were exported by the dozen. Newport, a strong rival of Boston and New York in commercial activity and as a seaport, sent such cargoes as the following:

Sloop *Sally* to North Carolina — 42 chairs, 2 tables

Sloop *Defiance* to South Carolina — 3 maple desks, 14 maple tea tables

Sloop *New York Packet* for Virginia — 2 desks here made, 1 clock

Clearances from Providence included:

Sloop *Hannah* for Charleston — 3 dozen chairs, 2 desks, 8 small tables

Ship *General Washington* to West Indies — 5 desks, 4 tables, 25 chests,
 14 dozen chairs

Brigantine *Providence* to Baltimore — 20 boxes of furniture, 42 dining chairs

Ship *Union* to Charleston — 10 maple desks, 4 dozen Windsors [chairs]

In the year 1771 hundreds of chairs, desks, and tables were shipped from Portsmouth to cities along the coast as far as Charleston. In the preceding year the customs reports reached the peak of activity of shipments from New England and Philadelphia: to Baltimore went some 784 chests, 74 desks, and 68 tables; to Virginia, 879 chests, 45 desks, and 35 tables; to North Carolina, 619 chests, 78 desks, and 39 tables; and to Charleston, 315 chests, 48 desks, and 13 tables.

In a Report of the Commissioners for Trade and Plantations laid before Parliament in 1733 "to ascertain the Laws made, manufactures set up, and Trade carried on, in any of His Majesty's Colonies and Plantations in America which may have affected the Trade, Navigation, and manufactures of this Kingdom," the part concerning Virginia states:

"The People of New England, being obliged to apply themselves to manufactures more than others of the Plantations, who have the Benefit of a better Soil and warmer Climate, such Improvements have been lately made there in all Sorts of Mechanic Arts, that not only Scrutores, Chairs, and other wooden manufactures, but Hoes, Axes and other Iron Utensils are now exported from thence to the other Plantations, which, if not prevented may be of ill Consequence to the Trade and Manufactures of this Kingdom, which Evil may be worthy the Consideration of a British Parliament."[28]

Tobacco was the chief commodity of trade in Maryland and Virginia, the report declared, and gave no cause of complaint.

By British standards the American colonies were expected to supply only raw materials to the mother country and to take in exchange her manufactured goods. The restrictions of commerce between the colonies and the limitations of their industries finally became a major cause of the Revolution.

Extant trade records between England and her American colonies from 1697 to 1780 give some account of the English furniture imported by New England, New York, Pennsylvania, Maryland, Virginia, and Carolina. From 1720 to 1728 the valuations were:

Chairs	£1232
Looking Glasses	3969
Clock Cases	234
Escritoires	5
Upholstery Ware	2606

Between 1740 and 1747 the figures show:

Chairs	£ 377
Looking Glasses	1402
Clock Cases	26
Escritoires	7
Upholstery Ware	6744

From 1760 to 1767 the records show:

Cabinetware	£ 3983
Upholsteryware	9879

Imported luxuries had long been sought for the American background and contributed an Old-World atmosphere, described by a traveler in 1741 ". . . that a Gentleman from London would almost think himself at home at Boston, where he observes that Number of People, their Houses, their Furniture, their Tables, their Dress and Conversation, which perhaps is as splendid and showy, as that of the most considerable Tradesmen in London."[29]

After the mid-century, importations from England declined as more cabinetmakers became active and war clouds gathered.

Although Samuel Powel, who attended the coronation of George III in 1761, was advised by his uncle and guardian, Samuel Morris, against importing English furniture to Philadelphia for his new house because of public sentiment, Governor John Penn's furniture at Lansdowne included some that was English. The original appraisal of it reads:

List of English furniture at Lansdown	277.2.3 Sterling
American furniture	581.9.0 Currency
Farming Utensils & Stock	429.8.9 Currency

Although in the room-by-room inventory curtains and floor coverings represented much of the English contents, there were also of English origin:

In the Hall
    10 elbow chairs, matted seats
Small dining Parlour
    A looking Glass
In the Nth Chamber
    A Chest of drawers
    A Mahogany table
    A looking Glass
    8 green chairs
Sth West Chamber
    A Mahogany bedstead
Nth West Chamber
    A Bedstead
    A Walnut Table
    A looking Glass
    3 green Chairs

Woods

In the eighteenth century the virtues of mahogany (*Swietenia mahogani*) were recognized as a wood unsurpassed in durability, rich pattern, close grain, and fine color, which offered an ideal medium for the highest expression of carving and cabinetwork. First discovered in the sixteenth century in the West Indies by the Spaniards, who used it for ship building, the name *Spanish mahogany* described the wood cut in Santo Domingo and adjacent Spanish-owned islands. Logs from the oldest trees were sometimes 12 feet in diameter, and provided timbers of unmatched size for furniture making. The early mahogany was heavy, solid, and became nearly black with age. Cuban mahogany, imported before 1750, was prized for its figured pattern of curls and "fiddle back" stripe absent in the Santo Domingo wood; another admirable quality was its golden-brown color which did not darken with age.[30] Regular shipments of mahogany were made early in the eighteenth century to England and the American colonies; one of the first records here was in 1708 in the inventory of Charles Plumstead, a cabinetmaker in Philadelphia;[31] it was well known in New England by the second quarter of the century. In the latter part of the eighteenth century Honduras mahogany, one of several varieties cut in Central America, was in general use.

By 1803 Thomas Sheraton wrote:

"Hispaniola or Santo Domingo produces mahogany not much in use with us. From [Honduras] is imported the principal kind of mahogany in use amongst cabinetmakers, which generally bears the name of Honduras mahogany, and sometimes Baywood from the bay or arm of the sea which runs up to it. The grain of Honduras wood is of a different quality from that of Cuba, which is close and hard, without black speckles, and of a rosy hue, and sometimes strongly figured; but Honduras wood is of an open nature, with black or grey spots, and frequently of a more flashy figure than Spanish. The best quality of Honduras wood is known by its being free from chalky and black speckles, and when the colour is inclined to a dark gold hue. The common sort of it looks brisk at a distance, and of a lively pale red; but on close inspection is of an open and close grain, and of a spongy appearance."[32]

Linings of small drawers for fine American and English furniture were made of the Honduras wood, and veneers were cut from the branch grain. The excellence of the early West Indian mahogany is thought to have been due to the poor, dry soil of those islands, unlike the Honduras variety, lighter and softer in texture, grown in rich moist soil. A typical newspaper notice in the New York *Gazetteer* of July, 1774, notes:

> "Now landing from on board the brig *Content*, Captain Benjamin
> Stammers from Honduras Bay, and to be sold by Anthony Van Dam
> 30,000 feet of Mahogany
> 30 tons of Logwood
> 1500 weight Sasparerilla
> Also, Molasses, West-India Rum, Madeira Wine, Guatamala In-
> digo, Cocoa &c."

Before mahogany was available, black walnut *(Juglans nigra)* served the purpose of a dark, close-grained medium for fine turning, carving, and veneering to express the nuances of a more elegant fashion than the coarser woods employed in the seventeenth century could do. The black walnut was plentiful all along the eastern seaboard and often grew to 8 feet in diameter.[33] The branch figure or swirl crotch of walnut wood enriched plain surfaces, and the root and burl cuts provided an intricate figure for veneering the fronts of desks, chests of drawers, and clock cases frequently seen in northern furniture in the Queen Anne period. The nuts of the walnut were valued for food, and their husks produced a brown dye. Walnut continued to be used south of New York throughout the colonial period in spite of the widespread popularity of mahogany. Only in Charleston did mahogany gain an early lead because of its easy importation there. Many Philadelphia high chests of drawers and chairs made in the fully developed Chippendale style are of walnut, carefully selected for its handsomely figured grain. Quantities of that wood were exported to England before 1700; John Evelyn's *Sylva* favorably compares its qualities with those of European walnut, and extant bills of lading preserved in the British Museum prove the source of the shipments.[34]

In a *Catalogue of Cabinetware* made in Philadelphia as late as 1786, Benjamin Lehman furnished prices for work in both mahogany and walnut.[35] Among the long list of items were:

	Mahogany	Walnut
Easy chair claw feet, leaves on knees	£3. 5.0	£3. 0.0
Sofa, leaves on knees	6.10.0	6. 0.0
Side Board Table with bases and brackets 5 ft. by 2 ft. 6 in.	5. 0.0	2.10.0
Chest Drawers and frame claw feet and quarter columns	15. 0.0	11. 0.0

Less important was white walnut *(Juglans cinerea)*, or butternut, native from New England to Maryland. The wood is open grained, of a light-brown color, without much figure. It may be seen in country-made pieces or upon the sides and backboards of case furniture The nuts are edible and produce an oil similar to linseed oil. Colonial dyes were made from the bark of white walnut, ranging from purple to brown and fawn color. During the Revolution, army doctors found the inner bark a remedy for dysentery.

Second only to walnut in the early part of the eighteenth century were several kinds of maple employed in earlier Pilgrim furniture for turnings and "jewels" on oak chests and upholstered chair frames. The sugar, or hard, maple *(Acer saccharum)* is pre-eminent in the maple family and is native from Canada to North Carolina, a symmetrical tree of great beauty often 100 feet high and 4 feet in diameter. It is still one of the most useful American woods; "rock" maple well describes its tough, close-grained texture. From its sap comes the major crop of maple syrup and maple sugar. Especially sought after by colonial cabinetmakers for their important pieces were the figured maples, the so-called curly, bird's-eye, and blister markings, more frequent in the maples than in any other trees, as unaccountable freaks of nature. Bird's-eye maple, named for its resemblance to the eye of a bird, is more common than the blister figure, and the twisted fibers resemble pins radiating from the heart wood. Pits in the bark of the growing tree mark the bird's-eye grain. The blister figure in maple resembles a landscape of mountains and valleys in irregular waves, often combined with a bird's-eye grain. An experienced observer can identify the blister figure in a growing tree by the elevation of its warty bark; the finest pattern is near the surface, and nowadays the log is shaved around and around with a huge lathe, until the heart of the log is reached. Plain-figured maple was the customary wood for the underframing of fine mahogany chairs and sofas in New England.

Queen Anne maple furniture more often shows the curly grain than the other figures. It was found in the white, or silver, maple *(Acer saccharinum)* and the red, or swamp, maple *(Acer rubrum)*, both soft varieties having the same habitat as hard, or rock, maple. The curly figure is produced by fibers which develop spirally, without any known reason, giving a tiger-stripe pattern much prized by collectors. In New Hampshire, Massachusetts, and Rhode Island, both hard and soft maple shared honors with walnut and to some extent with mahogany. In Pennsylvania it was sometimes the preferred medium for fine furniture even in the Chippendale period. Old maple wood takes on a dark honey color inimitable in new wood, all too often destroyed by the scraper.

The wild black cherry *(Prunus serotina)* grew mightily from Southern Canada to the Carolinas, sometimes 4 feet in diameter and 100 feet tall.[36] The wood is hard, strong, and close grained, pale red when new and dull red-brown when aged. Its fruit made cherry brandy, as well as food for frugivorous birds. In Connecticut and New York State, cherry was a favorite wood for furniture; in the former state it surpassed maple and even mahogany in the last half of the eighteenth century. The interior lining of furniture in New York was often cherry, soft pine, and tulipwood. The Pennsylvania Germans made many household wares of cherry; in Lancaster County Jacob Bachman and his son John used cherry almost entirely for their ornately carved furniture. On June 27, 1772, John Caldwell, a deceased joiner late of Chester, left "Some Walnut & Cheree Boards, A Wild Cheree Tree Chest." Southern furniture is often made of cherry, especially in Virginia and Kentucky.

The tulip tree *(Liriodendron tulipifera)* is among the finest native trees, sometimes growing 150 feet high and 6 feet in diameter. It is easily recognized in May or June by its yellow and orange tulip-shaped flowers, whence comes the name *tulipifera,* from the Persian *toulyban,* a turban.[37] It grew from southern New England to Mississippi. The wood is light, strong, compact, and satiny in texture, pale green when cut, and aging to nut brown on long exposure. In early times it was called *canoewood* because the Indians made dugout canoes of it, sometimes large enough for thirty passengers. Today *tulip-poplar* is a name frequently used; in the colonial period poplar often is listed with walnut and mahogany on joiners' inventories, both as lumber and as furniture, and almost certainly refers to tulipwood. It seems erroneous to describe tulip only as poplar, inasmuch as poplar *(Populus alba)* and whitewood, or cottonwood *(Populus deltoides)* — used now for packing boxes and paper pulp — are so inferior to it. Tulipwood was a favorite lining for mahogany and walnut furniture from Rhode Island to Maryland and to some extent in Virginia and the Carolinas all through the eighteenth century and well into the Victorian era. It braces the inside corners of New York chairs, along with white pine. In Connecticut it sometimes replaces the ubiquitous white pine for interior finish and for furniture made along the Sound; in Guilford the early houses are sheathed and paneled in tulipwood, and the well-known decorated chests made there, four of which are in the Winterthur Collection, are likewise tulipwood. In 1726 David Williams in Chester County had on hand "107 Feet of Poplar Boards, 4 pieces of Curld Wall Nuttboard, 38 Feet of Oadk Boards." In Charleston there are frequent records of poplar used for beds.

Less known, but equally fine, was the red, or sweet, gum *(Liquidambar styraciflua),* generally called *bilsted* in colonial New York. Its tall, straight trunk sheathed in light-brown bark is often 5 feet in diameter; its star-shaped leaves turn brilliant scarlet in autumn. The wood is heavy, close grained, and silky; red-brown in color with less figure than cherry, it warps and twists in drying unless steamed after sawing. Like tulipwood, it was plentifully used for trimming rooms and for furniture in the Hudson Valley. For turnings and moldings it was ideal. A fine wall of red gum paneling from the Hasbrouck house, built in 1752 at High Falls, Ulster County, is now in the American Wing, in New York. Quite a different wood is another red gum *(Eucalyptus rostrata)* naturalized in California from Australia, with a dense hard texture, almost like mahogany and variously used today.

Black, or sweet, birch *(Betula lenta),* yellow birch *(Betula lutea),* and white, or canoe, birch *(Betula papyrifera),* grew from Canada southward along the eastern seaboard, to a height of 80 feet and often 3 to 4 feet thick. The wood was found useful because it was strong, close grained, and hard; it was used with maple and, when stained, was substituted for mahogany in country-made furniture. The bark of sweet and yellow birch gave flavoring for sweets and beverages; the bark of white birch made canoes for the Indians.

The scarcity of American beech *(Fagus ferruginea* or *grandifolia)* in furniture of the eighteenth century is puzzling because of the early and continued use of beech *(Fagus sylvatica)* in England and the continent.[38] Here, the large, handsome trees with bluish-gray, smooth bark grew plentifully from Canada south to Georgia. The limbs of the fern-leaf variety send out flying buttresses, like medieval thrusts, for support to hold one limb to another. The wood is smooth, close grained, and hard, with little figure except for the tiny pink specks in the radial cut of the wood. In New York furniture of the Chippendale period, beech appears with pine, oak, and cherry on the underframes of easy chairs and tables. Perhaps John Evelyn's warning, first published in *Sylva* in 1664 and reprinted by Dr. Hunter in 1776, became a tradition against its use here "... were this Timber [walnut] in greater plenty amongst us, we should have far better utensils of all sorts for our Houses as Chairs, Stools, Bedsteads, Tables, Wainscot, Cabinets, etc. instead of the more vulgar Beech, subject to the worm, weak, and unsightly . . ." In any case walnut, maple, and cherry served to better purpose for American furniture.

The wood of sycamore *(Platanus occidentalis)* is often confused with beech by its flecked grain, but is actually much coarser and more pronounced. The tree is known, too, as plane and buttonwood, one of the largest of the deciduous family. Its bark, flaking off to expose white patches, easily identifies the sycamore along roadsides, from Southern Canada as far down as the Gulf Coast. It has been called the *ghost tree* because of its white trunk. The wood is heavy, reddish-brown in color, but difficult to split and work, and its uses were confined to the "quartered" cut of the radial section for veneers and for small articles of decoration. Unlike beech, it was rarely used as a secondary wood for furniture in the eighteenth century.

The kind of wood in drawer linings, backboards, braces, and corner blocks is of first importance to ascertain the regional origins of furniture, inasmuch as the craftsmen carefully chose the most serviceable material available, which repeats time and again like a formula in a given area. In mahogany and walnut furniture the secondary woods have much to say in identification. In the Queen Anne and subsequent periods many principal woods, formerly of equal rank with oak, like pine, ash, and chestnut, were relegated to obscure uses in fine furniture. Of these the coniferous woods — the pines, cedars, and cypresses — rank first.

The white, or soft, pine *(Pinus strobus)* is rightfully called the king of the American forest for its majestic height and straight trunk, often growing 160 feet tall and 8 feet in diameter. It is native from Canada southward to the Alleghanies and westward to the Great Lakes region. From the earliest days of the colonies it found constant use for building, spars, and ship masts, where its light weight, straight grain, and lack of shrinkage were valuable factors. It shared honors with oak and maple for seventeenth-century furniture in New England and continued to be used there almost entirely for drawer linings of case pieces until modern times. The paneling and often the framing of New England houses was largely of white pine and, when left unpainted, took on a bloom of inimitable soft brown. In New York it is common as a secondary wood in structural members of furniture. White pine grew in England, too, where it was named *Weymouth* pine for Lord Weymouth, who introduced it there; it was restricted in its use by Queen Anne in 1711 as an attempt to encourage its growth. American white pine was exported to the South and to England after the mid-eighteenth century in increasing quantities.

Among the hard pines there were several which were favored for secondary woods in furniture in the walnut and mahogany period. The short-leaf, or yellow, pine *(Pinus mitis or echinata)* grew from New Jersey southward; its wood is heavy, coarse grained, and light orange colored. This wood is most often found in New Jersey and Pennsylvania furniture, as well as in Virginia, where strength in underframing was required. Drawer linings and gates of tables and backboards were made of it. It was the accepted material for paneling in the fine Philadelphia houses prior to the Revolution and is still one of the most important American pines for interior finish.

Another yellow pine is the pitch pine *(Pinus rigida)*, one of the smaller varieties, growing from 40 to 70 feet tall, from Maine to northern Georgia. The wood is coarse with a reddish-yellow grain and is rarely seen in New England furniture of the eighteenth-century period, although six-board chests of the Pilgrim Century often were built of it. As its name implies, the wood is highly resinous. South of Pennsylvania it was used as a secondary wood in Chippendale furniture.

The loblolly pine *(Pinus taeda)* grew to 125 feet and is variously known as southern yellow pine, Virginia pine, and heart pine, among other names, from Delaware to Florida. It, too, found wide use in building and furniture in the southern colonies, where its strongly marked radial-cut grain lent a distinguishing pattern to the unpainted wood.

The longleaf pine *(Pinus palustris)* was an important tree from Virginia southward, known now as hard yellow pine, Georgia heart pine, and southern hard pine, among a score of other regional names. Growing to 80 or 90 feet tall and 3 to 4 feet in diameter, it had great economic value for interior finish and cabinetwork. The wood is heavy and coarse grained, of a pinkish-brown color. This wood found particular use in early Virginia furniture and in the Carolinas for interior finish.

White cedar *(Chamaecyparis thyoides)*, an evergreen of the pine family, was native along the East Coast from Maine to Florida. The largest trees often reached 3 to 4 feet in diameter. The wood is light, close grained, and aromatic, nearly white when cut. It is found in drawer bottoms of much fine Philadelphia case furniture, combined with tulipwood, oak, or chestnut for the sides. Entries of *cedar* are recorded between 1763 and 1777 in Benjamin Randolph's receipt book in Philadelphia and earlier by other cabinetmakers. In 1737 Joseph Hibbard, a joiner in Darby near Philadelphia, included in his stock "50 ft pine & poplar Bord, 260 foot Wallnut Bord, 1 piece Mahogany, Some split cedar for drayor bottome."

Red cedar *(Juniperus virginiana)*, native from New Hampshire to Florida and along the Gulf Coast, was called *baton rouge* or *red stick* by the Canadian French. It is unmistakable for its aromatic, dark reddish-brown, smooth wood. Slow in growth it rarely attained a diameter of 4 feet. Both northern and southern colonial furniture was made of it, and venture pieces shipped from New England are so described. One of its principal uses was for linings of drawers; Josiah Quincy's fine mahogany desk is entirely cedar within, and several Newport block-front pieces are lined with it.

Bald cypress *(Taxodium distichum)* was one of the most valuable southern woods, much used in the Carolinas during the colonial period. Unlike the evergreen *cupressus*, it was deciduous and derived the name *bald cypress* from its winter bareness. It grew to an impressive size from Delaware southward, buttressed with spreading knees when growing in swampy soil perhaps for greater stability. The wood is light, smooth, and non-resinous with a grain less pronounced than that of hard pine. It is pale colored when grown on high, dry ground, and dark brown in swampy soil, which accounts for its gamut of names from black to white cypress.[39] Its resistance to decay is notable. Linings of drawers, as well as entire pieces of furniture, were often made of cypress. Thomas Elfe, perhaps the leading cabinetmaker in Charleston before 1775, opened his account book in 1768 with "mahogany and cypress to the value of £350."

In the eighteenth century several of the hard, coarse woods of first importance in the preceding century served for frames of upholstered furniture, the swinging gates of card and dining tables, and similar obscure uses where especial strength was required. Among them were chestnut *(Castanea dentata)*, red or gray ash *(Fraxinus pennsylvanica)*, and white oak *(Quercus alba)*, or swamp oak *(Quercus palustris)*, and burr oak *(Quercus macrocarpa)*. These were combined with pine, cherry, and other native woods, as the craftsmen judged best. In the famous block-front case pieces made in Newport, ash and chestnut made up the drawer linings or were combined with tulipwood and red cedar. Oak was used for the entire interior of Philadelphia high chests of drawers in more than one instance, although tulipwood and white cedar are more frequently seen. It is observed on the frames or gates of gaming and dining tables, where added strain was to be expected. In Philadelphia the frames of fine easy chairs and sofas were built of ash, chestnut, and yellow pine instead of the soft pine and maple seen in New England. White oak was combined with southern hard pine or tulip in Virginia; and in the Carolinas it was used with ash, cypress, and poplar as a secondary wood.

The site of Charles Town in South Carolina was described in 1682 by Thomas Ash. Sent by the King to "Enquire into the state of that country," he reported: "It is cloathed with odoriferous and fragrant woods, flourishing in perpetual and constant Verdures, viz. the lofty Pine, the sweet-smelling Cedar and Cypress trees, of both of which are composed goodly Boxes, Chests, Tables, Scrittores and Cabinets."

NOTES TO THE INTRODUCTION

1. *The Encyclopedia Americana*, 1948 Edition, Vol. 4, p. 297.

2. Adams, C. F., *Works: With a Life of John Adams.* Boston: Little, Brown and Company, 1856.

3. Flynt, Henry and Helen, *The Ashley House in Old Deerfield.* Privately printed, 1948.

4. Swan, Mabel M., "Boston's Carvers and Joiners," *The Magazine Antiques*, March and April, 1948.

5. Illustrated, with Editorial Note, in *The Magazine Antiques*, March, 1930.

6. Cummin, Hazel E., *Handbook Concord Antiquarian Society.* Concord, Mass., 1937, p. 46.

7. Swan, Mabel M., "The Goddard and Townsend Joiners," *The Magazine Antiques*, April and May, 1946.

8. Downs, Joseph, "The Furniture of Goddard and Townsend," *The Magazine Antiques*, December, 1947.

9. Brewster, Charles W., *Rambles About Portsmouth*, First Series. Portsmouth, 1873.

10. Notes and illustrations in *The Magazine Antiques*, November, 1950.

11. Symonds, Robert W., "The English Export Trade in Furniture to Colonial America," *The Magazine Antiques*, June and October, 1935.

12. Hoopes, Penrose R., "Notes on Some Colonial Cabinetmakers of Hartford," *The Magazine Antiques*, May, 1933.

13. Davis, Emily M., "Eliphelet Chapin," *The Magazine Antiques*, April, 1939.

14. *Three Centuries of Connecticut Furniture.* An Exhibition at the Morgan Memorial, Hartford, 1935.

15. Singleton, Esther, *Social New York Under the Georges, 1714-1776.* New York: D. Appleton & Company, 1902.

16. Adams, *op. cit.*

17. Hornor, W. M., Jr., *Blue Book Philadelphia Furniture.* Philadelphia, 1935. Plates 258-265.

18. *Ibid.*, Plate 95.

19. Vickers, Philip Fithian, *Journal and Letters, 1767-1774.* Edited by John Rogers Williams. Princeton, New Jersey: The University Library, 1900.

20. *The Encyclopedia Americana*, 1948 Edition, Vol. 6, p. 331.

21. Elfe, Thomas, *Account Book 1768-1775.* Manuscript in the Charleston Library Society. Published in the *South Carolina Historical and Genealogical Magazine*.

22. Rose, Jennie Haskell, "Pre-Revolutionary Cabinetmakers of Charles Town," *The Magazine Antiques*, April and May, 1933.

23. *Baltimore Furniture: The Work of Baltimore and Annapolis Cabinetmakers from 1760 to 1810.* Catalogue of An Exhibition at the Baltimore Museum of Art, 1947.

24. Comstock, Helen, "Furniture of Virginia, North Carolina, Georgia, and Kentucky," *The Magazine Antiques*, January, 1952.

25. *Ibid.*

26. Burton, E. Milby, "The Furniture of Charleston," *The Magazine Antiques,* January, 1952.

27. Swan, Mabel Munson, "Coastwise Cargoes of Venture Furniture," *The Magazine Antiques,* April, 1949.

28. Symonds, *op. cit.*

29. *Ibid.*

30. Payson, William F., *Mahogany: Antique and Modern.* New York: E. P. Dutton, 1926.

31. Hornor, *op. cit.*, pp. 8-9.

32. Sheraton, Thomas, *The Cabinet Dictionary.* London, 1803.

33. Hough, Romeyn B., *American Woods.* Lowville, New York, 14 Volumes, 1888-1928.

34. Symonds, R. W., *English Furniture from Charles II to George II.* London: The Connoisseur, Ltd., 1929, pp. 42-45.

35. Lehman, Benjamin, *A Catalogue of Cabinetware.* Philadelphia, 1786. In The Historical Society of Pennsylvania.

36. Sargent, Charles Sprague, *Manual of the Trees of North America.* Boston: Houghton Mifflin Company, 1922.

37. Elliott, Simon B., *The Important Timber Trees of the United States.* Boston: Houghton Mifflin Company, 1912.

38. Kelsey, Harlan P., and Dayton, William A., *Standardized Plant Names.* Prepared for the American Joint Committee on Horticultural Nomenclature. Harrisburg, Pa.: J. Horace McFarland Company, 1942.

39. Hough, *op. cit.*

AMERICAN FURNITURE

Queen Anne

and Chippendale Periods

A GROUP OF QUEEN ANNE

AND CHIPPENDALE INTERIORS

The close relationship of the several elements in this room lends to it a suave congruity that is a triumph of composition. Both the background and the furnishings reveal a knowing derivation from European sources. The English delft pottery and lighting fixtures and the Asia Minor carpet express the colonial taste for Old-World refinements not available from domestic sources. The low-ceiled woodwork on the fireplace wall, divided into heavily fielded panels to give strong accents of light and shade, is intercepted by stop-fluted pilasters of renaissance derivation. The woodwork came from a house in Derry, New Hampshire, built about 1760; but in style it might be twenty years earlier.

The furniture, all of Queen Anne design, shows marked innovations of shape and ornament from the Dutch and English forms which inspired it. The carved chairs were first owned by the Van Cortlandt family in New York. Those with stuffed backs, likewise New York made, are covered with resist-dyed linen, indigo blue on white, contemporary with the chairs; the floral pattern was adapted from French and English silks, then in high fashion for costume and upholstery.

The table is dominated by a great Bristol delft punch bowl painted in blue and inscribed *George Skinner Boston 1732*. Similar plates around the table and bowls on the kas beyond are probably from the Wincanton factory; they are richly painted with blue fish on an aubergine ground and provide a striking color scheme with the green painted woodwork and blue upholstery. Flanking the plates are silver pistol-handled knives and forks. A pewter tankard of the earliest American form has the mark of Joseph Leddell, who was a freeman in New York in 1716; five colonial pewter beakers and a pair of Dutch candlesticks of the William and Mary period complete the table.

On the entrance wall four mezzotints of well-known colonial figures enliven the walls — the two divines, Cotton Mather and Thomas Prince, the latter "the most learned scholar, with the exception of Cotton Mather, in New England"; Jonathan Belcher, distinguished for his style of living and hospitality when Governor of Massachusetts and New Hampshire, and later, in 1747, when Governor of New Jersey, as the chief benefactor of the College at Princeton; and George White-field, Methodist evangelist, famed from New England to Georgia for his eloquence. Near the door hangs a parchment certificate of "Joseph Kingston, Joyner admitted Received and allowed a Free-man and Citizen of New York. [signed] Jacobus V. Cortlandt Esqr. Mayor 1720."

Between the windows a fine silver coffeepot, sugar bowl, and cream jug have the mark of Myer Myers, who was working in New York in 1746. Nearby is a porringer made by Henricus Boelen and a two-handled bowl by Jacobus Vanderspiegel in Manhattan about 1700.

Over the mantel in a gilded shadow box are three carved and painted wooden fish — a smelt, a mackerel, and a cod, all mainstays of early New England. They recall the mansion of Captain Loring in Essex Street, Salem, where each stair end was carved with a miniature gilded codfish.

The flowers at the left of the fireplace are purple colchicum, a favorite September bloom in colonial gardens, listed in *The Flower Garden Display'd, London 1732* as ". . . Naked Boys, because the Flowers appear before the Leaves." Actually, the leaves fall before the flowers appear.

This small parlor came from Readbourne, built in 1733 in Queen Anne's County, Maryland, on the land granted to George Read in 1659. The plantation house, in the style of an English manor, was built for Colonel James Hollyday, who, tradition says, went to England for materials and furnishings; his wife Sarah, the widow of Edward Lloyd of Wye, remained at home to plan and supervise the building, after consulting with Lord Baltimore. The high-studded walls are lined with hard pine paneling of the plain stile-and-rail type; the corner fireplace, framed with a bolection molding in the William and Mary style, is faced with seventeenth-century Dutch tiles in lively colors.

The woodwork is painted gray-white as a foil for the rare eighteenth-century Italian velvet window hangings, the New York and Philadelphia Queen Anne walnut furniture, and the glowing Ispahan carpets. The larger carpet dates from the late sixteenth century and has been recognized as one of the finest weaves of Ispahan.* Here the palmettes, lancet leaves, and vines distributed around a central axis are a marvel of rhythmic design in deep crimson, moss green, gold, and sapphire blue. Some early carpets were sent from Persia to India, and then were carried by Dutch and Portuguese traders to Europe. In 1520 Cardinal Wolsey was among the first to own eastern floor coverings in England; Van Dyck's portrait of the children of Charles I shows an Ispahan carpet in the foreground.

Upon the tall chimney breast hangs a portrait by John Wollaston, who was painting in the middle colonies in the mid-eighteenth century, of Experience, the daughter of Mary and Joseph Johnson of Newark, New Jersey, who married Samuel Gouverneur in 1750. They lived at Mount Pleasant, their country home on the Passaic River beyond Newark, with their eleven children.

Above the sofa is a pair of sparkling quillwork sconces with their original silver candle branches marked by Jacob Hurd, one of the ablest colonial silversmiths of the early eighteenth century. They belonged to Parson William Smith of Braintree, "the richest clergyman in the Province," and Madam Elizabeth Smith, a descendant of the Sieurs de Quincy who signed Magna Carta. Their daughter Abigail married John Adams.* A double quillwork sconce near the window is lighted by a pair of silver candle branches stamped by Knight Leverett, a contemporary of Hurd's in Boston; they are engraved with the monogram of Ruth Read, the wife of John Read, a minister and lawyer who was admitted to the bar in New Haven in 1708 and died in Boston in 1749.

A shapely Irish silver chandelier in the center of the room was made as a memorial gift in 1742 at Galway and is inscribed: "Pray for ye soule of Mr. Lynch of Burdeux who dyed ye 4 of [October] 1737 . . ." The pair of silver wall sconces on the chimney breast, modeled with shells and engraved with a coat of arms, were marked by John Sanders in London in 1718.

The large japanned looking glass was an heirloom of the Bleecker family in New York; and the tea table, laid with an enameled salt-glaze tea-and-coffee service, is from the same region.

In the window are scarlet geraniums, described by Robert Furber in 1732 as "A Green-House Plant: It makes a Shrub of about two Foot high. It is raised from Seeds, which it brings plentifully, and must be sown in March on a Hot-bed."

III · THE MARLBORO ROOM

Climate and living customs decreed the form of southern plantation houses, which were markedly different from colonial mansions north of Maryland. In 1705 an English traveler wrote of them: "The Private Buildings are of late very much improved; several gentlemen there, having built themselves large Brick Houses of many Rooms on a Floor, and several Stories high, as also some Stone Houses: but they don't seem to covet to make them lofty, having extent enough of Ground to build upon; And now and then they are visited by high winds, which wou'd incommode a towering Fabrik. They always contrive to have large Rooms, that they may be cool in Summer. Of late they have made their Stories much higher than formerly, and their windows large, and sasht with Cristal Glass; and with in they adorn their Apartments with rich Furniture."*

The paneling of this room came from Patuxent Manor, in Lower Marlboro, Maryland. The iron fireback inscribed *Potuxent 1744* notes the completion of the house for Charles Grahame, who had arrived from England two years earlier.

The furniture is principally of walnut, made in Philadelphia and of generous proportions to suit a room of imposing size. An armchair labeled by William Savery stands at the window to the right. A set of four stools with shell-carved knees were made by John Elliott in 1756 for Stenton, in Germantown. Several easy chairs, backstools, and sofas are covered with leather or old sand-colored brocatelle. The five tall windows are hung with crimson brocatelle cut in conformity with the engraved patterns of Daniel Marot, designer to William III.

A graceful pair of chandeliers in wood and gilded tin, of the kind used in colonial ballrooms and churches, and several pairs of heavy English brass wall arms light the room, together with numerous American-made iron and brass standing lights.

Delft bowls from the Lambeth, Brislington, and Bristol potteries in England have deep, slanted sides indicative of the early period; one is inscribed: "Liberty and Property Without Any New Excise."

The subject of the crewelwork picture above the fireplace is the *Fishing Lady on Boston Common*, among the largest of about a dozen known examples of this subject. A few years earlier is a silk-and-wool needlework landscape with shepherds, embroidered in 1746 by Priscilla Allen in Boston.

The old pine floor is nearly covered by an immense Feraghan carpet representing the highest art of that district in the finely drawn trellised flowers and distinctive borders in red and blue on a pale-green ground.

Several portraits in this room have both historic and human interest. Over the sofa is Charles Willson Peale's dramatic likeness of Richard Lloyd Bennett, who was born at Wye House, Maryland, in 1750. As a young man, he joined the Coldstream Guards in England, and married Joanna Leigh of North Court, Isle of Wight. They returned to Wye House in 1783, where he died four years later. Between the windows is a three-quarter-length portrait of General Washington, with an encampment of soldiers in the background, painted by Charles Peale Polk after the War. Opposite is Robert Edge Pine's profile likeness, done at Princeton, October 10, 1783, of General Walter Stewart, distinguished as "the handsomest officer in the Continental Army." Other portraits in the room are of Anne de Montchanin and Samuel du Pont, and their son Pierre Samuel du Pont de Nemours, painted in France in the eighteenth century. The last-named subject arrived at Newport in 1800 and later settled in Wilmington.

IV · THE PORT ROYAL ENTRANCE HALL

In memory of his old home, Edward Stiles, a wealthy planter from the West Indies, chose *Port Royal* as the name for the new house which he built at Frankford, north of Philadelphia, in 1762. In plan and design the architecture followed that of Mount Pleasant, a neighboring mansion still standing above the Schuylkill River. The classical influence is dominant, continuing a traditional theme introduced into England a century and a half earlier. In Horace Walpole's words: "[England] adopted Holbein and Van Dyck; she borrowed Reubens; she produced Inigo Jones. Vitruvius drew up his grammar. Palladio showed him his practise. Rome displayed a theatre worthy of his emulation, and King Charles I was ready to Encourage, Employ, and reward his talents."*

The entrance hall and the adjoining parlor at Winterthur show Port Royal's finest interiors. The staircase was concealed at the left, giving an unbroken sweep through the house from the front to the garden door.

In the entrance hall the Greek Doric entablature follows the severe classic pattern of carved triglyphs alternating with plain metopes. Fanlights pierce the arch-topped door openings on the east and west walls and give a hint of the pierced shells to come in Chippendale ornament. A paneled dado skirts the lower walls; above it an eighteenth-century Chinese wallpaper painted with tree peonies, bamboo, birds, and butterflies in nebulous shades of green, white, and rose blends harmoniously into the original gray of the woodwork.

The furniture in the Chippendale style is large-scaled and formal in aspect to suit the background. Three marble "slab" side tables and a Philadelphia sofa occupy the principal spaces. Several pairs of armchairs have the sturdy lines favored by Philadelphia joiners. At the right of the door, the pediment of a fine double chest is richly carved with a bucolic scene. Opposite stands a tall clock distinguished by its great size and wealth of ornament; it is signed by Thomas Wagstaffe, an English Quaker who sent many clock works to his colonial Quaker brethren. At the east end of the hall, a pair of superb looking glasses, framed in walnut with gilded carving, has, since 1769, a long history of ownership in the Quincy family in Massachusetts. Reflected in the looking glasses are some of the eight gilt bronze wall branches which light the room. They have the airy asymmetry of Thomas Johnson's rocaille ornaments, published in 1761. One pair of branches came from Epaphroditus Champion's mansion at East Haddam, built about 1795; perhaps they were used in Colonel Champion's earlier house·at West Chester, Connecticut.

On the tables, the famille rose porcelain represents the early export wares brought from the Orient to Europe before American ships traded directly with the Far East.

In the center of the floor is a rare late-sixteenth-century Persian vase carpet named for the Chinese vase forms spaced at wide intervals in the field from which archaic-patterned flowers spring — a reminder that Shah Abbas I and his father were avid collectors of Ming porcelains. The scarcity of similar vase carpets is due to their limited production, which was always small, and to the toll of centuries.

V · THE STAMPER-BLACKWELL PARLOR

The woodwork and furnishings here epitomize the sophisticated life of eighteenth-century Philadelphia, famous in the colonies for fine houses and superb furniture. The house was built in 1764 at 224 Pine Street for John Stamper, Mayor of Philadelphia; later the Reverend Dr. Blackwell, assistant rector of St. Peter's and Christ Churches, occupied it until his death in 1831. No other colonial room matches this one for its wealth of carved ornament imposed on a background of classical pattern. On the cornice, pedimented doorways, mantel, and overmantel the carver's skill has been lavished unstintedly. The doors, mantelshelf, and chair rail are mahogany.

The plan and ornament of the room were adapted from English books; Abraham Swan's *Designs in Architecture*, published in London in 1757, provided the pattern for the overmantel and flanking panels.*

Here is the greatest assembly of rare Philadelphia-carved paw-foot furniture in any collection, numbering eight pieces in all — a card table, an easy chair, a firescreen, and five side chairs. Most famous of them is a *sample* chair at the left, one of a group attributed to Benjamin Randolph through family ownership. A looking glass between the windows hung originally in the Cadwalader house in Fourth Street and retains its original white-and-gold finish. At the right is Copley's self-portrait in pastel, a well-known likeness often reproduced.

On the round table stands a unique silver punch bowl, or monteith, with scalloped rim to hold the wineglasses. It was made by John Letelier in 1770 for the Thomas-Wallace family. Other ornaments here are five matched bowls and a set of Chinese porcelain, enameled in color with the *Cherry-Pickers*, a subject copied from Nicolas Lancret's design.

On the card tables "burnt image China," advertised in the Pennsylvania *Gazette,* is seen in the fragile Chelsea porcelain candelabra modeled with birds, figures, and flowering trees.

The cut-glass chandelier, like those assembled to light the Meschianza Ball in 1778, has unusual swags of drapery connecting each pair of arms.

The window curtains are lustrous salmon-colored silk of the Louis XV period and show the pre-eminence of French weaving in the eighteenth century; their wide floral borders of needle-point embroidery are contemporary in date. The chairs are covered with silk similar to the curtains.

In the center of the room an early Kuba carpet, woven in the sixteenth century, is a glowing masterpiece from the Caucasus, influenced by Persian weaving.

The book on the table is *Mēdicina Brĭtannica*, reprinted in Philadelphia by B. Franklin and D. Hall in 1751. On the title page is the signature of Elias Boudinot, the President of the Continental Congress who signed the Treaty of Peace in 1783.

Below the looking glass claret-colored carnations of variegated shades are arranged in a Chinese porcelain bowl. Robert Furber, a gardener in Kensington, described in 1732 a "Painted Lady Carnation or July-Flower. This brings its Blossoms large; the Flower-Leaves are white on the Back, but on the Upper Side are blotch'd with a Crimson Color upon White. There are many sorts of Painted Lady Carnation some blotched with Purple, others almost Blue."

VI · THE CHINESE PARLOR

This room takes its name from the old Chinese painted wallpaper that records the measured serenity of daily life in the eighteenth century. It is drawn with the incomparable taste of the oriental artist who created an enchanted world of peace and beauty. In the same spirit of imagination are the black-and-gold lacquer screens in the corners, brought from China before 1800 for Elias Hasket Derby, a famous merchant, shipowner, and patron of the arts in Salem; and the carved rhinoceros horn near the window, brought home by Admiral Samuel F. du Pont a century ago and described in 1857 by Anna Brinclé who wrote of the Admiral's Chinese collection: "The carving exceeds anything I ever saw of the kind. The most curious piece of work I think is a rhinoceros horn about four feet long, entirely cut in flowers and fruits, and set up, cornucopia fashion on a carved ebony stand."

In the shell-topped cupboard a Chinese porcelain tea set decorated with western figures penciled in black is earlier than the export wares bearing patriotic devices of the American Republic. Religious and secular engraved subjects were introduced to the Chinese artists by Jesuit missionaries who had been accepted for centuries in China for their learning in the arts and sciences, and often acted as interpreters for the foreigners there. The porcelain flower vases and bowls, enameled in color, are other appropriate ornaments for a Chinese parlor.

The marble-top tables follow the Chinese Chippendale spirit in the use of rectangular supports and pierced fret brackets, reminiscent of the summerhouse on the wallpaper above the mantel. Two sets of Philadelphia chairs in the rococo style express the ability of two equally skillful craftsmen, James Gillingham and Benjamin Randolph.

The mantelpiece came from the Stamper-Blackwell house in Philadelphia and, like the parlor from that house, shows a dependence on the published designs of Abraham Swan, especially for the consoles carved with tattered leaves. Standing on the mantel is a seven-piece garniture of Derbyshire spar, a mineral endowed with crystalline amber and amethyst depths.

The yellow antique silk window hangings are draped from carved wood pelmets in accordance with the authority of Chippendale's *Director*, and the same silk is used for upholstery. This fabric is for autumn; and in winter early-eighteenth-century green damask, trimmed with blue fringe, dresses the windows and furniture. On the old pine floor a large Feraghan carpet, similar to one in the Marlboro Room, serves to hold together various elements in the room with its intricate and even-toned pattern.

A sparkling English cut-glass chandelier and wall branches of the mid-eighteenth century furnish a magic source of light for this exotic scene.

VII · THE BERTRAND PARLOR

This room was brought to Winterthur from Belle Isle, William Bertrand's house at Boer, Lancaster County, Virginia. The house, built before 1760, was occupied in later years by Mary Ball Washington's niece Fanny, the wife of Rawleigh Downman.

The high-paneled dado and the diminished cornice show the change from the tall, fully paneled rooms in the Virginia plantation houses that were a legacy from the William and Mary period. The painted mantel came from Springfield, an estate in Montgomery County, Virginia, built at the close of the century. English delft tiles decorated with chinoiserie figures trim the fire opening.

The walls are painted oyster-shell white, a new fashion spreading in England when the Chippendale style was at its height in the colonies. The mode was noted by travelers, among them Benjamin Franklin, who relayed instructions from London to his wife Deborah for finishing their parlor in Philadelphia.

The furniture is almost all of New York origin; the gaming table and set of four chairs, arranged for play, are fine expressions of the vigorous scale and curve of Manhattan design. The lavish carving on the tea table has some features of a pair of chairs nearby which were owned by Sir William Johnson, Superintendent of Indian Affairs for George II.

Above the chairs hangs a portrait of Hannah Farmar painted by John Durand in New York between 1767 and 1768. A portrait of her aunt, Hannah Farmar Peck, hangs opposite; Peck's Slip had been a part of her dowry, and a shop façade from that waterfront landmark is in the Winterthur Collection. Near the window a rare mezzotint, scraped by Charles Willson Peale, of William Pitt (dressed in a Roman toga), one of America's heroes who defended in England the colonies' fight for freedom, bears the legend: "Worthy of Liberty, Mr. Pitt scorns to invade the Liberties of other People." The parents of the children in the canvas above the fireplace are shown in two unidentified portraits in the Stamper-Blackwell parlor.

The easy chair by the fireplace and several other chairs are upholstered in cherry-red moreen, a fabric coveted in the eighteenth century for its watered pattern applied to the wool surface by hot irons. The sumptuous window hangings in two shades of crimson silk show a serpentine lace pattern framing floral clusters; they were woven probably about 1725. Softer in color is the carpet of Turkish weave, made about the same time.

On a piecrust-top table stands a silver tankard of extraordinary size, having a gallon capacity. It was marked by Benjamin Hiller, active in Boston from 1711 to 1745.

The five-piece armorial mantel garniture and the flowerpots are of Chinese origin and, like the fabrics and brass lighting fixtures, show how imported luxuries augmented the native arts for domestic decoration.

VIII · THE MAPLE ROOM

When Port Royal was demolished over twenty years ago, three rooms, as well as the entrance hall described in Plate IV, were saved for the Winterthur Collection. Illustrated here is one of the two bedrooms, plainer than the principal rooms on the first floor. The paneled chimney wall and dado have wide, fielded panels relieved by the simple crosseted frame of the fire opening and by the Wall-of-Troy molding pierced in the deep cornice. The woodwork, like that in the entrance, retains its original colors, here a faint green, buff and salmon, to set off the panels from their frames. A wide facing of mottled gray Chester County marble frames the fire opening. Within is an arched fireback cast with the British lion, unicorn, crest, and crown, and the legend of the Garter, a product of the Oxford Furnace, Warren County, New Jersey, between 1745 and 1758.

A pervading harmony in the rich color of the background, hangings, floor covering, and furniture serves to make this room memorable. It is a symphony not achieved with much license in the choice of material, but only with meticulous regard for the credible relationship of each element to the other.

The Chippendale furniture is made of honey-colored maple, often curly-grained, a wood rarely used when mahogany had largely superseded native woods. A Philadelphia high chest of drawers, a dressing table, and a desk and bookcase stand against the north and south walls. The hangings of the bed are homespun umber-colored glazed wool combined with a quilted, green wool bedspread.

The carpet is a rare survival of the English Wilton looms, daring in its large figures and bold color. On a black ground, rococo scrolls and eighteenth-century garden favorites — lilies, roses, bluebells, and tulips — spread over the surface, in shades of orange, wine red, blue, and green.

Above the mantel is a conversation piece painted in brilliant colors by William Williams, who worked in the middle colonies for nearly thirty years and returned to England during the Revolution where he died in poverty. A pastel portrait of Catharine Herring Brickerhoff, drawn by Nathaniel Smibert, hangs near the bed. As a pendant to it, a hatchment, embroidered in silver thread and blue silk on black, depicts the arms of the Hodges and King families.

At the right of the fireplace a Jackfield tea-and-coffee set is laid out on a dished-top table; its mirror-black surface repeats the background of the carpet, as the golden colors of the pattern echo the dark amber tone of the furniture.

On the desk from Philadelphia, the city where John Hancock's name stood first among the Signers, are two of his signatures. The fly leaf of *A New Version of the Psalms of David*, printed in Boston, 1765, is inscribed: *John Hancock's Thou shalt not Steal Saith the Lord.* Nearby is a letter Hancock wrote to his wife: "2 Octo. 1783. My Dear, I Arrived very safely in Town just before 3 o'clock, took Knox in my Carriage, & went home, Din'd upon Neck of Veal & Goose, went to Council & in the Eveng went to Mrs. Balch's . . . I have Sent you A Basket of Potatoes from Roxbury, the finest I ever Saw, Six Lemmons Six Loaves Bread a Roast Sirloin of Beef A large Speaking Trumpet for Johnny — I Should have Sent you a four Rib piece of Beef Roasted, but I had it taken off the Spit and the Barge Men with my self Devour'd the whole that you must be Content with the Sirloin.

"God Bless You, I wish you very happy. I am, My Dear, Yours Affectionately John Hancock."

IX · THE HAMPTON ROOM

Hampton Court was built in Elizabeth, New Jersey, in 1761, and subsequently became known as the Winfield Scott house, where "Fuss and Feathers," as the illustrious general was known because of his punctiliousness in dress and decorum, spent nearly twenty years prior to the Mexican campaigns and where he returned for a short time in 1846 before ending his days at West Point. Hampton Court became hemmed in by domestic dwellings in later years and was demolished in 1928, at which time this room was removed to Winterthur.

The woodwork is like the parlor at Woodford, built five years earlier as a country seat for William Coleman in the Northern Liberties of Philadelphia. These two rooms have only a hint of the pierced and carved rococo ornament of the Stamper-Blackwell house and Mount Pleasant, then about to be built in Philadelphia. The stirring of new influences, visible in the carved tabernacle overmantel marks a link between the plain, high-ceiled rooms of Virginia and the urbane rococo style which flowered on the eve of the Revolution.

The landscape above the mantel was painted for Fancy Hill, the home of Samuel Ladd Howell at Gloucester, New Jersey, and shows a view from the house, across the Delaware to the present League Island.

The New England furniture is largely of Newport origin. A desk and bookcase, a kneehole chest of drawers, a tall clock, and a high chest are carved with the flamboyant shells which have made the names *Townsend* and *Goddard* famous. A tea table, a breakfast table, and an easy chair belong to the same group. The bed, the finest one of the Chippendale period in the collection, and perhaps unmatched elsewhere, is of Massachusetts origin. The bed furniture or hangings are blue and white printed linen in the French taste, which aptly describes the spirited sweeps of rococo detail at the command of the English engraver on copper.

The carpet is an eighteenth-century Asia Minor weave probably from Ushak and shows the influence of Egyptian carpets in the geometric framework of the field and border panels.

Tutenag, an alloy of zinc, nickel, and copper, was brought from China in the mid-eighteenth century and became popular for fire grates, lighting fixtures, and other domestic hardware. Here it provides a silver-colored metal for seven candlesticks on the tables and chests in the same shape as contemporary silver.

Other ornaments keyed to the quiet tone of the room are a miniature Holland Delft garniture on the mantel and a collection of Worcester porcelain, transfer-printed in black with idyllic and chinoiserie subjects, that fills the cupboard.

On the desk is an early brass standish and a snuffer stand; near the bed is a copy of "Practical Discourses Delivered on Occasion of the Earthquakes in November, 1755. Wherein is particularly shown, by a Variety of Arguments, the great Importance of turning our Feet unto God's Testimonies, and of making Haste to keep his Commandments; Together with the Reasonableness, the Necessity, and great Advantage, of a serious Consideration of our Ways. By Jonathan Mayhew, D. D., Boston 1760."

X · THE ESSEX ROOM

The paneling of this room was taken from the plantation house of the Ritchie family at Tappahannock, in Essex County, Virginia, where it was installed about 1740. The house had been in existence prior to 1690 on land granted to Bartholomew Hoskins by Charles I in 1645, but passed through several changes of ownership before this room was added.

The high-ceiled room has an arched fire opening, flanked by tall pilasters, and a heavy chair rail which is carried around the fully paneled walls, all of which are features of early-eighteenth-century wainscoting.

The furniture runs the gamut of variety made by Connecticut cabinetmakers of the Revolutionary era in the tawny-brown cherry wood especially favored by them. The bed has the turned and square fluted posts which mark the peak of elegance in this period of cabinetwork; the block-front chest of drawers carved with shells is among the best of its kind; the desk and bookcase and the double chest of drawers have the multiple-arch paneled doors or the pin-wheel carving which serves as a signature of their origin. A carved easy chair and an armchair in dark mahogany stand by the fireplace and, like the matching side chairs in the room, represent the quiet perfection of Massachusetts Chippendale furniture. On the chest by the bed is one of three bombé or serpentine-shaped dressing stands in the collection, made in New England in the Chippendale period.

The curtains at the windows and bed as well as the carpet evoke the distant relationships through trade and commerce with Europe and the Far East. A selvage of the printed linen is marked: *Soehnée L'Ainé & Cie à Munster près Colmar.* Soehnée, the Elder, of Paris, formed a partnership in 1799 with the founders of the textile manufactory at Munster, which had been started in 1776. This continued the long tradition of fine textiles produced at Lyon, Jouy, and elsewhere which made France pre-eminent in that field in the eighteenth century. The design of this linen repeats the exotic shapes of the fabrics imported into Europe from the Orient by the Compagnée des Indes for a century or more. The eighteenth century Ushak carpet is one of the luxurious carpets brought from Asia Minor by way of Europe for fine colonial rooms.

On the chimney breast hangs a three-quarter-length portrait of William Verstille, a self-assured youth in a plum-colored suit and blue satin waistcoat; the artist was William Johnston, a recently recognized painter from Boston, who worked in Hartford. Verstille, born in 1757, likewise was a Bostonian who settled in Wethersfield, and served as a second lieutenant in Colonel Samuel Blachley Webb's regiment. He became a miniature painter, and two fine examples with his signature are in this room; one is an ingratiating likeness of Catherine Sewell Orne (1780-1818), who married Thomas Cushing and, later, Elisha Mack.

Several rare contemporary books and newspapers on the desk and tables are of interest. *Domestic Medicine or the Family Physician* was printed by John Trumbull at Norwich in 1778; Elijah Eldredge's *Book of Receipts for Painting & Staining Wood* is in manuscript. Among the old newspapers is the Boston *Gazette* for June 24, 1771, its back pages advertising imported fabrics, runaway apprentices, and "Umbrilloes made and sold by Isaac Greenwood of all sizes for Ladies . . . and Oyl Cloth and neat jointed for men."

AMERICAN FURNITURE

Queen Anne

and Chippendale Periods

ILLUSTRATIONS FROM THE

WINTERTHUR COLLECTION

1 · BED
Maple
Rhode Island 1735-1750

Few American four-post beds of the Queen Anne period are known today. This example is an exceptionally fine one. The wood is maple, and all four posts are alike, having bold cabriole legs and deeply cut pad feet. Usually only the foot posts of American beds are shaped and carved. The headboard and rails are likewise of maple, a wood often favored by Job Townsend, the first of the famous cabinetmaking family.

An extant bill rendered to Samuel Ward, later the governor of Rhode Island, by Job Townsend in 1746 includes some maple items:

a Mahogany High Chest of Drawers	£30: 0:0
a Mahogany Dressing Table	13:10:0
a Mahogany Dressing Table	17:17:6
a Mahogany Dining Table	15: 3:4
a Mahogany Tea Table	8:10:0
1 Square Kitchen Table	5:10:0
a Maple Tea Table	2:10:0
a Maple Stool	2: 0:0*

The bed hangings and spread are contemporary in date. They are of homespun linen embroidered in crewels, chiefly in shades of rose, blue, green, and yellow. The strapwork trellis pattern of the spread is rarely seen in American crewelwork. The embroidery is an exceptionally fine example of New England work. The bedspread was originally owned by Thomas Hancock in Boston and later by his nephew and heir, the patriot John Hancock.

Height 8' Width 4' 11½" Length 6' 8"

1

2 · BED
Mahogany
New York 1760-1775

The excellence of this bed shows in the stop-fluted posts, the leaf-carved knees, and the large claw feet. The square, tapered headposts end in round clubs and, like the side and footrails, are of mahogany. The lavish use of expensive imported wood is most unexpected where native woods were customary; in this instance cost must have been of little consideration. The stop-fluting occurs on Connecticut, Newport, and New York furniture (see Figure 311 and Figure 147), an architectural detail borrowed from classic columns. Long, straight-lobed leaves on the knees are cut with a series of crescents along their ribs, a device that recurs on Gilbert Ash's signed chair, made in Wall Street, New York.*

Bed furniture, so prized in colonial days that often it is listed in wills, is here fashioned of crewel embroidery in varying shades of blue on homespun linen; it is a rare survival of American origin. Two other sets, used alternately on the bed, are indigo resist-dyed linen, popular in New York for its bold pattern of birds and flowering branches and its rich blue color.

In his will proved August 30, 1754, Nathaniel Townsend, of Jericho, in the town of Oyster Bay, New York, directed: "Being this 18 day of 5th month called May in the year 1754 very sick and of exquisite pain of body, but my understanding pretty well . . . I leave to my wife Martha one of my choicest beds & full furniture thereto belonging and my cupboard which I had by her and a brass kettle & £130."

Height 7′ 3″   Width 4′ 6″   Length 6′ 5½″

2

3 · BED
Walnut
Philadelphia 1750-1760

A bed was among the most valued household possessions in colonial America, and since the seventeenth century often was used in the parlor. Besides the frame, made to match the companion pieces in a room, the so-called bed furniture or upholstery was costly and often elaborate. Long, cold winters and ill-heated houses made heavily curtained and feather beds a necessity. In 1769 John Mason, a Philadelphia upholsterer, offered hair mattresses to replace the traditional feather beds: ". . . for Sale Mattrasses, or wool beds, which are so beneficial to mankind for when a constitution grows weak through inadvertency, or any waye thrown into Confusion, these beds are of great use to rest on, therefore I would advise every Constitution to be provided with one of them . . . [it] gives a greater spring to the nerves than feather beds."

The plain foot posts of the bed pictured here end in shapely curved cabriole legs and strong claw-and-ball feet; the rear posts stand on simple club feet. Rails of stained softwood show peg marks along the upper rabbeted edge where the sacking bottom was fixed.

The bed coverings are embroidered in blue crewels on homespun linen, American, about 1750.

Height 7' 9½"   Width 4' 10½"   Length 6' 6"

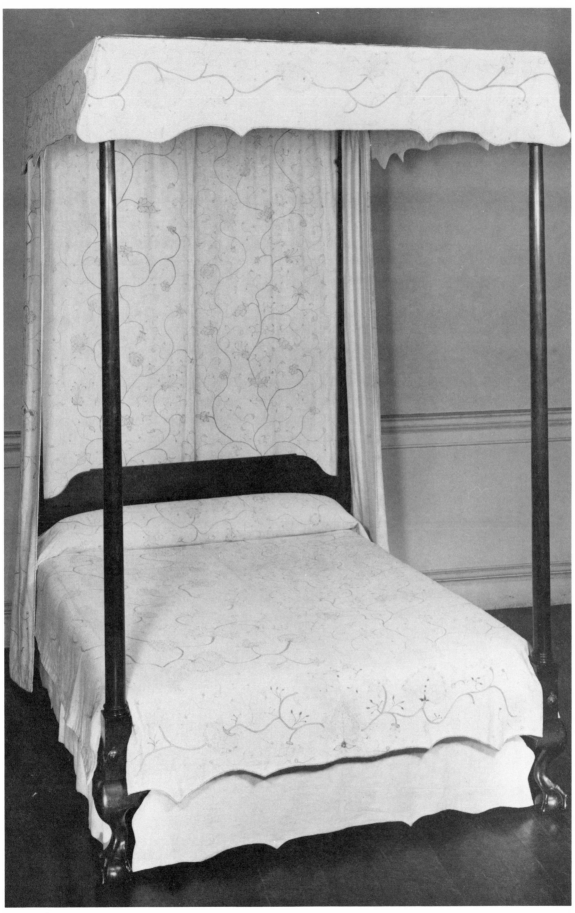

4 · BED
Mahogany
Massachusetts 1760-1775

The hazards of fire and the changes of fashion through the years may best explain the rarity today of fine colonial beds. A bed wrench and canvas bag for silver, stored in a leather fire bucket under the staircase, to guard against sudden emergencies may not have been certain protection. Furthermore, in the mid-nineteenth century when fashionable low beds of the sleigh, spool, and panel form made cornices, curtains, and valances seem outmoded, doubtless many early beds were sacrificed. This example, one of the handsomest known, was acquired from a descendant of the Whittemore family in Massachusetts. The carving upon the knees of the foot posts is straight-lobed acanthus leaves, set off by a punched, snowflake background that is a hallmark of Salem wood carvers. The delicacy of the fluted corner posts, and square headposts and rails of maple (painted here to simulate mahogany) are other characteristics of the same origin. The headboard is stained softwood. The canvas bottom was nailed to the upper rabbeted edge of the rails. A rare feature here is the original tester frame of pine, rounded at the corners.

The hangings are sea-green silk damask, Italian, mid-eighteenth century. The coverlet is green quilted satin of similar date.

An inventory, dated October, 1775, in Boston lists: "Things divided between W^m & Nath: Coffin, T. Amory & G. Deblois, who are to account with John & Eben? Coffin for their Proportion of the same. Viz!

Check — Bed, Furniture & Bed stead	£22..10..—
1 Carpet	13..10..—
3 Looking Glasses	24.. 0..—
6 Red Bottom Chairs	3.. 0.. 0
Copper drinking Pot & Ladle	0..18..—
1 Brass Bason	0..12..—
Pine Table	1.. 0..—
Red Bed & Bedstead	40.. 0.. 0
Round Table & Carpet	9.. 0.. 0"

Height 7' 5"   Width 4' 8"   Length 6' 4"

5 · BED
Walnut
Philadelphia 1750-1760

Low-post beds of double size were almost unknown in the eighteenth century; a few oak ones remain which date before 1700. This form possibly found a welcome use in warm weather, when hangings were gladly dispensed with. Here the bold cabriole legs and club-shaped rear feet match the tall-post bed, Figure 3. The headboard is walnut instead of softwood, which in a tall-post bed often was covered by the back curtains.

The coverlet is silk brocade in polychrome, French, Louis XV period. The valance is similar, but of the Louis XVI period.

In the *Pennsylvania Gazette*, July 4, 1754, James White, "Upholsterer and Undertaker, lately arrived from London," advertised:

"Makes all sorts of furniture for beds, window curtains, either festoon or plain, all sorts of chairs, either French or India back, sofa's settees and settee-beds, feather-beds, mattrasses, and all other sorts of household furniture, after the newest taste, either in the Chinese or Venetian, likewise paper hangings put up, so as not to be affected by the hottest weather; also funerals furnished, and shrouds ready made, pink'd as in London, or plain and plaited, and sheets."

Height 30½"   Width 4' 10"   Length 6' 6"

6 · BED
Curly Maple
Massachusetts 1760-1780

Only one other bed of the colonial period in this collection is made of maple (Figure 1) among so many others of walnut and mahogany. It indicates the early restriction of this handsome wood, which later became appreciated in widely different regions during the Federal period and after, until the pall of machined-carved walnut gave it pause. This bed is maple throughout, even on the rails, headposts, and headboard, no birch, ash, or pine being used for those customary parts. The design of the posts is well suited to the grain of the honey-colored wood.

The hangings of the bed are old yellow homespun glazed wool to match the window curtains. The coverlet is green wool quilted in a pattern of raffle leaves, mid-eighteenth century in date.

The bed was owned by descendants of Richard Derby in Salem and was acquired from them in 1939.

An inventory of the Amory family in Boston dated July 1775 reads:

1 Check Bed. Furniture & Bedstead
1 Red Bed & Bedstead
1 Cot Bedstead
1 Green d°
1 Field d° & Curtain
9 Chairs
6 d° (Red bottom)
2 d° (Round)
6 d° & 2 great Chairs
9 d° (Chamber)
1 Table
1 d° (Round) & a Carpet
1 d° (Bureau)
1 d° (Pine)

Height 7′ 5″   Width 4′ 10″   Length 6′ 8½″

7 · BED
Cherry
Connecticut 1770-1785

The bed pillars illustrated in design books are faintly echoed in the posts of this shapely and unusual bed from the school of cabinetmakers that included Hartford, Middletown, and New Britain. The square, Chinese Chippendale legs, nicely fluted and chamfered, stand on double-tiered Marlborough feet. The tall posts to carry the tester frame and curtains are turned in perfect proportion. On the top inside edge of the rails wooden pegs are fixed for roping.

The old French cotton hangings are printed in blue with whimsical chinoiserie figures and scenes well suited in date and character to the bed. The spread is blue silk damask, early eighteenth century.

A contemporary bill, written in Boston, November, 1769, records "Bought at the Vandue Mr Wells made of Mr Spooners Furniture . . .

A Copper plate Bed with 4 window Curtains & Chair bottoms	£145.—.—
1 Red Silk Quilt	30.—.—
1 Mohoggeny 4 post Bedstead	32.—.—
1 finnered [veneered] Chest of Draws	12.—.—
Nature Displayed 7 Vol 30	10.10.—
1 folio Bibble	42.—.—
Guardian 1 Vol	1.—.—"

Height 7' 2"   Width 4' 5½"   Length 6' 8"

7

8 · BED
Mahogany
Philadelphia 1780-1790

This bed, of great size, shows the last phase of the Chippendale style. The bottom of the posts remain square; but the elongated vase form above and the reeded shaft rising from it, carved with raffle and water leaves, nevertheless may be seen among the bed pillars on Plate 106, dated 1787, in Hepplewhite's *Guide*. Both the headposts and headboard of this bed are uncommon; the former are mahogany and are shaped exactly like the foot posts, but without carving; the latter is likewise mahogany, shaped in reverse curves, and not meant to be covered by the back curtain as a headboard of softwood would be.

The curtains of emerald green taffeta silk are contemporary in date; they are hung on cords and pulleys and, when released, enclose the bed. The design was adapted from Plate XXVII in Chippendale's *Director*. The curtains may be similar to those offered by Hyns Taylor in Philadelphia in 1782: "A fine green Moreen Furniture to a four post Bedstead, made compleat, to draw in double drapery, with tassels, lines and brass pins."

The rails are mahogany and still retain the small wooden knobs inside the upper, rabbeted edge, to hold the sacking bottom. Original wooden pulleys are in the cornice.

Height 8′ 2″   Width 6′ 3½″   Length 7′ 6″

9 · BED
Black Birch and Soft Pine
New England 1770-1785

The wood and design of furniture are ready indications of its probable origin and importance. In smaller towns, metropolitan styles were followed, sometimes belatedly, and often became only faint echoes of the parent inspiration when the limitations of cost and space, as well as the abilities of the maker, were finally met.

In this bed, the choice of birch for the posts, nicely fluted on four sides at the foot, and on two sides at the head, is a country cabinetmaker's wood. White pine provided an easy, smooth surface to cut the curves of the painted Chippendale cornice; it still has the original wooden pulleys for cords to adjust the curtains. The headboard is of the same wood, stained.

The bed furniture is contemporary, of Massachusetts origin. It is homespun linen, embroidered in various shades of red, green, blue, and yellow crewels, a well preserved set of rare colonial needlework.

A sale of furniture is recorded at Danvers, October 18, 1781; "Know all men By these presents that I Benjamin Balek of Danvers in the County & State of Massachusetts Bay in consideration of the sum of one hundred pounds Lawfull money to me cash in hand paid the Recp^t whiere of I do hereby acknoledge Do sell bargen & convea unto Samuel Sairt of Danvers in County & Ste fores^d gentilman — that is to say

one Black walnut Desk
two parlor tables maple
one Dozen of maple parler chears
one Brass kettel
a Quantity of pueter plates and platters
fore fether Beds & furniture Belonging to y^e Same
one Looking glass   Skaile and weights"

Height 7' 1"   Width 4' 3¾"   Length 6' 1"

9

10 · DECEPTION BED
Mahogany
Philadelphia 1780-1790

Concealed beds were as much needed in the eighteenth century as they are today; although houses were larger then, families were, too, and visitors stayed indefinitely. Early in the century, half-tester beds that folded up against the wall behind a curtain were popular in New England. Built-in beds, with folding doors to conceal them, were customary in New York. The bed here is a so-called press bed, and simulates a chest of drawers; the detachable front allows the sack-bottom frame to be unfolded. The waning Chippendale style is apparent in the choice of oval brasses and concealed tapered square legs. A Philadelphia upholsterer, William Martin, advertised in 1770 ". . . all sorts of chairs, sofas, couches, deception beds. . . ," the last-named well describing the bed here. The hinged top of the chest when raised releases the false front. The folding frame is made of ash, and the back is pine.

In the Philadelphia inventory printed in 1788 "of the Plate, Houshold Furniture and other goods, of the Hon. John Penn, jun. Esquire, which are to be exposed to Sale . . . at his House the corner of Market and Sixth streets . . ." the bedroom furniture included two deception beds:

> 1 set of hair colour furniture cotton bed curtains, pattern William Penn's treaty with the Indians
> 3 window curtains to match ditto, with cord, tassels and screws
> 5 common poplar bedsteads and 2 ditto that shut into the form of drawers
> 1 elegant Wilton carpet 20 by 12, with some spare pieces
> A tin shower bath

Height 3′ 7½″   Width 4′ 2¼″   Length (open) 6′ 4″, (closed) 23¾″

10

11 · ARMCHAIR
Walnut and Cane
Probably New England 1700-1725

Here is an early use of the cabriole leg, as it emerged from the Carolean style; the shape of the block and turned rear legs originated in the latter period. The same squared cabriole leg, edged with an incised line, was used in Connecticut, and some English caned chairs show a similar design.*

Height 48½″   Width 23″   Depth 17″

12 · ARMCHAIR
Maple and Cane, Painted
Probably New England 1700-1725

This chair is similar to Figure 11, but the flattened cresting and rounded arms of this chair are more familiar in New England than are those of the former example. The stretchers are shaped like the turnings on Connecticut side chairs of the Queen Anne period.

Cane chairs were mentioned in many eighteenth-century inventories such as an early Boston inventory of ". . . the Estate of Jonathan Remington Esq. Deceas'd

7 Cane Chairs	£8 . . — . . —
Governour Belchers picture	1 . . 10 . . —
A Small Ovel Table	1 . . 10 . . —
7 Leather Chairs	4 . . — . . —
A Standing Candlestick	3 . . — . . —
A Folding Board	— . . 5 . . —
A Suit of Curtains	8 . . — . . —
A Bed quilt	3 . . — . . —
2 Blanketts	— . . 10 . . —
7 Knives & Forks 23 Oun. 17 dwt. 12 grs. Silver at 58/	69 . . 2 . . —″

Height 44¾″   Width 24″   Depth 18¼″

12

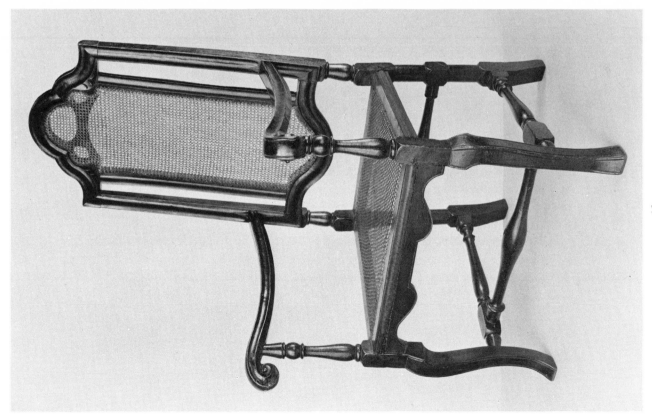

11

13 · ARMCHAIR
Walnut
Philadelphia 1740-1750

High-backed upholstered armchairs often show in early eighteenth-century portraits by Smibert, Greenwood, and Kühn. Several similar chairs of northern origin are in the collection (Figures 15, 16, and 20), but only this one is Philadelphia made. The walnut frame is typical of Queen Anne chairs there; the long-toed web feet and incurved arm posts often appear on solid- and pierced-splat armchairs.

Large triangular blocks of hard pine brace the corners; the strips of poplar under the slip seat originally held the commode form.

The upholstery is old cowhide.

Height 41¾″ Width 22″ Depth 19″

14 · ARMCHAIR
Walnut
Pennsylvania 1730-1750

This sturdy armchair was found in Bethlehem and has the forthright simplicity and rugged strength of the Pennsylvania German folk from whose locale it came. The heavy legs and arms carry easily the broad expanse of home-cured leather; the forward-standing ears lend a whimsical air of arrested attention. The arm supports echo distantly the architectural baluster in stone and marble native to Renaissance palaces which gradually filtered down to humbler uses.

Thin vertical strips brace the corners of the seat frame. The frame of the slip seat is hard pine.

Height 46½″ Width 22¾″ Depth 21¼″

14

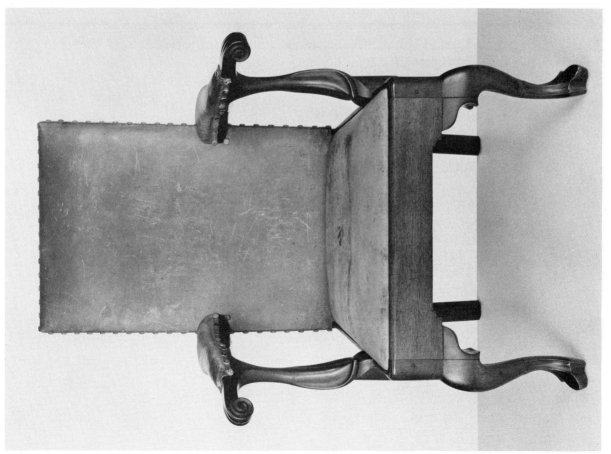

13

15 · ARMCHAIR
Walnut
Newport 1740-1750

This chair is a rare contemporary of the more numerous side chairs with solid splats and claw-and-ball feet. The arms are somewhat abrupt for this style of chair and lack the suave curves of New York and Philadelphia ones.

The stuffed back and seat are covered in plum-colored moreen, eighteenth century.

Height 41″   Width 23½″   Depth 18¼″

16 · ARMCHAIR
Walnut
New York 1735-1750

This might well be considered unique among the group of stuffed-back armchairs (Figure 17 and Figure 18) that were popular in New York about the middle of the eighteenth century. The high back, shaped like a woman's bodice of the period, and the sloping arms are departures from the customary pattern of this style. The rear legs vary from the smaller armchairs inasmuch as they taper and then widen into rounded feet. The upholstery is rare plum-colored moreen, eighteenth century.

Although walnut was used much more than mahogany in the first half of the century, the latter wood is mentioned in the "Inventory of Capt. John Deane Dec. 14, 1733, in New York:

1 large Sconce, 4 old Pictures, 10 old Cain Chairs, 1 small empty case	
1 Mohogany Table, 1 pr. handirons, 1 pr. tongs, 1 shovel,	
1 pr. Bellows, a case with twelve Bottles	£15.—
230½ ounces of old wrought Plate	92.12
3 old Pictures, 4 China Basons, 3 old Guns	
1 pr pistols and holsters, 1 Desk, 1 looking	
glass, 6 leather Chairs, 1 old Watch,	
1 pr handirons 1 pr Tongs, 1 Shove, 8 earthen	
plates, 18 China Cups & Saucers, 6 knives, 6 Forks	
1 pr bellows, 1 powder horne, 1 old Tea Table	
1 glass Decanter, 1 glass Beaker	15.15
1 pr. handirons, 1 coffee Mill, 1 Sugar box,	
1 old Chest of Draws, 2 earthen Bowls,	
1 prospective Glass, 1 old Tea Table	2. 5
Several Books of Navigation, 1 old Bible	
15 old books on several Subjects	1.—"

Height 41″   Width 23½″   Depth 20″

Ex Coll. MRS. FREDERICK S. FISH

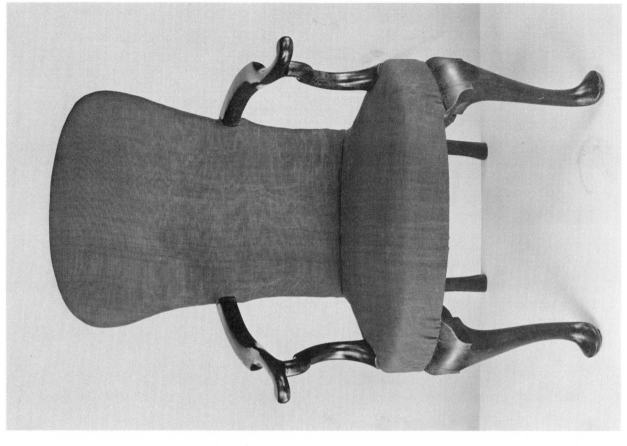

16

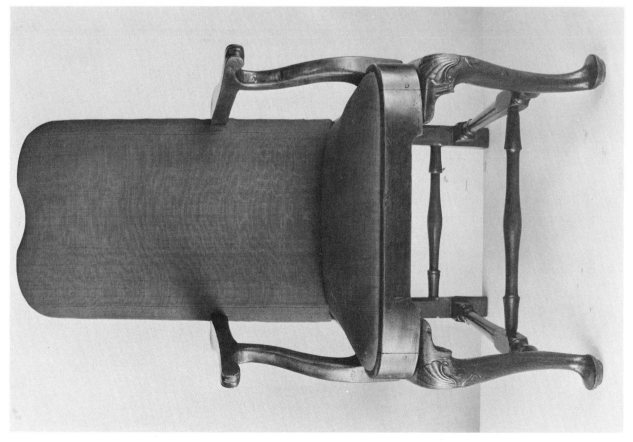

15

17 · ARMCHAIR
ONE OF A SET OF SIX
Walnut
New York 1730-1750

This armchair in the Queen Anne style, one of six, has handles to the outcurving arms and a higher back than a similar chair (Figure 18), but retains the bold, reversing curves and compact proportions that are features of Manhattan chairs.

The upholstery is resist-dyed linen, indigo blue on white. It is American, perhaps like that advertised in 1761 by the wife of John Haugan in New York, ". . . stamped linen china blue or deep blue, or any other colour that gentlemen and Ladies fancies."

This set of chairs belonged to the Tibbits family in New York. A matching pair of armchairs were heirlooms of the James family in Flushing, New York, and are now in the American Wing of the Metropolitan Museum.

Height 35½"   Width 26¼"   Depth 20½"

18 · ARMCHAIR
Walnut
Newport 1730-1750

This armchair serves as a reminder of the close connection in design of English and American furniture even before engraved pattern books were available for colonial guidance. English-trained craftsmen were numerous in this country. The shapely curved, stuffed back and seat, the reversed scroll arms round in section, the plain cabriole legs and pad feet repeat the outlines of early Georgian patterns. Abraham Redwood, who founded the famous library in Newport in 1747, is shown in his portrait seated in a chair with arms of this shape; the portrait was painted by Samuel King.*

Here, instead of needlework often used on English chairs, the original cowhide upholstery is fixed with brass nails. Wide seat rails of cherry follow the outline of the stuffed seat.

Height 35"   Width 22½"   Depth 19½"

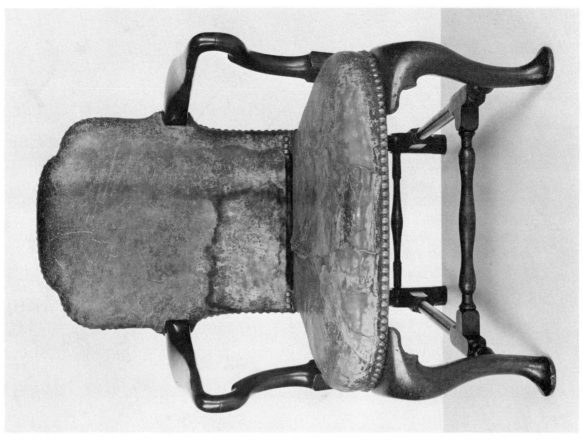

18

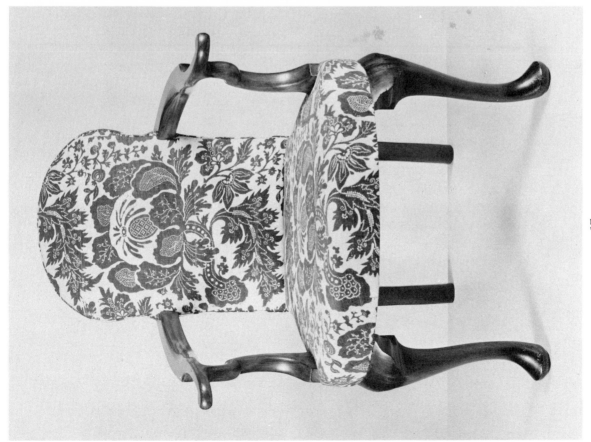

17

19 · ARMCHAIR
Walnut
Massachusetts 1730-1750

Glimpses of high-backed stuffed chairs may be had in New England portraits by Greenwood and Smibert, chosen as "properties" by the artist for their color and pattern. For the same reason, as well as for comfort, they had been used in rooms since the time of Charles II to satisfy an acute sense of scale and textural contrast in the architectural setting of Renaissance origin. Details of arms and stretchers and legs changed with the times until in the Federal period the Martha Washington armchair emerged with slender, tapered outlines. In this chair, function and style combine happily in a perfect design.

The covering is cherry-red wool moreen in a "watered" pattern achieved with heated irons. It is probably English, early eighteenth century.

Height 41″   Width 24½″   Depth 20¾″

20 · ARMCHAIR
Walnut
New England 1740-1760

This *lady's chair* has a low seat just above fourteen inches high which justifies the name *Martha Washington chair*, used by cabinetmakers to describe this shape of back before 1800. The shod pad feet, turned and block stretchers, and ram-horn arms are often associated with Newport chairs during the working years of Job Townsend.

The upholstery is silk brocade, the floral sprays in polychrome on a white ground, English Spitalfields, eighteenth century.

Height 39¾″   Width 28½″   Depth 20″

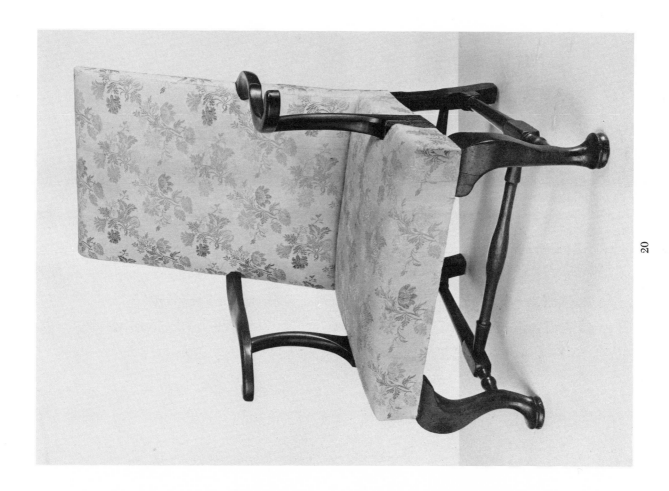

20

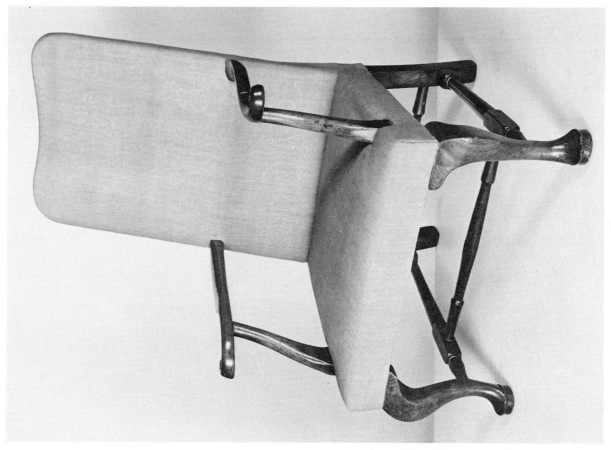

19

21 · ARMCHAIR
Mahogany and Walnut

Massachusetts 1750-1760

The combination of walnut, the wood most used in the Queen Anne period, with mahogany, which largely replaced it after the mid-century, is a noteworthy transition in material as well as style. For this chair, walnut was relegated to the turned stretchers, and the finer-grained mahogany made the arms and legs. Bird's-claw-and-ball feet, borrowed from England by many Newport, New York, and Philadelphia chairmakers before 1750, were belated in Connecticut and Massachusetts, and are hardly seen there before the genesis of the Chippendale style.

The seat frame of this chair is maple.

The upholstery is cream-colored silk damask, Italian, late seventeenth century.

Height 38½″	Width 22¾″	Depth 19″

22 · ARMCHAIR
Walnut

Connecticut 1730-1750

In the eighteenth century, chairs often were made with low seats to conform to the short stature of their colonial owners. *Slipper chair* or *lady's chair* is the description now given to them. Here the seat is fourteen inches from the floor. Two features of this chair often recur in Connecticut Queen Anne chairs; namely, the square seat, instead of the more unusual balloon shape, and the long, thin splat.

The upholstery is printed cotton, French, mid-eighteenth century.

Furniture was sometimes moved, especially by boat, in the colonial period. A bill dated "Boston, 16ᵗʰ May, 1747" reads: "Shipped by the Grace of God, in good Order and well condition'd by James Monk in and upon the good Ship call'd the Neptune whereof is Master, under God, for this present Voyage, Francis Bramham and now riding at Anchor in the Harbour of Boston and by God's Grace bound for Norwalk in Connecticut, to say,

"Twelve Cases. five Trunks — Three barrils, two Bedsteads, three beds, one chest — three tables, one Box, a bundle of pictures, 20 chairs, a cradle, a childs stool, a bundle Curtain Rods . . . and Sundry other Small things."

Height 38″	Width 21″	Depth 17″

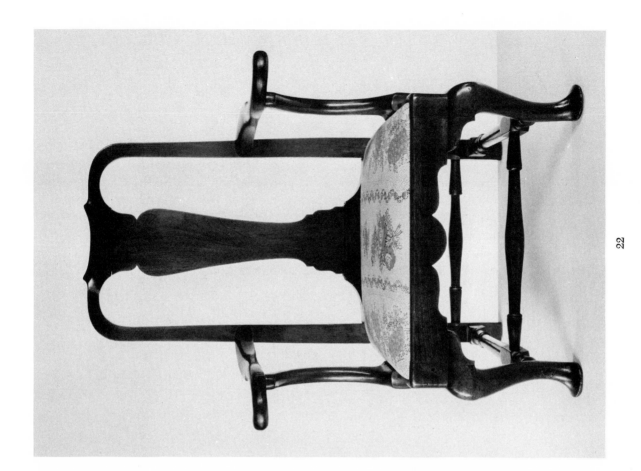

22

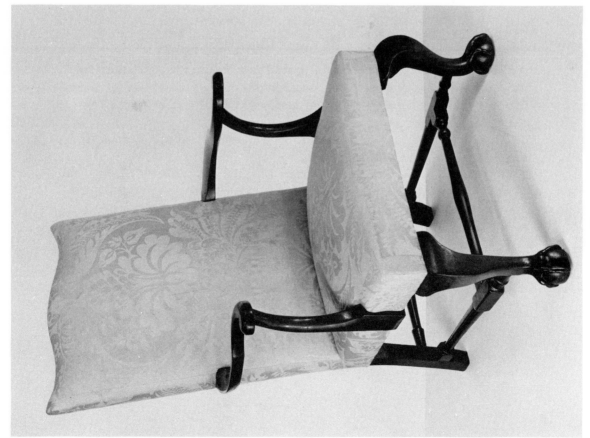

21

23 · ARMCHAIR
Maple, Painted Black
Connecticut 1725-1740

This chair presents a combination of the provincial and urban styles in a unique and graceful, if somewhat naive, design. The back is found on rush-seated chairs with turned legs and sometimes Spanish feet; the lower part follows the conventional Queen Anne style. On the latter, the maker has introduced a novelty in the turned bosses at the sides of the knees, to replace the conventional cyma-curved blocks on other chairs.

The seat rails are oak and maple. The upholstery is cowhide.

Height 43" Width 23½" Depth 17½"

24 · ARMCHAIR
Maple and Cherry, Painted
New York 1720-1740

Turned chairs of the Queen Anne period with trumpet legs ending in pad feet were made in New York State from Long Island to the upper Hudson Valley. A similar style made in New England is narrower and usually has straight turned legs. This provincial style is of American genesis.

Dutch hospitality seems to emanate from this wide-armed, sturdy chair. It is painted to imitate walnut and has a rush seat.

In the inventory of Isaac Willis, of New York, dated October 29, 1736, there were:

A great chair & 8 small chairs	£0/11/0
A set of Blew Linnen Curtains	0/2/10
a high bedstead old	0/10/0
Chest with a drewer in it	0/15/0
31 p^{ds} best pewter	3/0/0

Height 45¾" Width 25" Depth 18½"

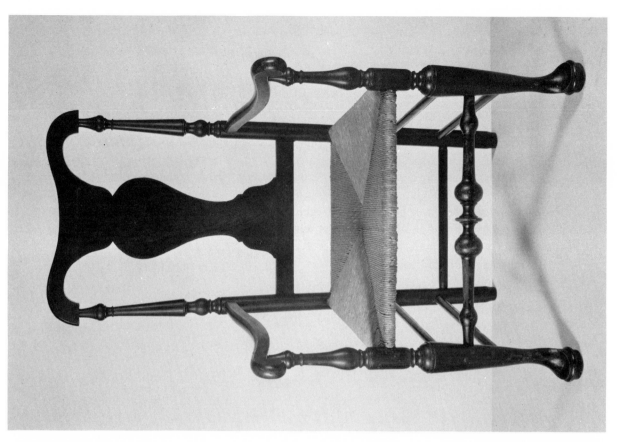

24

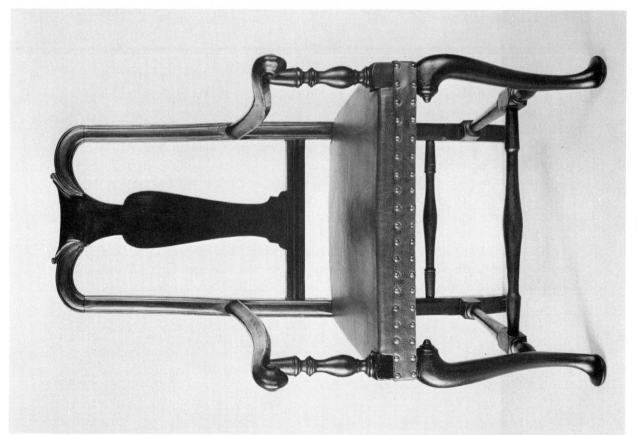

23

25 · ARMCHAIR
Maple, Painted Black
Philadelphia 1740-1750

Here the repetition of the cyma curve on splat, seat front, and legs coordinates the parts of this chair into a fluid pattern which shows a master's hand. The very wide seat is balanced by a sturdy stretcher and rising back. The various parts of this chair match the labeled work in maple of William Savery, whose long career began in 1742 and continued for forty-five years.

The seat is old rush.

Height 41″   Width 25½″   Depth 16″

26 · ARMCHAIR
ONE OF A PAIR
Walnut
New York 1730-1750

Because of its lack of identification, no less than its rarity, the colonial furniture of New York only lately has been collected by connoisseurs. This armchair, one of a pair, embodies the best qualities of the Queen Anne style. Its generous proportions, decisive, reversed curves, and bold, undercut cresting have a marked Dutch quality; yet the chair is quite distinctive in design.

The splat is made of pine veneered with walnut, and the cresting above it is carved from the solid rail. The eagle-head arms were adapted from English chairs of the George I period. The rear legs are braced by a baluster-shaped stretcher just below the seat rail. Triangular pine blocks strengthen the seat frame under the leather slip seats.

This pair of armchairs belonged to a large set (this one is No. X) made for the Stephanus Van Cortlandt house in Manhattan; some of the side chairs are still owned by descendants of that family.

Height 39½″   Width 23″   Depth 19⅝″

26

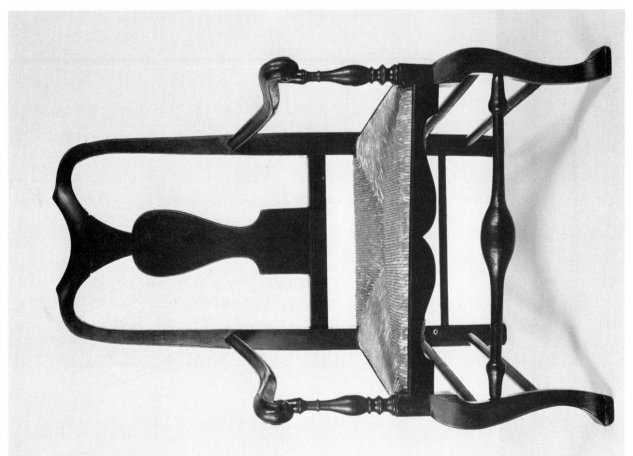

25

27 · ARMCHAIR
Walnut
Philadelphia 1740-1750

The outstanding feature of this Queen Anne armchair is the theme of repeating, sinuous curves which hardly tolerates a straight line in its composition, and the repetition of carved spirals and shells, curvilinear in themselves, to produce a harmonious co-ordinated design of calculated subtlety. The outline of the back is formed by stiles, round in section, an unusual detail, instead of the customary flat-surfaced ones. The carved trifid feet were favored by Philadelphia chairmakers as an alternate of claw-and-ball and slipper feet.

Inside the seat is inscribed: "This chair made in 1725 sent from England to John Heale Esq. Bought by J. Jay Smith Esq. in 1878 & presented to his Dau: Eliz^th P Smith, July 29th 1878 born 1825."

The slip seat is covered with flame-stitch crewelwork, American, early eighteenth century.

Height 45½″   Width 33½″   Depth 19″

28 · ARMCHAIR
ONE OF A PAIR
Walnut
Philadelphia 1740-1750

Perhaps less spectacular than the armchairs in Figure 27 and Figure 29, this example nevertheless has a rare grace in the curves of the top rail, the back stiles, and the rear legs of which few others can boast. This knowing use of congruent lines and the smaller scale of the chair make an arresting pattern which would be difficult to match.

The back splat is veneered, to secure a rich grain of walnut.

The slip seat is covered with green cut velvet, probably Italian, seventeenth century.

This pair of chairs was owned by the Latourette family in Bound Brook, New Jersey.

Height 39½″   Width 24″   Depth 18½″

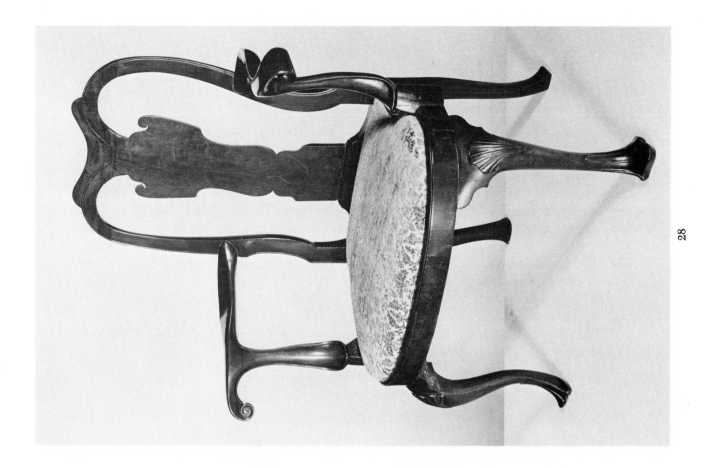

28

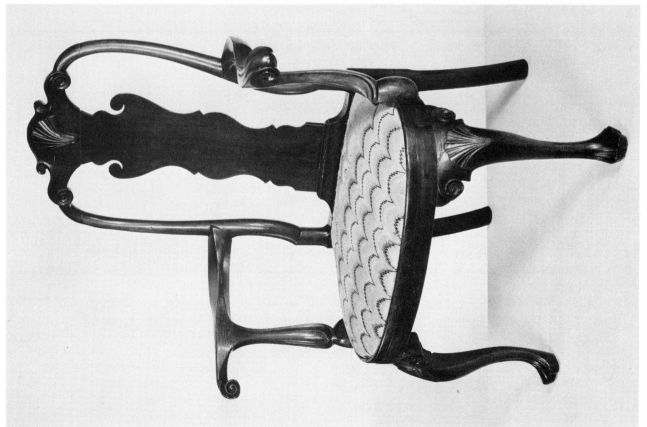

27

29 · ARMCHAIR
ONE OF A PAIR
Walnut

Philadelphia 1740-1750

This handsome armchair is typical of Philadelphia, but has borrowed widely for the elements incorporated in its design. Easily recognized are the claw-and-ball foot from ancient China, the double spirals derived from cloud forms, the solid splat based on porcelain vase shapes, and the bowed cresting from mandarin chairs. These motifs had long been familiar in Europe, and they found their way into English furniture before the turn of the eighteenth century. Here they have a fresh interpretation by their combination in this chair, remarkably vigorous in line and mass. The horseshoe-shaped seat has a spur on the side rails, making a cyma curve unlike any other Queen Anne style chairs of similar origin.

The petit-point crewel seat cover represents a bucolic scene of a huntsman and milkmaid framed by a wide border in clear shades of red, blue, yellow, and green.

This pair of armchairs was acquired from descendants of Robert and Abigail Griffiths Smith, who were married in Philadelphia in 1760.

Height 41⅜″   Width 23½″   Depth 18⅞″

30 · ARMCHAIR
Walnut

Philadelphia 1740-1750

Occasionally the vestiges of English tradition are clear in furniture that seems emphatically colonial. In this chair the contours and ornament are easily recognized as Philadelphia in origin until the arms are scrutinized; here a departure was made from the usual practice (Figure 28 and Figure 29), and instead the looped handles of Queen Anne English chairs were adopted. This circumstance is noteworthy as the foliation of the knees, the concaved line of the seat rail, and the S-shaped spirals on the cresting are marks of the highest development of mid-eighteenth century colonial chairmaking.

The splat is veneered branch walnut on hard pine.

The upholstery is woven silk in polychrome, Italian, early eighteenth century.

In the *Pennsylvania Gazette* for August 9, 1739, a notice was printed as follows: "MADE and SOLD By Robert Barton, near the Post-Office in Philadelphia, at the most reasonable Rates, Walnut, Mohogony, Easy, Close-stool and Ship-Chairs, and Stools, Couches and Settees, Backgammon Tables, with Men, Boxes, and Dies. Who has a likely Negro Woman fit for Town or Country Business, with a Child about one Year and an half old, to dispose of. Also right good Neatsfoot Oyl for Coach and Chaise Leather and Harnesses to sell reasonably by the Gallon or larger Quantity."

Height 42⅜″   Width 23⅞″   Depth 18⅜″

30

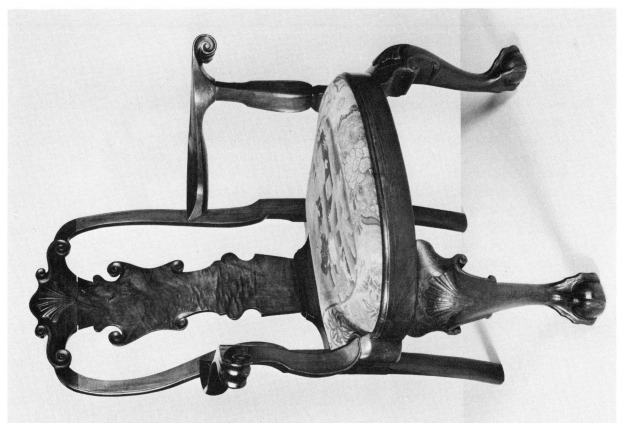

29

31 · CHILD'S ARMCHAIR
Maple and Ash
New England 1740-1750

No American style appeared full fledged, but each emerged from earlier fashions which show in structure and turning. Here the block and baluster legs and the carved Spanish feet are in the style of 1700, but the vase splat and the bow top rail bring the date to nearly 1760. An endless combination of forms in American furniture lend it a variety unknown in other countries.

At Mendon, Massachusetts, the inventory of Margery White on May 26, 1759, included a "Maple Chest and Round Table   40/."

The four turned stretchers of this chair are ash. The rush seat is original.

Height 26″   Width 15¼″   Depth 11½″

32 · ARMCHAIR
Maple
Philadelphia 1745-1755

The mingling of old forms with newer ones adds many variations to American furniture. Here the turned ball stretcher and arm supports and the flattened undercut arms current at the start of the eighteenth century fuse easily with the curves adopted at the mid-century.

The rush seat is old, but not contemporary with the frame.

The "estate of Ruth Harlan late of Kennett in the County of Chester and Province of Pennsylvania, Widow and Relict of Ezekiel Harlan in February 1743" listed:

Six flag bottomed Chairs	£0.15.0
One Framed Chair	0. 5.0
One Bedstead, Bed Tick and Pillows	4.15.0
One Chaff Bed & Bolster	0.10.0
One Copper warming Pan	1. 0.0
Five old Pewter Porringors	0. 3.0
Two iron Candlesticks & flesh fork	0. 3.0

Height 44¾″   Width 23¾″   Depth 17″

32

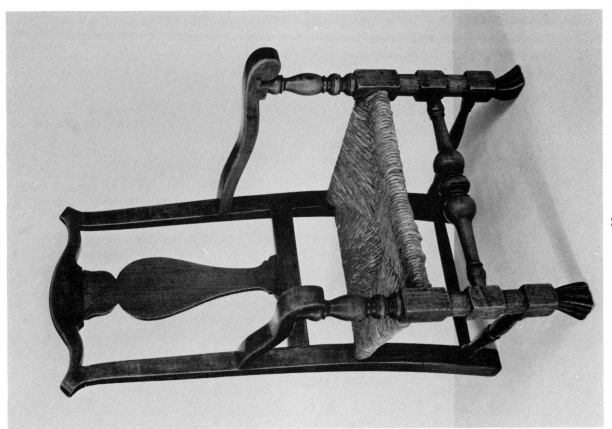

31

33 · ARMCHAIR
Maple
Pennsylvania 1745-1755

The artistry of Philadelphia chairmakers is foretold in this transitional chair. Its fluid lines hold the memory; the seeming lightness of the chamfered legs and the splat accented in curly maple are skillfully contrived.

This chair may have been made by William Savery inasmuch as early labeled work of his shows the same shaped feet, stretcher, and splat. The combination of several styles is often a hallmark of provincial furniture.

The rush seat is probably a replacement.

Maple, as well as walnut, found important uses in Pennsylvania. In 1759 John Lea's estate in Chester included:

> Pair of walnut high drawers
> 1 low pair of Walnut draws
> 1 Walnut cradle
> 1 Walnut Stand
> 1 walnut desk
> 1 case of maple drawers
> 1 maple dressing table & tea table
> 1 walnut oval table
> Walnut desk
> Walnut tea chest

Height 40¾″   Width 21″   Depth 16″

34 · ARMCHAIR
Curly Maple
Philadelphia 1745-1755

This armchair is transitional in style, like Figures 32 and 33, but is more urbane in form. Most advanced in style is the serpentine-shaped top rail of the Chippendale period. The carved feet accord with the attenuated splat, both typical of Queen Anne furniture. A commode form was fitted under the slip seat, accounting for the unusually deep skirt.

The commode set into a hard-pine frame is a very rare example of American pewter and was made by John Fryers, of Newport, Rhode Island. Fryers was born in 1685, and the first record of his name appeared in Newport records in 1735. He died in 1776. Only two other pieces of pewter are known by him, one being a porringer with the same maker's mark, *I. F.*, as upon this commode. In the Brooklyn Museum and Yale University are the only other American pewter commodes, made by Frederick Bassett in New York.

The upholstery is olive-green linsey-woolsey, quilted.

Height 41″   Width 23″   Depth 18″

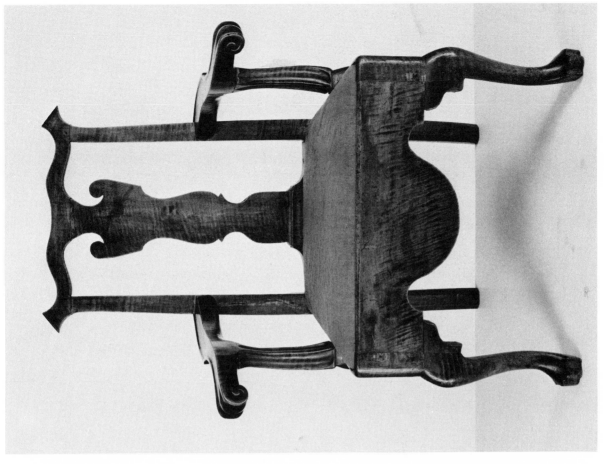

34

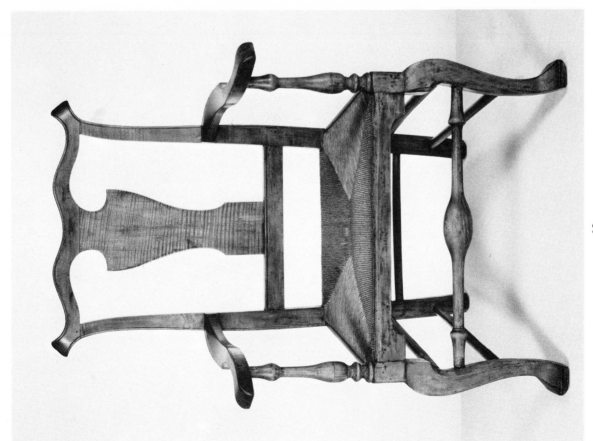

33

35 · ARMCHAIR
Mahogany
Philadelphia 1755-1765

This rare transitional design is a graceful example of the Queen Anne splat retained in a Chippendale chair. The shells on the top rail to form ears are carved in triple overlays, and the stippled background on the legs is unusual. The chair shows the stylistic development from a slightly earlier one (Figure 116).

The upholstery is silk brocade, French, Louis XV period.

In the *Pennsylvania Packet* October 5, 1772, a workman is sought: "Carpenter and Joyner by trade . . . Thirty Pounds Reward — Run away on the 6th of July . . . a mulattoe Slave who goes by the name of Charles Harding . . . some scars on the small of his legs, occasioned by wearing of Irons . . . Samuel Owings jun, Alexander Wells."

Height 41¼″   Width 22¾″   Depth 18½″

36 · ARMCHAIR
ONE OF A PAIR
Walnut
Philadelphia 1760-1770

This armchair, with matching side chairs, embodies the essential features of the Philadelphia style as it emerged from the mid-eighteenth century. The square seat, bow-shaped top rail with pronounced ears, and pierced splat are its Chippendale details. The bold scalloping of the seat front is unusual. The seat frame was fitted for a commode form. This shape of arms and of shell-carved legs is carried over from the Queen Anne period.

The upholstery is printed linen, English, eighteenth century.

Height 40¾″   Width 23½″   Depth 17¾″

36

35

37 · ARMCHAIR
Mahogany
Maryland or Pennsylvania 1755-1770

This armchair, another one (Figure 38), and a side chair (Figure 123) are closely allied in design. The exaggerated scrolled ears and heavy members indicate some provincial origin, and the name *Chester County chairs* by which they long have been known sets them apart. Those features and the interrupted fluting on the stiles may be observed on the chairs owned by Governor Bowie's family in Maryland, which point to a possible origin other than Pennsylvania.

One of the problems of the craftsmen of this period can be understood from notices such as the one printed in the *Maryland Gazette* on September 6, 1770: "Ran away ... Mansfield Lewis Gwym, who professes to be either a Carpenter, Painter, or Cabinet Maker by Trade. He is about 24 years of age ... Edward Maw"

Height 41″   Width 24½″   Depth 20½″

38 · ARMCHAIR
Mahogany
Maryland or Pennsylvania 1755-1765

A group of Chippendale furniture thought by some to be of Philadelphia origin is more provincial in line and ornament than the typical Philadelphia style patterned on London designs. The chairs are tall and narrow with heavy rails, exaggerated ears, and thickened splats. There is a vitality in the emphatic curves and large proportions that suggests an early date, a step between the Queen Anne and the Chippendale period.

In this particular chair the Queen Anne rounded loop arms of English origin are grafted to vertical supports, familiar in Philadelphia, creating a novel profile. The deep scalloped apron once covered the utensil under the removable slip seat; its presence indicates that the chair was for bedroom use. The inside seat frame is tulipwood.

The upholstery is moss-green cut velvet, probably Italian, seventeenth century.

Height 44″   Width 26½″   Depth 19½″

38

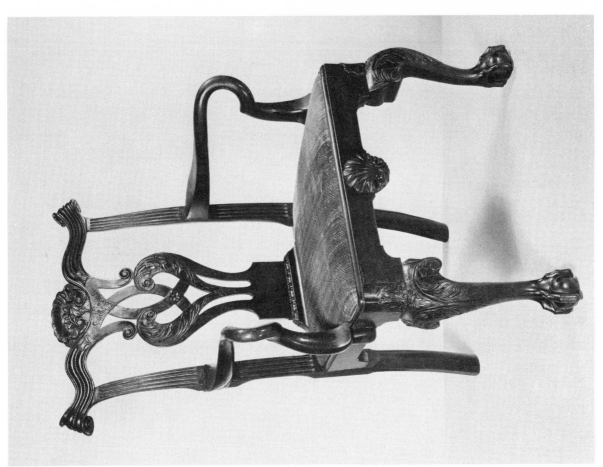

37

39 · ARMCHAIR
Walnut

Philadelphia 1755-1760

Made by William Savery

The attribution of furniture to specific cabinetmakers has been carried to unreasonable extremes, inasmuch as few labeled pieces exist as a basis of judgment. The label on this plain Chippendale armchair is inscribed: "All Sorts of Chairs and Joiners Work Made and Sold by William Savery at the Sign of the Chair a little below the Market in Second Street Philadelphia" (see Figure 389).

Although a simple design, the shape of the arm supports, the pronounced ears, and the stump rear legs are characteristic features of Philadelphia Chippendale chairs. A carved lowboy by Savery was the first labeled piece of Philadelphia furniture to be published and resulted in a fabulous reputation for that craftsman. His standing has since diminished by the discovery of several more ambitious, documented pieces by various cabinet and chairmakers, but none has exceeded William Savery for sound craftsmanship. He worked in Second Street for more than forty years, until his death in 1787.

From his Second Street address he advertised frequently in the *Pennsylvania Journal* and the *Pennsylvania Packet* between 1750 and 1772 different items of interest such as a loaded fowling piece found by him, which could be reclaimed by the owner if said owner would describe the marks and pay the charges; a good beaver "hatt" found by him; the considerable loss in household furniture, merchandise, etc., suffered by him and three neighbors in a fire, during which "the activity and public spirit of the inhabitants never appeared more conspicuous upon occasions of this nature than on the present"; the arrival of Joshua Brook from England with "a neat assortment of Forest cloths" to be sold in Savery's house.

The slip seat of the Savery chair shown here is covered with sand-colored brocatelle, Italian, early eighteenth century.

This chair was owned by Hannah P. Laurence, whose ancestor was a brother of Lewis Morris, a Signer of the Declaration of Independence.

Height 40″   Width 23⅛″   Depth 16″

40 · ARMCHAIR
Walnut

Philadelphia 1760-1770

Although similar to the armchair in Figure 36, this particular interlaced back is so characteristic of Chippendale chairs, not only in Philadelphia, but also in New England and New York that it takes its place in the history of the colonial development of the style.

The upholstery is printed linen, English, eighteenth century.

Height 41½″   Width 24″   Depth 18¼″

40

39

41 · ARMCHAIR
Mahogany
Philadelphia 1760-1775

Several chairs with the same back and seat skirting as this one were labeled by James Gillingham, a Philadelphia cabinetmaker. Although the back was taken from Chippendale's *Director*, Plate X in the first edition, and was available to any chairmaker then, it was especially favored by Gillingham. The sharp-edged arm posts are less typical than those in Figure 50. The sprays of husks festooned over the knees were individual touches of the carver not often repeated. Under the slip seat is a frame to hold the commode form.

The upholstery is purple and white copper-printed toile de Jouy, French, eighteenth century.

Height 38⅜″   Width 24½″   Depth 19⅝″

Ex Coll. HOWARD REIFSNYDER

42 · ARMCHAIR
Mahogany
Philadelphia 1765-1780

The pierced back of this armchair makes use of the Gothic arches which the last edition of Chippendale's *Director* made popular, especially in Philadelphia after 1762. The curves of the arms and legs are strong and well shaped.

Under the slip seat, strips of hard pine once held the commode form and are supported by old quarter-round blocks of cedar. One curious detail of construction is the double tenons of the side rails which pierce the back legs.

The upholstery is green silk damask, eighteenth century.

In the *Pennsylvania Packet* for March 13, 1775, the following appeared, making repeated mention of mahogany chairs:

"To be sold by William Martin, Upholsterer, next door to the City Vendue-store, in Front-street, Philadelphia. Part of his stock and Household Furniture, consisting of twelve stuffed back and seat chairs, three sofas and three easy chairs in canvas, six mahogany Gothic back chairs covered with hair cloth and brass nailed, one French elbow ditto, two four feet dining tables, a handsome Pembroke ditto, six neat mahogany chair frames, a pair of handsome hand-irons, some trimmings, &c. &c."

Height 39″   Width 24½″   Depth 19″

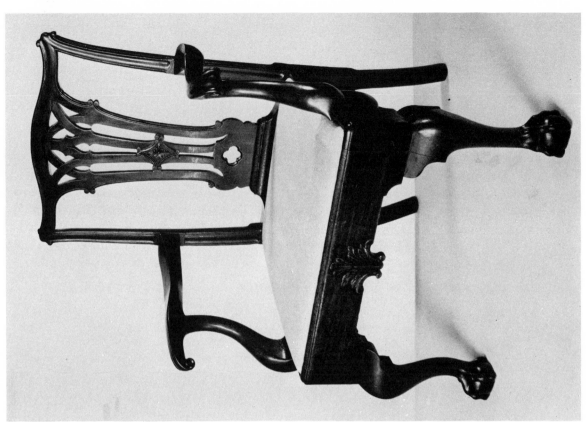

42

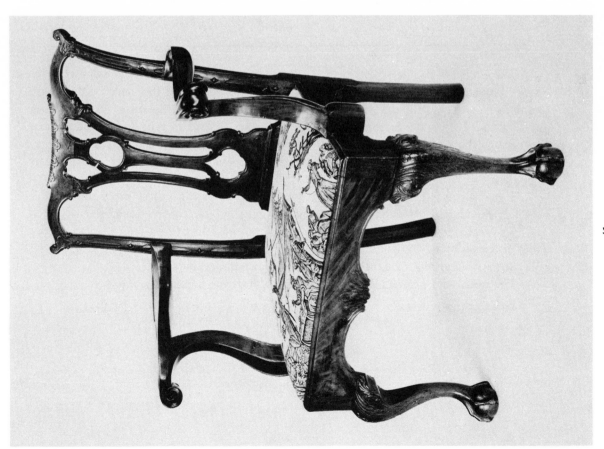

41

43 · ARMCHAIR
Walnut
Philadelphia 1760-1770

The advance of the Chippendale style is noticeable here in the interlaced splat and the carved crest of the top rail. The curves of the arms are more developed than in Figure 39, and they here assume a shape that was peculiar to Philadelphia chairs in the Queen Anne period. Small three-cornered walnut blocks brace the seat.

The seat frame of hard pine is covered with peach-colored brocatelle, probably Italian, about 1700.

Height 40″   Width 25½″   Depth 17¾″

44 · ARMCHAIR
Mahogany
Philadelphia 1770-1780

The Gothic fantasies exploited in the last edition of the *Director* were adopted with caution by colonial furniture makers; they were never as popular as the rococo and Chinese patterns more plentifully shown earlier. Perhaps the complaint of the author in his preface of 1762 that ". . . some of the Profession have been diligent enough to represent them (especially those after the Gothick and Chinese manner) as so many specious Drawings, impossible to be worked off by any Mechanick whatsoever" determined him to force their popularity.

This chair and the one pictured in Figure 45 represent the fullest expression of the style in Philadelphia, where it was more often smuggled into rococo patterns.

The seat rails, which are not tenoned through the rear legs, make an exception to the rule of construction.

Strips of hard pine once held the commode form under the seat.

The upholstery is green figured silk, French, Régence period.

Height 39½″   Width 22½″   Depth 18½″

44

43

45 · ARMCHAIR
Mahogany
Philadelphia 1765-1775

The especial importance of this chair is that it matches the sixth Randolph *sample* side chair now in the Garvan Collection at Yale University. This chair may have been part of a set, unlike the other five, which are all isolated designs (Figure 138). The rear stump legs are a novelty here in combination with square front legs; they are associated habitually with the cabriole style in Philadelphia.

The seat blocks are quarter round, of hard pine. The upholstery is silk brocade, French, Louis XV period.

Height 37″   Width 23⅜″   Depth 19″

46 · ARMCHAIR
Mahogany
Boston 1765-1780

In recent years several distinctive Chippendale chairs have been identified as Massachusetts, comparable in quality to those made in other colonial cities or in England. Often the designs may be traced to Robert Manwaring or other designers' books published in the third quarter of the eighteenth century.

The splat of this chair, arranged in four vertical uprights which are interrupted by Gothic quatrefoils, is a familiar English pattern also adapted to Philadelphia chairs (see Figure 143); here the top and bottom elements are treated in an original way, and the carved leaves on the cresting are repeated on several Massachusetts chairs (see Figure 155 and Figure 156). The shapely arms and molded legs are enriched with excellent carving; even the concaved seat has unusual elegance of line and finish.

The inside seat rails are hard maple. The upholstery is wine-colored cotton.

A Boston bill of sale dated in December, 1771, shows that Mrs. Margaret Spooner bought the following:

8 Mohog^y Chairs at 21/4	£ 8.10.8
8 Bottoms	1.17.4

Another bill shows that in August, 1769, Mrs. Spooner had bought:

1 Japan'd Tea Chest	£10.16.0
1 Chaf^g dish	1. 4.0
1 Red Silk Quilt	30. 0.0
Mohog^y Bedstead	32. 0.0

Height 35″   Width 23″   Depth 20½″

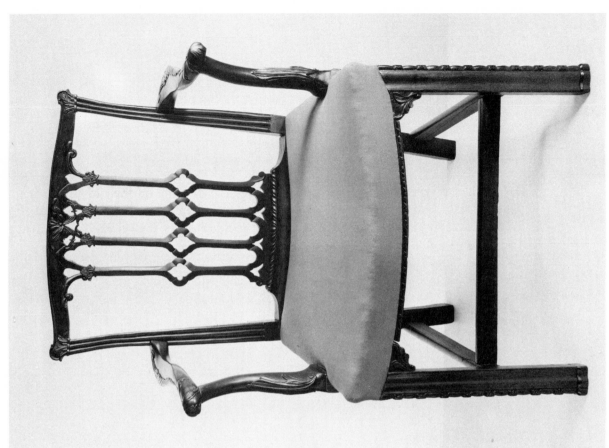

46

45

47 · ARMCHAIR
Mahogany
Philadelphia 1765-1775

Here the flat arm rests are cut with a sharp, right-angle edge on their inside curve, unlike the Massachusetts armchair Figure 46, but repeated on many Philadelphia chairs as in Figure 45 and Figure 49. The openwork splat is a variant of that in Figure 131. Its Gothic tracery combines well with the squared lower structure.

The seat frame is braced with quarter-round blocks of hard pine.

The upholstery is silk brocade, French, early eighteenth century.

Height 38½"   Width 23¾"   Depth 19"

Ex Coll. HOWARD REIFSNYDER

48 · ARMCHAIR
Mahogany
Philadelphia 1770-1785

The "pretzel back" design of chair was developed after English models in Philadelphia with numerous variations. Two makers of them, Ephraim Haines and Benjamin Trotter, contributed several distinctive patterns.* In New England a simpler version of ladder-back chair was less popular in the Chippendale period, as if the slat-back style, changing with time since the Pilgrim century, had worn itself out.

The seat frame is fitted for a commode. The side rails of the seat are mortised through the back, as most Philadelphia-made chairs were constructed. Quarter-round blocks of hard pine brace the inside seat corners.

The upholstery is blue silk damask, French, mid-eighteenth century.

Height 38"   Width 28½"   Depth 19½"

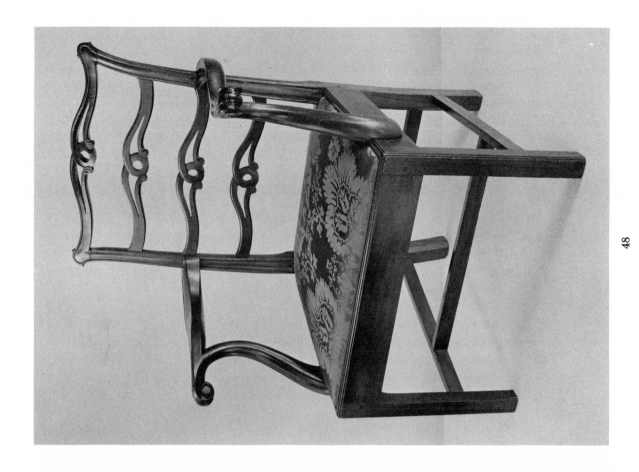

48

47

49 · ARMCHAIR
Mahogany
Philadelphia 1760-1770

Serpentine-curved arm posts were consistently used on Philadelphia Chippendale chairs. The difference is made clear by comparison with a Massachusetts chair, Figure 46. The pierced splat and top rail in silhouette are like Benjamin Randolph's chairs, Figure 142.

The tall back retains the proportions of the earlier style typical of Queen Anne chairs. The seat was fitted for a commode.

The upholstery is silk brocade, French, early eighteenth century.

Labor troubles are not only of the present day. On August 14, 1775, the *Pennsylvania Packet* offered its readers "Ten Dollars Reward. Ran away from the subscriber, Cabinet-maker, in Pine-street, Philadelphia, an Irish servant man named John M'Cean, by trade a cabinet-maker, but most accustomed to chair making; about 24 years old . . . Matthias Hand."

Height 39¾″   Width 23¼″   Depth 18¼″

50 · ARMCHAIR
Mahogany
Philadelphia 1765-1775

This armchair and six side chairs (Figure 133) have the same back as a side chair labeled by Benjamin Randolph in the Karolik Collection.* None has the straight seat rails of this chair. The arms are especially well shaped and, like the close-set claws of the feet, exemplify Philadelphia details of design. The cabriole legs are thinner than those used on most Philadelphia chairs.

The upholstery is cream-colored silk damask, French, early eighteenth century.

Height 39″   Width 24″   Depth 19″

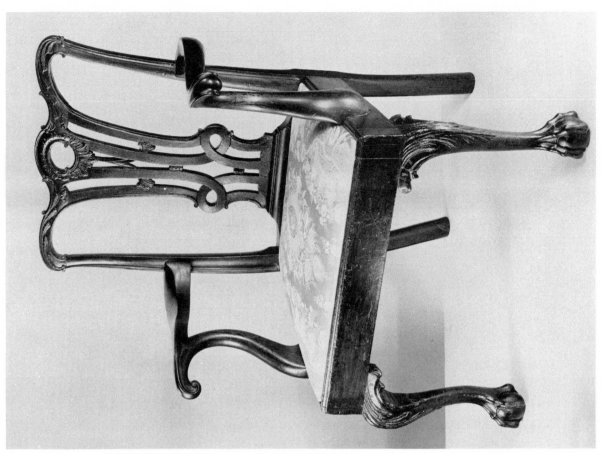

50

49

51 · ARMCHAIR
Mahogany
Maryland or Philadelphia 1760-1775

The heavy scale of this chair and the broad splat flanked by stop-fluted stiles is comparable to several others (Figures 37, 38, and 123) which may be of Maryland origin. It is an ambitious and handsome chair, although lacking the delicacy of proportion which the typical Philadelphia Chippendale chairs show.

The upholstery is green silk damask, Italian, early eighteenth century; two quarter-round blocks of poplar remain in the seat frame.

Height 41½″   Width 24″   Depth 19¼″

52 · ARMCHAIR
Mahogany
New York 1765-1775

The splat of this chair, carved with a tassel and ruffle flanked by wide, foliated scrolls, appears on several sets of chairs in New York families. One of them belonged to Whitehead Hicks, Mayor of New York from 1766 to 1776. Another was owned by Jacob Harsen, a Manhattan merchant.

This chair (No. IX of the set) was owned by Stephen van Rensselaer, last patroon of the Manor in Albany; with six matching side chairs it was acquired from that family. The bird's-head arm terminals, often seen on English walnut chairs of the George II period, were occasionally used by Boston chairmakers, too.

The slip-seat frames are cherry, and heavy three-sided blocks of white pine are nailed across the inside corners.

The upholstery is brown cowhide.

Much was imported to supplement the native-made articles for houses. There is the "Invoice of One Case Merchandize Shipped in the Amelia Capt. Sinclair for New York Consigned William Livingston Esqr on his own Acco^t Viz^t

3 Pair Large Silver Candlesticks	£53 . . 16 . . 6
1 Large Silver Waiter	10 . . 8 . . 1
1 Silver Coffee Pott	12 . . 3 . . 6
12 Polished Table Spoons	6 . . 12 . . 0
Making the Spoons	1 . . 10——
2 Mohogany Cases with . . . Furniture	3 . . — —
12 Knives & forks	7 . . 10——
Graving 48 Crests & Arms	2——
53 y^{ds} Sky Sattin	24 . . 1 . . 5
1 Gold Watch Cas'd & Jewelled, name Geo: Prior	21 . . ——
1 yd Baize to Wrap this Silk	. . 2 . —"

Height 39¼″   Width 23½″   Depth 19½″

Ex Coll. PEYTON VAN RENSSELAER

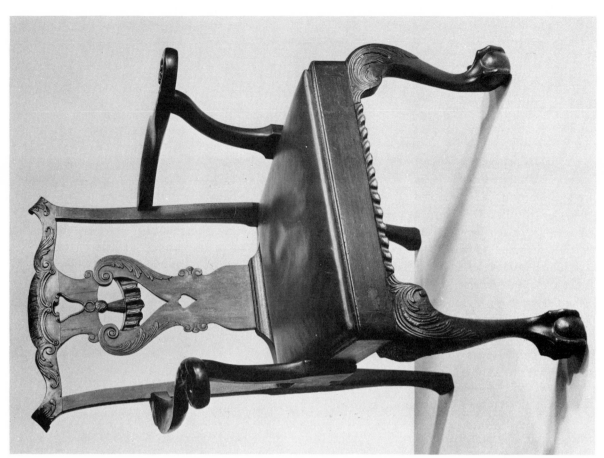

52

51

53 · ARMCHAIR
Mahogany
Probably Baltimore 1755-1765

The concave-shaped arm posts and wide splat of this chair are the same features found in several Baltimore armchairs, one originally owned by Governor Bowie, now in the Breckinridge Long Collection, and another owned by Mrs. Miles White, Jr.* They differ markedly from Philadelphia designs. The sweeping lines and bold details make this chair memorable. It was originally owned by Francis Scott Key's family and was known as the "Washington chair" because it was used by Washington on his visits to Key's father, John Ross Key, a Revolutionary officer.

Three quarter-round cedar blocks brace the seat frame. The upholstery is yellow silk damask, Italian, early eighteenth century.

A prosperous Baltimore cabinetmaker perpetuated his name for us by a notice in the *Maryland Journal*, November 3, 1778, as follows: "To Be Sold, A neat convenient well built brick house and lot adjoining the Methodist Meeting house. The Lot subject to a ground rent of 4£ 10s per year. For terms apply to Robert Moore, Cabinet Maker."

Height 39⅝″   Width 24¾″   Depth 18″

Ex Coll. R. R. BARRETT, Warrenton, Virginia

54 · ARMCHAIR
Mahogany
Baltimore 1765-1780

This unusual chair is a rare design, allied to the Baltimore school by its wide splat with involved tracery, low seat, and thick molded legs. The carved garrya elliptica, or husk pendants, on the center of the back are a prophecy of the classical style to come, the golden age of Baltimore furniture.

Small quarter-round blocks of hard pine remain in the seat frame. The undulating lines of the stiles were probably inspired by a chair in Plate XV of the *Director*, 1754.

The seat is covered with yellow silk damask, Italian, early eighteenth century.

An early portrait by Thomas Sully shows Charles Carroll, of Carrollton, Maryland, seated in a Chippendale armchair which has similar rounded arm ends and square legs.

Height 39″   Width 24″   Depth 20½″

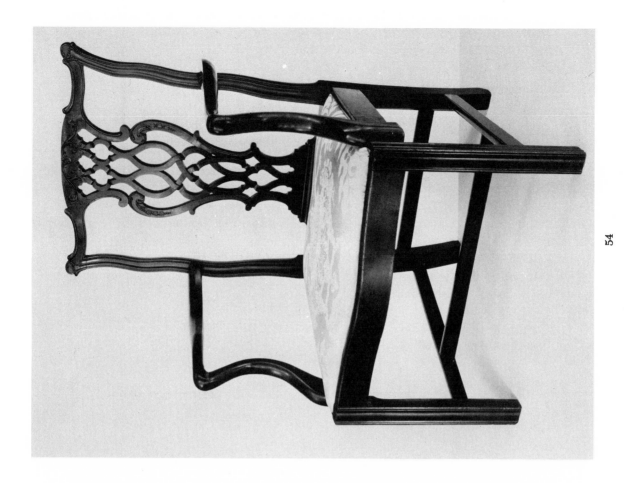

54

53

55 · ARMCHAIR
Mahogany
Massachusetts 1770-1780

This is one of the finest New England chairs known. It is richly carved, even on the arm posts and the shoe of the splat. The spiral arm handles are probably unique. The hairy paw-and-ball foot, like that on the side chair, Figure 151, is shown in Chippendale's *Director* on a bed, Plate XXVII, in all three editions. The stopped fluting on the back stiles occurs on a Connecticut desk by Benjamin Burnham and the tables signed by John Townsend in Newport and on several New York chairs.

A matching side chair is in the collection of Dr. C. Ray Franklin, Westchester, New York.*

The seat frame is beech, and a thin strip of beech is nailed across each corner instead of being mortised, to follow an English practice.

Height 37¼″   Width 25½″   Depth 20½″

Ex Coll. FREDERICK BECK, Boston

56 · ARMCHAIR
Mahogany
Massachusetts 1765-1780

The lean mass and lively curves of this armchair easily identify it as an example of the Massachusetts Chippendale school. It is a plainer version of the side chair seen in Figure 152. The arms are particularly well designed.

The seat rails are rock maple; no corner blocks were used.

Bills of sale often indicate the furnishings of a colonial house. "Mrs. Howard Bo^t at Gould's Vendue, Boston, 22^d April 1774:

4 China Bowles	£ 1..16..0
12 Views of Athens	19..16..0
1 suit Green Curtains	17..10..0
1 large Floor Carpett	21.. 0..0
2 Needle Worked pictures	1.. 3..0
1 Walnut Chamber Table	6..15..0
1 Sett Burnt China Tea Cups & saucers	2.. 7..0
1 Table cover	3..15..0
1 Mahogany Dining Table	10..10..0"

Then on May 20, 1774, Mrs. Howard "Bo^t of Jos: Russell 6 Mohogg^y fram^d Chairs for £5..3..0."

Height 38½″   Width 25½″   Depth 19¾″

Ex Coll. NORVIN H. GREEN

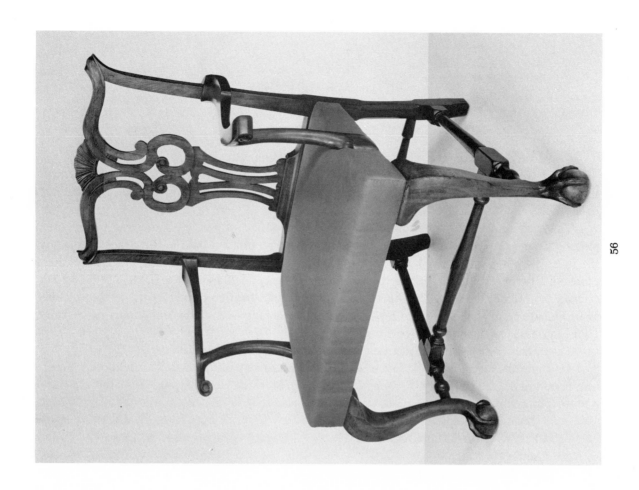

56

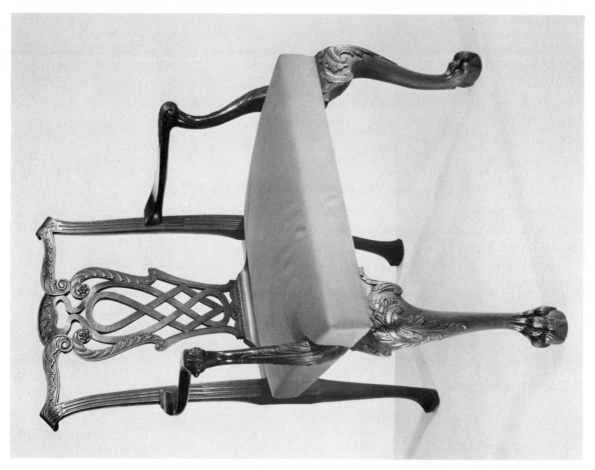

55

57 · ARMCHAIR
Mahogany
Philadelphia 1760-1770

Lansdowne, the country seat of Governor John Penn, stood on the opposite bank of the Schuylkill River from Mount Pleasant, a contemporary mansion less ambitious in design than the vanished Lansdowne. To match the rich background of rococo carving, the furniture was equally elaborate, as some of the scattered contents prove.

This armchair, part of a set owned by Penn, is a variant of two designs made in Philadelphia by Thomas Affleck between 1763 and 1766.* One has Chinese frets in the paneled insets of the legs; the other, represented here, is carved with husks and strapwork and was chosen from Plate XIX, two French chairs in the third edition of Chippendale's *Director* of 1762. Stuffed-back armchairs were not developed to the same degree of sophistication in other parts of the colonies as in Philadelphia, and even there few were made in comparison to the ubiquitous easy chairs (see Figure 92) with wings and enclosed sides.

The upholstery is yellow silk damask, Italian, late seventeenth century.

At Winterthur is an original "List of English furniture at Lansdown £277.2.3 Sterling, American furniture 581.9.0 Currency, Farming Utensils and Stock 429.8.9 Currency." In the Hall are

A large Vase Lamp with paste Ornaments	
brass branches, vase ballance &c	£9.9.0
10 elbow Chairs, Matted seats	9.10
2 settees to match	9.9
2 flower Stands	2.10

Height 42⅜″   Width 28¾″   Depth 24½″

Ex Coll. Mrs. FREDERICK S. FISH

58 · ARMCHAIR
Mahogany
Massachusetts 1790-1795

Although the exact origin of this chair is uncertain because of its unorthodox details, the similarity of the arm posts to those on chairs made by Joseph Short (1771-1819), of Newburyport, makes it reasonable to attribute this chair to him.

The back fulfills his statement that he "makes Martha Washington chairs" and was a shape often repeated in Sheraton and Hepplewhite armchairs.* The seat rails are maple, braced by diagonal strips of cherry.

The upholstery is cream-colored silk damask, Italian, about 1700.

This chair was owned originally by the Davenport family in Newburyport.

Height 42½″   Width 23″   Depth 18½″

Ex Coll. PHILIP FLAYDERMAN

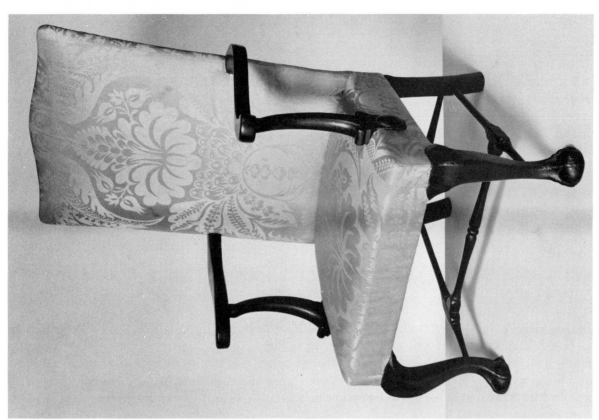

58

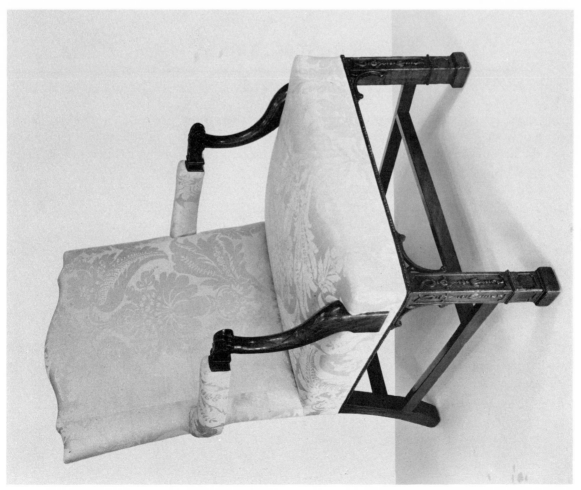
57

59 · CORNER CHAIR
Maple, Stained
New England 1725-1740

Corner chairs were made in the American colonies for almost a century beginning about 1700. The earliest ones have block and vase turned supports without any splats in the back. No American prototype of the Flemish scrolled and caned chairs is known to match those of European origin. The pad feet of this chair are its latest feature, and they encroach on the block and vase turned legs of the seventeenth century style. Over the rush seat is a cushion of figured maize-colored wool.

Height 28¼"   Width 25½"   Depth 25¼"

60 · CORNER CHAIR
Walnut
Philadelphia 1740-1750

The Philadelphia features of this chair are the short slipper feet overlaid with carved tongues, the inverted cabriole arm supports, and the simple urn-shaped splats, the last named similar to those on chairs labeled by William Savery. The front seat rail, made of narrow interlocking strips, was repeated on a contemporary chair of Philadelphia origin, formerly in the Louis G. Myers Collection. The frame of the slip seat is hard pine covered with leather.

Height 30½"   Width 27"   Depth 22"

61 · CORNER CHAIR
Walnut
Philadelphia 1740-1750

Although repeating the general lines of Figure 60, this chair offers a study in variations within the same area and period. The higher back gives more sweep to the sinuous arm supports, similar to Figure 66, and balances well the heavy skirt, which conceals the commode form, and the spreading trifid feet. The slip-seat frame of tulipwood is covered with leather.

Height 32½"   Width 28¾"   Depth 25½"

62 · CORNER CHAIR
Mahogany
New York 1740-1750

This chair has an expansive air lent by its outcurving seat, a quarter circle in plan, unlike any other one. Different, too, is the deep seat rail upon which the legs are imposed. The pointed and shod feet are typical of New York design (see Figure 108). The slip-seat frame of tulipwood is covered with blue and white resist-dyed linen, eighteenth century.

Height 32⅛"   Width 29½"   Depth 19½"

59

60

61

62

63 · CORNER CHAIR
Walnut

Rhode Island 1740-1750

The corner chair is practical for comfort, compactness, and mobility — all good reasons for its many variations and long popularity. The tête-à-tête chair of the eighties, spool-turned and gilded, is a revival of the corner chair in a double form.

Here the shape of the back splats, the turnings of the stretchers, and the heavy knuckled claw feet match those on a side chair (Figure 103) typical of Newport origin. The soft pine seat frame is covered in yellow silk damask, Italian, seventeenth century.

Height 35¾″   Width 31⅝″   Depth 25¾″

Ex Coll. GEORGE S. PALMER

64 · CORNER CHAIR
Walnut

Newport 1735-1750

The shape of the top comb and of the splats below it is the first clue for the attribution of this chair. The seat rail is cut on the inside to follow the upholstery unlike the squared inner rails of New York and Philadelphia chairs. An old inscription there reads: "Large Round about chair with top Belonged to Elizabeth Wentworth wife of Joseph Haven Grandmother Thacher's uncle." The cherry seat frame is covered with blue cut-wool velvet, French, early eighteenth century.

Height 44½″   Width 30″   Depth 24½″

65 · CORNER CHAIR
Mahogany

New York 1750-1760

The simple piercing of the back splats (see also Figure 99) and the heavy claw feet are features of New York chairs. Beneath the leather slip seat the commode form has a round wood cover, a ten-petaled flower carved at its center. The side rails are ash, and the underframing is tulipwood. The chair originally belonged to the Wright family at Oyster Bay, New York.

Height 32″   Width 31″   Depth 23″

66 · CORNER CHAIR
Mahogany

New York 1750-1760

The curved arm supports, perhaps more ingratiating than the turned vertical ones of Figure 65, were more often used in Pennsylvania than in New York, and by adoption are variants of Figure 60 and Figure 61. The splats and seat plan of both chairs here are alike, and the carved knee compares closely to Figure 105. The cherry seat frame is covered with red wool moreen, stamped in a ribbon pattern, English, eighteenth century.

Height 32″   Width 27½″   Depth 24″

63

64

65

66

67 · CORNER CHAIR
Walnut
New York 1750-1760

Corner chair is a name found in colonial newspaper advertisements; sometimes it was called *roundabout* and *writing chair*, and a *barber's chair* in England. Like other arm and easy chairs, it often was fitted for a commode.

This chair has some features of New York chairs, Figure 68 and Figure 106, and even of a Newport one, Figure 64; but the inner framing of the seat, an important detail, is like New York construction, as in Figure 68. Occasionally the overlapping of Newport and New York design is confusing. The slip seat is covered in varicolored crewelwork.

| Height 29¾″ | Width 29″ | Depth 24¾″ |

68 · CORNER CHAIR
Walnut
New York 1750-1760

The thick intertwined splat and thin, straight inner seat rails make this chair of likely New York origin. The very deep serpentine curves of the seat are further clues of locality. The slip seat is covered in brown cowhide.

| Height 29¾″ | Width 29″ | Depth 24¾″ |

69 · CORNER CHAIR
Mahogany
New York 1760-1775

The craftsmen of New York followed English patterns in unexpected ways. Here the straight legs ending in claw feet are more often associated with English work; so too is the cabriole leg, flanked by scrolls. The cup-shaped turning of the arm supports is found on New York furniture from 1700 onward. The slip seat is covered with yellow silk damask, Italian, about 1700.

| Height 31½″ | Width 25¾″ | Depth 23½″ |

70 · CORNER CHAIR
Mahogany
New York 1760-1775

The design of the pierced splats resembles that of two other New York chairs owned originally by the Livingston-Parson and Webb families (Figure 150). The arm supports are similar to Figure 62. The seat lined with white pine was fitted for a commode, which fact explains the deep scallops on both sides; the latter are cherry. The seat frame is covered with sand-colored brocatelle, Italian, about 1700.

| Height 31¾″ | Width 31″ | Depth 23″ |

67

68

69

70

71 · EASY CHAIR
Maple, Painted Black
Massachusetts about 1725

The beginning of the cabriole style of furniture is shown here by the square section of the curved legs and the heavy ball medial stretcher. As the Queen Anne period advanced, the block and turned underframing became thinner, and the curved legs rounded. The shape of the arms and the height of the back later became wider and lower, as in Figures 74 and 80.

The upholstery is cowhide.

In an inventory of the goods of Mrs. Mary Bull in Boston on August 12, 1718, there were these items:

To a Desk & Stool 5ˢ and old chest 1ˢ	£0. 6.0
To 2 Tables 8ˢ four joint stools 6ˢ	0.14.0
To one greatt Chair	0. 2.6
To a Cupboard Drawers & Table	1.10.0
To a flock Bed	1. 5.0
To a Table Board and old frame	0. 5.0

Height 47½″ Width 33″ Depth 21″

72 · EASY CHAIR
Maple, Painted Black
Massachusetts 1720-1730

Curved lines were grudgingly admitted to early eighteenth-century furniture and were crowded by older forms unwilling to give way to them. Here the first shape of the cabriole leg compromises with the heavy turned and block stretchers and Spanish feet of the preceding century. The cylinder-rolled arms are lesser interpretations of the mighty Carolean upholstered and fringed chairs in Castle Howard and Ham House in England. The black paint that covers the maple frame shows the same ancestry, when lacquered furniture demanded a similar finish in its proximity.

The upholstery is faded red wool velvet, late seventeenth century.

Height 48″ Width 33½″ Depth 21½″

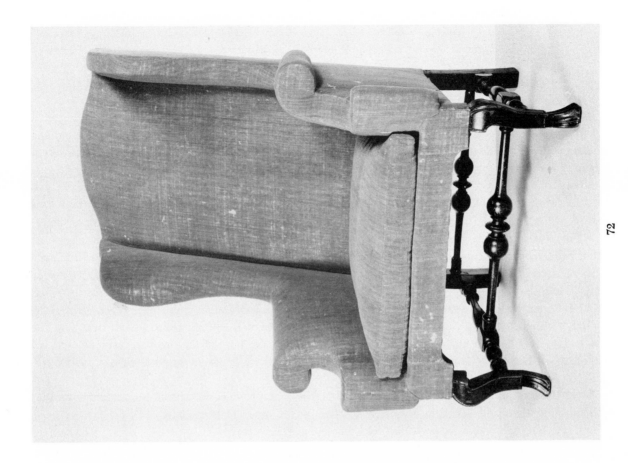

72

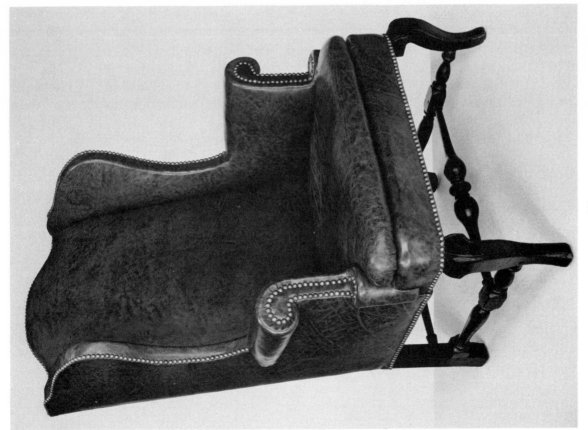

71

73 · EASY CHAIR
Walnut
Philadelphia 1740-1750

This easy chair belongs in the same group as the sofa seen in Figure 269. Here the carving of the legs and the shaping of the flattened stretchers are carried to a greater degree of development than in the sofa, and this chair stands as one of the finest examples of this group of Philadelphia chairs in the Queen Anne style.

The upholstery is the original crewelwork embroidery, early eighteenth century.

On February 4, 1755, Edward Weyman, upholsterer, advertised "At the Sign of the Royal Bed, the Corner of Chestnut and Second Streets, Philadelphia, makes all Kinds of Upholsterer's Work, viz.

"Furniture for beds and window curtains, either festoon or plain, stuffs all kinds of settees, and settee beds, easy chairs, couches and chair bottoms, either of silk, worsted, or leather, likewise feather beds, matrasses, cabin stools, and puts up paper hangings in the neatest manner; he also makes umbrelloes suitable for the sun, and mends those for bad weather. He will either find materials suitable for the above mentioned furniture, or will make up ladies and gentlemens own; he likewise can supply persons with all sorts of joyners work; those ladies and gentlemen who please to favour him with their custom, may depend on having their furniture made up in the neatest and newest fashions, and with immediate dispatch at the most reasonable rates, by their most obedient humble servant, EDWARD WEYMAN.

"NOTICE is hereby given to the tanners, and others, who have cows tails, or horses manes and tails to dispose of, that said Weyman gives the best prices for those sorts of hair."

Height 46¼″	Width 34½″	Depth 24½″

74 · EASY CHAIR
Maple
New England 1720-1740

This easy chair, probably of Massachusetts origin, is in the Queen Anne style which is characterized by outflaring, rolled arms, cabriole legs, and turned stretchers — a style that became so firmly entrenched that it continued in New England with minor variations until the end of the century. Claw-and-ball feet and carved knees were later developments upon the same theme without any change in the upholstered frame.

The covering is flame-stitch wool embroidery in shades of yellow, blue, red, and green.

In an inventory of the estate of Mrs. Mary Fay, "late of Boston, Widow Dece'd — taken July 29th 1730" there were:

1 Walnut frame Looking Glass	£6- 0-0
1 Oval Table 35/. 12 Turkey-workᵈ Chairs 96/	6-11-0
3 Brass Candlesticks Snuff Dish & Snuffers	1- 5-0
62 lb of Pewter @ 3/ pˡᵇ	9- 6-0
An Easy Chair 90/. a Couch & Squabb 60/	7-10-0
1 Small oval Table of Maple & a Table Board	1- 0-0
1 Joint Stool Table 8/. high Candlestick, &c 40/.	2- 8-0
6 Leather Chairs 48/. 1 pair of Doggs, Shovel &c 20/.	3- 8-0
51 oz of wrought Plate at 18/ pᵒᶻ	46- 6-0
22 yᵈˢ of Silk 14 yᵈˢ Ditto	13- 0-0

Height 47″	Width 35½″	Depth 22″

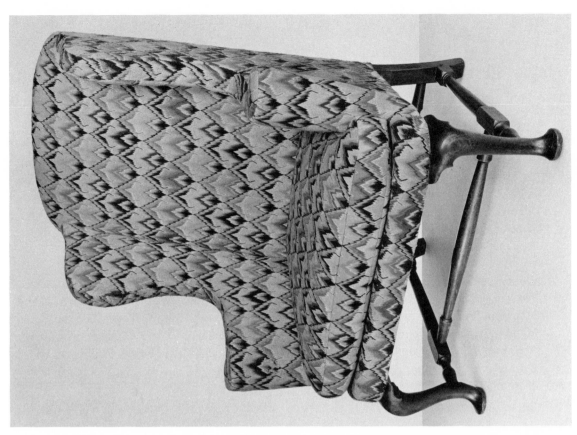

73

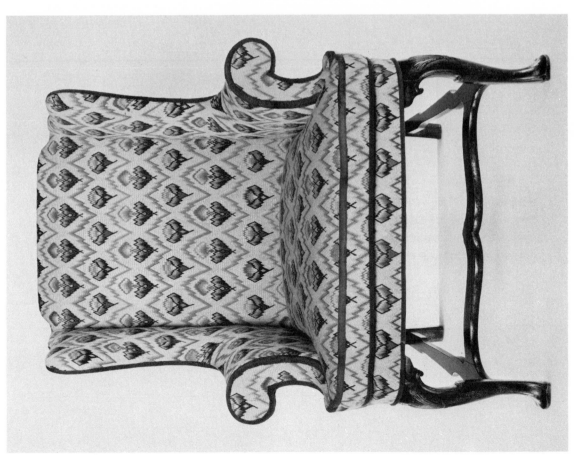

74

75 · EASY CHAIR
Walnut

Philadelphia 1735-1750

Upon this easy chair the slipper foot, overlaid with a slender tongue, is an indication of its Pennsylvania origin. The large rolled armrests are a departure from the upright, cone-shape supports or the widely projecting scrolls of the Stuart period, from which the arms of this chair developed.

The upholstery is silk damask, French, Louis XV period.

One of the most active craftsmen in the heyday of the Queen Anne style, Plunket Fleeson, advertised as early as August 1, 1739, in the *Pennsylvania Gazette*, "Plunket Fleeson, Upholsterer, lately from London and Dublin, at the Sign of the Easy Chair, near Mr. Hamilton's in Chestnut-Street; makes all Kinds of Upholsterers Work after the best Manner: Where any Person may be furnish'd with Feathers, Bed ticks, Blankets, Sacking-Bottoms, &c. at the most reasonable Rates"; and in 1755, "Pike-heads, Halberd-heads, Drums and Colours, for compleatly furnishing a Company of Foot, may be had reasonably of Plunket Fleeson, in Fourth-street."

Height 46⅛″   Width 28½″   Depth 24½″

76 · EASY CHAIR
Walnut

Philadelphia 1740-1750

Contemporary in date with Figure 75, this armchair has cabriole legs which are likewise typical of the Philadelphia region. They are more elongated than those of northern easy chairs and are finished with carved web feet; the latter were used too by New Jersey chairmakers and cabinetmakers. The scrolls flanking the legs were adopted from English designs and appear on fine New York chairs and tables as well (see Figure 107, Figure 351, and Figure 354).

The upholstery is silk brocade, probably Spanish, early eighteenth century.

Height 45¼″   Width 30½″   Depth 22½″

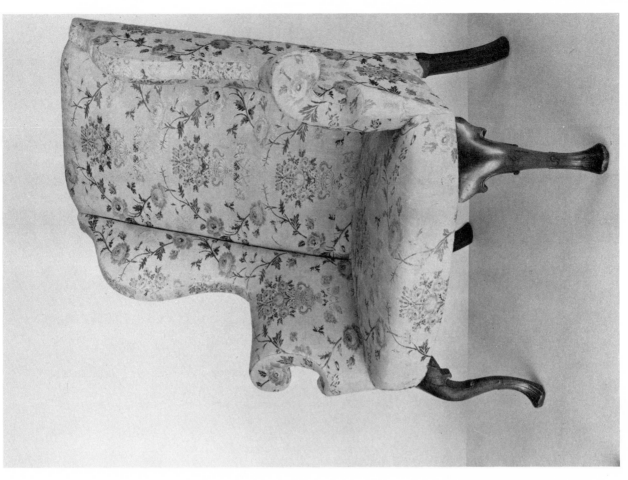

76

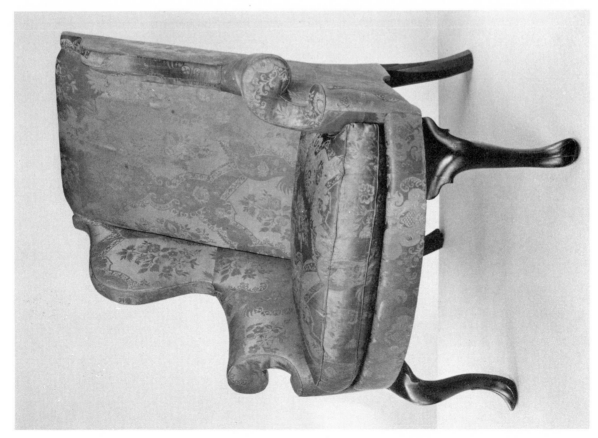

75

77 · EASY CHAIR
Walnut
Philadelphia 1740-1750

This easy, or wing, chair and another one with which it is almost a pair except for size are believed to be unique because of their shell-carved cabriole legs at the rear to match those at the front. The design is a happy one lending to the profile view a balanced stability not often attained in any period of chairmaking. The suave curves of the body complement the supports in a way that could hardly be improved upon.

The covering is coffee-colored brocatelle, Italian, about 1700.

Height 47¼″   Width 27⅜″   Depth 25″

78 · EASY CHAIR
Walnut
Philadelphia 1735-1750

Although walnut was the favored wood for furniture in the Queen Anne period, documentary evidence shows other varieties were not neglected by cabinetmakers. When Joseph Hibbard, a *Joyner*, died in Darby, near Philadelphia, in 1737, part of his stock included:

> Wallnutt Spice Box
> Spice box of sweet gum
> One Screen Candlestick of Cherri Tree
> 3 Walnut Chaires & a Gum one
> 118 foot Wallnut bord
> 50 foot pine & poplar Bord
> 1 piece Mahogany
> Some split ceder for drayor bottome
> One pine Table
> 24 foot pine Bord in ye place
> 6 short bords cut out of Wallnut Roots

The chair pictured here, smaller than any similar ones, has cabriole back legs to be seen only on one other easy chair, Figure 77.

The upholstery is cowhide from Winterthur Farms.

Height 49″   Width 27¾″   Depth 22¾″

78

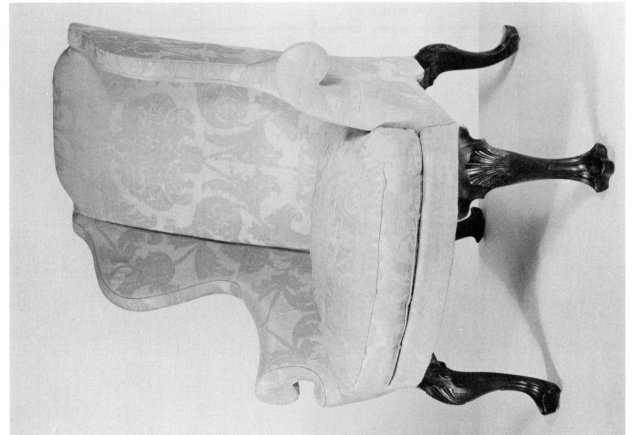
77

79 · EASY CHAIR
Maple and Walnut
Rhode Island 1740-1750

This easy chair shows to best advantage the flat, serpentine stretchers often used by Newport makers and offers, too, a comparison with those in the Philadelphia region (see Figure 73). Unlike other examples of this form of underbracing (see Figure 110), the edges are molded to lighten its weight. The tapered, round legs are skillfully shaped to join the stretchers. The chairmaker selected maple for the rear legs and the turned medial brace, perhaps to lend greater strength than walnut might have done. They are stained to match the other wood. The inside seat rails are hard maple.

The upholstery is brown cotton.

Chairs of this quality were "bespoke" or made to order, unlike those bought for speculation in lots, for export to other cities.

Height 44"　　　　　　Width 31"　　　　　　Depth 22"

80 · EASY CHAIR
Walnut
Rhode Island 1735-1745

The broad low seat of this easy chair and the turning of its understructure are both characteristic of New England upholstered chairs. The stretchers were functional elements repeated throughout the eighteenth century; here the block and spindle stretchers were the customary form of brace, refined from the heavy ball underpinnings of the William and Mary chairs. The cone-shaped arm rests long were favored in New England and New York Chippendale easy chairs, but less often in Philadelphia ones (see Figure 87 and Figure 89).

The green velvet upholstery is probably Italian, eighteenth century.

Height 46½"　　　　　　Width 31"　　　　　　Depth 24"

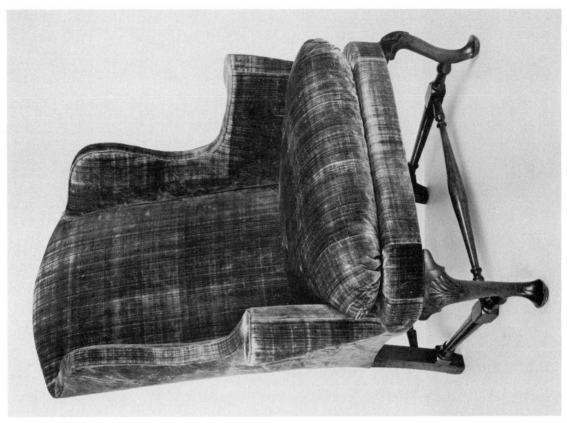

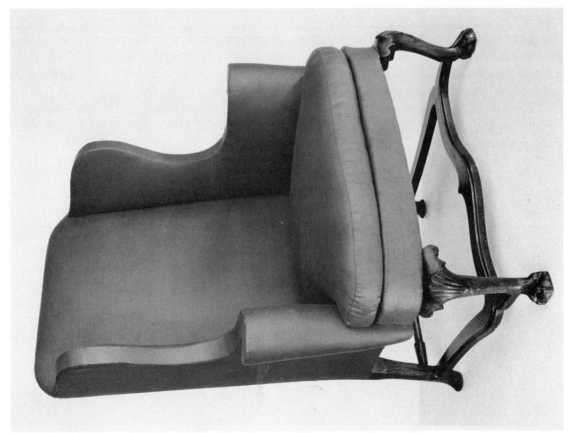

81 · EASY CHAIR
Walnut and Maple

Newport 1765-1780

The shape of the upholstered frame is familiar in New England chairs; here the long claws without webbing and the form of the stretchers are earmarks of the Newport school.

The upholstery is cherry-red wool moreen, probably English, early eighteenth century.

Many valuable possessions were abandoned by fleeing Tories during the War. An "Account of Sundʸ Articles Left at Ashford on March yᵉ 1ˢᵗ, 1775" included:

1 Green Harrateen Easy Chair — 1 Windsor Chair

1 Toilette Table & Muslin covering

1 Bed Bolster & Pillows   1 Bedstead and full Suit of Chince Curtains blue & White — & 1 pʳ Window Curtains

1 Toilette Table with Covering and dressing Glass.   1 pʳ Transparent work Sconces.   1 Coat of Arms glaz'd & Framed.   1 Windsor Chair

1 pʳ Brass Tongs & Shovell & andirons

3 large Homespun Carpets

1 Mahogony Fram'd Couch, with a Red Harrateen square and Check'd Casing — 2 Mahogony Tables

1 Mahogony Fram'd Compass Chair Leather bottom

Height 47½″   Width 30″   Depth 21¾″

82 · EASY CHAIR
Mahogany

Massachusetts 1765-1780

The carved legs of this chair are the most exact clue to its date; the straight-lobed acanthus leaves and small claws were carved on many Salem- and Boston-made Chippendale side chairs. Turned stretchers, almost never found on contemporary cabriole chairs south of New England, are the expected procedure in the Northern states.

The upholstery is blue and red printed linen on white, French, mid-eighteenth century.

In Boston in 1775, "An Account of the Personal Estate of Henry Dering Esqʳ decᵈ sold at Publick Oction" included:

1 Red Easy Chair	£ 13 . . — . . —
a Cace Cedar Draws	16 . . 10 . . —
1 Bewrow Table	25 . . — . . —
12 Blue & White China Plates	2 . . — . . —
1 Blue & White Delph Bowl & 6 Stone patty panns	1 . . — . . —
11 White Delph wash Basons	1 . . — . . —
1 White Gallepott Caudlecup & mugg	. . . .
1 Suit old Grean Curtains	3 . . — . . —
1 Suit Brown Serge Dᵒ	12 . . — . . —
1 Suit Red China Dᵒ	5 . . 5 . . —
a Suit Callico Dᵒ	16 . . — . . —
4 Painted Canvas Pictures aᵗ 31/	6 . . 4 . . —

Height 46½″   Width 31½″   Depth 20″

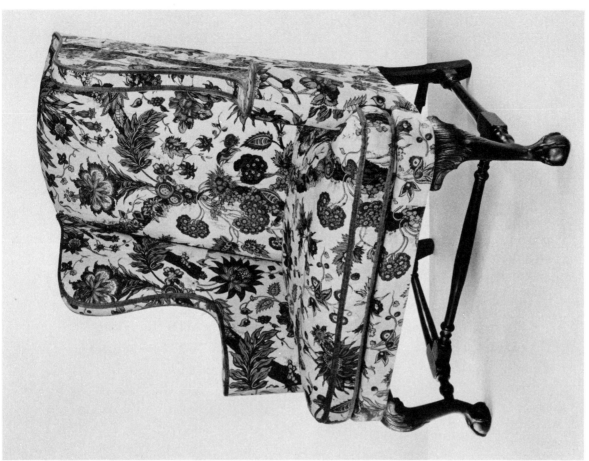

82

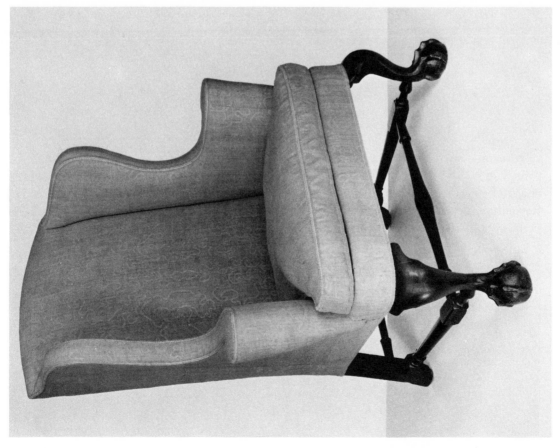

81

83 · EASY CHAIR
Walnut

Probably Virginia 1745-1755

Although this chair has the rolled arm posts of New England chairs (Figure 81) and the rear pad feet familiar in New York (Figure 147), they are "worn with a difference" to present a new picture. The bravado of the flaring arms, the wide knees, the extended smooth claws, and the high-shod back feet are significant. The underframing, entirely built of walnut, is unlike other easy chairs in the collection, where maple, pine, ash, and chestnut are to be seen. The chair was owned originally by the Lewis family in Virginia. Fielding Lewis married General Washington's sister Betty.

The upholstery is maize-colored brocatelle, Italian, early eighteenth century.

Height 44″   Width 28½″   Depth 23″

84 · EASY CHAIR
Mahogany

New York 1760-1775

Some features of earlier furniture were carried over into later styles for practical considerations of strength and personal comfort. This easy chair, although carved with Chippendale ornament, has the cone-shaped arm supports and square rear legs without benefit of chamfered corners. That chairs of this type were popular in Boston, too, on the eve of the Revolution is evidenced by the fact that chairs with similar arms appear in two of Copley's portraits, Mrs. Moses Gill painted in 1759 and Mrs. John Powell painted in 1764.

The upholstery is yellow damask, probably Italian, early eighteenth century.

Height 46½″   Width 31½″   Depth 25″

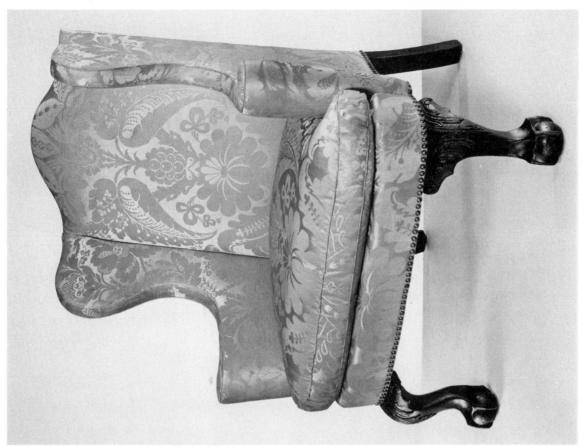

84

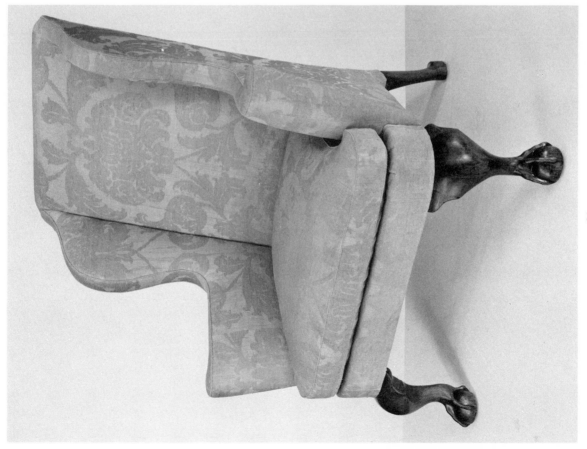

83

85 · EASY CHAIR
Mahogany
Philadelphia 1750-1760

The fluid lines of the wings and arms and the rolled arm ends are old-fashioned details of Philadelphia easy chairs that were repeated by chairmakers until the Revolution. The scallop shells, standing out boldly on the knees, match those carved on the stool (Figure 294), one of a set originally at Stenton in Germantown, the house built for James Logan between 1727 and 1734.

The back thrust of the stump legs and the wide, hospitable arms promise comfort and stability to the occupant.

The upholstery is red silk damask, Italian, late seventeenth century.

Height 44½″   Width 28¾″   Depth 21¾″

86 · EASY CHAIR
Mahogany
Philadelphia 1775-1780

The straight seat front and flattened arm supports resemble those on Philadelphia sofas with paw feet (like Washington's sofa now in Independence Hall) and claw-and-ball feet (Figure 273). This form is distinctly different from the typical Philadelphia easy chairs which have a horseshoe-shaped seat and scrolled arm supports (Figure 87 and Figure 91) that perpetuated the Queen Anne form of easy chair all during the Chippendale period. The carving represents the finest design and workmanship and carries the development of the colonial easy chair to its apogee.

The upholstery is sea-green brocatelle, Italian, late seventeenth century.

Height 49¼″   Width 26¼″   Depth 21½″

Ex Coll. ELLA PARSONS

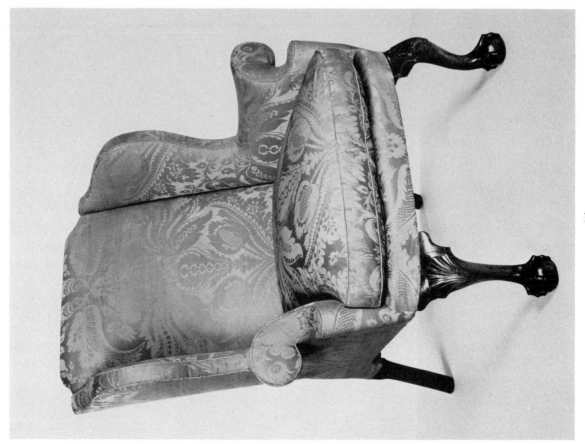

87 · EASY CHAIR
Mahogany
Philadelphia 1765-1780

A chairmaker often gave distinction to his work by changing an accepted practice, as was done in this chair. The high arch upon the narrowed back and outsweeping rear legs ending in ovoid feet are calculated innovations for added grace. On the knees, the carved lambrequin pattern surrounded with leaves matches the well-known Cadwalader easy chair in Philadelphia, and a high chest of drawers (Figure 195).

The upholstery is moss-green silk velvet, Italian, eighteenth century.

Height 51″ Width 27¼″ Depth 22¾″

88 · EASY CHAIR
Mahogany
Philadelphia 1765-1775

The emphatic curves of this chair can be seen also in Figure 91; the carving of the knees has an added grace in the curling ends of the dependent leaves which are arranged in a novel manner, around an uncarved center.

The upholstery is yellow silk damask, Italian, late seventeenth century.

An inventory, room by room, gives a picture of the interiors of houses as they were lived in; ". . . the Goods & Chattles rights & Credits of William Miller late of the Township of Newgarden in the County of Chester & Province of Pennsylvania . . . ye 9th mo 1768" included:

In the Hall	To a Feather Bed & Furniture	£12	0	0
	to a Walnut Ovel Table £1..8. to Twelve Chairs £1..16	3	4	0
	to a Looking Glass £1..15, to hand Irons 12/	2	7	0
In the	To a Feather Bed & Furniture	16	0	0
Chamber up	to a high Case of Drawers £4..10, a little Walnut Table £1..0	5	10	0
Stairs	to Seven Chairs £5 to an Elbow Chair £1..5	6	5	0
	to a little Tea Table 12/ to a Looking Glass £1..15	2	7	0
	to Brass hand Irons Shovel & Tongs, & hand Bellows	1	15	0
	to a Trunk 5/ Glass Furniture on the Mantle Shelf 12/	0	17	0
	to Window Curtains	0	15	0

Height 47″ Width 28¾″ Depth 23″

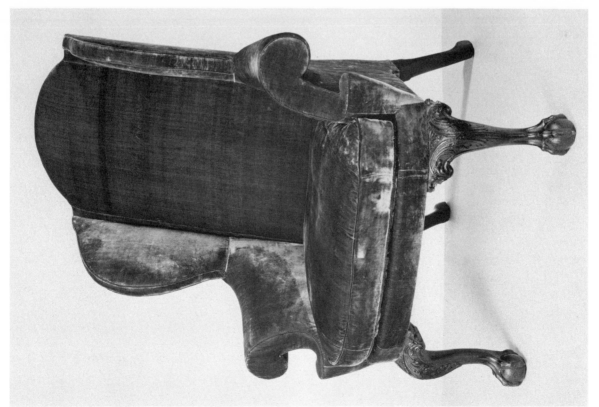

87

88

89 · EASY CHAIR
Mahogany
Philadelphia 1765-1780

The vertically rolled arms, like those of Figure 90, are rarely found in Philadelphia, but in New England and New York they are customary. Another parallel with New York and Massachusetts chairs is the tapering, square rear legs (see Figures 55, 146, 149, 154). This is a shape often seen on English Queen Anne chairs.

The upholstery is blue and white silk, probably French, early eighteenth century.

Height 46″   Width 30″   Depth 20½″

90 · EASY CHAIR
Mahogany
Philadelphia 1765-1780

The carved front legs of this easy chair recall the unique sample chair now in the Philadelphia Museum of Art.* These two chairs are more nearly alike in this respect than any others known and are the only Philadelphia easy chairs with carved paw feet. The old finish, now nearly black, still covers the superb carving.

This chair was owned originally in southern New Jersey.

The upholstery is salmon-colored silk, probably Italian, mid-eighteenth century.

Height 48½″   Width 36¾″   Depth 24⅛″

90

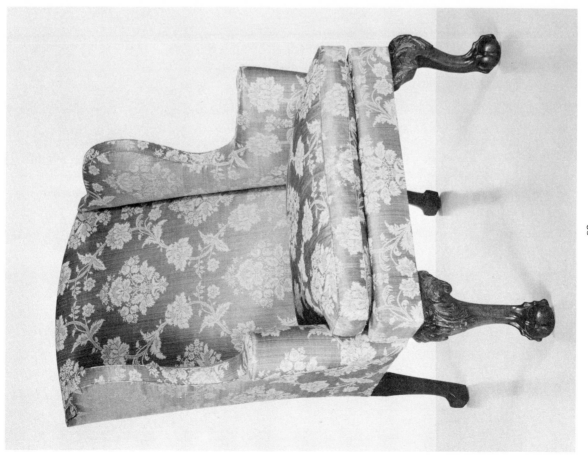

68

91 · EASY CHAIR
Mahogany
Philadelphia 1765-1775

It is certain that this style of chair was familiar to readers of the *Pennsylvania Gazette* in the mid-1760's because of the woodcut illustrations advertising Thomas Hewes' upholstery shop in Chestnut Street, Philadelphia. The chair embodies the essential features of fine Philadelphia design.

The covering has been replaced with green silk damask, Italian, early seventeenth century.

Height 47½″   Width 28″   Depth 22″

92 · EASY CHAIR
Mahogany
Philadelphia 1760-1775

In Philadelphia the C-scrolled arm supports and close-set front legs were habitually followed as a pattern on so-called wing chairs. Northern chairmakers were apt to retain the cone-shaped arm (Figure 74) and the corner-set legs of the Queen Anne period. The modified stump rear legs and the details of the fine carving on the knees in front are likewise characteristic of the Philadelphia school.

The covering is yellow silk damask, Italian, late seventeenth century.

Height 47⅝″   Width 29″   Depth 24½″

93 · EASY CHAIR
Mahogany
Philadelphia 1780-1790

The serpentine-shaped wings of this chair are the latest evidence of its date, repeating the lines of an *Easy Chair* reproduced in Hepplewhite's *Guide* and dated 1787. The mahogany structure below has not been touched by the custom of tapering and inlaying supports for furniture which are prime evidence of classic period furniture. Chairs of the late eighteenth century often are very broad, a fact which has earned them the name of *drunkards' chairs*, to describe their roomy proportions for lolling occupants. In any case, spaciousness points toward greater interest in human comfort, and the new invention of ingenious sleeping and folding chairs among other mechanical devices of furniture, toward which Thomas Jefferson directed his fertile mind with good purpose.

The upholstery is silk brocade in polychrome shades, French, mid-eighteenth century.

Height 46"   Width 30"   Depth 27½"

94 · EASY CHAIR
Mahogany
Philadelphia 1760-1775

This unique easy chair, or so-called wing chair, has the outstanding features of Philadelphia design with the same plan as the more famous *sample* easy chair formerly in the Reifsnyder Collection. The latter has a wealth of elaborate detail unfamiliar to other Philadelphia work. However the relationship between the two chairs is unmistakable. Few other easy chairs show a skirting or arms of wood, but are made like Figure 86 or Figure 92, all upholstered except for the legs.

The frame of this chair is ash and oak, and the side rails of the seat are mortised through the back legs, as most Philadelphia chairs were.

The upholstery is peach-colored silk lampas, the pattern woven in several colors. It is French, early eighteenth century, Regence period.

This chair was originally owned by the Biddle family in Philadelphia.

Height 49⅜"   Width 38¼"   Depth 24"

94

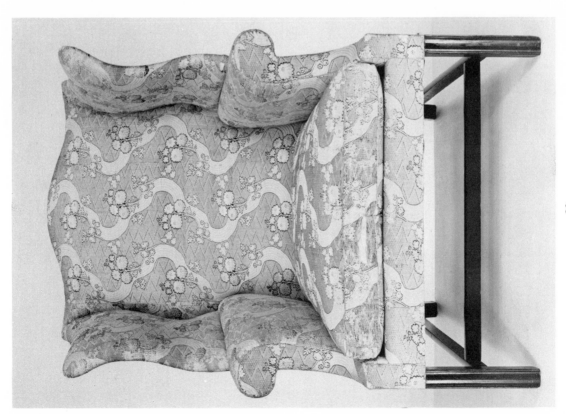

93

95 · SIDE CHAIR
Walnut
Newport 1730-1740

This low-seated or slipper chair, twelve inches from the floor, is typical of the comfortable furniture that was unknown until the Queen Anne style developed. No doubt it found many and frequent uses; its name indicates only one of its purposes.

The upholstery is yellow glazed wool with white lace floral sprays in appliqué, early eighteenth century.

An inventory of John Hebon's modest estate dated December 13, 1727, indicates the possession of certain luxuries:

2 Looking glasses & one ovall table	£4.19.0
1 pr. brass headed andirons	1. 7.0
Pewter	1.15.7½
6 high back Matted Chairs	
8 old dº & small case with drawers	1. 7.8
1 brass chafing dish & frying pan	0. 9.3
4 Linnen Window curtains & Chimney cloth	0.18.0
1 Elbo Chair	0. 6.0
One Iron Back wt. 85	1. 6.6
1 pr. Silver buckles	0. 9.0
1 pr. gold earrings	1.15.0
1 cradle	0.19.0

Height 59″   Width 39″   Depth 22″

96 · SIDE CHAIR
Cherry
Connecticut about 1725

This chair shows the beginning of the Queen Anne style, when the cabriole supports were first grafted to chairs with a high back and rolled cresting, and heavily turned stretchers, a legacy of William and Mary chairs. The angular legs, as though unwilling to adopt the full curves of the high-style cabriole shape, may be seen on several Connecticut chairs with yoke-shaped top rails and solid vase splats. The incised outline on the legs was a customary finish for them.

The seat blocks are heavy triangles of cherry.

The upholstery is old plum-colored moreen, eighteenth century.

Height 43½″   Width 20″   Depth 17″

96

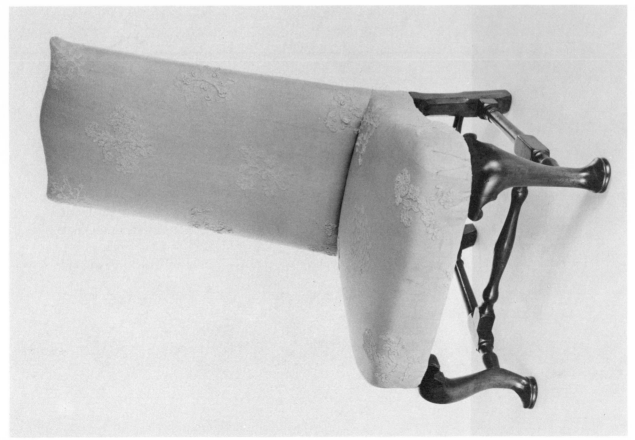

95

97 · SIDE CHAIR
Walnut
Pennsylvania 1720-1740

In France as the reign of Louis XIV declined, the first gesture was made to domestic comfort when the curves of the human form were adapted to seating furniture. Other countries soon followed the curving line, and by way of Holland and England the colonial furniture called *Queen Anne* appeared. In New England and the Southern colonies low-seated, stuffed chairs were made; they are now called *slipper chairs* to explain their height, no doubt adapted to the small stature of women. Feminine costumes prove their wearers' shortness. This chair has pointed feet overlaid with a carved tongue. The side stretchers match those of a sofa, Figure 269, and are typical of the Philadelphia Queen Anne period.

The upholstery is black leather trimmed with brass nails.

This chair came from Stenton, James Logan's house in Germantown. The famous library there was bequeathed to the City of Philadelphia in 1751, and the house is now owned by it and is open to the public.

Height 43″ Width 22½″ Depth 15¼″

98 · SIDE CHAIR
Walnut
Rhode Island 1730-1750

This rare chair is both a back stool and a slipper chair and is related to the small stuffed armchairs designated as ladies' chairs. The tall back is a carry-over from the William and Mary period.

A newly discovered English inventory of 1436 mentions *Bacstowylls* — or stools with stuffed backs, until now thought to be of seventeenth-century origin like those at Knole, in Sevenoaks. Robert Manwaring's *Chairmaker's Real Friend and Companion* offered back stool designs in 1765, and colonial chairmakers adopted the name for their printed trade notices.

The fabric is silk and silver metal brocade on grey and pink ground, French, Louis XV period.

Height 35½″ Width 20″ Depth 17″

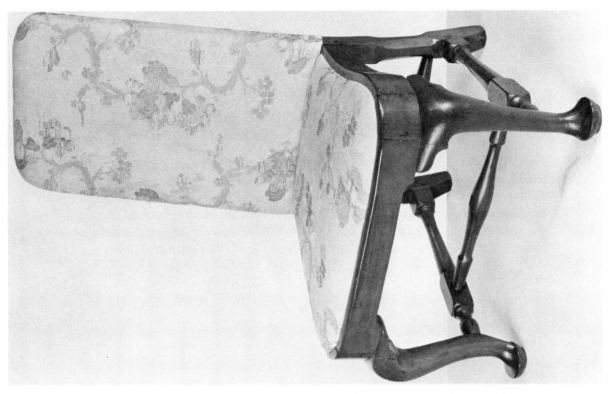

98

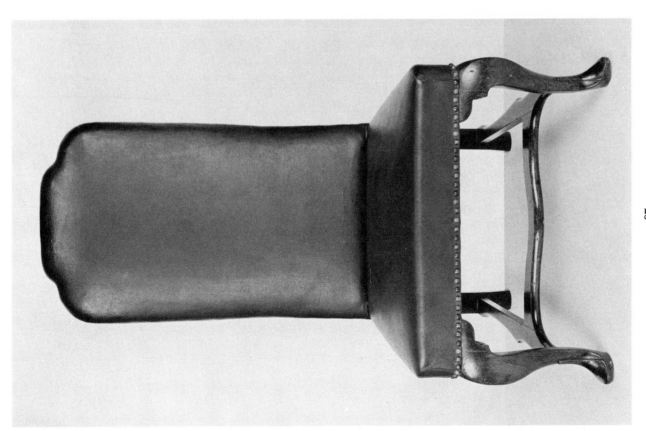

97

99 · SIDE CHAIR
ONE OF A PAIR
Maple and Cherry
New York 1720-1740

The pierced heart in the cherry back splat shown here is found on several Hudson Valley chairs and recalls the corner chairs Figure 65 and Figure 66 with the same ornament.

Hannah Nicoll, widow of John Nicoll, deceased, of New Windsor, New York, bequeathed ". . . To my dau. Frances . . . six fiddle back chairs . . . one case of mahogany drawers . . . one chest of black walnut drawers, one stand candlestick."

Height 39½"   Width 20½"   Depth 15½"

100 · SIDE CHAIR
ONE OF A SET OF THREE
Maple
Portsmouth, New Hampshire 1720-1740
Attributed to John Gaines

A fresh pattern of Queen Anne chairs which originated in Portsmouth is unique for its strong outline and ornament. Earlier caned Flemish and bannister-back chairs have many of the same features, but none has combined them with the solid splat of this period. Armchairs with carved scroll handles were made to match the side chairs.

The upholstery is red wool moquette, French, late seventeenth century.

Height 41"   Width 18½"   Depth 14½"

101 · SIDE CHAIR
Walnut
Newport 1740-1750

The aspect of this chair is not emphatically a Newport design, but the wide convex shell on the cresting forecasts the larger, more decisive ones to come on chests and desks by the Townsend-Goddard clan. The splat, although elongated, has the solid vase shape of medium width, typical of those on lower and broader Newport side chairs. The stretchers and horseshoe seat contribute to the definite attribution of Newport origin. The inside seat rails are thin and conform to the outer ones.

The upholstery is worked in crewels and shows lambs and dogs in a verdure setting. It is American, early eighteenth century.

This chair was No. I of a set.

Height 37″   Width 20″   Depth 17″

102 · SIDE CHAIR
Cherry
Connecticut 1730-1745

The Queen Anne style of chairs in Connecticut might well be epitomized by this one, tall and slender of splat, square seated with scalloped skirting, and having generous ball-turned stretchers. Those details are distinctly different from other New England chairs which they most nearly resemble. Here the profile of the back is serpentine in shape as a concession to greater comfort. Cherry wood, favored in Connecticut throughout the century for the finest cabinet and chair work, is one more assurance of origin.

A set of painted cherry wood chairs matching this one, formerly owned by William B. Goodwin, of Hartford, and lately presented by Mrs. J. Insley Blair to the Metropolitan Museum of Art, has been identified as the work of Southmayd, of Middletown, Connecticut.*

The seat is chain-stitch crewel embroidery worked in a diamond pattern of green, rose, and yellow.

Height 41¼″   Width 19″   Depth 14⅞″

101

102

103 · SIDE CHAIR
Walnut
Newport 1740-1750

A group of nine side chairs at Winterthur, of which this is one, although varying slightly in their turned stretchers and splats, have salient features of the Newport school. The carved shells on the top rails and knees match essentially; on only two chairs the latter shells are eight-lobed instead of seven. The back splat, inspired by Chinese porcelain vase shapes, is cut with scrolls not found in Massachusetts and Connecticut chairs. The thickened claw over a small ball foot somewhat resembles that on New York furniture, but has less thrust in profile.

All nine chairs have walnut back rails and few show a sign of having had seat blocks to brace the underframe. The slip-seat frame is maple covered with cowhide grown at Winterthur.

This side chair was No. I of a set.

Height 39″   Width 20¾″   Depth 17¼″

104 · SIDE CHAIR
ONE OF A SET OF TWELVE
Walnut
Rhode Island 1745-1755

This transitional design is one of two differing slightly in the pierced openings of the back, but otherwise alike. They are probably of Newport origin.

The slip-seat frame of maple is covered with cowhide. This one was No. III of a set.

Height 38¼″   Width 20½″   Depth 16¼″

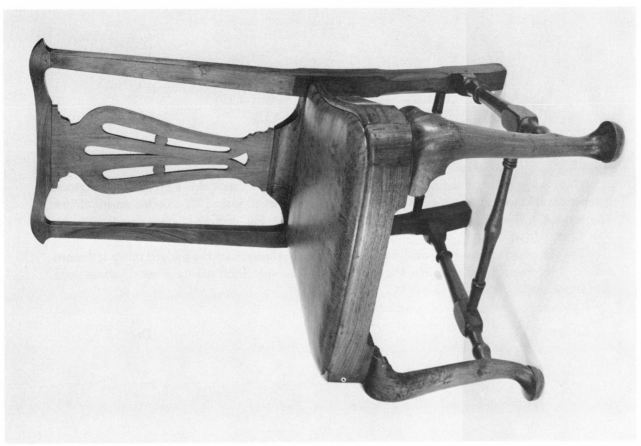

104

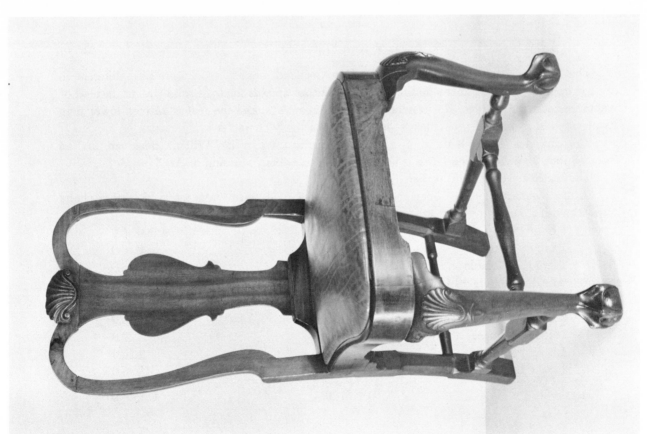

103

105 · SIDE CHAIR
Walnut
New York 1750-1760

This chair is perhaps slightly later in date than the Van Cortlandt chairs because of the cross-hatched lambrequins on the knees, which Gilbert Ash employed after 1757 so often on his chairs. The top rail, although not piérced through, is carved with the shell and leaves familiar on the Van Cortlandt set.

The slip-seat frame is red oak. The back seat rail is cherry, and the underframing is braced with quarter-round pine strips. It was customary to number each one of a set of chairs with Roman numerals. This one was No. IV.

The seat is covered with blue brocatelle.

Height 39″   Width 20″   Depth 17½″

106 · SIDE CHAIR
Walnut
New York 1730-1750

This chair is a variant in design of the Van Cortlandt chairs (see Figure 26), different in carving upon the top rail, knees, and feet. Here the wider splat is made of solid walnut, instead of walnut veneered upon pine. No stretcher braces the rear legs, and the seat is an inch lower than its prototypes. In both, a spontaneous vigor imparts a lively character to the chairs.

The carved legs match those of a settee originally used by Dr. William Beekman, in Van Brugh Street, New York. The settee is now in the Metropolitan Museum of Art.°

The seat is covered with leather.

In the inventory of John Collins, New York, April 4, 1738, mention is made of leather chairs together with a variety of other items:

9 Negroes	£390. 0.0
1 Elbow Chair	0. 4.0
1 large plank table	0.15.0
6 Leather Chairs & 1 Couch	7.10.0
6 old d.° d.°	1.16.0
2 Beds & Bedsteads	20. 0.0
1 silver porringer	4. 0.0
1 silver pepper box	1.10.0
1 silver teapot	12. 0.0

Height 38½″   Width 20½″   Depth 20½″

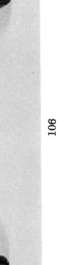

106

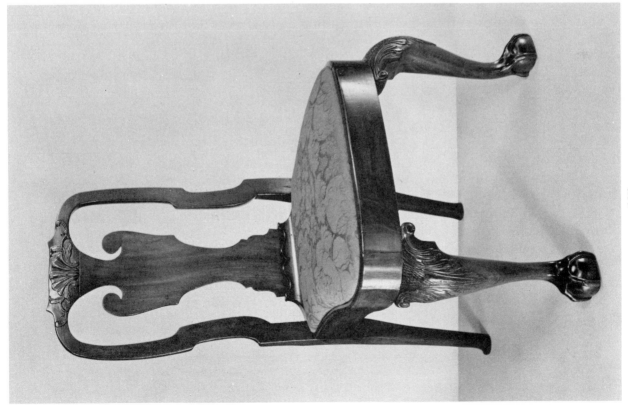

105

107 · SIDE CHAIR
Walnut

New York 1730-1750

Another chair with rounded stiles is noteworthy for the rear legs of cabriole shape, almost unknown upon an American chair. The carved lambrequin on the knees of the front legs is a refinement unmatched on other New York chairs.

The upholstery is plum-colored cotton. The cherry slip-seat frame is marked *XII*.

William Crawford's inventory at Eastchester, in Westchester County, on February 25, 1748, lists:

5 Leather Chairs and Six red ones	£ 2.14
19 Old Black chairs	2.
6 Tables and a Stand	2.17
1 Desk and Book Case	6.
1 Cubboard	2.10
2 Beds Bedsteads bedding and a Couch bed	11.10
1 Bed and Furniture	15. 0
2 Chests a close stool and a small bed	0.14
Remnants of Check linen	2. 0
Remnants of plush	2. 0
Remnants of Camblet	7. 0
Remnants of Shalloon	3. 0

Height 31″   Width 20″   Depth 16⅞″

108 · SIDE CHAIR
Cherry

New York 1740-1750

The sense of line and form, as well as the ability to realize them, was not restricted to a few early craftsmen. Nowhere can they be seen better than in this chair, where the back curves sharply to fit the human form and balances in reverse the shape of the cabriole legs. No ornament is needed to enrich the shape of the splat or legs or to emphasize their sweep. The front feet are like those of the Beekman dining table (Figure 318), shod and pointed, a local variant of the round foot of the Queen Anne period.

The slip-seat frame is cherry. Soft-pine vertical strips brace the corners of the inside.

The upholstery is resist-dyed linen in blue and white, American, eighteenth century.

Height 39½″   Width 21″   Depth 16″

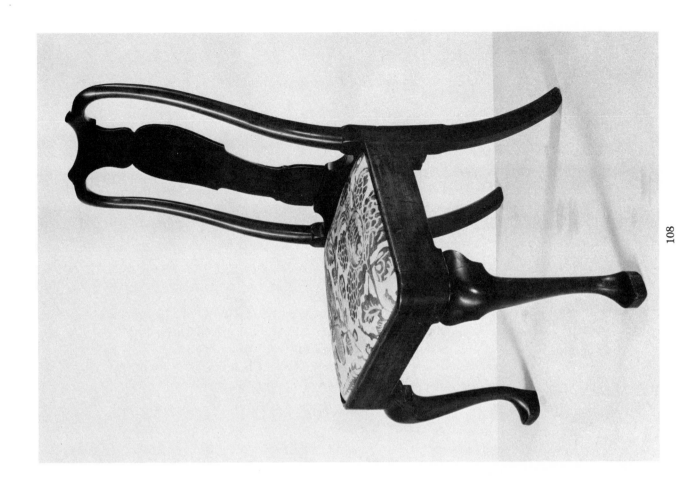

107

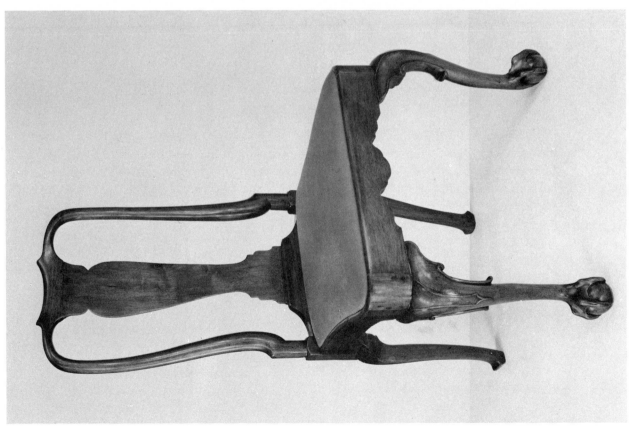

108

109 · SIDE CHAIR
ONE OF A PAIR
Curly Maple
Philadelphia 1745-1755

Several of William Savery's early labeled chairs follow the pattern of this one. The chamfering of the corners of the legs to lighten their appearance is an ingenious device — no less than the tiger-striped maple to embellish the simple splat.

Maple was relatively rare for early furniture in Pennsylvania. For example, the inventory of Caleb Cowpland in Chester County in 1757 is an average one for this date:

> Two Walnut Table
> One Rush bottom Couch
> One Small Walnut Table
> One ash tub One Wild-Cherry tree Desk
> One Wooden Couch and two Wooden armed Chairs
> A Quantity of Ceder boards
> A Cart Rope, and a large Timber Chair
> One pair of High Chest of Drawers Walnut

Height 38¾″   Width 20¼″   Depth 14½″

110 · SIDE CHAIR
Maple
Newport 1745-1755

The reason for the widespread popularity of Queen Anne furniture today is apparent in this chair, a model of graceful lines, comfortable proportions, and functional simplicity. Innumerable repetitions of it were made, and even now, after two hundred years, they are fairly numerous. Most of the New England chairs have block and spindle-turned stretchers, instead of this flat, scalloped underbracing, which may be seen on an easy chair (Figure 79), a characteristic Newport custom.

The seat is covered with printed cotton in shades of brown and yellow, English, eighteenth century.

Height 41″   Width 20¾″   Depth 16½″

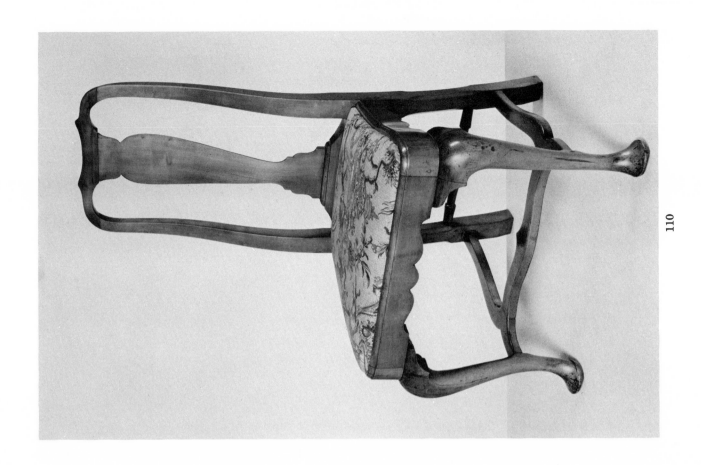

110

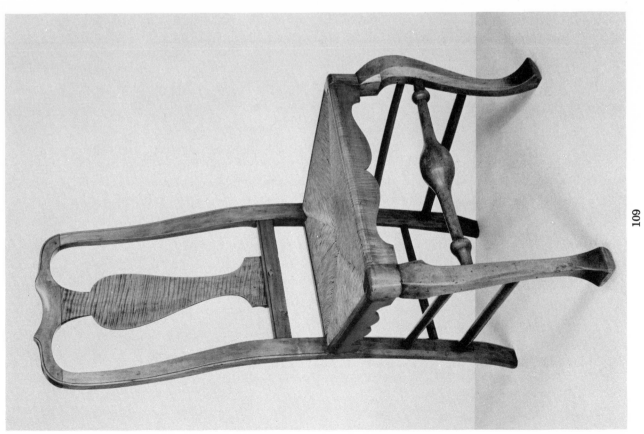

109

111 · SIDE CHAIR
Walnut

Philadelphia 1740-1750

The veneered splat and front seat rails and the incurving rear legs are outstanding differences from the average chairs of this group and are details more often observed on English chairs of the Queen Anne period. The armchair in Figure 28 probably was one of the same set.

The upholstery is silk brocade, French, Louis XV period.

Height 41″   Width 20″   Depth 16½″

112 · SIDE CHAIR
Walnut

Philadelphia 1730-1750

The variation of design in the same school is shown in the base of this chair, differing in several aspects from Figure 111, although the backs are identical. The use of stretchers is rare, and their shape is an interesting contrast with Figure 98, of Rhode Island origin. Under the seat, a partly obliterated inscription reads: "This chair was made . . . and originally . . . Schumachers. Given to E. H. Holt in 1891 by Hannah Yerkes one of the descendants of the Schumachers."

The upholstery is green cut velvet, Italian, seventeenth century.

Height 40″   Width 19¾″   Depth 16″

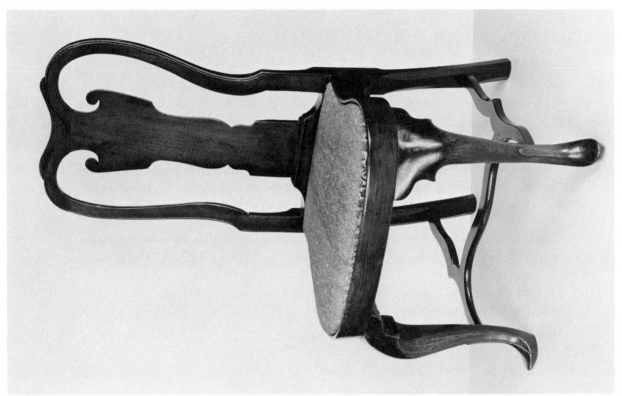

112

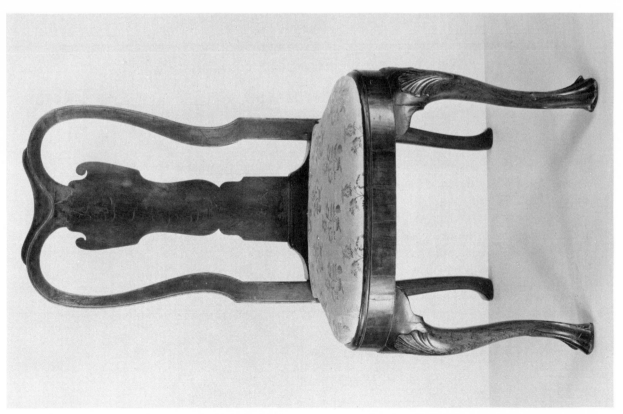

111

113 · SIDE CHAIR
ONE OF A PAIR
Walnut
Philadelphia 1735-1745

The rare judgment shown in the shaping of this chair and the restraint used in the distribution of the carving make it a memorable addition to the history of American furniture. It is one of the basic designs from which the richer, more involved conceptions sprang.

The rear legs are round, or stump shaped. As on many similar Philadelphia chairs, the edge of the seat frame is made in a separate piece, to hold the slip seat. The back rail is hard pine.

This chair, with No. V cut in the seat frame, is one of an original set.

The upholstery is cowhide.

Height 40½"   Width 20"   Depth 17"

114 · SIDE CHAIR
Curly Maple
Philadelphia 1740-1750

The wood of this chair sets it apart from the customary walnut ones which are its contemporaries. The curly maple has become an admirable honey color without benefit of scraper or refinish.

The width of the chair and the line of its curves are somewhat more delicate than usual, imparting to it an especial elegance. The rear legs are tapered and shaped into square feet at the ends, which are noteworthy for their rarity.

The upholstery is cowhide.

This chair was No. VI of a set. It was owned formerly in Moorestown, New Jersey.

Height 41"   Width 19¼"   Depth 16"

113

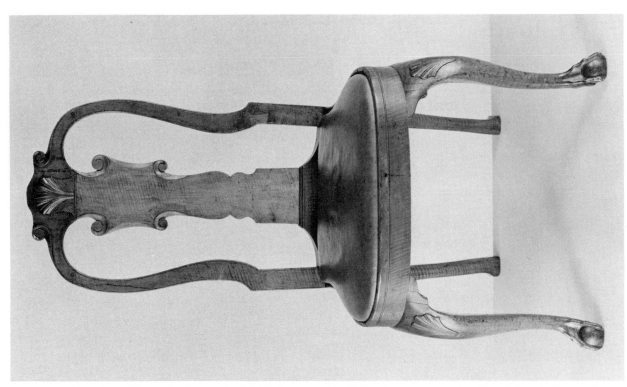

114

115 · SIDE CHAIR
Walnut
Philadelphia 1745-1755

This is the last phase of the Queen Anne style, in which the carving takes on the Chippendale character of furniture in the following decades. The plain splat, without the rich walnut veneer of Figure 116, and the outline of the back are earlier than the ornament; and they accord with the horseshoe seat. The bird's claws are remarkably long and wide for this early period; the rear legs are chamfered to make an octagonal section in plan.

The upholstery is cowhide.

William Lewis, who died in Haverford in 1754, had numerous pieces of walnut furniture, then in high fashion:

> To 1 Walnutte Arm'd Chair and 9 others
> To a Walnutte Oval Table and 1 Oak ditto
> To 1 Walnutte Oval Table and 2 Tea Tables
> To 1 Walnutte Oval Table   1 Chamber dressing Table
> To 1 Walnutt Arm'd Chair and 3 others
> To 1 Wallnutte Chest, 2 Chairs and 1 Cloaths-Press
> To Wallnutte Case of drawers and desk Trunk

Height 40″   Width 20″   Depth 17″

116 · SIDE CHAIR
ONE OF A PAIR
Walnut
Philadelphia 1740-1750

Perhaps slightly earlier in style than the chair in Figure 115 because of the long, dependent leaf ornament on the knees and the S-shaped scrolls of the cresting outlined with heavy moldings, this chair is another superb example of the best in colonial chairmaking. It is part of the matching set of which No. 656 in the Reifsnyder Collection was one. The chair pictured here was No. V of the original set.

The concaved front rail, embellished with a shell, was employed only for the finest Philadelphia chairs of this style. Another pair at Winterthur varies only in the details of the shell carving.

The splat is veneered to secure a richer pattern of walnut where it would count for the most. The inside seat frame is cut not in the usual square, but in fanciful ogee curves.

The upholstery is crewelwork floral embroidery, American, eighteenth century.

Height 39¼″   Width 20½″   Depth 17″

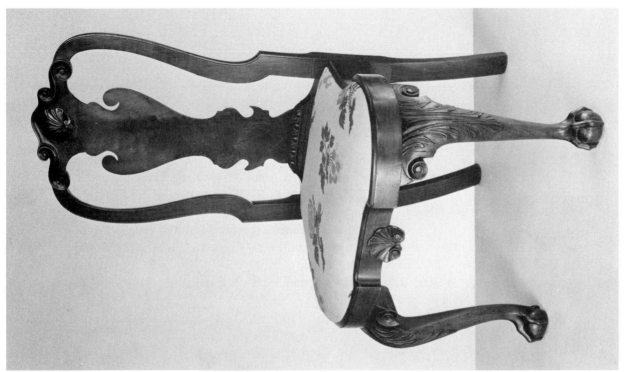

116

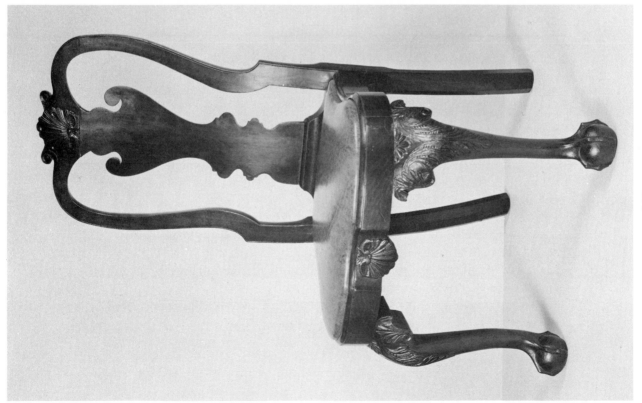

115

117 · SIDE CHAIR
ONE OF A SET OF SIX
Walnut
Philadelphia 1750-1760

The beginning of the Chippendale style, revealed in its pierced splat, must place this chair among the last of that fine group of Queen Anne chairs made in Philadelphia. The lower part of the frame carries on, in comparison to the development of the back, an older style, without the foliation and pierced shells associated with the rococo period.

The inside seat is constructed as a square, formed by wide rails. The long outward rake of the rear stump legs and serpentine profile of the back required an extravagant use of walnut timber, from which the curves were cut.

The upholstery is old American crewelwork embroidery in flame stitch; the geometric pattern is red, green, yellow, and white.

Height 42½″   Width 19¾″   Depth 16¾″

118 · SIDE CHAIR
Walnut
Philadelphia 1750-1760

This chair is transitional in design, retaining the horseshoe-shaped seat and top rail of Queen Anne chairs, but introducing later rococo detail on the pierced splat and knees. The latter Chippendale ornament is large in scale, well matched to the volutes and cockle-shell of the cresting. The legs and feet resemble the carved detail of a pier table, Figure 359, that is possibly by the same hand.

The seat rails are mortised through the back legs. The seat framing follows the curve of the seat, unlike chairs Figures 113 and 117, which have heavy straight frames under their seats. The back seat rail is hard pine.

Only a few chairs of this type are known, and because of their quality they are prized by collectors. It was No. V of the original set.

The needlepoint seat is original to the chair and is a conventional floral design in varicolored crewels.

Height 40½″   Width 20¾″   Depth 17″

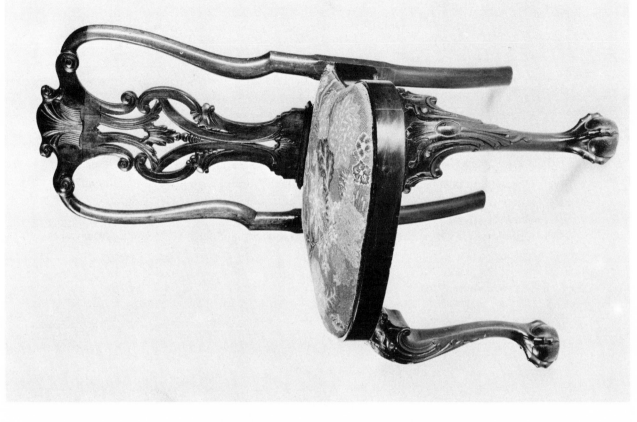

118

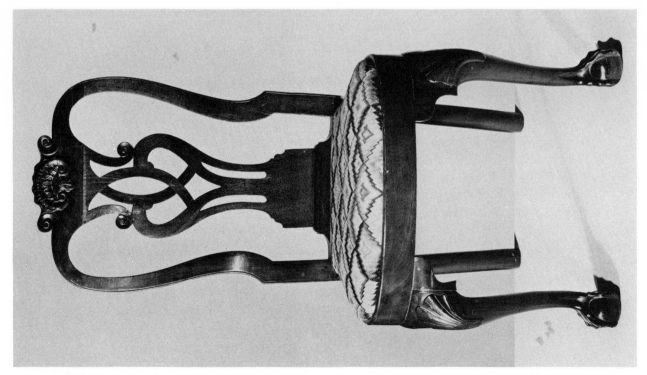

117

119 · SIDE CHAIR
Mahogany
Baltimore or Philadelphia 1750-1760

In the intermediate style of Queen Anne and Chippendale, this chair has the ornate carving of Figure 128, but retains most of the earlier structural outlines. Here the carving is superior in quality to the shape of the chair itself, but the design is an interesting comparison with other chairs in the development of the Chippendale style. The top rail and the splat are similar to those of an armchair, Figure 38, of possible Maryland origin.

The upholstery is a two-color green silk, probably Italian, early eighteenth century.

Height 42″   Width 20″   Depth 16¼″

Ex Coll. HOWARD REIFSNYDER

120 · SIDE CHAIR
Walnut
Rhode Island 1750-1760

This is a transitional chair; the open lacy splat and the ears grafted to the Queen Anne top rail provide a novel design which shows the beginning of the Chippendale style. The low seat suggests the name of *slipper chair*.

Number II is cut on the back seat rail. A matching chair is at the Van Cortlandt Museum, New York City, The National Society of Colonial Dames, and originally came from Kingston, Massachusetts.

The upholstery is yellow silk damask, Italian, early eighteenth century.

Height 36″   Width 21½″   Depth 17½″

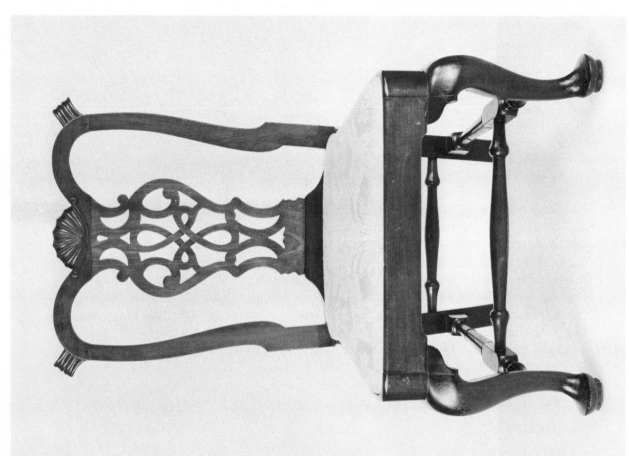

120

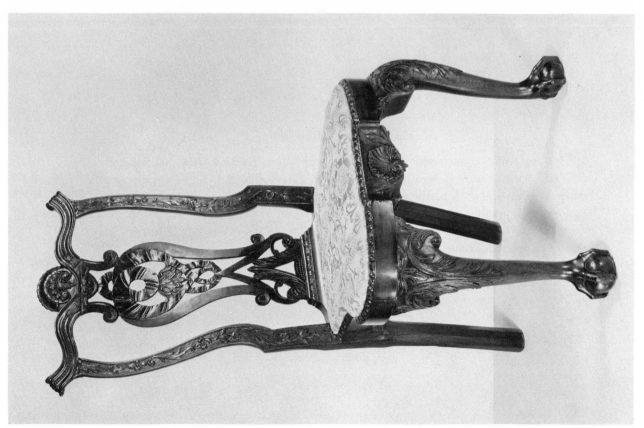

119

121 · SIDE CHAIR
ONE OF A PAIR
Walnut

Philadelphia 1755-1765

Some manuscript drawings of chairs by Jonathan Shoemaker, a joiner in Philadelphia in 1750, and his apprentice, Samuel Mickle, dated April, 1766, show the same bowed top rail and shell, and the same seat skirting as this chair. The solid splat shown in the ink drawing lacks the scrolls, and the feet are trifid shape. The designs give an approximate date for the transitional chairs from the Queen Anne to Chippendale style. Several other extant drawings show claw-and-ball-foot tables, and bookcases and desks with bracket feet and broken pediments. Shoemaker died in the yellow fever epidemic in 1793. After his apprentice Mickle became a journeyman cabinetmaker, he remained with his master for several years and then returned to his birthplace in Haddonfield, New Jersey, in 1776. Three years later he gave up cabinetmaking and started as a merchant in Woodbury, New Jersey.*

This chair was No. III of the original set.

The upholstery is light-blue silk damask, probably English, mid-eighteenth century.

Height 39½″	Width 21″	Depth 15¾″

122 · SIDE CHAIR
Walnut

Philadelphia 1755-1765

This chair may be the work of John Elliott, well known for his labeled looking glasses. He billed Charles Norris for similar chairs in 1756. The design of this chair is memorable for the asymmetrical shell on the cresting and for the protruding scrolls inside the knees. It is a fine example of a transitional chair well balanced in its proportions and ornament.

Individual touches rarely repeated on other chairs are the five-petaled flowers incised inside the scrolled ears and upon the shell.

The side rails are not mortised through the back legs, an omission of Philadelphia practice seen, too, on some of Benjamin Randolph's labeled chairs.

The seat is covered with sand-colored silk damask, probably English, mid-eighteenth century.

Height 41″	Width 21½″	Depth 17″

122

121

123 · SIDE CHAIR
Walnut
Maryland or Pennsylvania 1760-1770

This chair, like those in Figures 37 and 38, has some features of Maryland furniture, particularly in the scrolled ears of the top rail, the wide splat, and the fluted stiles flanking it. In years past, some connoisseurs have designated this type of chair as Chester County in origin to set it apart from the more urbane Philadelphia Chippendale work. However, its quality, although different, is undeniable. Even though the Baltimore and Annapolis school of colonial furniture is still to be thoroughly explored, enough is known to make this chair of probable Maryland origin. The webbed claws are a minor difference, too, from Philadelphia carved feet.

The upholstery is silk brocade in polychrome, French, Louis XV period.

Height 37½″ Width 21½″ Depth 17½″

124 · SIDE CHAIR
ONE OF A PAIR
Mahogany
Philadelphia 1760-1770

This chair is a more elaborate version of the armchair Figure 51 and shows one of several different uses of the same back in the early Chippendale style. Its development from the Queen Anne period may be studied in Figure 118.

The upholstery is silk brocade, French, Louis XV period.

In 1768 the well-furnished house of William Miller, deceased, at Newgarden, in Pennsylvania, included "In ye Big Room up Stairs:

To Six Chairs £2. 10, to a high Case of Drawers £3	£ 5.10.0
to a Feather Bed & Furniture £9 to a dº £4	13. 0.0
to low Case of Drawers £1. 10, to a Box & Frame 15/	2. 5.0
to a Looking Glass 7/6 to a Trunk 7/6	0.15.0
to hand Iron & Tongs	0.10.0
to Three Coverlids £2..2, to Two Blankets 18/	3. 0.0"

Height 39¾″ Width 22″ Depth 17″

123

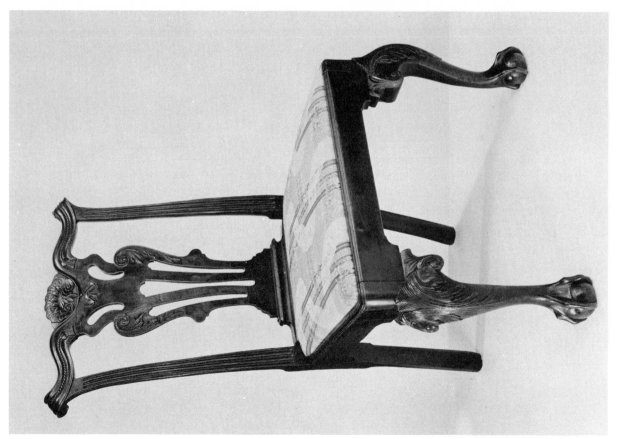

124

125 · SIDE CHAIR

ONE OF A SET OF THREE

Mahogany

Philadelphia 1760-1770

This well-known tassel-back pattern was often repeated and embodies the essentials of the Philadelphia style of Chippendale chairs. The stopped-fluting on the stiles of the back and the tassel motif in its center are contemporary details used in Newport (Figure 311) and New York (Figure 52) respectively.

The seat frame is braced with quarter-round blocks of hard pine. This chair was No. III of the original set.

The seat is covered with silk brocade, French, Louis XV period.

Height 39½″ Width 22½″ Depth 18″

126 · SIDE CHAIR

Mahogany

Philadelphia 1755-1760

This chair may be dated among the first in the Chippendale style; it follows the tall, narrow proportions of Queen Anne chairs. Even the same pierced strap splat occurs on chairs with outlines of the earlier period, like Figure 117.

The upholstery is blue silk damask, probably French, mid-eighteenth century.

Height 41½″ Width 21½″ Depth 17″

126

125

127 · SIDE CHAIR
Mahogany
Philadelphia 1765-1770

The popularity of this design carried it through several phases, each richer than the last. Here the rococo touches in the carving indicate the growth of a style that flowered ultimately in the full-blown Chippendale manner in Figure 137.

The upholstery is sea-green brocatelle, Italian, about 1700.

Height 40¼"   Width 21½"   Depth 17"

128 · SIDE CHAIR
Mahogany
Philadelphia 1770-1780

Here the apex is reached in the unstinted use of fine carving, where scarcely any surface is free. Several known chairs are so treated, as if to popularize an older pattern by a wealth of fashionable ornament.

The upholstery is silk brocade, French, about 1770.

This chair was originally owned by the Lambert family in Philadelphia.

Height 41¾"   Width 22½"   Depth 17¾"

Ex Coll. HOWARD REIFSNYDER

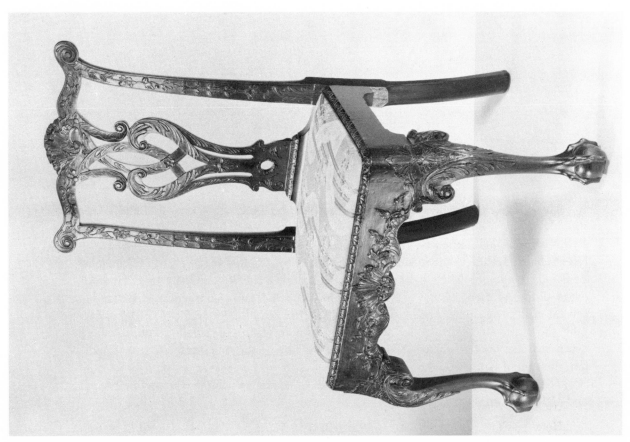

128

127

129 · SIDE CHAIR
ONE OF A SET OF FOUR
Mahogany
Philadelphia 1765-1780

The design of this chair ranks among the handsomest in the American Chippendale style. Here the Gothic arch and quatrefoil are subtly intermingled with rococo curves, a style that appealed particularly to Philadelphia craftsmen. In this collection are four different chairs, each with the identical splat outline. The simplest one (Figure 142) matches Benjamin Randolph's labeled chair (Garvan Collection), but it is unlikely that Randolph made all four of them, as they vary so much in proportion and construction. This chair has several rare features; viz., the hairy paw feet and the acanthus or "raffle" leaves overlapping the gadrooned skirting like the famous *sample* chair (Rockefeller Collection). It nearly matches another chair (Tiffany Collection) now in the American Wing, Metropolitan Museum of Art.

The upholstery of the stuffed seat is flowered silk in polychrome, probably French, mid-eighteenth century.

Height 38⅜″	Width 21½″	Depth 17¾″

130 · SIDE CHAIR
ONE OF A SET OF FOUR
Mahogany
Philadelphia 1760-1780

This chair is less ornate than several of its contemporaries with the same pattern of splat, but perhaps more nearly approaches the typical Philadelphia Chippendale style at its best because of its perfectly balanced proportions and elegance of carved details.

The upholstery of the slip seat is yellow silk damask, probably Italian, mid-eighteenth century.

Originally these chairs were owned by Elizabeth and Thomas Edwards, who were married in 1762. A chair was acquired for the Winterthur Collection from each of four of their descendants.

Height 38⅛″	Width 23½″	Depth 18½″

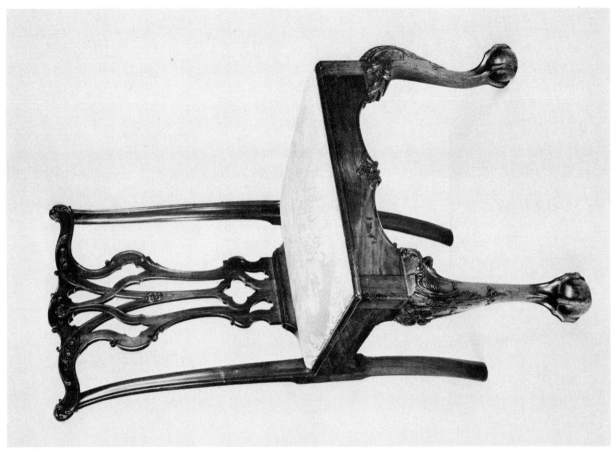

130

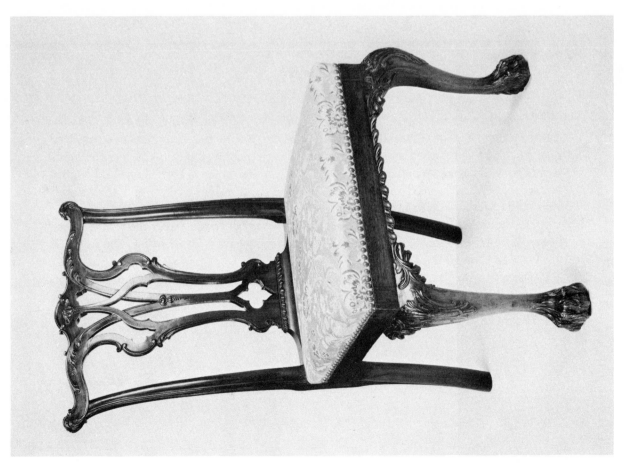

129

131 · SIDE CHAIR
Mahogany
Philadelphia 1765-1780

Although less ornate than some of its contemporaries, this chair ranks among the best for the urbanity of its shape and choice of carving. The back is patterned on Plate XIII of Chippendale's *Director*, 1762; therein, the scrolled ears, top rail, and pierced splat clearly show in the engraving. The fine detail of the carved legs has the same light touch and pattern as that on the Cadwalader easy chair; both have the distinctive lambrequin and flower center, from which delicate acanthus leaves curl away.

The overstuffed seat was used in Philadelphia on other excellent chairs, as Figures 129 and 138. The seat rails are ash, and small hard-pine blocks brace the corners.

The upholstery is yellow silk damask, Italian, late seventeenth century.

Height 38¼″   Width 22¾″   Depth 17″

132 · SIDE CHAIR
ONE OF A PAIR
Mahogany
Philadelphia 1760-1780

This side chair has several features of a similar chair, Figure 134, signed by Thomas Tufft; namely, the slender undercut knees, the scroll-trimmed knee blocks, a concaved seat rail, and the upturned ears that terminate the serpentine top rail. The cabochon-and-leaf carving of the knees and apron is also generally the same on both chairs, although it is improbable Tufft carved any furniture, but like other cabinetmakers and chairmakers employed carvers to embellish his work.

The underbracing of the seat is made like an English chair. Across the front corners, heavy diagonal strips of tulipwood are nailed in; none were used at the rear. The side rails are tenoned through the back legs.

The overstuffed seat is covered with yellow silk damask in a symmetrical foliate pattern, probably Italian, late seventeenth century.

Height 38⅛″   Width 22¼″   Depth 17½″

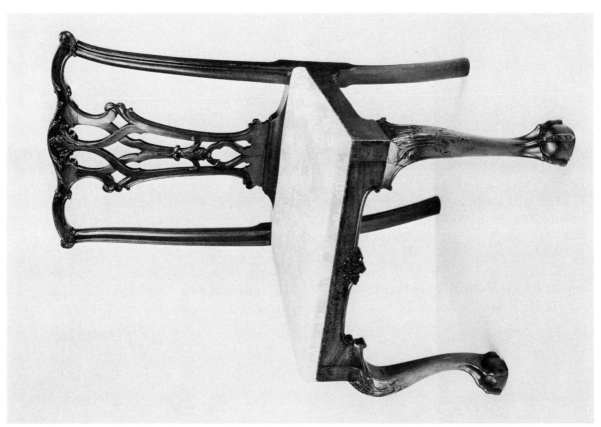

132

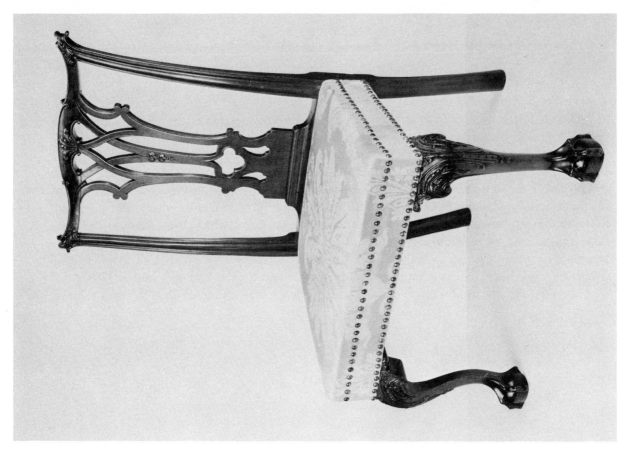

131

133 · SIDE CHAIR
ONE OF EIGHT
Mahogany
Philadelphia 1760-1775
Probably Made by Benjamin Randolph

This chair is attributed to Benjamin Randolph, whose label is fixed to a similar one in the Karolik Collection.* The skirt here is richer in carving. It is an urbane interpretation of the Philadelphia style, made probably in the early 70's before Randolph sold his tools and shop equipment in 1778. It is more characteristic of the proportions and carving of Philadelphia chairs than are other chairs attributed to the same maker (see Figure 50 and Figure 142). Randolph's fanciful trade card, engraved by I. Smither in Philadelphia, makes immortal his shop "at the Golden Eagle in Chestnut Street."

Unlike several chairs made by Randolph, the side rails of this set are mortised through the rear legs as in most Philadelphia chairs. The slip-seat frames are hard pine.

The upholstery is flowered brocade in a rococo pattern, French, mid-eighteenth century.

Height 38¾"   Width 22¾"   Depth 17½"

134 · SIDE CHAIR
ONE OF A PAIR
Mahogany
Philadelphia 1760-1780
Made by Thomas Tufft

This chair has a slim tallness of line lacking in many Philadelphia chairs of the Chippendale period. A greater distinction is the engraved paper label of the maker on the inside back seat rail, giving his name and address (see Figure 390).

Thomas Tufft is recognized for his able work; several of his signed case pieces, although less flamboyant than the Gratz and Van Pelt family highboys and lowboys, express the finest Philadelphia tradition. In adapting this chair from Plate XIII dated 1753 in Chippendale's *Director,* Tufft followed that author's advice, ". . . a variety of new pattern chairs, which, if executed according to their designs, and by a skillful workman, will have a very good effect. If you think they are too much ornamented, that can be omitted at pleasure." Tufft did omit a great deal of the original detail. He made chairs of the same design with straight legs for the Logan family in 1783.

The slip seat is covered with purple and white toile de Jouy, French, late eighteenth century.

Height 38¾"   Width 21½"   Depth 16⅞"

134

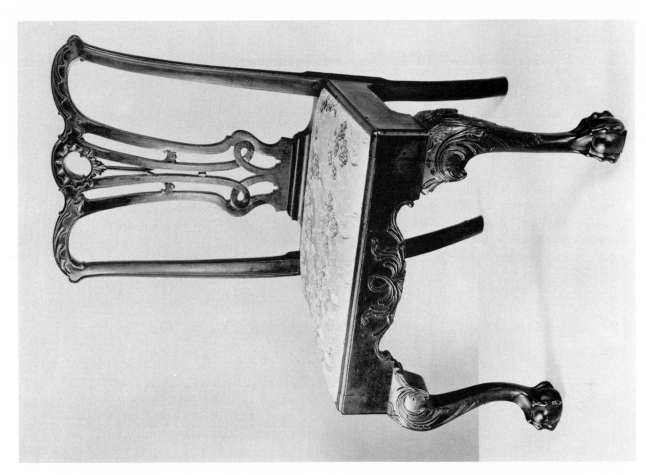

133

135 · SIDE CHAIR
ONE OF A PAIR
Mahogany
Philadelphia 1760-1780

These Chippendale side chairs are extraordinary for their exactness to contemporary engraved design. Inasmuch as colonial craftsmen borrowed and adapted freely, it is rarely possible to find American furniture completely faithful to the engravings that inspired it. For these chairs, the pattern was taken from Plate XII in the first edition of Chippendale's *Director*, 1754; in high style then were the cabriole legs ending in scrolled French feet, and the Chinese fret splat of the back. Noteworthy, too, is the carving in extreme high-relief of the knees and the back, with a suggestion of the heavy scale found in Irish furniture and repeated in Philadelphia on several marble-topped tables.

The slip seats are covered with green silk, probably French, eighteenth century.

Height 39¾"   Width 22¾"   Depth 18½"

136 · SIDE CHAIR
Mahogany
Philadelphia 1760-1780

This chair is another version of the same design as the foregoing, though less exuberant in line and carving. It is an interpretation executed with the most exacting skill. The shape and detail of the legs may be observed on many pieces of Philadelphia Chippendale furniture in the collection.

The upholstery is flowered brocade in polychrome, French, Louis XV period.

Height 40½"   Width 23"   Depth 18"

136

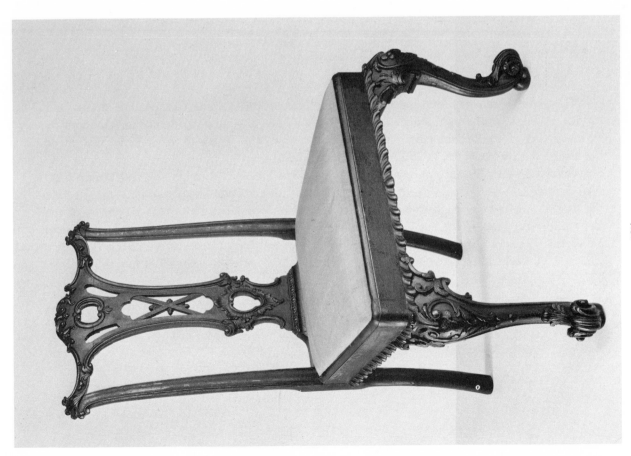

135

137 · SIDE CHAIR
ONE OF A SET OF FOUR
Mahogany
Philadelphia 1760-1775

One of the finest chairs of Philadelphia origin, heretofore unpublished, is this one, part of a set of four. It is similar to the well-known chairs made for John Dickinson and now at Stenton, the home of James Logan in Germantown. Certainly both sets are from the same workshop. Here the intertwined festoons on the back and the carved knees show a novel degree of elaboration. Certain parts of the back, the ears, the interlaced top rail, and the pendant garlands may be traced to Chippendale's *Director*, Plate IX in the 1762 edition; but these few fragments allowed the maker to improvise freely. The result could hardly be improved upon as a model of restrained elegance and beauty. The construction is routine in Philadelphia work; namely, mortised side rails through the rear legs, quarter-round seat braces of hard pine, and a slip-seat frame of the same wood. The upholstery is temporary.

A century ago the chairs were in the possession of Mrs. DeLancey Kane, who was directly allied to the Astor and Langdon families; her great-niece owned the chairs when they were acquired in 1950.

Height 37¾"   Width 22"   Depth 17¼"

138 · SIDE CHAIR
Mahogany
Philadelphia 1760-1775

This superb chair is unique and represents the best in Philadelphia Chippendale design and carving. It is one of the six *sample* chairs which have been attributed to Benjamin Randolph by reason of their descent in the family of Randolph's second wife. There is yet no proof who made the chairs, but the construction follows colonial practice.

Here the seat rails are entirely mahogany and are mortised through the rear stump legs; smooth quarter-round blocks of cedar brace the inside corners. These details would seem to refute the English attribution which formerly was given them. Significant, too, is the repetition of the Cadwalader card table, on a small scale, for the front of this chair, a rare analogy nowhere else paralleled. That card table is shown in a portrait of General John Cadwalader and his family by Charles Willson Peale; and the portrait, with the table itself, often has been lent to public exhibitions by his descendants.*

The upholstery of the chair is flowered silk, probably French, Régence period, about 1720.

Height 36⅞"   Width 21⅞"   Depth 18⅜"

Ex Coll. CHARLES A. CURRAN

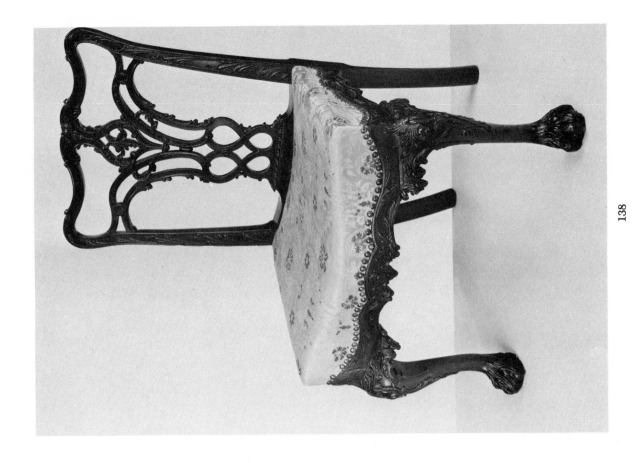

137

138

139 · SIDE CHAIR
ONE OF A SET OF EIGHT
Mahogany
Philadelphia 1770-1780
Probably Made by James Gillingham

This chair may with reason be called the work of James Gillingham, inasmuch as a chair with the identical back, now in the Mitchel Taradash Collection, has the label of that "joyner." The labeled chair was made after August, 1768, when Gillingham dissolved his partnership with Henry Clifton and moved his shop to Second Street. He used for this chair Plate XIII in Chippendale's *Director*, 1754, as a guide for the back, but added the novel corkscrew twist to the rolled-back top rail. The carved knees here are richer than the plain ones of the signed chair.

The frame of the slip seat is hard pine, and quarter-round blocks of the same wood brace the seat rails.

The upholstery is flowered brocade in a Louis XV pattern, French, eighteenth century.

Height 39″   Width 22½″   Depth 17¾″

140 · SIDE CHAIR
Mahogany
Philadelphia 1765-1775

The same chair back as Figure 139 is here enriched, as were other locally made chairs, with a Chinese lozenge pattern on its stiles and top rail, borrowed from Plate XII of the 1754 *Director*. The straight legs and the corner frets augment the Chinese Chippendale spirit.

The upholstery is red leather over a hard-pine seat frame.

Height 38″   Width 22″   Depth 17″

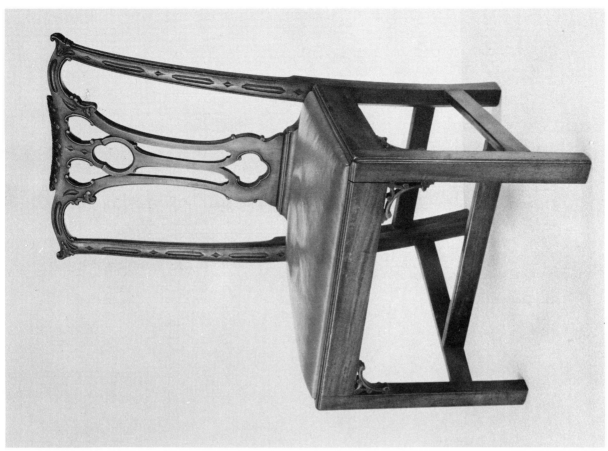

140

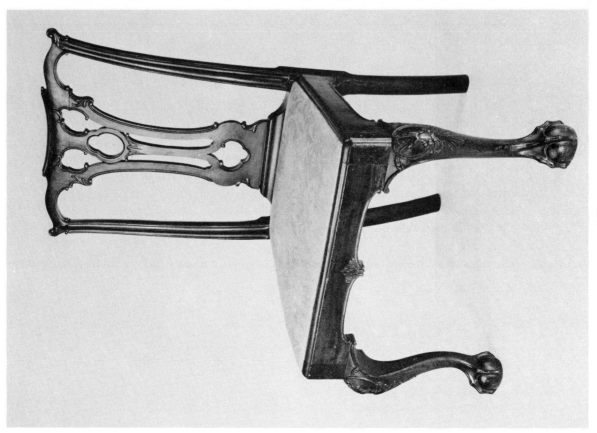

139

141 · SIDE CHAIR
Mahogany
Philadelphia 1770-1785

This chair combines all three of the salient themes of the Chippendale period — the Chinese, the Gothic, and the rococo. Manwaring's *The Cabinet and Chair Maker's Real Friend and Companion,* published in 1765, extended the range of the earlier *Director* and added numerous rustic subjects, which wisely were not attempted in wood. Here, the moderation of the exotic elements employed produces an original and successful result. Thomas Tufft's signed chair (Figure 134) has a similar splat.

The upholstery is red leather.

Height 38¾″   **Width 22″**   **Depth 17½″**

142 · SIDE CHAIR
ONE OF A PAIR
Mahogany
Philadelphia 1760-1770
Probably Made by Benjamin Randolph

This chair matches in every way one in the Garvan Collection which has the label of Benjamin Randolph, a cabinetmaker and carver who advertised upon an ornate trade card, replete with Chippendale ornament and furniture taken straight from the *Director.* This chair is atypical of Philadelphia workmanship in several ways — the unusual width of the back and seat, the lack of seat rail tenons mortised through the back legs, and the small mahogany strips inside the seat frame, instead of quarter circles of hard pine.

There are other pieces here associated with Benjamin Randolph's name (Figures 133 and 138), more elaborate in character. Randolph's receipt book from 1763 to 1777 is in the Winterthur Collection.

The slip seat is covered with sand-colored brocatelle, Italian, early eighteenth century.

Height 37″   **Width 22⅝″**   **Depth 19⅝″**

142

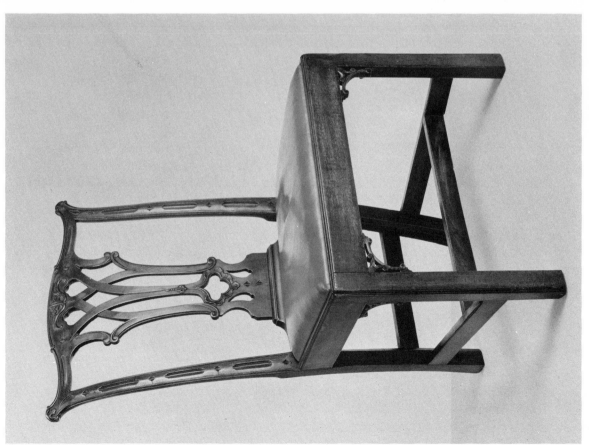

141

143 · SIDE CHAIR
ONE OF A PAIR
Mahogany
Philadelphia 1760-1770

When Benjamin Randolph issued his elaborate trade card, engraved in the French style, he took care to mention "Cabinet and Chairwork . . . Performed in the Chinese and Modern Tastes." The end of that statement is significant because the colonial fashion, as in England, turned from the pagodas and china gods that had so long amused Europe, to Gothic and rococo forms, novel if no more logical for domestic decoration than "the affectation of the Chinese taste . . . meer whim and chimera," as the architect Robert Morris described it. Here the old and new fashions combine with Gothic arches and Chinese rails smuggled in below the seat. The rear stump legs, customarily used in cabriole-leg chairs, are a novelty here. These various elements merge into a close-knit, vigorous pattern of peculiar distinction.

The slip-seat frame is made of hard pine.

The upholstery is purple and white toile de Jouy, French, late eighteenth century.

Height 37⅞″   Width 22⅝″   Depth 18″

144 · SIDE CHAIR
Mahogany
Baltimore 1765-1775

The wide splat of this chair composed of involved Gothic arches is different from any other known designs of the period. The carving has the overworked richness of many English chairs, but the mahogany in the seat rails under the upholstery indicates a prodigal use of that wood not customary in England.

Mahogany was often extravagantly used in the colonies for construction, as for example, under the armrests in Figure 58 and for seat blocks in Figure 44. A wide, closely interlaced back splat used on straight-legged chairs has become associated with Baltimore chairs, an attribution strengthened by long Maryland ownership of similar patterns.

The seat covering is plum-colored cotton.

Height 38¼″   Width 21¾″   Depth 17½″

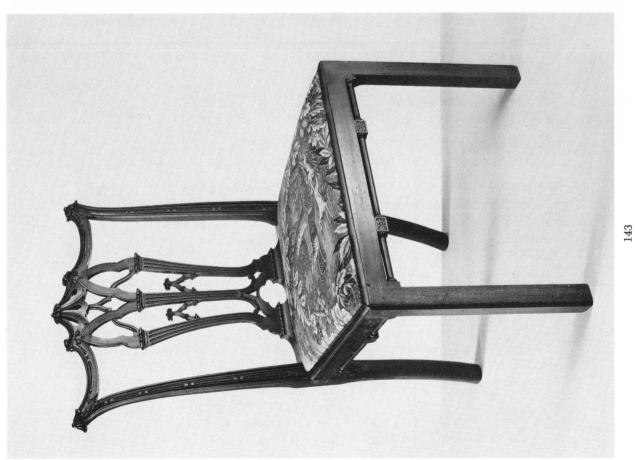

143

144

145 · SIDE CHAIR
Mahogany
New York 1765-1780

This chair is not so emphatic in its regional design as some New York chairs; indeed there are features that might be Philadelphia, as the round-knuckled claw feet or the tall back crested with "peanut" carving; or even Massachusetts, if the incurving rear legs and flattened top rail were a criterion of judgment. However, the broad leaf-carved knees, rounded seat corners, heavy ears, and splat centering a tassel are typical of New York and recall the well-known Van Rensselaer chairs.

The slip-seat frame is made of beech, a wood often combined with cherry and oak in the construction of Manhattan furniture.

The slip seat is red wool moreen, English, eighteenth century.

This chair was owned originally by Elias Boudinot, philanthropist, lawyer, and patriot. He was chosen President of the Continental Congress in 1782. He proclaimed the end of the War, and expressed the Nation's thanks to its Commander-in-Chief. As chief executive, he signed the Treaty of Peace in 1783. Boudinot's last service to his country was as Superintendent of the Mint for several years, starting in 1795. His *Great House* in Elizabeth, New Jersey, which he acquired in 1772, is now a public shrine.

Height 38½"   Width 20½"   Depth 17"

146 · SIDE CHAIR
ONE OF FOUR
Mahogany
New York 1765-1780

The back of this chair has the sophisticated shape and detail of fine Philadelphia Chippendale chairs and, like several of them, was inspired by an engraving in the *Director*; it follows Plate X, dated 1753, with faithfulness. The carving of the knees and the squared, tapered back legs are often observed on chairs of New York origin.

This chair was No. III of the original set.

The upholstery is quilted blue and white cotton, eighteenth century.

The chairs were owned until lately by the Wright family of Oyster Bay, Long Island. The original land deed to Peter Wright is dated 1667.

Height 38½"   Width 21¼"   Depth 17½"

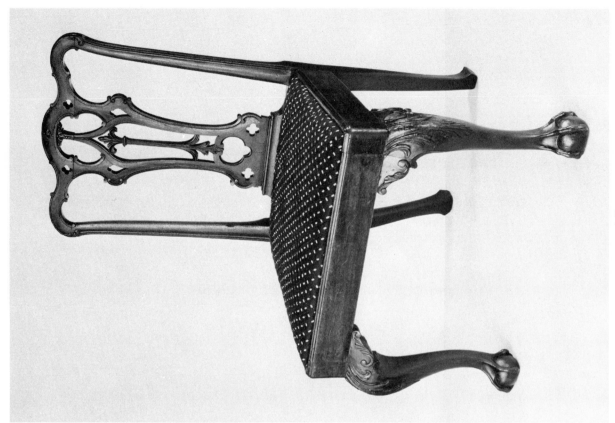

146

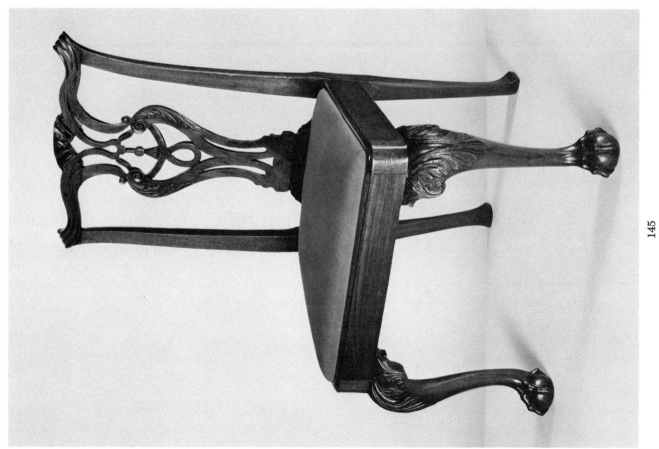

145

147 · SIDE CHAIR
Mahogany
New York 1760-1780

This design was used on English chairs as well as on those in New York. It is peculiarly delicate for the latter, but the cherry seat rails and the shape of the rear legs are typical New York details.

The same design was used for a set of chairs (the armchairs having eagle-head handles like Figure 52) that belonged to Judith and Samuel Verplanck, at 3 Wall Street, Manhattan, before the Revolution. The original diagonal strips of tulipwood brace the underframing of the seat.

The upholstery is plum-colored cotton.

This chair was published and illustrated as New England in 1931.*

Height 37¾″   Width 22¼″   Depth 18″

148 · SIDE CHAIR
Mahogany
New York 1765-1775

The design of this chair was adapted by the maker from an engraved plate in Robert Manwaring's *The Cabinet and Chair Maker's Real Friend and Companion,* published in London in 1765. The book was advertised in colonial newspapers from 1767 (and possibly earlier) and provided a Massachusetts chairmaker with the same pattern for a set of chairs made for the Loring family in Salem. Two chairs of the latter set are now in the American Wing. In the chairs here, the rugged aspect imparted by New York craftsmen is readily apparent. The wide proportions, thickened cabriole legs and squared claws on the ball feet, simple gadrooned molding along the skirt, and square rear legs are all Manhattan features. Two details here are often repeated on Philadelphia furniture; namely, the fine "fingernail" edging along the outline of the splat (Figure 132) and the seat rails mortised through the back legs.

The seat frame is braced with triangular blocks of white pine.

The upholstery is blue wool damask, in the style of the eighteenth century.

Height 38½″   Width 21¼″   Depth 17¼″

148

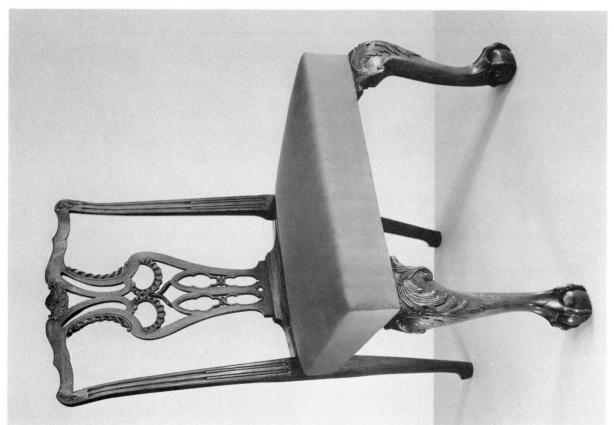

147

149 · SIDE CHAIR
ONE OF A PAIR
Mahogany
New York 1755-1765

In 1756 Gilbert Ash, a chairmaker "in Wall Street near the City Hall," New York, signed and dated a side chair closely allied in design to this one. It has an identical scrolled splat with a diamond center, dependent leaves on the ears, and crosshatched knee carving, each one a distinctive feature.

Gilbert Ash was born in 1717 and became a freeman joiner in 1748. New York newspapers advertised his cabinet and chair work until 1763. He died January 3, 1785, "an old and much respected inhabitant . . . an agreeable companion . . . possessed of an excellent mechanical genius."

In Martin Van Bergen's Account Book of goods carried between Manhattan and Albany on the Hudson River, one item under November 6, 1760, is significant: *To Wm Johnson to freight 6 chairs   £0.6.0.*

This chair, No. IV of a set, belonged to Sir William Johnson (1715-1770), an Irishman who was Superintendent of Indian Affairs in New York State. In 1755 George II created him a baronet following the victory of Lake George. His house, Johnson Hall, built in 1764 near Johnstown, New York, is now open as a museum. Another chair with this splat was owned by Hermanus Ten Eyck in Albany and is branded *H E* on the back.

The oak seat is covered in red wool moreen, English, eighteenth century.

Height 38½"   Width 21¾"   Depth 18½"

Ex Coll. PHILIP FLAYDERMAN (One of this set is in the Garvan Collection, Yale University)

150 · SIDE CHAIR
Mahogany
New York 1770-1775

This is No. II of a set of twelve chairs which belonged to General Samuel Blachley Webb, of New York and Connecticut, an aide-de-camp to General Washington. General Webb married an heiress, Elizabeth Bancker, in 1779; history states she made the needlework chair seats before her marriage.

The slip seat of tulipwood rests upon a narrow square frame, similar to other New York chairs (see Figure 149). The back rail is oak, as are the triangular seat braces.

The original cover is crewelwork embroidery in rose, blue, and tan shades.

Height 39¼"   Width 21"   Depth 18"

Ex Coll. MISSES ANNE R. and CAROLINE L. WEBB, great-great-granddaughters of Samuel Blachley Webb

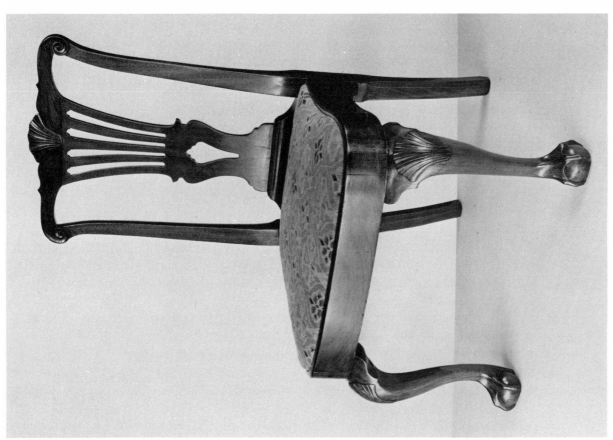

150

149

151 · SIDE CHAIR
Mahogany
Massachusetts 1770-1780

This side chair, marked *VII* of a set, is an ambitious variation of the Chippendale style that, in Massachusetts, was habitually simpler. The maker gave especial heed to the design of the lower part, carving the knees with rococo scrolls and the feet with very uncommon five-toed paws. In the splat, the figure-eight and diamond, the drapery, and tassel are found on several different Philadelphia chairs; but there the likeness ends. The blunt ears of the top rail are typical features of Salem and Boston chairs. The carving of the knees and the shape of the rear legs match a settee (Figure 270) of the same origin, one of a known pair.

The slip-seat frame and the triangular seat blocks are cherry; the rear seat rail is oak, veneered with mahogany.

The upholstery is yellow silk damask, Chinese, eighteenth century.

Height 37″   Width 21½″   Depth 17¾″

152 · SIDE CHAIR
Mahogany
Massachusetts 1760-1770

The turned and block stretchers and the thin, spread claws of this chair are clues to the Massachusetts school of chairmaking.

The carving and punched star ground of the top rail are rare on chairs of this type, so often plain. A fine bed (Figure 4) has a background of similar punch work around the carving.

The upholstery is crewelwork embroidery on white linen, American, eighteenth century.

Height 37½″   Width 19¾″   Depth 16½″

152

151

153 · SIDE CHAIR
Mahogany
Massachusetts about 1795

This chair and that in Figure 154 were probably made at the close of the eighteenth century, although the vigor of the Chippendale style remains unabated. The same outline of splat was used for several Philadelphia chairs, one of which is in the Winterthur Collection (Figure 123). Other chairs more nearly like this one, with the same shaped legs and feet, and punched background for the carving, are owned in Salem and Newburyport; one of them has the family tradition of having come from the shop of Joseph Short (1771-1819), whose printed trade card reads "Warranted cabinet work of all kinds made and sold by Joseph Short, At his Shop Merrimack Street, between Market Square and Browns Wharf, Newburyport."*

The seat frame is made of maple, braced with triangular blocks of white pine.

The upholstery is wine-colored cotton.

Height 38″   Width 21¼″   Depth 17½″

154 · SIDE CHAIR
Mahogany
Massachusetts about 1795

There are parallels and differences in this chair and Figure 153, but obviously they are from the same shop. They are a little-known pattern of Massachusetts origin. This example is more orthodox in the shape of the upturned ears and square seat than is Figure 153. Nathaniel Silsbee, a prosperous shipowner and merchant in Salem, owned a set of chairs like this one.

The slip-seat frame is maple and is covered with purple cotton.

Height 37½″   Width 21½″   Depth 18″

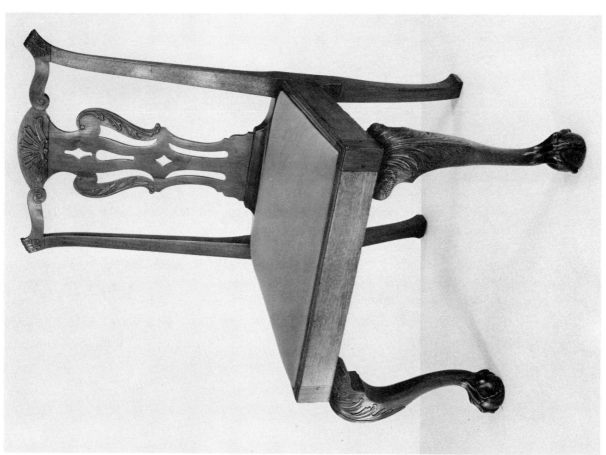

154

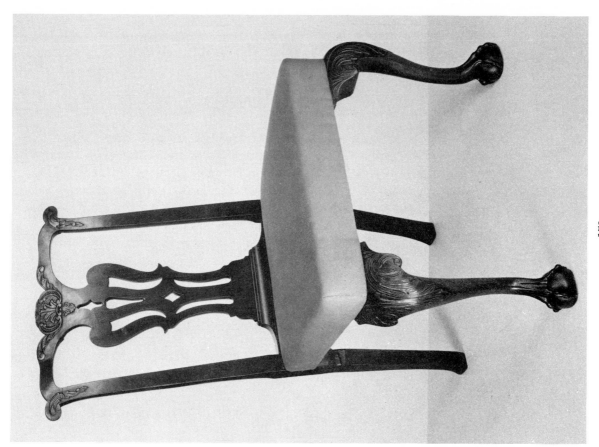

153

155 · SIDE CHAIR
Mahogany
Massachusetts 1770-1780

The Gothic Chippendale style found little favor in the American colonies and is barely noticed except for an occasional pointed arch intertwined with rococo scrolls in a chair back. In New England, Gothic design is particularly lacking, and this forthright instance of it is remarkable.

The delicate, widespread claws may be seen on labeled Massachusetts furniture (Figure 349). The sharp corners of the front legs are repeated on many Salem and Boston chairs. One triangular seat brace of white pine remains.

The upholstery is plum-colored cotton.

Height 38″   Width 22¼″   Depth 18½″

156 · SIDE CHAIR
ONE OF A PAIR
Mahogany
Massachusetts 1760-1780

Lightness of scale, almost a wiry quality, marks this chair as of New England and particularly of Massachusetts in origin. The undercut knees and widespread claws upon the ball feet are distinctive, and the turned and block stretchers were rarely added to New York and Philadelphia chairs of contemporary date. This pattern of splat is occasionally found with straight square legs and plain stretchers; examples of it are in the Winterthur Collection and in the Bolles Collection in the Metropolitan Museum of Art.

The upholstery is blue and white printed cotton, probably English, about 1750.

Height 36¾″   Width 21½″   Depth 17¼″

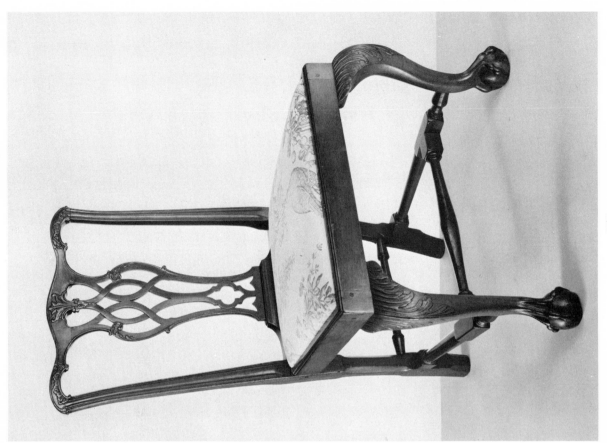

156

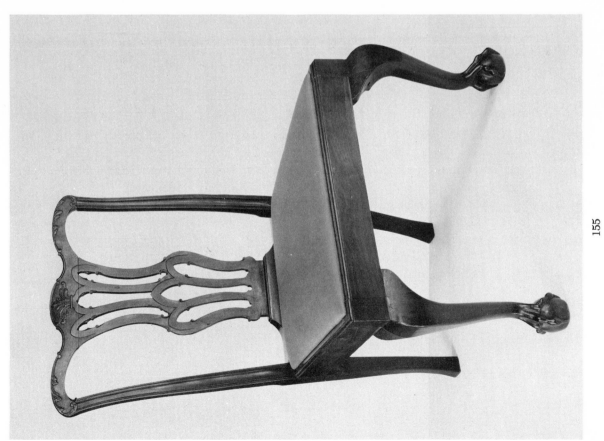

155

157 · SIDE CHAIR
Maple, Painted Blue
New Hampshire 1775-1790

Sometimes one family, by the impress of its creative ability, established a style of furniture that became an individual school within a period. The Dunlaps worked in Chester and Salisbury, New Hampshire, carving on woodwork and furniture concaved fans, S scrolls, and interlaced straps, which are unmistakably their own choice. This chair shows the fans, a repetition from Queen Anne furniture in New England, and the S scrolls, in this case pierced in the splat instead of carved, as upon a high chest of drawers, Figure 193.

The wide, molded stretchers and elongated back further indicate the Dunlaps' personal touch. This chair, matching a pair in the Metropolitan Museum of Art, has a similar crewelwork seat stitched in shades of blue and brown.

Height 45″   Width 21¾″   Depth 15¼″

158 · SIDE CHAIR
Cherry
Connecticut 1785-1790

Chairs with this splat have been attributed to Aaron Chapin, who worked in Hartford from 1783 until his death in 1838. Other examples with this back have cabriole legs and claw-and-ball feet; a record of claw-foot chairs by Eliphalet Chapin is dated 1781.*

The side rails are mortised through the rear legs, similar to Philadelphia construction. The frame of the slip seat is soft pine. The upholstery is temporary.

Beyond Connecticut, furniture in other parts of New England was made of cherry wood; one instance appeared in the inventory of James Caldwell, Esq., of Rutland District, Massachusetts, on May 31, 1764:

One Douzen of black Cherry Tree Chairs	£3: 4:0
One round Ditto 10/8 one Maple round Table 8/	0:18:8

Height 38″   Width 21″   Depth 16½″

158

157

159 · SIDE CHAIR
Mahogany
New York 1765-1780

The interlaced figure-eight and diamond design of this splat is found on several Philadelphia and New England chairs too (Figure 151), but with variations of the surrounding outline. Joseph Willard, president of Harvard College on the eve of the Revolution, owned a set of chairs of this design. The seat is fourteen and one-half inches high, which makes the name *slipper chair* or *lady's chair* appropriate.

The upholstery matches that of Figure 160.

Major John André, soldier, gentleman, and artist, sketched his own portrait while sitting on a side chair which had sharply scrolled ears similar to this one. It was the day before he was hanged as a spy, following his capture near Tarrytown, New York, September 3, 1780.

Height 35″   Width 20½″   Depth 17″

160 · SIDE CHAIR
Mahogany
Massachusetts 1765-1780

This plain version of the New England school is distinguished by its low seat, thirteen inches high, which suggests the name *slipper* or *lady's chair*.

The upholstery is blue and white printed linen, probably English, eighteenth century.

Height 34¼″   Width 21½″   Depth 17½″

160

159

161 · SIDE CHAIR
Mahogany
New York 1765-1780

This chair is more graceful in the use of curved and tapering lines than other back stools (Figures 162 and 164), which have broad, simple contours.

The seat rails are cherry. The upholstery is silk lampas, crimson and white, probably French, early eighteenth century.

William Van Wyck, a distiller in New York and the father-in-law of the well-known New York chairmakers and cabinetmakers, Edward and Thomas Burling, bequeathed in his will, dated June 7, 1773, "to my dau Mary £130 & my silver spoons, a Bed and Beding, a half duzzen of my chairs and a looking glass. My grandsons Walter Burling son of Thomas Burling and Charles son of Edward Burling to each £40."

Height 37″   Width 20¾″   Depth 18″

162 · SIDE CHAIR
Mahogany
New York 1760-1775

The comfort of this stuffed chair is apparent in its broad proportions similar to its English prototypes. The rear feet are cut vertically for alignment with the top, so that the chair may stand snugly to the wall.

The frame and the diagonal strips under the seat are beech. The upholstery is yellow silk damask, Italian, about 1700.

A portrait of Martin Howard, painted by Copley in 1767, shows the subject seated on a back stool similar to this one.

Height 39″   Width 23½″   Depth 22″

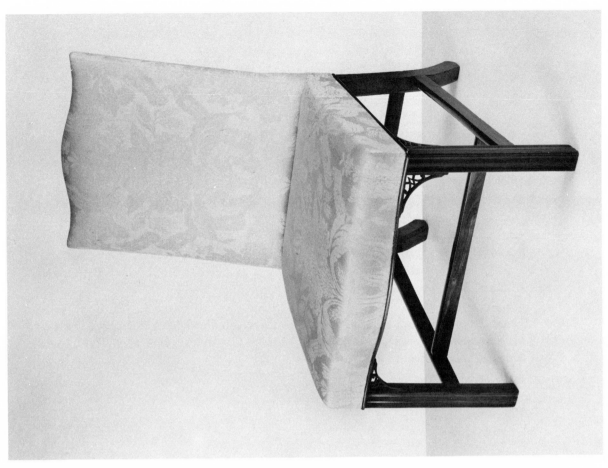

161

162

163 · SIDE CHAIR
Mahogany

Philadelphia 1760-1775

The demand for comfort brought more upholstery on seating furniture; *stuffed, French,* and *back stool* are various names applied to the upholstered chair frame by Ince and Mayhew, and Chippendale. In 1772 Richard Fowler, "upholder and Paper-Hanger from London . . . has six elegant French Back-Stools covered with very rich brocade . . . very cheap for cash." Here, the curved outline of back and seat are happy improvements on the severely rectangular frame more often seen. Similar chairs made for Governor John Penn by Thomas Affleck between 1763 and 1766 may be seen at Cliveden, the famous Chew Mansion in Germantown, Philadelphia.*

The upholstery is black leather.

There is a portrait in the Winterthur Collection which Matthew Pratt painted of Hugh McCulloch seated on a similar chair covered in green to match a table cover. The likeness was done in Philadelphia in 1773.

Height 39¼″   Width 24⅛″   Depth 25″

164 · SIDE CHAIR
ONE OF A PAIR
Mahogany

New York 1760-1775

The conversation pictures painted by Hayman and Zoffany in England often show the stuffed-back chairs that reappeared in the portraits of Copley and Earl in the following decades. Named "stool back chairs" in *The Universal System of Household Furnishing,* by Ince and Mayhew, for their obvious relation to upholstered stools, their popularity as comfortable chairs carried them through the century; lighter versions were illustrated in Hepplewhite's *Guide* in 1788. The rear legs are raked at the base to stabilize the thrust of the heavy back.

The seat rails are cherry; triangular seat blocks of soft pine brace the corners.

The upholstery is brown cowhide from Winterthur Farms.

Height 39½″   Width 22⅛″   Depth 20⅞″

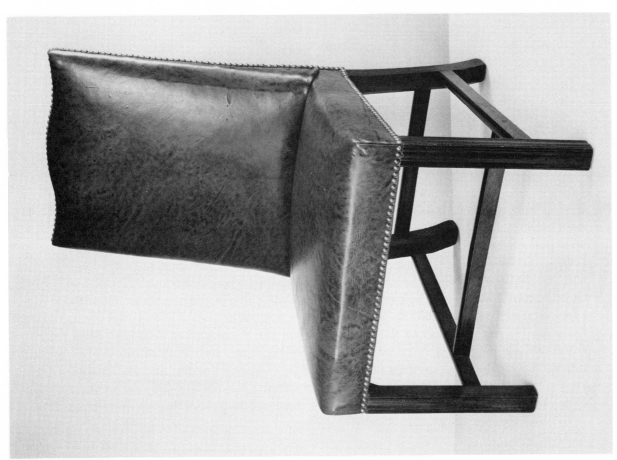

164

163

165 · CHEST OF DRAWERS
Mahogany
Massachusetts 1765-1780

The colonial cabinetmakers of New England excelled in making variations on straight-front case furniture. The ox-bow, serpentine, block-front, and bombé shapes were exercises for only the most skillful masters of wood. Rarely a combination of those forms was attempted, as on the block-front and bombé secretary originally in the Craigie-Longfellow house in Cambridge. Here an equally exotic combination of the serpentine and bombé shape was used for this small chest of drawers, which is a triumph of American furniture. The omission of any carving or even of the traditional scalloped brasses offers no distraction from the principal theme of curving lines.

Here the soft pine sides of the drawers are straight, the overlap of the fronts filling the curved outline. The upper drawers are divided into three sections by thin oak partitions. The cast bail handles show the beaded edges of classical origin; the side handles are earlier and exuberantly rococo. All the hardware has the old fire-gilt finish seldom seen on American furniture; that on the front is in the Adam style, which was in fashion in England then.

Height 33½"   Width 35¾"   Depth 21"

166 · CHEST OF DRAWERS
Mahogany
Massachusetts 1765-1775

Prosperity from the three-way trade in sugar, rum, and slaves between the West Indies, New England, and Africa, a source of many Yankee fortunes, is echoed in this bombé chest of drawers. The opulent curves of the body and the fancifully shaped base of this chest of drawers are contrived to satisfy the most exacting taste.

Cabinetmaking of a high order is required to shape not only the exterior curves, but also the drawer sides, which are mortised on a curved line. The top edges of the drawer sides have a double bead molding, like the rails between the drawer fronts. No dust boards were used here between the drawers. The noticeable projection of the top is 2⅝ inches, a continuation of the wide overhanging tops in the tradition of early New England tables.

Height 35¼"   Width 40"   Depth 22¼"

165

166

167 · CHEST OF DRAWERS
Curly Maple

Massachusetts 1760-1780

More reserved in form than the Newport and Connecticut block-front furniture are the chests from Boston and its vicinity. The absence of carving and the frequent use of straight bracket feet are typical of the northern pieces. Maple was a favorite wood of the provincial cabinetmaker in the Chippendale period, but its use for the intricate block-front style is rare. Here the blocks are cut from one thickness of wood and hollowed out inside to lessen the weight of the drawers. The curl of the wood, an inexplicable freak of nature, is well matched over the surface here.

The lining is soft pine.

A chest of drawers of this shape was labeled by Benjamin Frothingham in Charlestown.* (See Figure 349.)

Height 31″	Width 35½″	Depth 18½″

168 · CHEST OF DRAWERS
Mahogany

Massachusetts 1760-1780

The wide overhang of the top, narrow blocking of the drawer fronts, and compact size are familiar features of the best case furniture in Massachusetts from Boston to Newburyport, attested by several labeled chests by Abner Toppan, Jacob Sanderson, and others. The carved fan was a ubiquitous ornament in a more extended area of New England, on high chests, desks, and dressing tables. Here the concave shape fits the curve of the base.

The drawer linings are soft pine.

Height 31¾″	Width 34¾″	Depth 22⅝″

167

168

169 · CHEST OF DRAWERS
Mahogany
Massachusetts 1760-1780

The bowed shape of this block-front chest of drawers was employed less often than the flattened square pattern of Figure 167. It recalls the high chest (Figure 189) by Joseph Hosmer, of Concord, in the shape of the drawers, the raised moldings of the front, and the double-arched top edge of the pine drawer sides. The carved bird's claws are not curved back as they appear on the signed work of Benjamin Frothingham and John Cogswell, two other competent cabinetmakers in colonial Massachusetts. The soft pine of the lining is common to New England case furniture.

Height 32½″   Width 36″   Depth 21″

Ex Coll. PHILIP FLAYDERMAN

170 · CHEST OF DRAWERS
Cherry
Connecticut 1770-1790

This chest represents the Connecticut block-front style at its best, and may be from the shop of the Chapins. It has several features of their signed furniture. The shape of the feet, gadrooned skirt, and nine-lobed spreading shells are repeated on a chest in the Reginald W. Lewis Collection; these two chests are closer than any others known to the Newport style of block-front design. The shells are glued to the upper drawer fronts.

The lining and back are white pine.

Height 36½″   Width 40″   Depth 19″

169

170

171 · CHEST OF DRAWERS
Cherry
Connecticut 1770-1785

Any piece of block-front furniture carved with nine shells is a great rarity in Rhode Island, where the style originated and developed; three or six shells are more customary on the finest chests of drawers and desks there, as in Connecticut. The scalloped base here was peculiar to Connecticut and is nearly matched on a shell and block-front desk owned by Yale University. The centers of the shells are blunt, like Figure 172, and lack the cameolike exactness of Newport carving on Figure 175 and Figure 176.

The inside of the chest is white pine.

Height 33"   Width 35½"   Depth 19"

172 · CHEST OF DRAWERS
Cherry
Connecticut 1770-1790

The emphatic style created by the raised block front and large shells in Newport furniture was repeated in a lesser degree in contemporary Connecticut cabinetwork. In the latter, the size and shape of the blocking and shells do not conform to so rigid a pattern. On Figure 176 the shells have twelve lobes and on Figure 233 there are fourteen; here there are eleven. The shells are glued to the drawer front instead of carved from the solid.

This chest is a typical Connecticut shape; the use of short cabriole legs and claw feet is a marked difference from the Newport school. The scrolled brackets here resemble those on a cherry desk signed by Benjamin Burnham in Norwich in 1769.

The original hardware follows the Adam pattern then current in England, whence it was exported.

The lining is white pine. The heavy drawer sides are one-half inch thick, about double that of Figure 176.

This chest was acquired in Colchester, Connecticut.*

Height 37"   Width 38½"   Depth 20½"

171

172

173 · CHEST OF DRAWERS
Cherry

Connecticut 1793

Made by Kneeland and Adams

The long serpentine sweep of this chest front is impressive by its simplicity and unusual grace. The engraved label in the top drawer identifies its origin exactly; it was made by Kneeland and Adams, cabinet and chairmakers in Hartford (see Figure 392).

Samuel Kneeland (1755-1828) advertised in the Hartford *Courant* as a cabinetmaker in August, 1789. Several years later he formed a partnership with Lemuel Adams; two years after this chest was made, Kneeland and Adams made the carved shield-back armchairs for the State Capitol at Hartford, which had been completed by Charles Bulfinch in 1796. In 1798 Samuel Kneeland advertised his removal to Farmington "to the noted stand lately occupied by Mr. Thomas Bulkley, cabinetmaker deceased; where he intends to carry on the above business in all its various branches in the most modern fashions of cherry or mahogany."

The combination of bracket and claw-and-ball feet may be seen in Figure 172 and is repeated on other similar chests.

The drawer linings, of tulipwood, are unusually thin, being five-sixteenths of an inch through.

Height 35½″   Width 46½″   Depth 20¾″

174 · CHEST OF DRAWERS
Mahogany

New York 1765-1780

Thomas Burling and Samuel Prince were two of the colonial joiners in Manhattan who labeled mahogany chests of drawers and wardrobes trimmed at the front corners by a wide chamfer, cut with several flutes and ending in a lamb's tongue, which may be seen on this chest. The thick smooth claws on the ball feet and the drawer linings of tulipwood here are other details of a New York origin. No dust boards separate the drawers as in Philadelphia chests.

A sale in New York on June 28, 1775, of the possessions of G. W. Leslie included:

Chest of Drawers £8   Looking Glass £6
Teaset of China £4
Silver tankard £18
Dining Table £5   Tea Table £3   Card d⁰ £3
Silver pepper box £2
1 Easy Chair £3.4
Small Looking glass £2   Gold chair £2.6

Height 33¼″   Width 41″   Depth 21½″

173

174

175 · CHEST OF DRAWERS
Mahogany

Newport 1765-1775

This kneehole chest of drawers (sometimes called a dressing table) ranks with the finest block-front examples of Newport origin.

The recessed center and the three-dimensional drawer fronts present a powerful contrast of light and shadow. The shells, with crosshatched incising at their centers, are identical to the labeled work of John Townsend on a four-drawer chest made for the Slocum family. The cupboard is divided by a shelf.

Characteristic of Newport cabinetwork are the two strips of ash mortised under the top and showing on the back edge of the top, the purpose of the strips being to prevent warping. The backboards are ash, and the drawers are lined with tulipwood.

Height 34¼″   Width 36¾″   Depth 20″

176 · CHEST OF DRAWERS
Mahogany

Newport 1760-1775

Probably Made by John Townsend

This chest has the unusual combination of a center cupboard flanked by tiers of small drawers, a variant of the kneehole shape (Figure 175) made in New York, Massachusetts, and Rhode Island.

This is believed to be the work of John Townsend because it matches in moldings, shells, feet, brasses, and size a labeled chest of his, now privately owned.

Backboards and dust boards between the drawers are white pine, and the drawer lining is tulipwood.

Height 33½″   Width 36½″   Depth 19″

175

176

177 · CHEST OF DRAWERS
Mahogany
Philadelphia 1760-1780

Chests of drawers show less ornamentation than almost any other furniture. In that sense this chest is quite exceptional, having carved festoons of oak leaves and flowers at the corners, reminiscent of a similar treatment on the Howe-Steel highboy, on the set of Dickinson chairs at Stenton (two are in the Philadelphia Museum), and on the side chair shown in Figure 137. Of equal rarity is the leaf-and-dart carved molding on the top. Only one other known chest, in the Richard Wister Harvey Collection in the Philadelphia Museum of Art, has nearly identical carving and brasses.

The brasses have their original gilt finish and are made in the Adam style that was current with the Chippendale style in the American colonies.

The drawer bottoms are cedar, and the sides are tulipwood. The interior framing is hard pine.

Height 35½″   Width 41½″   Depth 23½″

178 · CHEST OF DRAWERS
Mahogany
Philadelphia 1775-1780
Made by Jonathan Gostelowe

The serpentine-front case pieces were developed in colonial New England, even with bombé sides, the ultimate test of skillful joinery. But in Philadelphia the form was an innovation that Jonathan Gostelowe, "cabinet and chair maker at his shop in Church Alley," tried with success, if judgment is based on two labeled chests of drawers that match this one, one at the Chew Mansion in Germantown, the other in the Philadelphia Museum of Art. A table desk made for the Wister family is probably Gostelowe's work; it is now in the Metropolitan Museum of Art.

When the Hepplewhite style supplanted "that burden of barbarous ornaments," as Thomas Jefferson castigated the rococo style, serpentine and bow-front case furniture became popular in Philadelphia, as it was in other cities of the new United States.

Drawer linings are tulipwood. Dust boards are hard pine. The Adam-style brasses are original.

Height 35¾″   Width 45″   Depth 25¾″

177

178

179 · DOUBLE CHEST
(OR CHEST-ON-CHEST)
Cherry
Connecticut 1730-1750

Parti-colored star inlay was an inheritance from English furniture upon fine Queen Anne pieces in several of the colonies; to name a few, there are a Philadelphia walnut child's desk, a Massachusetts high chest and dressing table in the Bolles Collection, a New York side table from the Verplanck house at 3 Wall Street, and Peter Faneuil's needlework-top gaming table from Boston.

The Connecticut features of this chest match those on a desk, Figure 231; namely, the chamfered corners, carved petal rosette, concave lunette, and square ribbed feet.

The drawer linings are butternut and tulipwood.

Height 7′ 7½″   Width 41″   Depth 21½″

Ex Coll. GALE CARTER

179

180 · DOUBLE CHEST-ON-FRAME
Cherry
Connecticut 1770-1790

The seventeenth-century method of building a chest or desk on a frame continued into the next century, but after 1750 the custom declined. A double chest on its original frame of this period is most unusual, rarely duplicated in any collection today.

In the Chippendale period, cherry wood was more often used by Connecticut cabinetmakers than was mahogany. It had a smooth, close-grained texture, well suited to carving, and colored a rich reddish-brown with age. Cherry offered an inconspicuous surface without the figure of branch mahogany or walnut, and served as a better foil for applied ornament. This is evident here where the carved pin wheels and fluted pilasters would appear timid in competition with a richer wood. The stout candy-twist finials are typical of Connecticut and are different from those of Massachusetts, the so-called corkscrew shape (Figures 190, 225, and 229).

The interior is white pine.

Height 7′ 5″   Width 42¾″   Depth 20″

180

181 · DOUBLE CHEST
Cherry

Connecticut about 1800

Made by Reuben Beman, Jr.

The chalk inscription *Ruben Beman Junr* on the inside back of this chest proves the exactness of its origin and brings to light a new name among Connecticut cabinetmakers. Beman's name is recorded in 1785 as a cabinetmaker in Kent, Connecticut, where he was born in 1742. His father, Ebenezer Beman, born in 1719, may have been a cabinetmaker, as an inventory of his estate lists joiners' tools. Another inscription in pencil reading *Bought Dec. 1801* may indicate the time the chest was made, which, although belated for the Chippendale style, would not be unusual in Connecticut, when Aaron Roberts and the Chapins were then turning out their finest chests and desks.

One peculiarity of construction here is the soft-pine drawer sides which taper from five-eighths of an inch at the bottom edge to five-sixteenths of an inch at the top. The backs of the drawers are seven-eighths of an inch thick, an extreme weight even in Connecticut. The roof is cut from paper-thin ash.

Height 7′ 4⅜″   Width 43″   Depth 22″

181

182 · DOUBLE CHEST
(OR CHEST-ON-CHEST)
Curly Maple
Massachusetts 1770-1785

A lean refinement is a pervading quality of the average Massachusetts furniture, giving way to the imperious demands of the merchant prince or governor. Restraint in size and ornament is one of its virtues, exemplified by this chest. The "broken" pediment, without scrolled and carved volutes so much used in Connecticut and the fluted pilasters flanking the upper drawers were favorite devices in eastern Massachusetts.

The pulvinated caps above the pilasters are a special turn of design, to be seen on a double chest originally in the Jonathan Warner house, and upon a desk and bookcase owned by Colonel Thomas Dawes (1731-1809) of Revolutionary fame.

The literal interpretation of the carved fan is rare; it occurs again on a desk and bookcase now in the Manse at Deerfield.

The drawer linings are white pine.

Height 7′ 2″   Width 41½″   Depth 21″

183 · DOUBLE CHEST
(OR CHEST-ON-CHEST)
Mahogany
Newport 1765-1780

This impressive block-front double chest is one of several carved with nine shells. Like the profile of the moldings, the shells differ in shape from those on John or Edmund Townsend's case furniture (Figure 175 and Figure 176); on the latter the lobes turn down in a cyma reversa curve, but here they curve upward like plants growing to the light. The ten-lobed shells are cut from the solid drawer fronts, which are hollowed on the reverse side. On several of John Townsend's signed chests of drawers, the shells are glued on the drawer fronts — a custom likewise followed in Connecticut.

On the pediment, the boxed sides recall the stepped platform used to display china on high chests earlier in the century. John Goddard made a similar pediment on a desk and bookcase for Joseph Brown, of Providence; that desk and bookcase is now in the Rhode Island School of Design.

Height 8′ Width 40″ Depth 21½″

Ex Coll. MRS. HENRY W. BURNETT

183

184 · DOUBLE CHEST
(OR CHEST-ON-CHEST)
Mahogany
Philadelphia 1760-1775

Comparable to the high chest of drawers, but apparently made in fewer numbers, the double chest in several instances was carved in the richest manner of the Philadelphia rococo style. The central theme here is a lamb and her ewe, a variant of Aesop's fables employed by Philadelphia carvers (the dog and the meat on the mantel of the Powel house ballroom, the fox and the grapes on the Howe-Steel high chest, and the two pigeons on the Pompadour highboy and lowboy in the American Wing). In every case the lower body is plain, save for the traditional fluted quarter columns at the corners that serve as a foil for the carving above. On this double chest the plainness is compensated by the fine Cuban branch grained mahogany veneered to the drawer fronts.

The drawers are lined with oak, and the bottoms are white cedar.

Height 7′ 2″ Width 42⅞″ Depth 22¾″

184

185 · DOUBLE CHEST
(OR CHEST-ON-CHEST)
Mahogany
Philadelphia 1760-1780

Not all Philadelphia high chests made in the Chippendale style have the same degree of carved ornament. Here is an example of the lesser style, but still carrying typical evidence of its origin. The heightened proportions add to its happy effect, and the hollowed brasses are a rare variation of the usual willow-pattern handle. The fluted quarter column is almost the rule on case pieces from the Quaker City, although one contemporary cabinetmaker, Jonathan Gostelowe, substituted wide chamfered and fluted corners on several of his chests of drawers (Figure 178).

The drawer bottoms are of cedar, the sides of tulipwood. The interior framing is of hard pine.

Height 7' 6" Width 43½" Depth 22½"

185

186 · HIGH CHEST OF DRAWERS
Maple and Pine
Connecticut 1720-1735

The colonial craftsman sometimes departed from routine forms to give greater emphasis or strength to his work. The cabriole legs of this chest have wide curves and broad flattened feet; and, although exaggerations of the usual sinuous supports, they seem appropriate here as they bend to the weight of the massive bulk, bold scalloping, and wide moldings above them. The painted ornament in shades of brown on a black ground is of especial interest for its design and rarity. The subjects resemble contemporary crewel embroideries interspersed with storybook animals and hunting scenes. A matching chest, except for minor details of decoration, is in the Blair Collection, Metropolitan Museum of Art, and came originally from Windsor, Connecticut.

This chest was acquired in Hartford, where it had been owned for generations.

Height 4′ 11″ Width 39″ Depth 22″

187 · HIGH CHEST OF DRAWERS
Maple and Pine

JAPANNED DECORATION

Boston 1725-1735

The "mania for things Chinese" that spread from Europe to America before 1700 found early encouragement in Boston, where Nehemiah Partridge advertised "all sorts of Japan work" in 1712 and William Randle's notices appeared in the Boston *News Letter* in 1715. Thomas Johnson's (sic) engraved trade card in 1732 offered ". . . Japan Work of all Sorts, As Chests of Draws, Chamber & Dressing Tables, Tea Tables, Writing-Desks, Book-Cases, Clock Cases, &c." A favorite background for the medley of fabulous beasts and birds, pagodas, flowering trees, and personages was a black and red imitation of tortoise shell.

Lacking the true gum lacquer of the *Rhus vernicifera* tree, and perhaps the patience and knowledge to apply it, the colonial japanner with whiting, paint, and gold-leaf, and a protective coat of varnish, produced what he believed "no damp air, no mouldring worm or corroding time can possibly deface." Several books provided him with designs and formulas for his work, principally *A Treatise of Japanning and Varnishing*, by John Stalker, Oxford, 1688; William Salmon's *Polygraphice*, London, 1685; *Instructions in the Art of Japanning with the True India Varnish*, 1736; and *A New Book of Chinese Designs*, by Edwards and Darly, 1754.

The original drops on the skirting of this high chest match a detail on Thomas Johnson's trade card.

In Boston in 1734 an inventory of the property left by the late Thomas Fairweather mentioned: "1 Japan Chest Drawers & Steps for China & dressing table £14."

Height 5′ 9½″   Width 40¼″   Depth 22″

Maple and Pine

JAPANNED DECORATION

Boston 1740-1750

Made by John Pimm

The East India Companies spread the exotic wares of the Orient through the colonies as early as the seventeenth century. These riches leavened the bare and rugged interiors with gay and whimsical ornaments and created an insatiable appetite for foreign treasures. Homemade copies of lacquer became popular, contrived in whiting, gold-leaf, and varnish on painted grounds. Thomas Johnson (sic), who engraved his own trade card as a *Japanner At the Golden Lyon in Ann Street Boston* in 1732, was active until 1767; several extant pieces of fine japanned furniture may rightfully be considered his work, including this high chest.

The name *Pim* is inscribed on the back of each drawer. John Pimm was a cabinetmaker in Fleet Street, Boston, as early as 1736; he billed Michael Trowlett, shipowner and merchant for a long list of furniture in 1735 including:

Mahogany Tea Table	£19:0:0
A five foot Table	36:0:0
Two Card Tables	64:0:0
Two Bedsteads	17:6:0
One stand Table	15:0:0
One Cloues Horse	5:0:0

Pimm died in 1773.

This unique chest was made for Commodore Joshua Loring; born in Boston in 1716, Loring married Mary Curtis in 1740. He was active in the Siege of Louisburg and was wounded at Quebec. Retired from service, he acquired 200 acres of land in Jamaica Plain, adjacent to Boston, and built a handsome mansion which still survives. As the King's agent, he was a loyalist and joined other exiles abroad in 1775. This high chest descended by ownership in the Curtis family, kin of Mrs. Loring.*

The drawer fronts are made of hard maple, and the other parts are white pine. A rare detail is seen in the thin mahogany strips which edge the skirting.

Height 7′ 2″   Width 41″   Depth 24½″

188

189 · HIGH CHEST OF DRAWERS
Cherry and Maple
Massachusetts about 1770

As the design, wood, and history indicate, this unique high chest was almost certainly made by Joseph Hosmer in Concord, Massachusetts. Hosmer was a descendant of builders, and learned cabinetmaking from a Frenchman, Robert Rosier, who was related to him by marriage. He produced handsome and unusual furniture of cherry and other native woods. In 1775 after his house, barn, and shop had been burned by the British, Joseph Hosmer, as a lieutenant of Minute Men, led the attack on Concord Bridge with the taunt: "Will you let them burn the town down?"

This chest was made in 1769 for the new house of the young minister of Concord, William Emerson, and his wife Phoebe. The house, later known as the Manse, was occupied by their grandson, Ralph Waldo Emerson, and in 1847 was rented to Sophia and Nathaniel Hawthorne.

Perhaps this chest was among "the dark mahogany . . ." and prints of "sooty-faced divines" that the newly wedded Hawthornes relegated to the attic then.* Until the Old Manse became a public shrine recently, the chest stood in the second floor hall.

Certain features of the design are unique; namely, the blocked front surface, the small pyramids applied at the center of the hood and skirt, and the brass "doges cap" fixed at the center of the carved fan. There are no short drawers in the customary positions; instead three divisions were made inside each of the two lower drawers. The taut cabriole legs seem to make a whimsical gesture of toe-dancing, as if to relieve a New England primness.

Cherry was used for the drawer fronts and hood, maple for the sides and base, and white pine for the interior.

| Height 7' 4¾" | Width 40¼" | Depth 19¾" |

189

190 · HIGH CHEST OF DRAWERS
White Walnut, or Butternut
Massachusetts 1725-1740

Stringed, feneerd, and *star and scalup* are mentioned on joiners' bills in Massachusetts before 1750 to describe the veneers and patterns of inlay used for fine furniture in the Old-World tradition. This high chest of pale-colored butternut, sometimes called white walnut, has inlays of birch and dyed sycamore to accent the stars on its front and sides and the *scalup* on the lower center drawer. The *stringed* inlay here forms a triple border for the face of the hood and drawers.

The interior wood is all white pine. The drawer sides are fixed with a single heavy dovetail at each corner, and their top edges are cut with a double arch molding.

The brasses are small and plain — the earliest shape of the post and bail type of hardware.

Contemporary in date is the account John Mudg rendered of work done for "Mr. Nathaniell Holmes, Maldon (sic), Massachusetts, January the 6 1737/8

To a case of dros soled ends and stringed	£9. 0.0
To a desk with piler dros	2.12.0
To a desk with wolnot ends for Adam Knox	2.19.0
To a larg sedor desk with a star and scalup	
dros no well rume lap beeded and pilor dros	3. 3.0
To a three foot desk bracet feet and pilor dros	
fore long dros brased of	3. 9.6
To a three feet and half tabell fraim	1. 3.0"

Height 7' 2"   Width 41¾"   Depth 21"

190

191 · HIGH CHEST OF DRAWERS
Mahogany
Newport 1750-1760

The earliest detail of this fine, compact high chest of drawers is the carved shell, confined within an arc, like those on a dressing table, and a desk and bookcase documented by Job Townsend as early as 1746.* Neither of them has the bird's-claw feet with the rare undercut talons which match John Goddard's two tea tables, Figures 372 and 373; he made the latter in 1763 for Jabez Bowen. Wall furniture made in Newport invariably combined the pad and claw-and-ball feet as upon the gaming table seen in Figure 348 and another unique one made for Mrs. Abraham Redwood, now in the Library at Newport.

A similar high chest of drawers, but without the same refinements of carving upon the shell and feet as this example, has been mistakenly published as the labeled work of Job Townsend. It was presented to the Newport Historical Society by Miss Ellen Townsend, a descendant of the famous cabinetmakers.

On the high chest of drawers pictured here, the raised panels below the arch are molded at the edges to match the drawers. The lining is tulipwood.

Height 6′ 9″   Width 39″   Depth 21¼″

191

192 · HIGH CHEST OF DRAWERS
Walnut
Philadelphia or Maryland 1740-1750

Although this high chest of drawers is of an earlier style than that in Figure 199, some unusual details of its design, such as the fluted and chamfered corners and the complicated scrolled apron, show some alliance to it. The drawer linings of white cedar and tulipwood are the same in both chests. The design is of great dignity, in which the diagonal line of the corners, carried up to the finials themselves, lightens the mass of the broad plain front in a way seldom contrived in southern furniture. An approach to this design may be seen in a double chest, Figure 179. The pattern of the branch walnut grain was chosen to compensate the absence of ornament. The trifid feet and six-lobed shells are familiar on Queen Anne furniture in Philadelphia.

In the *Maryland Gazette*, April 4, 1754, Gamaliel Butler advertised: "Living in East Street, near the Dock in Annapolis, Having engaged a very good Workman in the Cabinet-Way, hereby gives notice to all Gentlemen and others, that he will supply them with all sorts of Cabinet Work, such as Desks, Escrutores, Tables, Chairs, Bedsteads etc. etc. in a very neat Manner, and at the Cheapest Rates."

Height 7′ 9″   Width 43″   Depth 22½″

192

193 · HIGH CHEST OF DRAWERS

Maple

New Hampshire 1775-1790

Probably Made by Samuel Dunlap II

One of the most distinctive regional designs evolved in American furniture is the work of Samuel Dunlap. This high chest of drawers summarized the individual details found on numerous pieces made of maple which have become identified lately as the work of the Dunlap family of Chester and Salisbury, New Hampshire. Among the Dunlaps — John I, John II, Samuel I, and Samuel II — the last named is the best known; he lived from 1751 to 1830.[*]

The paneling of a house on the outskirts of New Boston is also attributed to the Dunlaps; a paneled room with a carved corner cupboard from the Zachary Taylor house at Bedford, New Hampshire, is now at Winterthur.

Removable panels give more emphasis to the interlaced cornice. The drawer linings, of white pine, are one-half inch thick and have equally heavy dovetails, four on each corner.

Height 6′ 11″   Width 42″   Depth 20¾″

193

194 · HIGH CHEST OF DRAWERS
Curly Maple
Philadelphia 1765-1780

Walnut and mahogany were the favorite woods of the Philadelphia Chippendale period. Curly maple was used infrequently, and its rarity is mysterious because it too offered the joiner and carver a hard, fine-textured, and richly grained wood comparable to the others. Scarcely any mention of maple appears in Pennsylvania inventories.

Narrower than many of its contemporaries, this high chest has more grace of proportion than they. Augmented by the competence of the carved ornament and the rare use of the curly maple, this chest is of especial interest as a unique and important document. The cartouche and finials on the pediment are likewise maple, and original.

The drawer linings are white cedar and hard pine.

Height 8′   Width 42½″   Depth 22½″

194

195 · HIGH CHEST OF DRAWERS
Mahogany
Philadelphia 1765-1780

This is one of the famous examples of Philadelphia furniture and is well known to the public for its exceptional qualities of design and carving, no less than for its history. It was made probably between 1765 and 1780.

The ornament upon the pediment and base, derived from the engraved designs of Chippendale's third edition of the *Director*, 1762, is a unique expression of the rococo style in colonial furniture and is likewise distinguished by the crisp, cameolike touch of the woodcarver. It represents the highest development of the Philadelphia Chippendale school of furniture. The curvilinear piercings of the brasses echo the fantasy of the carving.

The history of this highboy began with William Turner and his wife Mary King Turner, the first owners. Their house, Walnut Grove, was the scene of the famous Meschianza Ball in 1778 given by the British Officers then occupying Philadelphia, an occasion distinguished alike by its lavish entertainment and the presence of nearly fifty Philadelphia belles who were the guests of the visiting enemy. Early in the nineteenth century the Turners and Van Pelts intermarried, and the highboy descended by inheritance in the latter family until 1921.

In the eighteenth century a highboy was known as a high chest of drawers. John F. Watson, the chronicler of early Philadelphia, notes in his *Annals* of 1829: "Every householder in that day deemed it essential to his convenience and comfort to have an ample chest of drawers in his parlour or sitting room, in which the linen and clothes of the family were always of ready access. It was no sin to rummage them before company. These drawers were sometimes nearly as high as the ceiling."

The wood of the exposed structure is Cuban mahogany; the drawer linings are tulipwood and white cedar; the drawer runners are oak strips; and the backboards are yellow pine.

Height 7′ 6″   Width 42¾″   Depth 23⅛″

Ex Coll. HOWARD REIFSNYDER

196 · HIGH CHEST OF DRAWERS
Mahogany
Philadelphia 1760-1775

Philadelphia cabinetmaking in the Chippendale period varied remarkably, from superlative to mediocre, predicated upon the skill and "eye" of the craftsmen engaged. Nowhere can the difference be studied better than in the high chests where the proportions are sometimes squat and graceless, the carving turgid and niggardly. When the quality of proportions and design reach the ultimate of perfection, nothing finer can be realized in the American rococo style.

This high chest, although not carried to the pitch of elaboration of several others, expresses, in spite of its size, the airy delicacy and refinement that is the essence of its period. In the relationship of the parts and distribution of the ornament, no less than in the excellence of the carving, this piece seems pre-eminent.

The drawer sides are tulipwood, and the bottoms are white cedar.

Height 7′ 6″　　　　　　　Width 41¾″　　　　　　　Depth 21½″

196

197 · HIGH CHEST OF DRAWERS
Walnut

Philadelphia 1765-1780

In the Chippendale period, when the rococo style demanded of the carver the ultimate in skill and taste, the results of his work are widely different. On some the carving is inadequate and ill disposed. This high chest required the most acute judgment and experienced hand to co-ordinate the lavish pediment with the base to give a comparable balance of richness for consistency in design. Here the performance was equal to the task.

Almost identical to this chest is one in the Garvan Collection, Yale University.

The lining of the interior is tulipwood and cedar.

In 1777 when William Lewis died in Haverford, his furniture was inventoried thus:

1 Case and draws, and One Black walnut desk

1 Walnut Tea Table   2 Black Walnut Leather bottom'd Chaires

1 Armed Chair   6 Other Rush botom'd, One Oake Chest

1 Walnut table frame and Chaier, 1 gum tubb

1 Blew painted Chest

2 Small tables One walnut the other poplar

1 Case & draws   One small Walnut Oval table, 1 bedd Steds & furniture

2 Walnut & 2 rush bottom'd Chaiers

1 Square table painted read

Height 8′ 3″   Width 45¾″   Depth 22¼″

198 · HIGH CHEST OF DRAWERS
Mahogany
Philadelphia 1769

Few examples of American furniture can equal the extraordinary quality of this high chest (and its matching table, Figure 333). They epitomize the elaborate Chippendale furniture for which Philadelphia was famous. They emphasize, too, the purely colonial development of the so-called highboy and lowboy which are unknown forms of this period in foreign furniture.

These pieces were made in 1769, the year Michael Gratz married Miriam Simon, of Lancaster. He had come from Lagensdorf, in upper Silesia, in 1755, and with his brother made a fortune as merchant and banker. A daughter Rebecca, born in Philadelphia in 1780, was well remembered after her death in 1869 as "beautiful in face, aristocratic in bearing, dignified in manner, noble of soul and pure of heart." She did not marry, but devoted herself to welfare work; she founded the Philadelphia Orphan Society, the Hebrew Sunday School Society, and for forty years was secretary of the Female Association for Relief of Women and Children in Reduced Circumstances. Sir Walter Scott made her the heroine of *Ivanhoe*, having learned of her unusual qualities from Washington Irving, their mutual friend. As the Gratz family prospered, its business activities extended westward, and Benjamin, a younger brother of Rebecca, settled in Lexington, Kentucky, where he married Maria Gist and became a leading citizen. A granddaughter inherited the highboy and lowboy; they were acquired from her lately.

The lining of the drawers is tulipwood and white cedar.

Height 8′ 5″   Width 46⅛″   Depth 21¾″

198

199 · HIGH CHEST OF DRAWERS
Walnut

Probably Maryland 1760-1780

The characteristics of Baltimore and Annapolis Chippendale furniture are not yet fully recognized, but some features emerge from contemporary Maryland furniture which have documented histories, to give some basis for attribution. The chamfered corners with lamb's tongue ends, sunburst-carved drawer fronts with stiff streamers, and flattened leaf-covered knees, recur in combination occasionally, and are unlike Philadelphia designs, which they most nearly resemble. Here four flutes are cut in the lower corners, and three in the upper ones, as in the high chest Figure 192.

The white cedar drawer bottoms, nailed from front to back, and the finely dovetailed tulipwood sides and backs are in the Pennsylvania tradition of construction.

In the *Maryland Gazette,* No. 1126, April 9, 1767, appeared the following:

"Gerrard Hopkins son of Samuel, Cabinet and Chair-Maker from Philadelphia at the sign of the Tea Table and chair in Gay Street Baltimore-Town

"Makes and sells the following goods in the best manner, and in the newest Fashions in Mahogany, Walnut, Cherry-tree and Maple viz. Chests of drawers of various sorts Desks, Bookcases, Scruitores Cloth-Presses, Tables of various sorts such as Bureaus, Card, Chamber, Parlor, and Tea Tables Chairs of various sorts such as easy, arm Parlour, Chamber or Corner Chairs, Settees, Clock-cases, Couches, Candle stands, Decanter stands Tea Kettles Stands, Dumb-Waiters, Tea-Boards, Bottle Boards, Bedsteads &c. &c.

"N.B. Any of the above Articles to be done with or without carved work."

Height 8' 10"   Width 43½"   Depth 24"

199

200 · SPICE CHEST
Walnut

Pennsylvania 1720-1740

The name *spice chest* is an old and an apt description of a miniature chest holding innumerable small drawers. In 1737 the stock of Joseph Hibbard, "Joyner" in Darby, included two spice chests, one of sweet gum and one of walnut. Spices were rarities then, brought from the far Indies by sailing ships and, like tea and coffee, were safeguarded from children and household slaves by lock and key.

The half-round moldings that frame the inner drawers are survivals of the seventeenth century. The squared foot with an anklet follows closely after the date of the Spanish foot (Figure 322), popular in the William and Mary period about 1700.

The lining of the drawers is walnut, except for cedar bottoms. The dovetails are heavy, indicative of an early date.

Height 27½″   Width 16¼″   Depth 9½″

201 · SPICE CHEST
Walnut

Philadelphia 1740-1750

During the Queen Anne period of furniture design, the double-door cabinet, enclosing numerous small drawers, was favored by Pennsylvania cabinetmakers. Usually they assume a miniature size, made to stand upon a table or chest of drawers; this comely example is as large as a small bookcase, scaled to other furniture. It has rarely graceful cabriole legs and very large, knuckled feet. Twenty small drawers of varying sizes are lined with tulipwood.

By and large, walnut was the principal wood used in Pennsylvania in the first half of the eighteenth century. One of many similar estate inventories reads: "John Hall (deceased) Springfield, 1760

> Square Black walnut table
> Black chairs
> Black walnut chest
> Walnut chest"

Height 58″   Width 25½″   Depth 11¼″

201

200

202 · TALL CLOCK
Walnut

Rhode Island about 1750
Dial Inscribed: James Wady, Newport

The brass face of this eight-day clock is uncommonly fine. In the arch, above the phases of the moon is inscribed *James Wady, Newport;* and below it are engraved baskets of fruit, vines, and birds. The dial is silvered, and at each corner are cast spandrels of the Queen Anne period centering female masks among arabesques. Three small dials are for the alarm, silent-strike, and minutes.

James Wady married on May 27, 1736, Mary, the daughter of William Claggett, famous Newport clockmaker. Wady may have been apprenticed to Claggett and was listed in 1740 and again in 1752 as clockmaker.*

The double cornice on the hood of this clock is found on other cases signed by William Claggett in Newport and on English examples. The gilt tracery with a black ground is made of heavy paper; a double row of it is rarely seen. The simple shell carved on the door is an early form of Newport carving, repeated on a desk and bookcase labeled by Job Townsend.

The hood is backed with ash and poplar; the backboard is soft pine.

This clock was formerly owned by the Noyes family.

Height 98¼″	Width 17″	Depth 10″

203 · TALL CLOCK
Walnut

New Jersey 1723
Dial Inscribed: Isa. Pearson, Burlington

This clock has the simple dignity which is an attribute of well-made early furniture. The handsome face is brass, mounted with cast spandrels displaying cupid supporters to a royal crown. The engraved and silvered dial is inscribed: *Isa. Pearson, Burlington.* Isaac Pearson, born about 1685, was a Quaker of several abilities in addition to clockmaking. He was proprietor of the Mount Holly Ironworks from 1730 to 1749, and a member of the General Assembly in 1738.*

Two other clocks with domed hoods are signed by the same maker.

Inside the door is inscribed: *Made for Elisha Laurence 1723.* The back of the case is hard and soft pine.

Height 80½″	Width 17½″	Depth 9½″

202

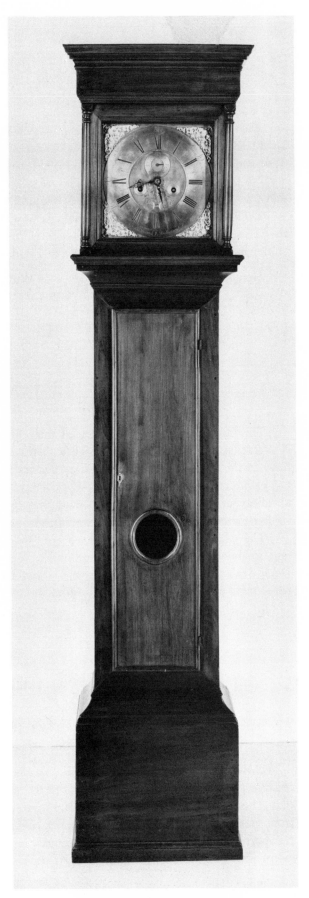

203

204 · TALL CLOCK
Mahogany

Philadelphia 1765-1775

Dial Inscribed: Edw. Duffield, Philadª

This carved clock case vies in richness with the famous Drexel clock whose works were signed by David Rittenhouse; and the tracery around the door matches the doors on the unique Cadwalader desk and bookcase. The swirled volutes are likewise rare; the lavish carving of the hood gives balance to the scalloped panel below. The brass and silvered face is mounted with cast rococo spandrels, and phases of the moon are painted in the arch. The silvered dial is inscribed: *Edw. Duffield, Philadª*

Duffield advertised in the Philadelphia newspapers from 1756 to 1775 and during that time kept the State House clock in order. He made numerous fine tall clocks and is also remembered as the friend of Benjamin Franklin and the executor of Franklin's will in 1790.

Height 99″   Width 23½″   Depth 11½″

205 · TALL CLOCK
Mahogany

Newport 1770-1785

Dial Inscribed: David Williams, New Port

The "handwriting" of the design of this tall-case clock suggests the name of John Townsend, of Newport, as the maker. Another clock with the label of that craftsman is the same, from the arched hood to the bracket feet. Here greater richness is given to the base and frame around the dial by the use of branch mahogany veneered over cherry. The urn-shaped finials are not carved upon the back, an idiosyncrasy of Newport carvers, and here the stop-fluted colonnettes of the hood are treated in a similar manner. The lining of the case is chestnut.

The white-painted and gilt dial, a type more often used for Hepplewhite-style cases, has openings to show the phases of the moon and calendar, above the signature of the maker of the works: *David Williams, New Port.* Williams worked in the early 1800's. He was not the patriot of the same name who fought at Quebec under General Montgomery and in 1780 captured the traitor Major André.

Height 96″   Width 21¼″   Depth 7½″

206 · TALL CLOCK
Mahogany

Philadelphia 1770-1780

Dial Inscribed: Thomas Wagstaffe, London

This clock case is behemoth, standing nearly ten feet high, but carries well the amount of carved ornament lavished upon it. The face is brass, mounted with pierced rococo spandrels. The silvered dial is inscribed with the maker's name and city. Wagstaffe was an English Quaker working in London from 1756 to 1793, who shipped clock works frequently to his American brethren in Philadelphia and Newport for American-made cases. The face records the days of the month, but not the phases of the moon, as does Figure 207, another Wagstaffe clock in a Philadelphia-made case.

Height 118″   Width 22¾″   Depth 11″

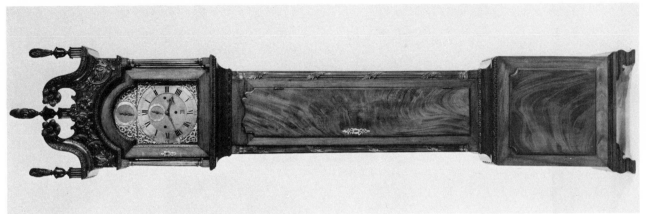

206

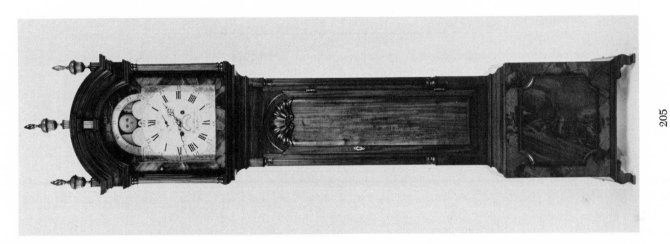

205

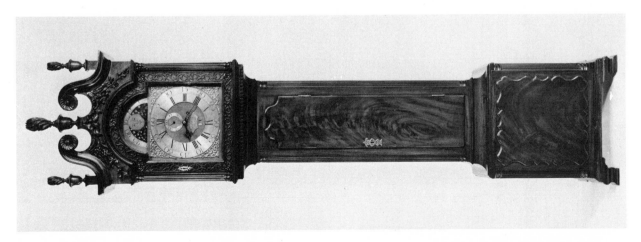

204

207 · TALL CLOCK
Mahogany
Philadelphia and London 1770-1790
Dial Inscribed: Thomas Wagstaffe, London

Some of the best colonial craftsmen produced cases for imported clocks, including Edward James, of Philadelphia; John Townsend, of Newport; and Thomas Johnson (Johnston), a japanner, of Boston. Meanwhile able clockmakers were active in the American colonies, but used imported faces for their clocks.

The tall case here was labeled on the back by William Connell, a cabinetmaker at Third and Spruce Streets, Philadelphia. He signed Benjamin Randolph's receipt book March 31, 1769, for "three pounds 1 Shilings (sic) & three Pence in full of all accts" and was listed as a joiner on the local tax lists in 1774.

The engraved brass dial is mounted with cast spandrels of elaborate rococo design; in the lunette above it are painted the phases of the moon, and on the rim the maker's name is inscribed: *Thomas Wagstaffe, London*. The back of the case is made of hard pine.

Height 104″   Width 17¾″   Depth 9½″

208 · TALL CLOCK
Tulipwood, Painted
Norristown, Pennsylvania 1760-1770
Dial Inscribed: David Rittenhouse, Norriton

The simple case of this small so-called grandfather clock is painted in black and brown to imitate walnut. At the corners of the case a fine chamfer is cut, the forerunner of the quarter-fluted column on Philadelphia clocks.

On the brass dial the name of the most famous colonial clockmaker is inscribed. David Rittenhouse (1732-1796) was a clockmaker, surveyor, astronomer, and inventor. An orrery which he made for Princeton College in 1770 was described by John Adams as ". . . a most beautiful machine . . . It exhibits almost every motion in the astronomical world." This was followed by a larger orrery, made for the University of Pennsylvania. Mr. Rittenhouse succeeded Benjamin Franklin as president of the American Philosophical Society, and after his death was succeeded by Thomas Jefferson, who wrote: "We have supposed Mr. Rittenhouse second to no astronomer living; that in genius he must be first because he is self taught."

There is no evidence of finials or feet ever having been used on this case. The works are made of steel and brass. The movement is for thirty hours, with a strike for each hour and half hour. The plain round brass dial has no spandrels, but is set behind a bezel of painted poplar to match the outside door.

Height 78¼″   Width 14⅜″   Depth 8″

209 · TALL CLOCK
Cherry
Connecticut 1785-1790
Dial Inscribed: Daniel Burnap, East Windsor

The moderate size and restrained ornament of this case, as well as the handsome dial, produce an excellent American clock. Daniel Burnap (1759-1835) was apprenticed to Thomas Harland in Norwich, the most able clockmaker in Connecticut.* The cresting of "whales' tails" around the hood is more literal in its shaping than on Harland's earlier cases.

The silvered face, engraved in graceful rococo lines, is a reminder that Burnap was an able engraver and silversmith as well as a clockmaker. The eight-day movement is made of brass. The pendulum is inscribed: *Elihu Colton*. The backboard is white pine.

Height 89″   Width 18″   Depth 10″

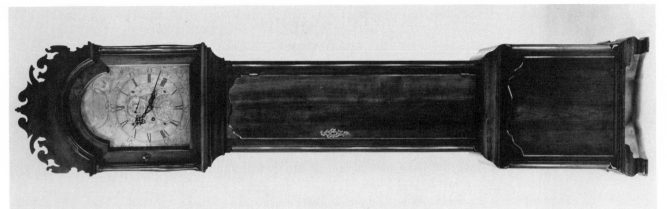

209

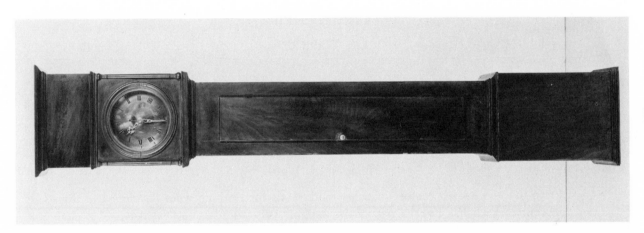

208

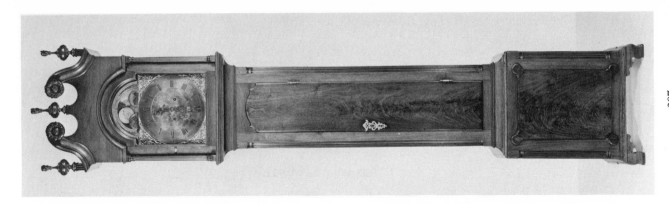

207

210 · COUCH
(OR DAYBED)
Maple
Connecticut 1710-1725

Maple chairs with tall narrow splats and carved yokes show the beginning of the Queen Anne style; the vertical block and vase supports terminating in Spanish feet show a transitional style from the seventeenth century. This rare daybed is contemporary with the chairs familiar to many collectors; here the back rest is strengthened with double stiles. The feet are carved from the same length of maple as the legs.

The cushion is covered with wool damask, early eighteenth century.

Among the property of Joseph Latham, a shipwright who died in New York in 1732, was:

> 1 Couch, squab & pillow
> 6 Cain Chairs
> 5 India Pictures
> 3 lackered Frames

Height 41"   Width 22"   Length 61"

211 · COUCH
(OR DAYBED)
Walnut
Philadelphia 1740-1750

From the seventeenth century, couches or daybeds for sleeping were developed in the style of contemporary chairs. The French chaise longue well describes the extension of a chair for reclining. As the colonial period waned, houses were larger and admitted more full-sized beds. Few couches in the Chippendale style are known, and none exist in the Federal-period style. Here the double chair splat and slip seat produce literally a long chair; the turned stretchers were not often used or needed for a Philadelphia Queen Anne side chair, but here they fortify the capacious width and length of the body.

The upholstery is cowhide from Winterthur Farms.

Height 41¼"   Width 28½"   Length 75"

212 · COUCH
(OR DAYBED)
Maple
Rhode Island 1740-1750

This daybed has a similar back and lower frame as one made for the Eddy family at Warren, Rhode Island, listed on Job Townsend's bill of 1743. Here the stiles end in scrolled ears, and scallops trim the seat rails to make another interpretation of Rhode Island design.

The cushion is cotton twill embroidered in crewels, about 1750.

Height 37¾"   Width 21¾"   Length 62½"

210

211

212

213 · DESK-ON-FRAME
Walnut
Probably Virginia 1730-1750

It is certain that many skilled cabinetmakers were slaves in the southern states and made considerable furniture which is only now becoming recognized. Thomas Elfe, a well-established craftsman in Charleston from 1751, listed among his assets in 1768 the names of a dozen or more "handy craft" slaves whose labor for other cabinetmakers brought him from £12 to £20 each a month.* More than one complaint by migrant white joiners in Virginia was made of the preference there for cheap Negro labor.

Cedar, hard pine, and cypress were native woods used alone or with walnut and mahogany in southern furniture. This sets apart those pieces from others transported from England and northern ports.

This desk of light walnut has yellow pine throughout its interior similar to furniture seen in Virginia. The blunt pad feet appear on walnut tables, with yellow pine underframing, which are scalloped at the ends in similar cyma curves. This desk may be Virginia made. It repeats on a broader scale the small desks-on-frames of the northern states.

The lid has side strips mitered at the corners to prevent warping.

Height 41½″   Width 35¼″   Depth 19½″

214 · DESK-ON-FRAME
Walnut, Inlaid
New England 1735-1750

This unusual desk has the familiar parti-colored star and triple bands of inlay on other Queen Anne pieces (Figure 190) of New England origin. The handsome blister walnut, more rare than blister maple, and the bird motifs on the skirt are not duplicated in the Collection. In the center of the writing cabinet two colonnettes conceal "secret" drawers; the sides are inscribed in ink: *Daniel W. True, Portland, Maine* and *This desk bought by D. M. True Jan 1884 and repaired. It is one hundred and fifty years-old or more.*

The interior is white pine.

Height 42″   Width 36″   Depth 20½″

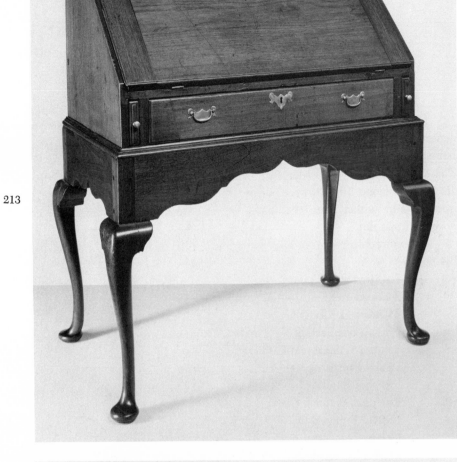

213

214

215 · DESK
Maple
Newport 1740-1750

This small desk shows considerable elegance for its period; the shells upon the legs and center drawer of the block-front cabinet are not often repeated on contemporary desks. The balusters flanking the shell cover the two secret drawers. In Holmes' *The Professor at the Breakfast Table,* the discovery of a secret drawer in the desk of a friend is described, with this conclusion: "Is there not one little drawer in your soul, my sweet reader, which no hand but yours has ever opened, and which none that have known you seem to have suspected? What does it hold? A sin? I hope not."

An eighteenth-century desk was often called a *scrutoir.* In 1736, the late Captain Andrew Bisset left:

1 Screwtor Desk	£2. 0.0
2 Cocoanut Shells footed with Silver	1. 0.9
12 Chairs 1 Elbow Dº	1. 2.6
2 Silver candlesticks	14. 7.6
8 Pictures the Royal Family	2. 9.0
1 Print Prospt. of New York	0. 8.6
1 Barber Bason	0. 0.10
1 piece of Spanish Cedar	0. 2.0
1 Silver Punch Bowl	12. 5.0
1 silver Tea Pott	9. 3.9
1 Silver Tankard	15. 7.0
1 Silver Snuff Box	1. 1.10
1 Silver Cup	3.10.8
1 Dº Tankard 7 spoons 2 Salts 4 Tea Spoons	20.12.6
1 Silver Box Round	2. 1.6
2 Silver Porringers	7. 9.10
1 Snuff Box with Silver Rimm	0. 6.5

Height 41½"   Width 35"   Depth 18¼"

216 · DESK-ON-FRAME
Maple, Stained Red
New England 1720-1740

Certain provincial furniture has a forthright character which imparts an individual personality to it. This derives from a rearrangement of accepted forms in new combinations from conventional urban-made furniture. This desk is an example of fortunate improvisation by a country cabinetmaker.

Inside the lid is a simple bank of shallow drawers, and pigeonholes with scalloped tops. The interior wood is chestnut, hard and soft pine.

Height 36¼"   Width 26"   Depth 13"

216

215

217 · DESK
Mahogany
Boston 1770-1785

The undulating curves of this desk give it the so-called oxbow shape, which takes its name from a similarity to an ox yoke. The form was favored especially in Massachusetts and Connecticut by Benjamin Frothingham, Aaron Chapin, and other able cabinetmakers for their best work.

In the writing cabinet here, the scalloped fans and concaved drawer fronts match those in a desk and bookcase, Figure 228, attributed to John Cogswell in Boston. The elongated hip blocks on the legs are likewise shaped to match.

Soft pine is used for the drawer lining.

Height 44″   Width 41″   Depth 25″

218 · DESK
Mahogany
New York 1765-1780

Case furniture in colonial New York was rarely shaped into bombé, block-front, and serpentine lines adopted by New England cabinetmakers. The last-named form was popular with Gostelowe in Philadelphia. But in Manhattan, if we observe the work of Thomas Burling and Samuel Prince, straight lines are the rule for desks and chests of drawers, compensated in a small degree by the bold, gadrooned edge carved along their base. Bird's-claw feet are the favorite shape of support and, as in contemporary Newport and Hartford furniture, are combined often with bracket or pad feet at the rear corners. Here the broad grain of the wood, probably Santo Domingo mahogany, is striking in effect.

The lining of this desk is tulipwood.

The desk was originally owned by the Post family in New York.

When William Loines, New York merchant, died in 1791, he owned:

1 Mahogany Desk & bookcase	£15. 0.0
1 Eight day clock	18. 0.0
1 do. Dineing Table	3.10.0
1 Cherry Round Tea do.	
7 Mahogany chairs	4. 4.0
12 Windsor	3. 0.0
1 Looking glass	4.15.0
1 Set White curtains	3. 0.0
1 cherry Dineing Table	2. 0.0
1 Looking Glass, Black Walnut Frame	2.10.0
1 Cherry Case of Drawers	5. 0.0
1 Bedstead, 1 set Callico Curtains	5.14.0
1 Cherry stand	0. 8.0
1 Turn up Bed, Beding, Curtains	5.16.0
1 Writing Desk	2. 0.0

Height 45″   Width 44″   Depth 22″

218

217

219 · DESK
Mahogany
Newport 1760-1775

This unusual "buro" or fall-front desk is built to resemble a chest of drawers. The shell-carved drawer front conceals five pigeonholes and a bank of small drawers; it may be pulled down to provide a narrow writing surface. The shells have "petal" centers which spring from a straight bar, like those on the signed Edmund Townsend chest.* Some differences from several signed Townsend pieces are the increased number of scallops and spirals on the feet and fewer lobes on the carved shells. These differences are indicative of the variety of details in one school of furniture.

The drawer linings are red cedar.

Height 34"	Width 35½"	Depth 19½"

220 · DESK-ON-FRAME
Walnut
Philadelphia 1755-1765

This desk is a transitional form, a faint reminder of the desk-box-on-frame of the seventeenth century. Its convenience recommended the long survival of a two-part construction.

The fluted quarter columns at the corners of both upper and lower sections and the serpentine lines of the writing cabinet are refinements beyond the average desk. The small drawers, lined with tulipwood, have a pair of spurs on the back of each drawer as stops. Four small drawers are concealed behind the center door.

The backboards and large drawers are lined with chestnut.

Mention of a desk of this shape may be found in Mary Waln's inventory, dated 1753, in Philadelphia:

> Walnut Desk up a frame
> Small wanutt Table
> Walnut Candlesticks
> One pare of walnut chest of Drawers up a frame
> Pine chest
> Pine corner cubberd
> Small looking glass
> Couch and bed
> One black wallnut Bed Steds Sacking bottom & Curtain rods

Height 42"	Width 37"	Depth 23½"

219

220

221 · DESK-ON-FRAME
Walnut

Philadelphia 1760-1770

The rugged scale of this desk in the Chinese-Chippendale style may be observed in the square legs, without the customary chamfered inner corners and elongated, pierced brackets at the corners.

The interior has a single drawer made to simulate four serpentine-front drawers, flanking the center door. There are no "secret" compartments. The drawer linings are tulipwood.

Height 41¼″   Width 41″   Depth 22½″

222 · DESK
Walnut

Pennsylvania 1740-1750

This buxom little desk is noteworthy for its practical size and shapely lines. The exposed dovetails on the top surface and the end strips on the lid to prevent warping are unabashed construction methods associated with early cabinetmaking.

The drawer linings are made of tulipwood and ash.

The contents of Stenton were listed, room by room, in 1752 after the death of its first owner, James Logan. "On the first Story in ye back Dining Room are:

1 Maple Desk	£2.15.0
1 Couch & Couch Bed & Cushion	1.15.0
2 Walnut Tables	1.17.6
10 Leather Chairs	4. 0.0
1 Armed with Cushions	0.17.6"

One of the leather chairs mentioned in Logan's inventory may well have been the chair pictured in Figure 97.

Height 38½″   Width 30¾″   Depth 18½″

221

222

223 · BOOKCASE
Mahogany
Philadelphia 1760-1775

The upper section of this rare bookcase recalls the famous case built by John Folwell to hold the orrery made by David Rittenhouse.* The fifteen-pane fenestration, patterned like a Chinese lattice, is earlier than the "thirteen colonies" paned doors, which are as mythical as Washington's cherry tree.

The adjustable shelves, of stained hard pine, are edged with mahogany. The enclosed cupboard is divided by a single shelf for tall books.

In the list of household property of Governor John Penn, advertised in Philadelphia for sale in 1795, were:

A Mahogany book Case	£20	10	..
1 Musick stand	1	17	..
1 Thermometer	2	.....	
1 Marble Chimney pˢ	7	10	..
10 Mahogany Chairs	30	10	..
2 Arm Ditto	6	2	..
1 Mahogany dining table	3	5	..
1 Ditto tea ditto	2	15	..
1 Ditto Card Ditto	2	17	6
1 turkey Carpet & piece	30	.....	
1 fire screen	..	19	..
2 Mahogany trays and 1 Knife tray	1	18	6
1 Mahogany Wardrobe	18	.....	

Height 99"   Width 43½"   Depth 12½"

223

224 · DESK AND BOOKCASE
Mahogany
New York 1770-1775
Probably Made by Samuel Prince

The only labeled work of Samuel Prince known at present is a desk and bookcase of the same shape as this; the pitched pediment, pierced fret cornice, and squat bird's-claw feet combined with similar expansive proportions are notably alike in each case. Only the glazed doors and carved knees, the latter matching the Hewlett family desk, are elaborations of Prince's labeled work. The diamond form in the Chinese fret is repeated consistently on cornice, pigeonholes, and center door, and even on the pierced brasses.

The top of this New York bookcase unlike others of local origin, does not fit down into the desk, but merely rests on its unfinished pine surface. The outside of the writing lid is framed by a wide veneered border.

The drawers are lined with tulipwood, and the backboards are soft pine and tulipwood.

Samuel Prince advertised in the New York *Gazette* and the *Weekly Mercury* from 1772 to 1776 "all sorts of cabinet-work . . . Orders for the West-Indies, and elsewhere, completed on the shortest notice." His engraved trade card, richly framed in rococo flourishes, announces a "Joyner at the Chest of Draws in Cart & Horse Street New York Makes and Sells all Sorts of Joyners Work on the Lowest Terms." Prince died in 1778 in Somerset County, New Jersey, and his will, proved October 26, left an ample estate to his wife Ruth and five children, including for the latter "an outset of furniture on their day of marriage as nearly equal as possible to each other."

Height 98½"   Width 44"   Depth 25"

224

225 · DESK AND BOOKCASE
Mahogany
Massachusetts 1760-1775

This shapely block-front desk is a slightly smaller version of one in the Bolles Collection which has female figures carved by Simeon Skillin on its pediment. The concaved shell above the arched doors is also repeated there. Within the small door of the writing cabinet is an engraved table of weights for silver coins embellished with figures of Justice in contemporary costume, a merchant, and a ship at anchor. It was *Engraved Printed and Sold by Nat. Hurd,* the Boston silversmith who engraved numerous richly bordered book plates.

An unusual wood here is white oak in the large drawer linings; it is supplemented with white pine in the bookcase above.

This desk was owned by Charles R. Waters, in Salem, and was purchased by his grandfather about 1770.*

A lately discovered inventory of James Bowdoin's large library in Boston which was taken over by Major General Burgoyne on September 9, 1775, included among several hundred volumes:

Johnston's Works	Lady Montagues letters 4 Vol.
The Holy Bible	Lord Bacons Essays
Rabelais's Works 4 Vol.	Novum Testament Graecum
Cott. Mather's life	Salmons Family Dictionary
Franklins Sophechles 2 Vol.	Hamiltons Observations on Mt. Vesuvuis
Daneby Dicto.ʸ of Greek & Rom. Antiquities	& Etnae
Houshold Furniture	Sᵗ Augustines meditations
Humes History of England 8 Vol.	Tolands Defence of Miltons Life
Mounteneys Demosthenes	Common Prayer Book
Enquire into the sublime & beautiful	Lex Parliamentaria
Millers Gardner's Dictionary 3 Vol.	Shakespears Plays 6 V. not compleat
Bradley on planting & Gardning	Moliers Plays Fr. & Eng. 2ᵈ Vol.
Reads enquiry into the human mind	Memoirs de Pompadour 1ˢᵗ Tome
Mallets life of Bacon	Fieldings Amelia
Claredons History of the Rebellion 6 Vol.	Addisons Works 1 V.
Trowell on Husbandry & Gardening	Swifts Dᵒ 5 V.
Turner's Art of Surgery 2 Vol.	Paradice Lost 2 Vol.
Diseases of the Skin	Clarks Homer
Boyle's Experiments on Cold	Shakespear illustrated
Clarkes Demonstration of Newtons principles	Tristam Shandi 2 V.
Fordius's Sermons to Young Women	Drydens Satires
The Tatler 4 V.	Young Mans Companion
Plutarchs morals 2 V	Locks Essay on Human Understanding

Height 90"   Width 41"   Depth 23"

225

226 · DESK AND BOOKCASE
Mahogany
Massachusetts 1765-1775

In this superb desk and bookcase the architectural style is more fully developed than in any other known colonial desk. The engaged Corinthian columns and pilasters, the voluted pediment, and the arched doors are Palladian forms inherited through England; the carved angels, festoons of flowers, and shells, set off by pitted backgrounds, are echoes of the same Renaissance theme.

In the writing cabinet a spring catch releases the center block to reveal a secret compartment; its base is inscribed: *This desk was purchased by Josiah Quincy Braintree 1778.* The Quincys, an ancient family related to the Earls of Winchester, came to Mount Wollaston, later Braintree, in 1633. Josiah (1709-1784) was graduated from Harvard in 1728 and negotiated with Thomas Pownall the barriers against the French at Ticonderoga in 1755. He was a merchant and built the mansion still standing at Quincy. His niece Dorothy married John Hancock; a son Josiah was the famous orator and patriot who with John Adams defended in court the British "Assassins" after the Boston Massacre. The younger Josiah died at sea while returning from England in 1775.

The raised drawer fronts are shaped from a solid plank. The lower interior is red cedar; the drawer linings are only three-sixteenths of an inch thick, or half the usual weight. Dust boards of white pine separate one drawer from another. The inside of the bookcase is mahogany.

This piece was purchased from descendants of the first owner in 1946.

Height 97"   Width 43"   Depth 22"

226

227 · DESK AND BOOKCASE
Mahogany
Massachusetts 1760-1780

Rarity adds much to the interest and value of American furniture today inasmuch as fire and neglect have taken heavy toll of much that was made. The form and construction of this desk indicate that it was made in Boston, and fortunately one documented piece of comparable design and quality is extant in private ownership. The one shown here may be the work of John Cogswell, whose shop in Middle Street, Boston, provided the famous Caleb Davis, shipowner and merchant, with some of his furniture. One other desk and bookcase (Figure 228) is probably of the same origin.

This desk and bookcase is of a more highly developed rococo style than any other known to have been made in Boston. Not only is the bombé or kettle-shape base elaborated with a serpentine front, but the Corinthian pilasters are augmented by a fanciful-looking glass frame and a reverse-scrolled pediment. The contemporary blue and white porcelain vases flanking the pediment are not the original finials, but seem appropriate in an age when the "chiny madness" of Georgian England had invaded colonial America.

An inscription on the slide below the lid states: "Bought this desk Oct. 15th 1828 of my Father . . .Total   Edward Brinley."

The interior wood is soft pine.

The estate of "John Cogswell late of Boston Cabinet Maker deceased" included:

Back	1 Desk & Bookcase	$10.—
Room	1 Mahogany Table	3.—
	6 Leather bottom Chairs	1.50
	1 " " " with arms	—.50
	2 Round Snap Tables	2.—
	1 Pembrook Table	3.50
	1 Pr Plated Lamps & Snuffers	1.50
	1 Old Stuffed Chair	—.25
	6 Old Pictures	—.50
	1 Looking Glass	8.—
	1 Small Mahogany breakfast Table	1.—
	1 floor Carpet	6.—
	1 Hearth Rug	—.50
	1 old Easy Chair	2.—
	1 Toilet Table	1.50
	1 Gilt Looking Glass	8.—
	1 Bed Bedstead Curtains & all the Beding	50.—
	1 Card Table	2.—
Front	2 Mahogany Card Tables	7.—
Room	1 " 4 foot do	7.—
	1 Looking Glass	10.—
	1 8 day Clock	20.—
	1 Pr Plated Candlesticks	1.—

Height 92″   Width 38⅜″   Depth 19¾″

Ex Coll. George S. Palmer

227

228 · DESK AND BOOKCASE
Mahogany
Boston 1770-1785
Probably Made by John Cogswell

The richness of Chippendale furniture in Philadelphia is taken for granted; far rarer is comparable carving of Boston origin. In this desk and bookcase the style is epitomized by the bombé form, the scrolled pediment, the rococo carving, the fluted pilasters, the Chinese frets, and the hairy claw feet. All of those rare features appear on a double chest signed by John Cogswell, cabinetmaker of Middle Street, Boston, and make plausible the attribution of this desk to him.

Certain facts about Cogswell are now available. He was married in 1762, and his son Samuel was born the next year. On November 4, 1769, he billed "to Mr. Caleb Davis, Merchant of Boston, a mahogany Beuro £5.6.8" and on the same day "Received of Mr. Davis 13/4 Lawful money in full for a mahogany tea board." The Cogswell chest, believed by the owners to have been made for their ancestor, Elias H. Derby, in Salem, is dated 1782. John Cogswell held town offices from 1778 to 1809 and was still active as a cabinetmaker in 1789. As surveyor of mahogany he passed on 10,000 feet of Santo Domingo lumber in 1809. In the same year his son John became the partner of Thomas Seymour, English-born cabinetmaker, famed with his father for the blue-lined tambour desks and sideboards of Hepplewhite and Sheraton design.

"John Cogswell, Cabinetmaker, late of Boston" died in 1818 intestate.

Height 95½"   Width 45½"   Depth 22⅝"

228

229 · DESK AND BOOKCASE
Curly Maple
Massachusetts 1765-1780

The curly maple that the observant traveler Peter Kalm noticed as a favorite native wood of joiners in the mid-eighteenth century was used widely in New England. In this small desk the pattern of the wood was selected to accent its flat surfaces on the lower drawers, the bookcase doors, and the center of the writing cabinet. The carved fans and corkscrew finials adequately supplement the ornamental stripe of the maple.

The lining is white pine.

In the estate of Captain Benjamin Hind, of Boston, appraised September 25, 1781, there were listed:

A maple desk 20/ a Mehog^y Table 45/ d° Side d° 20/	£4..5..0
a Small maple stand 2/ a set old Brushes 4/	6..0
6 Maple Chairs 24/ Pair Bellows 6/	1.10..0
A round Chair 20/ Six Leather Bottom chairs 60/	4..0..0
6 Delph plates 4/ Silver Watch 60/	3..4..0
a Mehog^y waiter 3/ a Tin scale & beam 6/	
3 brass scales 18/	1..7..0
a small maple Table 6/ Maple side Table 8/	0 14..0
a fire Screen 6/ Six Maple Chairs 18/ Cradle 8/	1.12..0
a Wicker Chair 6/ 2 pr Brass Candle sticks 12/	
2 old d° 3/	1..1..0
Six small Glass pictures 6/ a Small Trunk 3/	9..0
a Suit Old Blue Curtains 18/ a Suit Green d° 40/	2.18..0
a Black Velvett Jackett 54/ Black Velvett Breeches 30/	4..4..0
a Cotton Velvett old Suit 48/ a Crow Colour'd	
Suit Cloaths	5..3..0
a Huzza 80/ 2 Damascus Waistcoats 20/	5..0..0
3 Dozen Glass Bottles 9/	9..0
65 Ounces Plate at 6/8^d p^r ounce	21.13..4

Height 86″   **Width 38″**   **Depth 20½″**

229

230 · DESK AND BOOKCASE
Cherry
Connecticut 1765-1780

The recurring arches of the pediment, doors, and pigeonholes on this desk and bookcase seem to echo the Connecticut Valley doorways and paneled walls of mid-eighteenth century houses. Then the stark outlines and vertical sheathing of the first dwellings were softened by classical ornament of England's Restoration, details of Christopher Wren's rich vocabulary in provincial New England. Here the pin-wheel carving and the compact candy-twist finials are admirably suited to the simple character of the fielded paneling where the effect of light and shade is artfully contrived to repeat the broken surface of the writing cabinet. This is an excellent example of Connecticut furniture earlier than the New Britain-Hartford school of cabinetmaking developed by Aaron Roberts and Aaron and Eliphalet Chapin.

The interior is lined with white pine.

This desk and bookcase was owned by Colonel Jeremiah Halsey, who was born in Stonington, in 1743 and died in Norwich, Connecticut, in 1829.

The contents of John Dolbeare's bookcase, after he left Boston, August 12, 1776, comprised:

London Magazine 1770 ª 1773	4 Vol:
Lord Clarendon's Life	2
New Spanish Grammer	1
Stanhope's Christian Pattern	1
Seneca's Morals	1
Miltons Works	2
Pamela	4
Select Poems	2
Thompsons Seasons	1
Popes Works	4
Spencer's.Works	6
Duke Marlborough's Life	3
Monteiquieu's Spirit Law	2
Salmon's Geography	
Spectator Vol 8	
Guardian Vol 2	

Height 92¼″   Width 40″   Depth 22½″

230

231 · DESK AND BOOKCASE
Cherry
Connecticut 1750-1770

The proportions of this desk and bookcase are familiar in early Connecticut-made pieces. In the writing cabinet is a shell-carved door flanked by fluted colonettes; this section pulls out to show secret drawers inside. Left and right are banks of serpentine-front small drawers and scalloped pigeonholes. The carved "sunflower" on the lid, pediment, and corners was a favorite motif in the Connecticut River Valley, and it often appeared on mid-eighteenth century paneling. The short flame finials are likewise of local design. The heavy, raised molding which frames the arched door panels and the knuckled feet are reminiscent of an earlier period than the arched pediment and fluted chamfered corners. The outline of the entire piece is painted black to make a contrast with the natural cherry wood.

The drawers are lined with white pine.

Height 96″   Width 40″   Depth 21⅝″

231

232 · DESK AND BOOKCASE
Mahogany
Kingston or Newport 1770-1780

This is one of probably six similar desks associated with the Townsend and Goddard family of cabinetmakers. Except for the quarter columns here, it nearly matches a desk and bookcase probably made by Townsend Goddard, son of John, in Kingston before 1777, now in the Museum of Fine Arts in Boston.

The Revolution sadly interrupted the prosperous days of Newport. The Townsends and Goddards, as Quakers, were pacifists and found little welcome and few orders for furniture in the captive city. John Townsend lived in Norwich and Middletown, Connecticut, after escaping confinement in Newport; a labeled double chest gives his address as Middletown.

The lining of the drawers is red cedar.

This desk and bookcase was originally owned by the Updyke family.

Height 98″   Width 42¼″   Depth 25½″

232

233 · DESK AND BOOKCASE
Maple
Philadelphia 1760-1775

The rich figuring of curly and branch maple grain of this desk recalls the observation of Peter Kalm, who arrived in Philadelphia in 1748: "The Joiners say that among the trees of this country they chiefly use the wild cherry trees, and the curled maple . . . The wood of the wild cherry-trees (Prunus Virginiana) is very good, and looks exceedingly well, it has a yellow color, and the older the furniture is, of which is made of it, the better it looks. But it is already difficult to get at it, for they cut it every where, and plant it nowhere. The curled maple (Acer rubrum) is a species of the common red maple, but likewise very difficult to be got. You may cut down many trees without finding the wood which you want."

Behind the arched doors are three bookshelves. The fluted pilasters of the writing compartment may be used as secret drawers. The pair of drawers under the writing lid are locked by a wooden spring, manipulated from inside the drawer below.

The drawer linings are tulipwood, cherry and white cedar.

Height 95″   Width 39½″   Depth 21½″

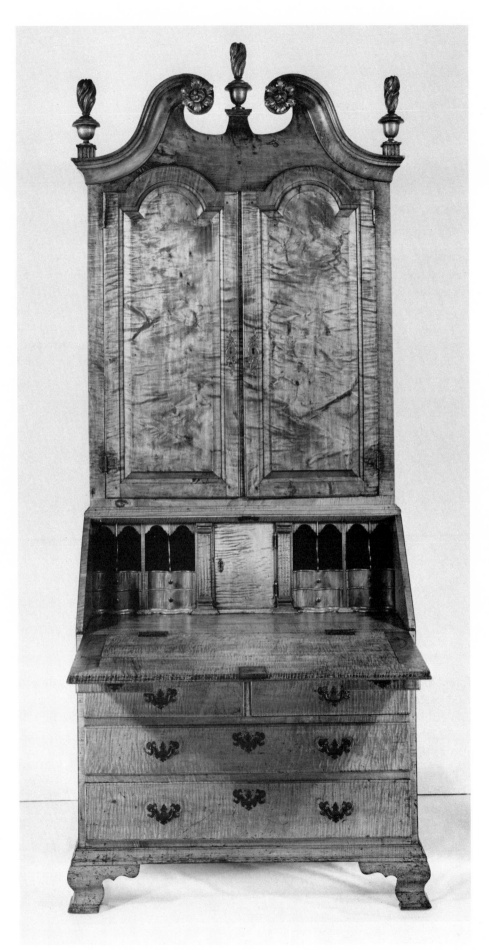

233

234 · FIRE SCREEN
Mahogany
Massachusetts 1765-1780

Screens were used in Europe since medieval times to give protection from drafts and heat from open fires. Folding and cheval screens are early, but the tripod pole screen is an eighteenth-century form, and it follows the pattern of tea tables and candlestands.

This pole screen, elegant in line and carving, follows the vase form of a tea table (Figure 383) for its carved pillar. The low-spreading tripod legs terminate in especially long rat-claw feet. The oval-shaped panel, more customary in the Hepplewhite period, shows a Chinese pheasant embroidered in chenille and plain silk thread in polychrome shades, on a cream-colored silk ground.

Height 50¼″   Panel 16½″ x 13¼″

235 · FIRE SCREEN AND CANDLESTAND
Cherry
Pennsylvania 1740-1750

Different from the fire screen with an adjustable panel, this combination screen and candlestand is stationary, fixed to an upright shaft. A raised molding frames the shelf.

Joseph Hibbard, *Joyner* in Darby, in 1737 listed "One Screen Candlestick of Cherri Tree."

Similar to this one may have been "a Table & Candle Skreen" owned by John Morgan in Uwchlan, Chester County, "first Day of ye Eleventh Month, 1744/5."

Height 45½″   Panel 15″ x 25″

235

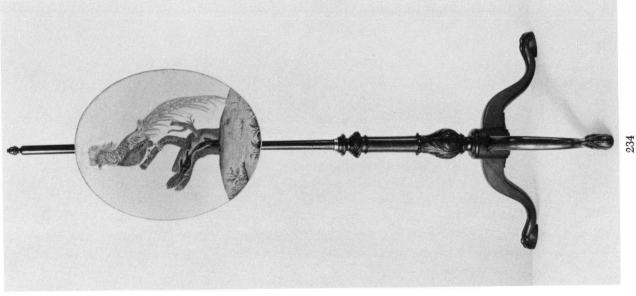

234

236 and 237 · FIRE SCREEN
Mahogany
Philadelphia 1765-1780

Probably not more than half a dozen screens of this pattern exist today; of four known, two are at Winterthur (see Figure 238), one matching this is in the Metropolitan Museum of Art, and one is privately owned. All are from one shop if judged by the similarity of the superlative carving that is lavished on them. One detail, the spray of husks that is superimposed over each leaf-carved knee, proves the virtuosity of the carver and the richness that is consistent with the whole conception. Even the minikin, plain fillets that border the elaborate carving have the precision of jewel work. The fact that no fewer than three engraved illustrations for fire screens appear on Benjamin Randolph's famous trade card would indicate their popularity in Philadelphia.

The panel is covered with painted Chinese silk, eighteenth century.

Height 62½"   Panel 19" x 22"

238 · FIRE SCREEN
Mahogany
Philadelphia 1760-1775

A group of four known fire screens of almost identical design epitomize the elegance of the Philadelphia Chippendale style. Minor variations in details of the feet — two have hairy paws — and the carving of the shaft and finials do not lessen their general homogeneity. A feature on this screen, unobserved elsewhere, is the scored knuckles of the claw feet.

The Chinese fret, flanked by the legs, is the same as in a chair back (Figures 135 and 136) inspired by Plate XII in Chippendale's *Director*, 1754. The panel is worked in crewels in muted colors; the design of a classical arch and rusticated masonry makes an unusual frame for the flowers.

Height 59⅞"   Panel 21⅝" x 19"

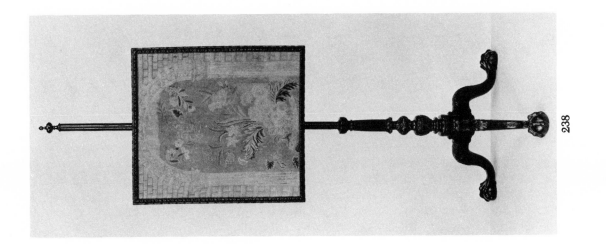

238

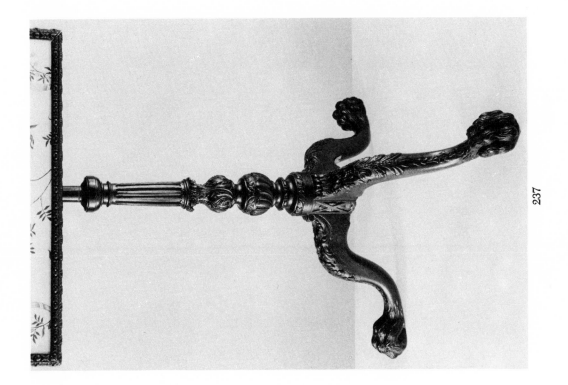

237

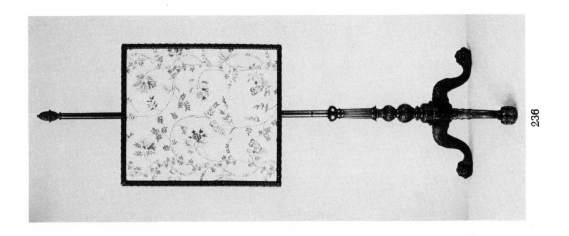

236

239 · FIRE SCREEN
Mahogany
Massachusetts 1765-1780

The spiral fluting carved on the shaft of this screen follows English furniture design and is frequently repeated on tripod tables in New England. The spiral-shaped finial may be seen repeated on a Massachusetts desk and bookcase, Figure 225. An elongated claw-and-ball foot, best described as a rat claw, was likewise favored in Salem and Boston.

The panel is covered with cherry-colored silk-and-metal brocade, French, Louis XV period.

Height 55″   Panel 24″ x 26″

240 · FIRE SCREEN AND CANDLESTAND
Mahogany
Massachusetts 1765-1780

Somewhat plainer than Figure 239, this fire screen shows alliances to it in the shape of the carved pillar and feet; the addition of an adjustable platform for candlesticks gives it greater usefulness. A satinwood fan is inlaid on the shelf top.

The panel is covered with painted silk in pastel colors on white, Chinese, eighteenth century.

Height 51½″   Panel 12″ x 8″

241 · FIRE SCREEN
Mahogany
New York 1760-1775

It is possible to distinguish regional features in furniture with as limited a structure as this pole screen. The bulbous pillar recalls similar forms on New York tea tables, and the panache of coarse leaves carved on the knees can be matched on several side chairs with New York histories. The sharply angular claw feet, best seen in profile, are a further clue for attribution.

The oversize crewelwork panel representing a shepherd and shepherdess tending their charges is now faded to shades of brown.

Height 61¼″   Panel 30″ x 21″

239

240

241

242 · LOOKING GLASS
Firwood, Gesso, and Gilt
English about 1705

Colonel Peter Schuyler, first mayor of Albany and Indian Commissioner of New York, took five Indian chiefs to London in 1709 to secure their loyalty against the French invaders. They were received with great courtesy by Queen Anne, entertained by nobles and statesmen, and given a banquet at Whitehall. The Archbishop of Canterbury presented each sachem with a Bible, and they reviewed four troops of horse and grenadiers. "They made a great bruit thro' the whole kingdom" before returning to Boston on the British man-of-war *Dragon* in 1710.

Among the gifts to the colonial visitors in England was this looking glass, which descended by inheritance in the Schuyler family until it was acquired for Winterthur in 1936.

Upon the lower part of the frame is centered an Indian head wearing war feathers, as an earnest of the famous London visit. The design is a spirited expression of the Queen Anne style, more ambitious than anything attempted by contemporary colonial craftsmen. Because of its unusual history and long New York ownership, it takes its rightful place among the American-made furniture here.

Height 56¼″   Width 29¼″

243 · LOOKING GLASS
Firwood, Gesso, and Gilt
English 1710-1720

This frame is a characteristic Queen Anne design, having the ornament built up in whiting or gesso, and gilded. The firwood backboard, set close to the glass, is inscribed: "This miror was bought . . . before 1821. It belonged to Col. Nathaniel Sparhawk who married Sir William Pepperrell's daughter June 10th 1742. It was probably brought from England for a bridal trosseau (sic) for his daughter . . ."

Although English, this looking glass takes its place (like Figure 242) among colonial furniture as one of the imported luxuries contemporary with it.

The brass sconces are of the same age. The beveled glass is original to the frame.

Height 40″   Width 23½″

243

242

244 · LOOKING GLASS
Pine, Painted and Decorated
New York 1725-1735

This frame and the one in Figure 245 are decorated in the tradition of japanned work copied from oriental lacquer. The pomegranate-colored ground is a foil for the black landscape and the gold animals of an exotic species. No attempt was made to build up the figures with gesso, a technique employed on larger colonial examples of japanning.

In New York during 1736 in the *Weekly Journal*, Gerardus Duyckinck advertised "Looking-glasses new Silvered and the Frames plaine, Japand or Flowered . . . made and sold, all manner of painting work done." Ten years later in the *New York Post Boy* a Gerardus Duyckinck continued "to carry on the business of his late Father deceased viz. Limning Painting Varnishing Japanning Gilding etc." Gerrit and Evert Duyckinck were *Limners* in the Freemen's lists of Manhattan for 1698; Gerardus was admitted in 1731.

Height 22½"   Width 12"

245 · LOOKING GLASS
Pine, Painted and Decorated
New York 1725-1735

Oriental inspiration provided the gold decoration of this frame, on a cerulean blue ground. The original beveled plate glass is intact.

The history on the backboard indicates the looking glass was originally used on the Luyster farm, in Middletown, Orange County, New York, in 1727.

The looking glass owned by Johannes Van Wyck in Flushing, listed on January 14, 1733, may have been painted:

Cupboard, chairs, Tables & Looking Glass	£ 11. 2.0
Tea Tackling	3. 4.0
Glass earthenware & Sundries	1.16.6
Sundry Negroes	210.——
Pewter	50.14.0
Chairs, candlesticks, potts, kettles	6. 6.6
70¾ bb. pewter	3.10.9

Height 21"   Width 11"

245

244

246 · LOOKING GLASS
Soft Pine

JAPANNED DECORATION

Probably New York 1729-1740

A rich source of designs for colonial lacquer was John Stalker's *Treatise of Japanning and Varnishing*, published in Oxford in 1688, which found its way into American libraries in the eighteenth century. The book teems with woodcuts of whimsical figures, fabulous beasts and birds, and tenuous pagodas, together with exact formulas and directions for japanning. Other books appeared later, and these guided the colonial decorator in his work, especially in New England.

This frame is the largest known with japanned decoration. The ground is black; and the ornament, raised with a ground of whiting, is gold.

On the back of the frame are burned the initials *I B I* for Jon Johannes Bleecker, from whose descendants the looking glass was acquired in 1940.

Height 60″   Width 24″

247 · LOOKING GLASS
Maple and Pine

JAPANNED DECORATION

Boston(?) 1720-1745

An important difference in the japanning done in Boston and in England is the technique employed. In Boston, decorators invariably chose a fine-grained maple for the principal surfaces of their work, and used whiting or gesso only for building up the raised ornament; then the whole surface was painted, gold-leafed where desired, and varnished. In England oak or firwood was the wood selected, which was first entirely coated with a layer of whiting to conceal the rough grain and knots. Now the wear and tear of years often shows these differences clearly.

Several japanned clock cases with New York works were made in the English manner on oak; the japanners were probably trained abroad.

Originally this frame probably had a cresting like that on Figure 246. It was made separately, and is now missing more often than not on many frames.

This looking glass was owned originally by Jacob Ten Eyck, a great-great-uncle of Henry F. du Pont.

Height 46½″   Width 19″

246

247

248 · LOOKING GLASS
Walnut
American 1725-1740

This frame of veneered walnut upon a pine carcass may be of New England origin and contemporary with the case furniture made there in the same way. The scalloped cresting is intact and, being removable, is missing on most frames of this era. The original beveled glass is in two parts.

On the backboard, fragments of an old Boston newspaper, but without a heading or date, are still evident.

Height 48″   Width 18″

249 · LOOKING GLASS
Walnut
Probably Philadelphia 1730-1750

This solid-walnut frame has the white cedar backboards used in much Philadelphia furniture lining. The upper section of the original beveled glass is cut with an archaic floral pattern.

An estate inventoried in Pennsylvania of "Archibald McNeile, late of Kennett . . . the first Day of March, 1762/3" consisted, in part, of:

Two looking Glasses 20/ a Quantity of brow sugar 25/	£2..15..
One pair of Gold Buttons	2......
One walnut Oval Table	2......
Eighteen framed wooden chairs	1..10..
Six black Chairs one of them armed	...15..
Two poplar Chests	...12..
Four Loaves of Sugar	1......
A Small parcel of Walnut Boards	1......
Seventeen flag bottomed Chairs	1 . 5..
A poplar Chest and two Walnut Boxes	...15..
One walnut Chest	1......
Three old Tables 8/ and one black walnut 3/	...11..
Two brass Candlesticks a pair of snufores and nine old iron Candlesticks	....7..

Height 48″   Width 17½″

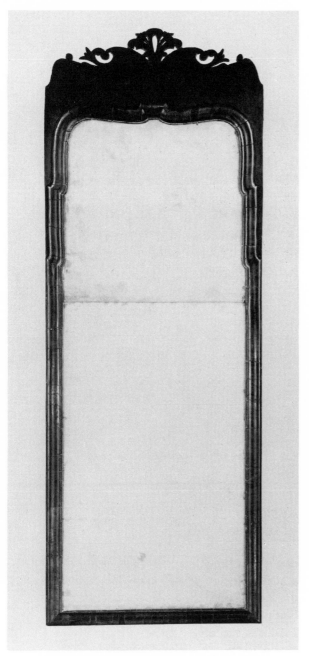

248

249

250 · LOOKING GLASS
Walnut
American(?) 1720-1730

The ground or carcass upon which walnut is veneered is a guide in determining origin. Here the deal or Norway spruce is more like English mirrors than American ones. This kind of furniture was more often imported than larger pieces and, whether English or American, belongs in any collection of the latter. The old beveled glass and candle sconces are intact, rare survivals of the Queen Anne period.

When Thomas Moone's will was proved on September 6, 1756, in Flushing, New York, it began: "To my wife Elizabeth slaves et silver, my best bed and one dozen best chairs, my pair glass sconces hanging in my parlor and my best oval table, and one dizen of my pictures the Seasons of the year, my pewter plates, shagreen case of ivory knives & forks, ¼ all my china."

Height 34¾"   Width 17½"

251 · LOOKING GLASS
Black Walnut and Gilt
Probably New York 1720-1730

Chimney looking-glass and *mantel-tree looking-glass* are contemporary names for the horizontal glasses made to fit the paneling above a fireplace or to rest upon the mantel shelf. This style was introduced into England in the last years of the seventeenth century; and, encouraged by the rebate of high taxes on plate glass in 1699, the size of blown glass plates at the Vauxhall and Southwark factories increased "to ninety inches . . . of lively color, free from Bladders, Veins and Foulness incident to the large plates hitherto sold."*

This frame does not take the reversed curve or arched shape of similar looking glasses in England; its narrow solid walnut frame, flanked by scrolled ears to hold the brass sconces is in the American tradition of sobriety. A carved and gilt inner border enlivens the dark wood.

The backboards are white pine.

Height 16"   Width 59"

250

251

252 · LOOKING GLASS
Walnut
American(?) 1710-1725

The half-round moldings of walnut, veneered on softwood, possibly cedar, are an early Queen Anne form of looking glass. The detachable cresting is made in a jig-saw outline that was repeated through the century on simple frames of mahogany and gilt. Whether imported or homemade, this simple version of tall, cut-glass-bordered frames that epitomized the style in England was widely used in the colonies. The long proportions of these frames carry on the tradition of the pier glass, hung between windows on a narrow wall.

Cornelius Kierstede, famous now as one of the ablest silversmiths before 1750 in New York, owned at his death in New Haven in 1753:

1 Looking Glass £8.   1 Three Legd Table 25/.

1 square Do 10/.	£ 9.15.0
1 round Do. broken 15/. 2 Pictures with Gilt Frames £6	6.15.0
1 Large old Picture, black Frame 40/. 1 round Table 60/	5. 0.0
1 Large Chest, with Lock & Key £9. 1 Chest of Draws	11. 2.0
Sundry old Chairs 90/. 1 Tea Kettle 80/. 1 Iron Pot 30/	10. 0.0

Height 50½″   Width 18⅝″

253 · LOOKING GLASS
Walnut and Gilt
American(?) 1725-1740

The technique of making looking glass from blown cylinders restricted its size until the third quarter of the eighteenth century, when the casting process allowed almost an unlimited size to be made in plate glass. Early claims from the English glass factories of single sheets 91 inches long were seldom realized when the limited facilities of blowing, grinding, and polishing glass were considered. For this reason early looking glasses invariably are in two parts and sometimes in three.

The shell and scalloped cresting are details favored by Philadelphia makers before 1750.

Looking glass was valuable, and old glasses were often reframed in later years. Looking glasses belonged with the luxuries treasured as heirlooms. In 1733 Lieutenant James Banks left: "One looking glass, two schonces, one bedstead & callico curtains, one Cubbort, one chest drawers, one picture, gilded frame, 9 old pictures, one pair scarlett breeches, one pair scarlett silk stockings, one box with knives & forks."

Height 59½″   Width 20½″

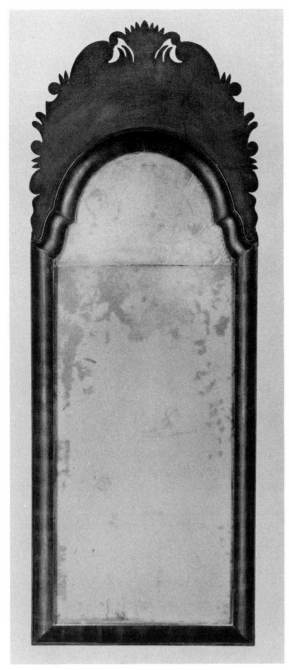

252

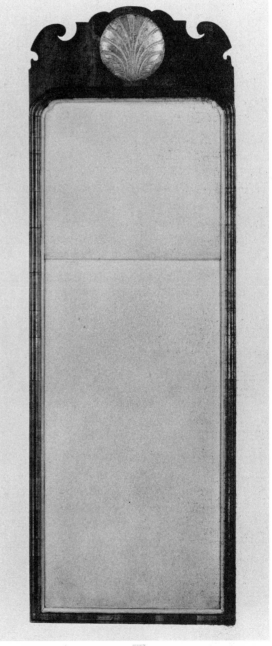

253

254 · LOOKING GLASS
Mahogany and Gilt
Philadelphia 1762-1767
Labeled by John Elliott, Sr.

Looking glasses in several periods were labeled by John Elliott, from the Queen Anne and pedimented (Figure 255) Georgian styles to the simple scalloped outline without carving or gilding (Figure 266). The label on the last-named looking glass includes mention of his sons, but omits the customary German translation. Elliott's first address was at Chestnut Street, Philadelphia, from 1753 to 1762, when he billed Edward Shippen, Jr., for his dining room furniture. His second shop, on Walnut Street, from 1762 to 1767, is the address upon this looking glass, written in over the earlier address (see Figure 395). The design combines the earliest shape of Elliott's frames with the pierced and gilded shell of the rococo period which followed.

Although Elliott's labels state that he "imports and sells all Sorts of English Looking glasses" at his store along with other merchandise including books, "fine worsted patterns for jackets, thread and cotton stockings," there is evidence that some of his labeled frames were Philadelphia made.

Height 57"   Width 20¼"

255 · LOOKING GLASS
Mahogany and Gilt
Philadelphia 1753-1761
Labeled by John Elliott, Sr.

In 1756 the first notice was published in the *Pennsylvania Gazette* of "John Elliott, Cabinetmaker in Chestnut-street, the corner of Fourth-street . . . A Neat assortment of looking glasses; viz, Piers, sconces, and dressing glasses . . ." In 1763 Elliott advertised, "He also quicksilvers and frames old glasses, and supplies people with new glasses to their own frames; and will undertake to cure any English looking glass that shews the face either too long or too broad or any other way distorted."

This frame is among the handsomest made by John Elliott; the printed label in English and German is the first used by him between 1753 and 1761, and it conclusively dates the looking glass. He advertised that he made and imported looking glasses; in this one the hard-pine carcass and backboards suggest a domestic origin. The frame is in the architectural style popular in England during the George II period; here the volutes of the scrolled pediment and the full-spread phoenix bird are carved with Chippendale flourishes. Elliott billed Edward Shippen for dining room furniture he made in 1753, and in 1784 he signed a deed as a "cabinetmaker."*

Height 62"   Width 28"

Ex Coll. HOWARD REIFSNYDER, 1929

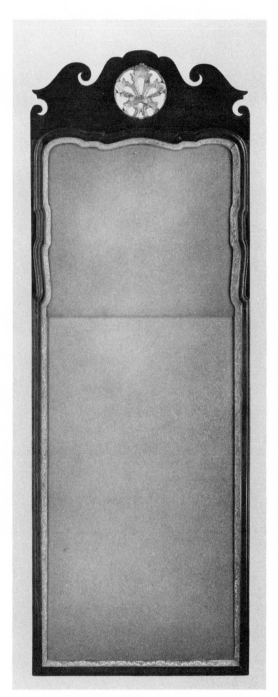

254

255

256 · LOOKING GLASS
Mahogany and Gilt
American 1750-1760

The name *tabernacle* aptly describes the frame of the architectural looking glass which took its shape from the early Georgian overmantels and doorways in the published designs of the British architects James Gibbs and Isaac Ware. In this frame the crossetted outline, pulvinated frieze, and arched pediment combine with familiar classical ornament of carved egg-and-dart moldings and pendant oak leaves and flowers. Set into the frieze, to lighten the formal symmetry of the frame, is a Chinese fret panel backed by glass — a hint of the fantastic chinoiseries yet to come in colonial decoration.

This looking glass was presented by Martha Washington to Mrs. John E. Van Alen in 1794 while her husband, the Hon. John E. Van Alen, was congressman from Rensselaer County, New York (1793-1799).

Height 61"   Width 25"

257 · LOOKING GLASS
ONE OF A PAIR
Walnut and Gilt
American 1760-1775

Two styles of looking glass frames are combined by the maker of this one. To the rectangular, narrow, molded frame of the Queen Anne period has been brought the fancifully carved detail and phoenix bird typical of the rococo style. A matched pair of looking glasses of this size is rarely seen.

The inventory of Maria Gerritse in Albany on August 7, 1749, listed:

> Too Looking glasses one large
> 2 small brass Shells for under a Looking glass
> 1 Schreen
> 3 Narrow boards with pins to hang Cloaths on

Height 68"   Width 25½"

256

257

258 · LOOKING GLASS
ONE OF A PAIR
Pine, Painted Gray and Gold
Massachusetts 1750-1760

This handsome and unique pair of American looking glasses are allied to English decoration in carving and finish. The long, sinuous raffle leaves which border the frame might be from John Vardy's *Designs*, published in London in 1744. The carver has imparted the spirit of that time to the movement and shape of his ornament; even the crosshatched background revived an early Georgian device as a foil for ornament in relief. The arched pediment is terminated in foliated volutes and streamers which resemble those on a Massachusetts desk and bookcase (Figure 226). It is significant, too, that the carving in softwood is painted and gilded in the same manner as much early Georgian furniture was finished. The parrotlike bird is a forerunner of the more realistic eagles which appeared in American decoration after the Seal of the United States was adopted in 1786.

Height 45″   Width 20″

259 · LOOKING GLASS
Yellow Pine, Painted White and Gold
Philadelphia 1760-1780

The American fashion for white-painted woodwork and furniture perhaps started in Philadelphia, a city which prided itself on "the newest taste from London" before hostilities interfered. Benjamin Franklin wrote from London in 1767* to his wife Deborah exact instructions for decorating a room in their Philadelphia house: "I would have you finish it as soon as you can thus: paint the wainscot a dead white; paper the walls blue, and tack the gilt border round just above the surbase and under the cornice. If the paper is not equally colored when pasted on, let it be brushed over again with the same color, and let the papier maché musical figures be tacked to the middle of the ceiling. When this is done, I think it will look very well." The next year James Reynolds, picture and looking glass frame maker, advertised in the *Pennsylvania Gazette*, ". . . looking glasses carved and white, carved and gold . . ."

The fanciful design of C scrolls, rockwork, and pendants of oak leaves and flowers was the nearest approach in America to the airy designs of Lock and Copeland, the pioneers in rococo in mid-eighteenth century England.

This looking glass belonged to the Cadwalader family and collateral descendants until 1949. It still has its original color.

Height 55½″   Width 28″

258

259

260 · LOOKING GLASS
Mahogany and Gilt
Probably Massachusetts 1760-1770

The scrolled pediment, frieze, and cornice used on contemporary overmantels and doorways were combined with rococo ornament for looking glass frames until the Federal period. The broken arch and tattered-shell carving shown here are repeated on a desk and bookcase, Figure 227. This frame is almost a pair with one formerly in the Louis G. Myers Collection and now in the Metropolitan Museum of Art.* The brass candle branches are contemporary.

In 1774 several looking glasses were among the possessions of "Mr. Samuel Collyer late of Marblehead merchant deceased":

"a large looking glass	£2. 8.0
a four foot walnut table 20/ 6 leather chair 12/	1.12.
a old greatchair 2/. 4 foot maple Table 12/	.14.0
6 Joiners chairs 18/. a dutch Looking glass 3/	1. 1.–
7 glass pictures 4 whole & 3 of them broke	. 8.–
round chair 2/. 2 Brushes 1/.	. 3.–
mehogany stand	.12.–
under bed, bedstead & cord	1. 2.0
trunkle Bedstead 2/. blue quilt 12/.	.14.0
walnut desk	.18.0
1 pine writing desk	. 4.–
a large looking Glass	2.———"

Height 54″   Width 27½″

261 · LOOKING GLASS
Mahogany and Gilt
Probably Philadelphia 1760-1770

The frivolous ornament upon the frieze of this handsome frame is made of papier maché, or chewed paper, popular for ceiling ornaments and woodwork in the colonies just after the mid-century. John Blott, upholsterer, offered in 1765 ".... Machee Ornaments for cielings, &c. to imitate Stoco Work." By 1783 it was outmoded and is not mentioned in newspapers except in derision as "a harbour of vermin." The other parts of gilded ornament on the frame are carved wood.

In the Pennsylvania *Gazette*, October 19, 1768, Plunket Fleeson, upholsterer, at the corner of Fourth Street in Chestnut Street offered "American Paper Hangings, Manufactured in Philadelphia, of all kinds and colors, not inferior to those generally imported; and as low in price. Also Paper Mache, or raised paper mouldings for hangings, in imitation of carving, either coloured or gilt."

Height 66″   Width 34½″

261

260

262 · LOOKING GLASS

Mahogany and Gilt

American 1780-1790

The last phases of the Chippendale style are represented in this veneered and gilt frame; festoons of beads replace the earlier pendants of oak leaves and flowers, and straight lines framing the glass encroach on the fanciful pediment and skirting.

In the *Royal Gazette* in 1781 Robert Stott advertised "Has a variety of Looking Glasses and Window Glass to be sold very cheap by the package, among which are, mahogany Sconces, dressing Glasses, Oval Serpentine dressing Box Glasses, Mahogany Swingers, Walnut Tree Ditto, Pole Glasses, Window Glass 20 by 14 and 19 by 14."

Height 63″   Width 30½″

263 · LOOKING GLASS

Mahogany and Gilt

Probably New York 1780-1790

The resemblance of this frame to one made by William Wilmerding for Jacob Everson in New York is apparent in the sparsely carved festoons, scrolled ears, and bird finial.* The applied rococo ornaments on the cresting were frequently resorted to for greater richness on American frames.

An instance of the high regard for household possessions in earlier days is the will of Theunis Van Vechten, of Catskill, Albany County: "To wife Judith the use but not the disposing of my large Cupboard or in Dutch called 'Groote Case' and furniture including the 'Looking glass she had from her father' said effects after wife's death to go to my dau. Elizabeth wife of Hezekiah Vanorden."

Height 29½″   Width 23″

263

262

264 · LOOKING GLASS
Mahogany and Gilt
Philadelphia about 1790
Made by James and Henry Reynolds

Frames for looking glasses of the colonial period seldom have the makers' labels to identify their origin. In Philadelphia John Elliott and his sons and James Reynolds fixed their printed labels to the backboards of looking glasses more often than other makers. James Reynolds advertised in the newspapers from 1768 to 1786 ". . . carved and white, carved and gold, carved mahogany pier, sconce, pediment, mock pediment, ornamented, or raffle frames, box, swinging, or dressing glasses, paper hangings, &c." Reynolds' sons succeeded him and labeled this frame "At their Looking-Glass Store, No. 56, Market Street." But they discontinued the business soon after their father's death in 1794.

Although this frame was made in the Federal period, the earlier Chippendale details have been retained; namely, the rococo curves, the phoenix bird (instead of the ubiquitous eagle), and the indented corners around the glass.

Height 49¼″   Width 24½″

265 · LOOKING GLASS
ONE OF A PAIR
Walnut and Gilt
Probably Boston 1760-1770

A pair of looking glasses of the Chippendale period are not often seen today; when they are nearly seven feet high and commensurate in quality with their size, they are indeed in the realm of rarities. This pair are made of light burl walnut veneered on pine. The carved and gilded rococo ornament, applied to the edges of the frames, is conceived and realized with masterly skill and vitality; it is more substantial in scale than the airy forms in the engraved designs of Thomas Johnson or of Lock and Copeland, by which the carver was guided, however remotely. Made as a pendant to each other, the asymmetry of the cresting and of the phoenix birds is arranged accordingly.

The glass is not beveled at the edges and is not contemporary.

The history of the looking glasses indicates that they originally hung in the Bromfield-Phillips house, near the Hancock house overlooking Boston Common, and were used as pier glasses between windows in the hall when Abigail Phillips married Josiah Quincy in 1769. They were removed to Dedham, Massachusetts, in 1805, and descended by inheritance to members of the Quincy family until 1947, when they were acquired for Winterthur.

Height 81½″   Width 37⅛″

265

264

266 · LOOKING GLASS
Mahogany

Philadelphia 1768-1776

Labeled by John Elliott

In the *Pennsylvania Gazette* on May 8, 1776, John Elliott, Sr., gave notice ". . . As he intends declining the importation of Looking-glasses on the future, and purposes to sell the house he lives in, which is properly fitted up for carrying on the Looking-glass business, particularly for quicksilvering; which art, with all other instructions necessary for carrying on said trade, he is willing to communicate to any person who may purchase said house . . . It hath been a noted and good accustomed store for looking-glasses near 14 years." But after the war, on July 14, 1784, his son John advertised "He has also just imported in the ship Pigou, from London, a very neat assortment of Looking Glasses in mahogany frames . . ."

The frame has the third type of label used by John Elliott, Sr., from 1768 to 1776 (see Figure 397).

Another looking glass at Winterthur with Elliott's second type of label (1762-1767) shows traces of japanned ornament. The shape of the frame is like this one.

Height 49"   Width 27"

267 · LOOKING GLASS
Mahogany and Gilt

Probably New York about 1785

This frame is similar to one made by William Wilmerding in New York in 1791 and billed to Mrs. Killian K. Van Rensselaer. The chief difference is in the oval piercing of the crest, where the Prince of Wales feathers and leaves have replaced the earlier phoenix bird. Several other fine looking glasses, richer in gilded ornament, are identified as the products of Wilmerding's shop.* After 1798, the New York directories list him as a merchant.

On the backboard is the label of Joseph White in Wilmington, Delaware, who sold it, along with drugs, medicines, painters' colours, etc.

Height 51¼"   Width 26½"

268 · LOOKING GLASS
Walnut and Gilt

American 1760-1775

The rich figure of the walnut veneers and gilded leaf inner moldings of this frame continue old methods of construction to be observed in the Queen Anne period; however the intricate profile of scrolls, pierced at the upper and lower corners, places the date after 1750. The brass sconces are contemporary.

Height 59"   Width 29"

268

267

266

269 · SOFA
Walnut and Cowhide
Philadelphia 1740-1750

This unique Queen Anne sofa has high, straight arms and flat, arrow-shaped stretchers that are rare features of Philadelphia furniture, not seen in the other few known sofas of the period. The carved web feet and scrolled knee blocks are reminiscent of a settee made about the same time for Stenton, the Germantown home of William Penn's secretary, James Logan, scholar and judge; some of his furniture is now in the Winterthur Collection (Figure 97 and Figure 294).

The seat rails are made of ash. There is one medial brace of hard pine.

The upholstery is cowhide from Winterthur Farms.

Height 36″   Length 84″   Depth 26″

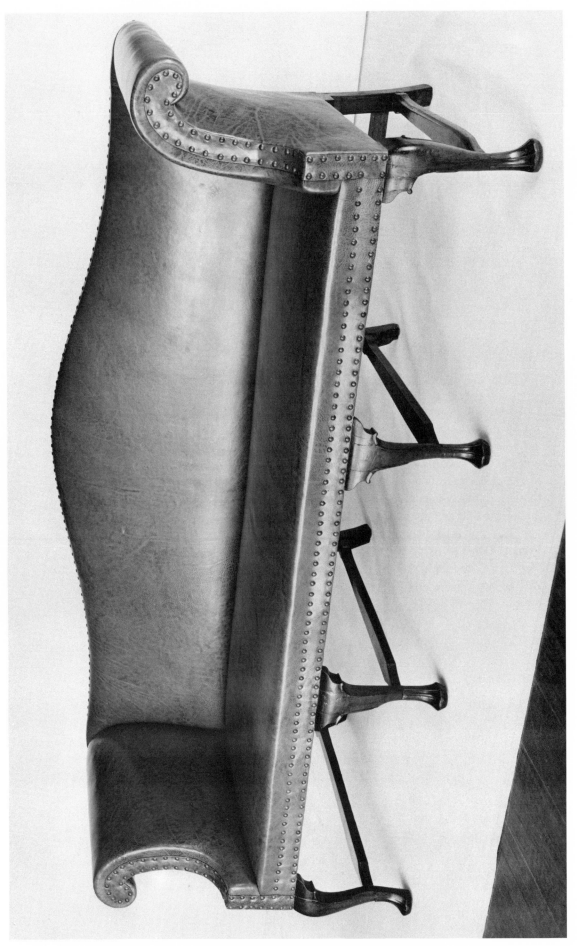

269

270 · SETTEE
Mahogany and Maple
Massachusetts 1765-1780

This settee, one of a known pair, has several features that indicate a New England origin, probably Boston. The attenuation of the cabriole legs, the elongation of the flaring claws over a large ball, the lightly curved, square rear legs, and the use of maple for the last-named supports and for the framing are all earmarks of northern design. The emphasis of the outturned wings and rolled arms, the latter a carry-over from the Queen Anne period, serve to strengthen the short line of the seat and gently serpentine top cresting.

The upholstery is flowered silk brocade in polychrome on a white ground, French, Louis XV period.

The mate to this settee is in the Graves Collection, Metropolitan Museum of Art, and was owned by the family of General Prevoost, an officer in the colonial forces.

Height 36"   Length 57"   Depth 24"

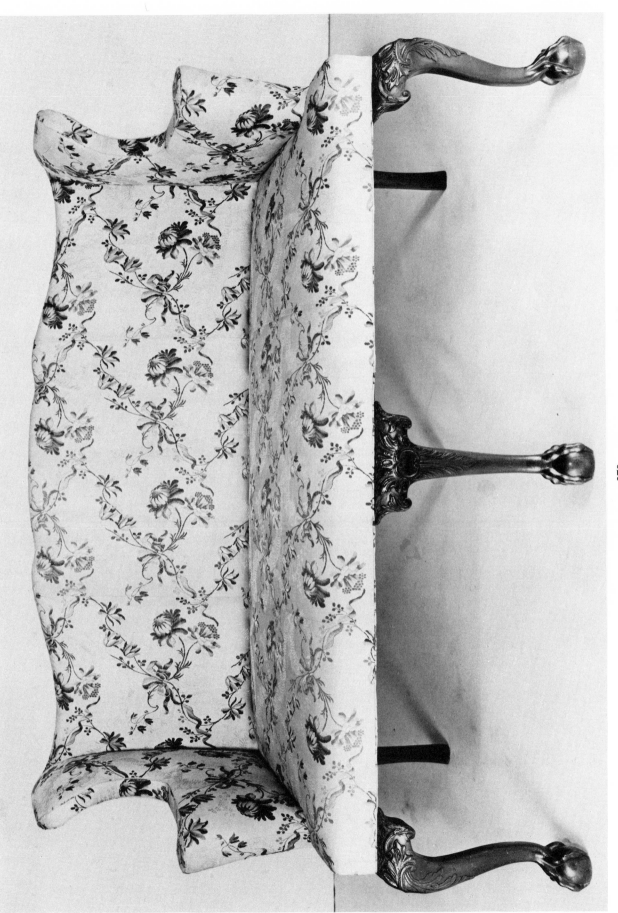

270

271 · SETTEE
Walnut
Philadelphia 1765-1775

Contemporary in date with the sofas in Figures 272 and 273, this settee is of an unusual design. The lower part is carved in the style of several Philadelphia chairs. The covered armrests, of oak, are reminiscent of the upholstered chairs occupied by the sitters to colonial limners; an example is the portrait of Mrs. John Edwards, wife of the Boston silversmith, which was painted about 1750 by Joseph Badger.

The underframing is built of walnut, oak, and hard pine; two medial braces of the last-named wood are fixed under the slip seat.

The covering is wine-red velvet, Italian, eighteenth century.

Governor John Penn's furniture, listed for sale in 1788, mentioned:

 3 elegant large settees, having hair bottoms, with sattin stripe, a double
   row of gilt nails and fluted legs
 2 ditto arm chairs to suit ditto ditto
 24 ditto chairs ditto ditto
 4 plain mahogany chairs for a hall
 1 writing table standing on brass castors, with drawers on each side
 1 large semicircular side board table, in which are three drawers,
   the middle drawer divided into eleven partitions, leaded for liquors

Height 39″   Length 66¼″   Depth 21⅜″

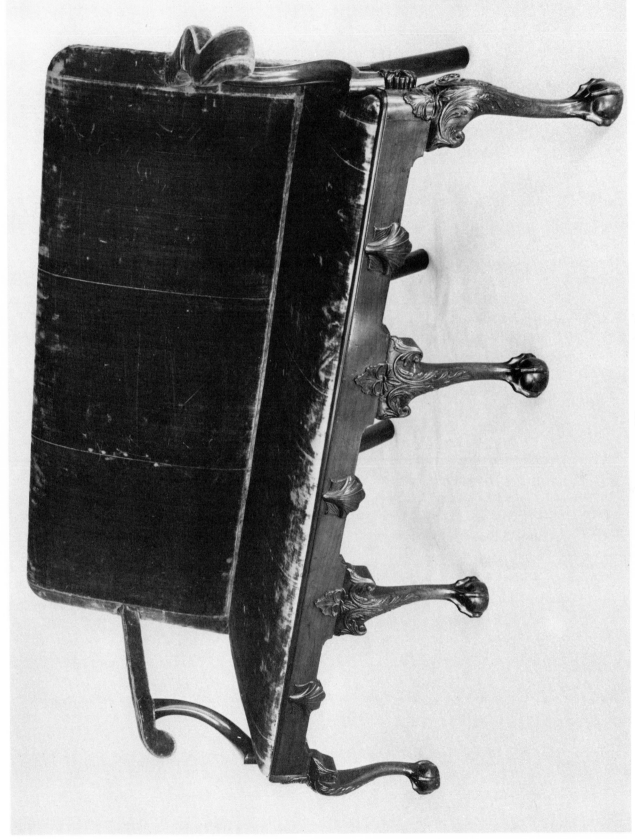

272 · SOFA
Mahogany
Philadelphia 1765-1780

The triple serpentine curves on the front seat rail of this sofa are probably unique on an American sofa. The molded legs and reverse curved back recall the stuffed-back chairs, like Figure 163, owned by Governor John Penn in Philadelphia. In an original manuscript list at Winterthur of his furnishings sold June 9, 1795, the North Drawing Room contained:

2 Chintz Curtains	£18.10.0
1 Large Looking Glass	26. 0.0
2 Settees & Covers	24.10.0
10 Japan'd Chairs	36.10.0
1 arm chair	0.12.0
1 My. T. Table	1.18.0
1 pr. Andirons S. & Tongs	7. 0.0

The covering of the sofa is cocoa-and-silver-colored silk, French, early eighteenth century.

Height 40″   Length 83″   Depth 29½″

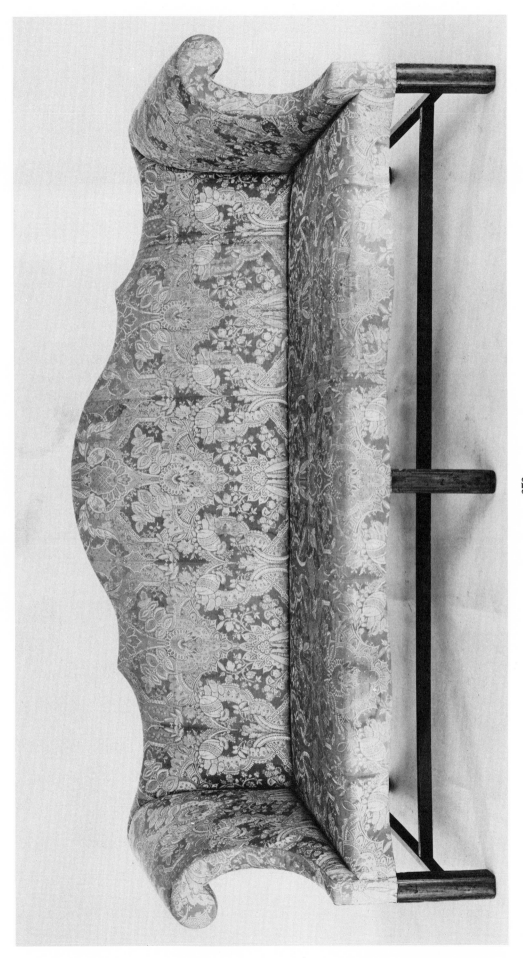

272

273 · SOFA
ONE OF A PAIR
Mahogany
Philadelphia 1775-1780

American Chippendale sofas are not plentiful today. Among the finest is this Philadelphia one, the carved supports matching numerous chairs of similar origin. The whole conception of the frame recalls the *sopha* now in Independence Hall that was used by President Washington in his Philadelphia house. The legs are mahogany, and the covered part is hard pine and ash. On the wood of the arched back the signature of John Linton is inscribed in chalk. He was a hitherto unidentified upholsterer who advertised in the newspapers of Charleston, South Carolina, in 1774 and removed to Philadelphia, where he was established again as an *upholder* in 1780. At the time of his death in 1831 he was the proprietor of a tobacco shop. The mate to this sofa has been published as the work of Thomas Tufft, completed in 1783 for £20.*

The upholstery is yellow silk damask, Italian, early eighteenth century.

The sofa belonged to John Dickinson in Philadelphia. It was John Dickinson who, through his famous *Letters from a Farmer in Pennsylvania,* published in 1768 by Benjamin Franklin, first gave to Europe the colonial viewpoint of unjust taxation. But Dickinson, like many other patriots south of New England, was against independence and held for reconciliation with the Crown. When he refused to join the Signers on that famous July 2, 1776, his enemy John Adams named him "that great fortune and piddling genius." Dickinson later served in the Continental Army, and spent his last years in Wilmington, Delaware.

Height 36¼″   Length 72¼″   Depth 28″

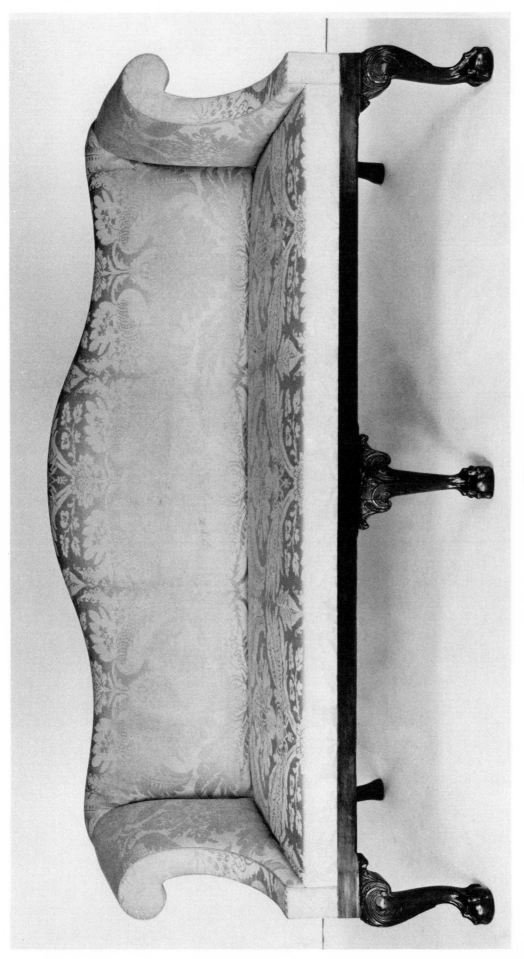

273

274 · SOFA
Mahogany
Philadelphia 1770-1780

The broad legs and rare Marlborough feet give a satisfying sense of stability to this sofa. The shape of the upholstered frame follows the undulating lines of a famous pair; one is shown in Figure 273 and is inscribed with the name of the upholsterer, John Linton. His name was known before he reached Philadelphia. In the *South Carolina & American General Gazette* on April 15, 1774, he advertised that he ". . . Makes and sells Feather beds, Mattrasses, Bed Furniture of different kinds, Window Curtains, Pavilions, Venetian Window Blinds: He also stuffs Sophas, Easy Chairs, French Chairs, and all other articles in that branch performed in the neatest manner, newest Taste, greatest Expedition, and at the most reasonable Rates.

"Paper Hanging also done in the neatest manner."

The covering is silk brocade in polychrome on a white ground, French, Louis XV period.

Height 38″   Length 81″   Depth 29″

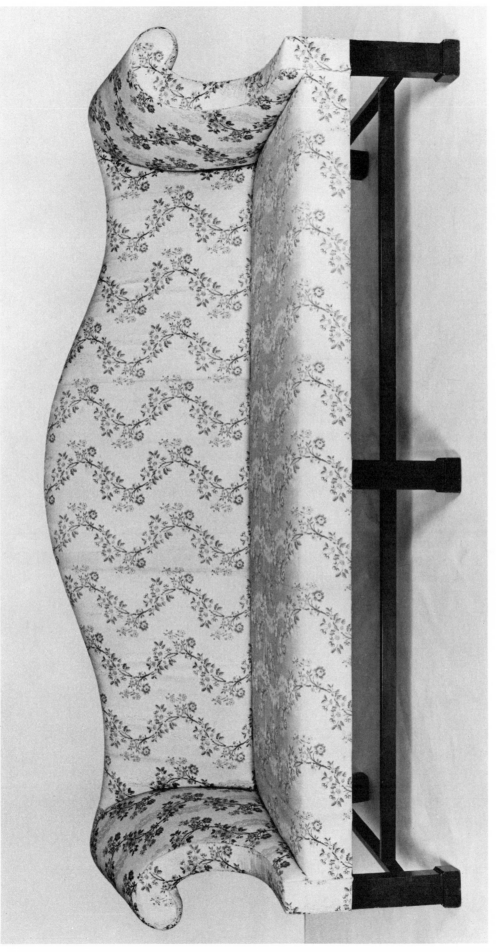

274

275 · SOFA
Mahogany
New York 1770-1780

Copley's portrait of Dorothy Quincy painted in 1772 shows a sofa of this shape, velvet covered, and nail trimmed. In the sofa pictured here the curves of the upholstered frame are more emphatic than those on the Philadelphia and Newport ones at Winterthur.

The sofa originally was owned in New York. In the long inventory of Dr. John Baker's house, taken in New York, June 17, 1797, the Drawing Room contained:

2 Mahogany Card tables, 1 oval glass	£ 8.10
9 Mahogony chairs, stuff'd seats white calico furniture	11.10
2 arm chairs, 1 Sopha same furniture	12.
1 fire screen, 3 window curtains same furniture	4.10
1 Wilton Carpet, 2 India fire fans	15. 0.0
1 pair brass hand Irons, brass fender	3.10.0
1 hearth brush, 2 mahog.y brackets	0.10.0
5 China Jarrs, Tin Cake Caddy	0.18.0

The covering is green and white satin lampas, French, about 1750.

Height 42"   Length 85"   Depth 33"

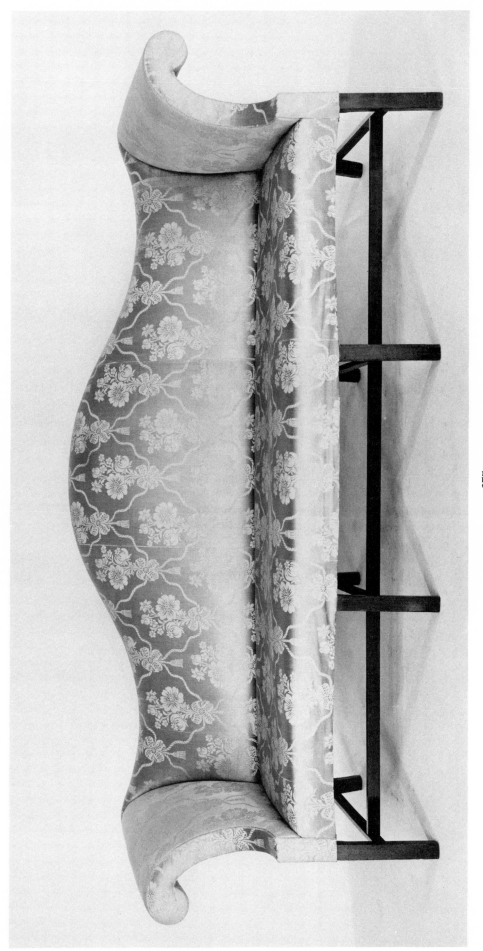

275

276 · SOFA
Mahogany
Newport 1812
Made by Adam S. Coe

This unique, documented sofa, the only known work of Coe, proves again that American furniture styles survived their allotted span by several decades, even in centers of expert craftsmanship. Here is no vestige of the classical revival upon the square molded legs and boldly curving lines, which typify the Chippendale era. Even the nails are the rosehead, hand-wrought type rather than the square-cut type invented about 1795. They fasten the original linen cover which partly obscures the inscription in red chalk: *Made by Adam S. Coe April 1812 for Edw W. Lawton.* Coe was born January 23, 1782. A Newport deed for land dated 1810 is inscribed *Adam S. Coe cabinetmaker.* In 1847 he sold the land *with a workshop to Simeon Hazard cabinetmaker.* Coe later joined the firm of Robert P. See and Company, lumber merchants, and died December 12, 1862.

Coe's patron, Edward W. Lawton, a merchant, was born in Providence on November 1, 1786. The Newport *Mercury* announced his marriage to Mary Engs on May 16, 1812, a month after this sofa was made; it was probably for his own use. Lawton died March 16, 1867.*

Most unusual is the construction of the upper frame, which may be disassembled by means of pegs and holes in the arms and back; this would facilitate shipment and upholstering, too.

The seat rails and backframe are hard maple, and the arms are white pine and cherry; the last-named wood matches the corner blocks and medial braces in the seat frame.

The upholstery is green silk damask, Italian, early eighteenth century.

Height 39½"   Length 78½"   Depth 26"

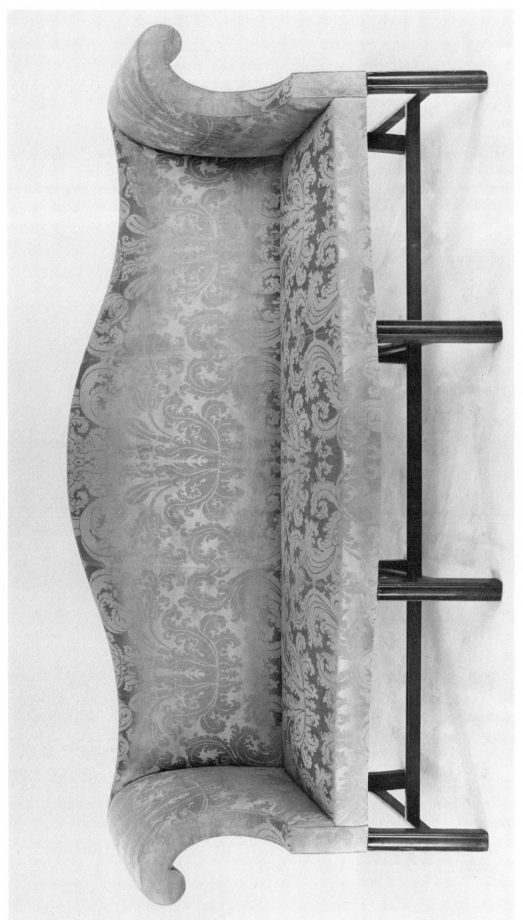

276

277 · BASIN STAND
Mahogany
Massachusetts 1770-1780

Portable washstands were English inventions of the mid-eighteenth century and were soon repeated in the colonies, taking on the features of regional furniture. The drawers were for wash-balls and other toilet articles, and often the soap was kept in a wooden sphere mounted upon the shelf above them. Public baths were open in large cities, and tin baths are mentioned in inventories of large households. But bathing facilities generally were scant.

In the furnishings sold by Aaron Burr to Sir John Temple in New York in 1797, an unusual mention of a washstand occurs:

> N⁰ 8 small Bed Room
> 1 Wash hand Stand
> 1 Venetian Blind
> 1 Carpet and Piece of dᵒ not received
> 1 Mahogany Bedstead and Crimson damask Curtains
> 7 Prints
> 1 Bed Quilt
> 1 Rose Blanket
> 1 Dressing Case, Glass &c.

Height 32″   Diameter 11¾″

278 · BASIN STAND
Mahogany
Newport 1760-1775
Probably Made by John Townsend

Bason stands illustrated in Chippendale's *Director* provided a new form for incidental furniture that was eagerly adopted, proof of which fact remains in the plethora of *wig stands* in use today, adapted to other uses.

Their form is stereotyped, but the Newport version here is quite different in the choice of successive fluted pillars and turned balusters and in the five-toed paw feet. Three horn bosses are fixed under the bottle shelf.

The raised panel on the pedestal was likewise used on the kettle stand Figure 288; and double concentric rings outline the soap-cup openings as they outline the slide of the kettle stand.

Height 32″   Diameter 10¾″

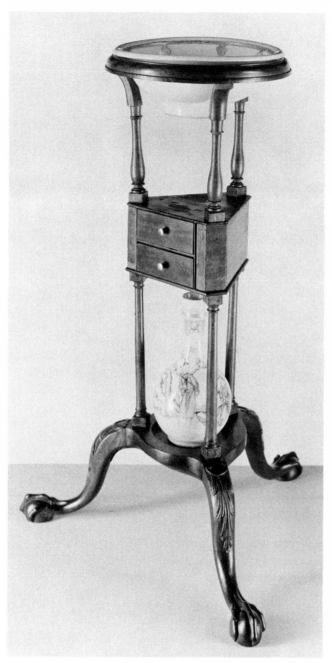

277

278

279 · CANDLESTAND
Walnut
Philadelphia 1740-1750

As characteristic as the shape of Figure 280, the heavy snake feet and club-shaped pillar of this stand are forms associated with mid-eighteenth century furniture.

John Paschall, "practitioner in Physick late of Darby," possessed in 1779: "A walnut Stand, five chairs, & Sweeping brush, a walnut oval Table, a small pine table, a walnut oval table, a small dᵒ, a small oak Chest."

Height 26¼″   Diameter 21½″

280 · CANDLESTAND
Walnut
Philadelphia 1740-1750

This candlestand is the epitome of conservative design that was repeated on larger tea tables contemporary with the tall-back chairs of Queen Anne pattern. The plain dish top and flattened ball at the base of the pillar were elaborated to conform with the Chippendale taste in the following decades.

When George Simpson died in Chester, Pennsylvania, in 1744, an inventory of his property showed:

One stand for a Candlestick	£0 .. 6 .. 0
6 Black walnut Chairs at 8/	2 .. 8 .. 0
one Walnut oval Table and dressing Box	2 .. 10 .. 0
6 Black Chairs at 6/ one Arm dᵒ at 8/	2 .. 4 .. 0
one Spice Box	1 .. 0 .. 0
6 red Chairs at 4/6 Chocklet Colour at 3/ one red one 4/	2 .. 6 .. 0
one white Arm'd Chair at	0 .. 4 .. 6
one Tea Kettle 18 a pewter Tea pot 5/ Coffee Pot 2/6	1 .. 5 .. 6
6 Cheny Tea Cupps & Saucers 12/6 Stone Dᵒ 3/	0 .. 15 .. 0

Height 27″   Diameter 22¼″

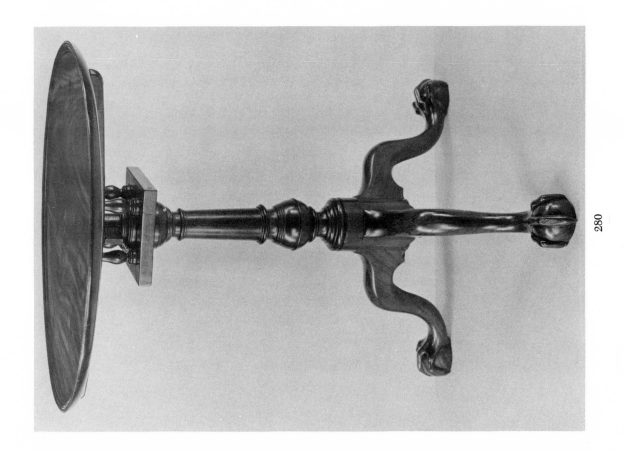

280

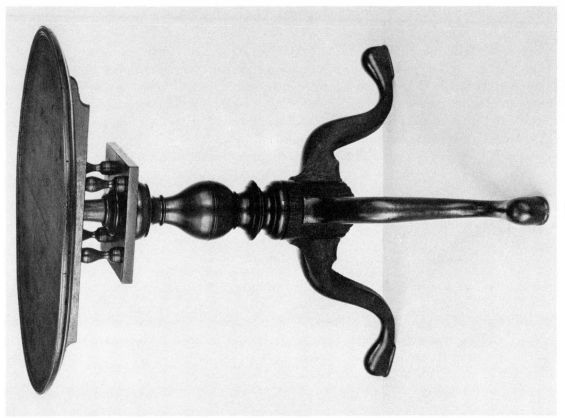

279

281 · WALL BRACKET
Yellow Pine, Stained
Philadelphia 1760-1775

Almost no small wall ornaments remain today by the colonial master carvers whose furniture is so well known. This rare and spirited example was inspired by an English engraving published in 1758 by Thomas Johnson, carver and designer of furniture. It first appeared in *One Hundred & Fifty New Designs Consisting of Ceilings, Chimney Pieces, Slab, Glass & Picture Frames, Stands for China, etc. Clock and Watch Cases, Girondoles, Brackets, Grates, Lanthorns, etc., etc. The Whole well adapted for Decorating all kinds of Ornamental Furniture in the Present Tastes*. No text or titles for the plates is included, but the book is dedicated to "Lord Blakeney, Grand President of the Anti-Gallican Association and the rest of the Brethren of that most Honourable Order." The latter is a gesture to the reaction then prevailing against the Louis XV style in England. A smaller book, *Twelve Gerandoles*, was designed by Johnson in 1755.

This wall bracket has been published before and described as mahogany, but the hard pine of its fabric makes its origin definitely American.*

Height 16½"　　　　　　　　Width 12¾"　　　　　　　　Depth 5⅜"

Ex Coll. CHARLES A. CURRAN

282 · DESIGN FOR WALL BRACKET
by Thomas Johnson
London 1758

This engraving, here identified as the pattern for the wall bracket in Figure 281, was first published in 1758 and again in 1834 by John Weale, who erased Johnson's name from the title page and from each of the illustrations and substituted that of Chippendale. The title of the latter became *Chippendale's One Hundred and Thirty-three Designs of Interior Decorations in the Old French and Antique Styles . . . London, published by John Weale 5 High Street Bloomsbury 1834*. Therein the order of Johnson's original pages was changed and a few were omitted.

To quote R. S. Clouston, who wrote of it in 1903: "This is perhaps the most daring and brazen piece of literary forgery extant . . . No one has to my knowledge ever before taken an important book published only about eighty years previously and re-issued it as by another author." Weale's edition has been the cause of endless confusion and misapprehension to writers and students in recent years. A comparison of Thomas Johnson's original book with that ascribed to Chippendale shows the graver's line on matching plates to be identical, proving that the old plates were reworked for the pirated edition.

This illustration was Plate 49 in both books and is one of five brackets on that page.

283 · CANDLESTAND
Mahogany
Philadelphia 1760-1775

In this candlestand may be seen all the essential features that are required to satisfy the demands of quality in a Philadelphia-made piece. The pillar rising from a flattened ball to a fluted shaft supports the revolving bird cage built of vase-shaped balusters — all significant for identification of origin. The top of strongly figured Cuban mahogany has eight divisions of cyma curves intercepted by a straight molding, as an English table might have. Its size is calculated to suit the base with an exacting nicety. Although lacking the elaborate carving of several larger tables, this candlestand is surpassed by none in elegance of perfection of outline.

Height 28½"　　　　　　　　　　　　　　　　Diameter 24¼"

283

282

281

284 · CANDLESTAND
ONE OF A PAIR
Mahogany
Massachusetts about 1778

This handsome candlestand, one of three examples known, is turned and carved with expert precision. An old inscription fixed under the pedestal reads: "This stand was made about the year 1778 for Samuel Hunt of Charlestown by an English soldier taken prisoner at the *Battle of Bennington* Aug. 16, 1777 by the N. H. and Vt. Militia under Gen. John Stark . . . The old Secretary is also his make."

Even without that clue to attribution, certain details of the design are unmistakably of Massachusetts origin; namely, the carved rat-claw foot grasping an egg, the slender, fluted Corinthian column, and the spirally reeded urn. Novel features are the scale-like pattern over the knees, the vertical row of tiny leaves edging the rim, and the pointed canopy beneath it. A pin-point punching on the background of the carving gives emphasis to it. As in other stands, a thick, threaded wooden screw holds the shaft in the tripod base.

Height 28″   Diameter 9½″

285 · CANDLESTAND
Mahogany
Newport 1760-1780

The fluted and reeded column that John Townsend adapted from classical architecture to shafts and legs of tables was repeated by Thomas and Stephen Goddard on their furniture in the Federal period. The spiral-fluted vase of this table's pillar was a further proof of the Townsend-Goddard hierarchy of skillful cabinet-work. The cockleshell-and-husk embellished the knees of many Newport chairs in the Queen Anne period.

Height 26¼″   Diameter 16¾″

286 · CANDLESTAND
Mahogany
New York 1760-1775

This candlestand is different in so many ways from all others in the collection that the regional features it presents are obvious. The club shape of the pillar, the squat bird-cage posts, and the lambrequin center to the leaf knee carving belong to many New York tables and chairs (Figures 149, 337, 382). The acanthus leaves are cut with graceful precision, without the ingratiating softness of Philadelphia carving. The dolphin feet and the carved surface of the top hark back to English furniture design. The simple triangle of iron under the pedestal omits the concave shape found on other tripod tables.

Height 27⅞″   Diameter 21¾″

287 · CANDLESTAND
Mahogany
Probably Charleston 1765-1780

This candlestand, like the tea table in Figure 382, is of especial interest because of its nonconformity to the orthodox design of Philadelphia pieces. The novelty of the turned pillar, round at the base and tulip-shaped above, the heavy molding of the close-scalloped top, and the oversized claw feet, when compared to Figure 283, of similar size, or to many larger tea tables, is apparent.

This candlestand has been tentatively attributed to Charleston because it was found there and because it has a different aspect. The work of many known southern cabinetmakers is yet to be identified; that of Thomas Elfe long has been known for its fine Chippendale design.

Height 27½″   Diameter 25½″

284

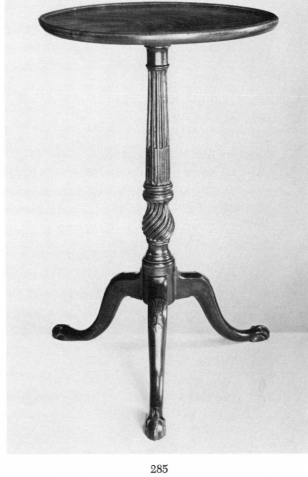

285

286

287

288 · KETTLE STAND
Mahogany
Newport 1770-1785

Following its early popularity in England, the ceremony of tea-drinking in the American colonies soon became a ritual that finally culminated in the famous Boston Tea Party.

The cabinetmakers were equal to the demands of their patrons and produced ingenious and special furniture for the service of tea.

This kettle stand was probably made by John Townsend, whose labeled Pembroke table (Figure 311) employs the same pierced frets, incised crosshatching, molding profiles, and long, wonderfully exact dovetails at the corner joints. The sliding teacup shelf is cut diagonally to parallel the incised ornament on the narrow frieze. The pillar screws into the pedestal by means of a wooden threaded post, and a wrought-iron brace strengthens the underframing.

Height 29⅛″   Width 8⅜″   Depth 8⅜″

Ex Coll. COLONEL JOHN COOKE, *Newport, R. I.*

Ex Coll. PHILIP FLAYDERMAN

289 · KETTLE STAND
Maple, Painted
New England 1760-1780

When John Adams' present of tea from Philadelphia to his wife Abigail in Braintree went by mistake to Mrs. Samuel Adams, "its prodigious cost" gave him concern to retrieve it; thus, even fervent patriots were unwilling to forego the delights of tea drinking during the embargo on imported luxuries. This kettle stand, although less ambitious than Figure 288 and Figure 290, has a marble top that indicates hot punch and posset were concocted there as well as tea. The open storage chamber and drawer, innovations here, suggest a French night table, but the phlegmatic stance of the fluted legs and deep drawer are indisputably American. The "tortoise shell" painting in black and red was a favorite decoration in Massachusetts since the seventeenth century.

Height 29″   Width 12¼″   Depth 12½″

290 · KETTLE STAND
Cherry
Probably Connecticut 1775-1785

Like a block-front, shell-carved cherry chest of drawers, Figure 171, this kettle stand, another version of Figure 288, has Rhode Island features, but may be of Connecticut origin. It has the same pierced gallery and paneled tripod base of the stand attributed to John Townsend, who spent several years during the Revolution in Connecticut. The refinements of the Newport example are lacking here.

Height 30″   Width 9¾″   Depth 9¾″

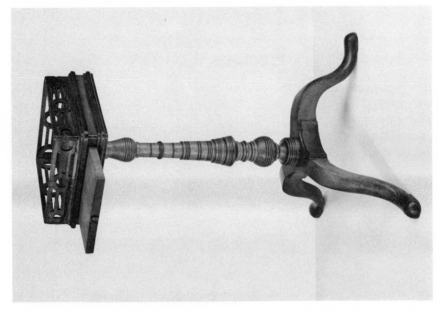

288

289

290

291 · STOOL

Walnut

Philadelphia 1730-1750

Early in the eighteenth century the role of stools and chairs was reversed; stools were then no longer as popular as they formerly had been. Stools continued, however, to follow the pattern of contemporary chairs with which they were made ensuite, as in England.

Here the web foot and knee carved with a pointed tongue are clues of the stool's origin.

The upholstery is silk brocade, French, Louis XV period.

Height 17″   Width 20⅝″   Depth 15″

292 · STOOL

Walnut

Newport 1720-1740

This is a fine early stool, lower than the average; it has characteristic details of Newport design in its pronounced curves and wafer-sharp pad feet (see Figure 98).

The maple slip-seat frame is covered with flame-stitched crewel embroidery.

Height 12½″   Width 18″   Depth 14½″

293 · STOOL

Walnut

Probably New Jersey 1740-1750

The slender frame and legs and the incised lambrequin upon the knees of this stool set it apart for the excellence of its conception. No blocks are used in the frame.

The upholstery is silk needlework, eighteenth century.

Height 15″   Width 18½″   Depth 14½″

294 · STOOL

ONE OF A SET OF FOUR
Walnut

Philadelphia 1755-1756

Made by John Elliott

The carving of this stool, one of a set of four, is more typical of Philadelphia work than is its pad foot; the latter was seldom used in Philadelphia, where the slipper, web, and trifid feet were favored. The stools were originally made for Charles Norris and later were used at Stenton in Germantown.

The upholstery is red leather.

Height 18″   Width 20¾″   Depth 16½″

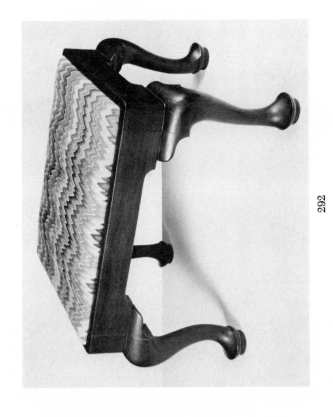

291

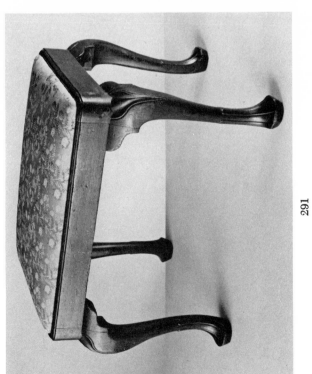

292

294

293

295 · STOOL
Walnut
New York 1730-1750

This stool is identified by its thickset cabriole legs and broad leaves flanking a plain yoke. Manhattan tables have the same details (see Figure 358).

The slip seat is covered in brown cowhide.

Height 16½″   Width 21″   Depth 17¼″

296 · STOOL
Mahogany
Philadelphia 1755-1765

After 1750 *ship and cabbin stools* were offered for sale by Philadelphia upholsterers, but their differences are obscure now. Colonial stools are rare and often are unrepresented in important collections.

This unique stool has the doweled leg and seat-rail construction and carving of the finest chairs (Figure 91) transitional in style between Queen Anne and Chippendale.

The upholstery is yellow silk damask, Italian, late seventeenth century.

Height 15⅝″   Width 20⅜″   Depth 15⅞″

297 · STOOL
Mahogany
New York 1770-1785

This simple version of the Chinese Chippendale style is a rare phase of colonial stools and is related to the back stools Figures 162 and 164.

The seat frame is cherry, braced with white pine blocks. The upholstery is wool moreen, probably English, eighteenth century.

Height 18″   Width 19½″   Depth 16¾″

298 · STOOL
Walnut
New York 1750-1760

The squared knuckles of the small claw feet and the carved pointed yoke, both repeated frequently on New York furniture, give this stool its special character. The seat frame and quarter-round blocks are walnut.

The overstuffed seat is covered with painted silk, Chinese, eighteenth century.

Height 16½″   Width 22″   Depth 16½″

295

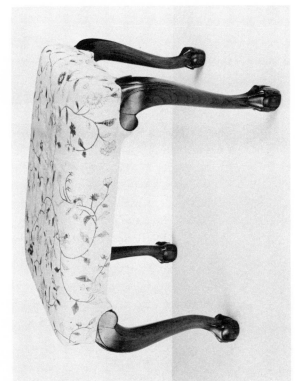

296

298

297

299 · BREAKFAST TABLE
Red Gum and Birch
New York 1725-1740

This sprightly table recalls the observation in the Journal of Madame Knight after she arrived in New York from Boston in 1704 by horseback: "They are not strict in keeping the Sabbath as in Boston and other places where I hae been, But seem to deal with great exactness as far as I see or Deale with; They are sociable to one another and curteos and civill to strangers and fare well in their houses."

The red gum of the turn-up top and frame was long known as bilsted in New York. One frequent record of it was made in the inventory of Effingham Townly, October 22, 1730, in Manhattan:

One Round Billstead Table	£0.10.0
One Bed stead, Curtains, Iron Rods Calico	6.10.0
One Billstead Cupboard	2. 0.0
One large table	0. 0.9

Another inventory, that of Elias Van Voorhees in 1779, included birch, not often mentioned:

Burch Table	£1.0.0
Lucking glass	4.0.0
Cubbord	5.0.0
10 Chairs	12.0.0

Height 26½"   Diameter 31"

300 · BREAKFAST TABLE
Walnut, Painted
New England 1720-1740

An endless variety of moderate-sized tables was invented by early eighteenth-century joiners in New England. These tables probably had as many uses as their changes of design; but, lacking the raised edge of the tea table top or the scale of a dining table, they may well be named *breakfast tables*. Here the chamfered legs, octagonal in form, give a slender outline that seems ubiquitous in New England furniture. The eight-sided top is cut to follow the same plan. The deeply molded skirt in cyma curves is well calculated to offset the angular forms of the top and base.

Height 26½"   Width 32½"

299

300

301 · BREAKFAST TABLE
Curly Maple
Newport 1735-1750

The cyma curves on the corners of the porringer top of this table are repeated on the skirt, making a more consistent design than a so-called tavern table usually displays. The result is a satisfying one, without any extraneous elements to impede its functional purpose. The maple surface is partly covered by black paint.

No blocks were used in the inside frame.

A portrait of Francis and Saunders Malbone painted by Gilbert Stuart at Newport between 1770 and 1772 shows the two young men seated at a table of this kind.*

Height 26″   Width 38″   Depth 24″

302 · BREAKFAST TABLE
Walnut
Newport 1735-1750

Their convenient size and shape recommended tables of this kind for many uses, and the venture cargoes of furniture taken from Newport by sea captains likely included many of them. Payment by barter and exchange was frequent; Job Townsend, Jr., in 1757 made three tables and a corner cupboard for Benjamin Dunham, the barber, for which he received: "A Year's Shaven, a Cutt Wigg, a foretop to the Wigg, and 24 feet of Mahogany."*

The corner blocks in the frame are thin strips of cedar.

Height 25½″   Width 33″   Depth 23½″

301

302

303 · BREAKFAST TABLE
Walnut
Probably Virginia 1710-1725

"From England, the Virginians take every article for Convenience or ornament which they use, their own manufactures not being worth mentioning." These words of a French traveler in Virginia suggest the different economy of North and South, the scattered craftsmen, and the lack of regional "schools" of design.*

Seventeenth-century features of this table are the turned stretchers and the heavy top, straight-edged, with ruled joints. The short drawers at either end are likewise early in construction, built of hard pine and walnut, with side runners to slide upon. The stout turnings and thick pad feet are unfamiliar shapes in northern furniture. The shape of the legs is the latest evidence to date the table in the Queen Anne period.

| Height 27½" | Width (open) 49" | Depth 43½" |

304 · BREAKFAST TABLE
Maple
Massachusetts 1725-1740

In Massachusetts and Rhode Island maple drop-leaf tables with cabriole legs and pad feet were made in a wide variety of sizes, from small tea tables to dining tables. The leaves when extended formed an oval or circular top and were supported by swinging gates, as the earlier turned tables were built. Many are known, and they are admirable for their practical design and graceful lines.

This one has two features not seen on some other tables; namely, the convex, scalloped skirt at the ends and the hocks on the ankles of the pad feet.

The gates are maple, and the inside frame is soft pine.

A maple table was listed in "An Inventory of the Estate of Mrs Mary Fay late of Boston Widow — Dece'd — taken July 29th 1730   Viz.

1 Small Oval Table of Maple & a Table Board	£1-0-0
1 Walnut frame Looking Glass	6-0-0
3 Brass Candlesticks Snuff Dish & Snuffers	1-5-0
1 pair of Wooden Sconces 3/. 2 Chairs & a Cushion 5/	0-8-0"

| Height 25½" | Width (open) 31½" | Depth 31¾" |

303

304

305 and 306 · BREAKFAST TABLE
Mahogany
New York 1750-1760

The unique aspects of this table propose some difficulties in its attribution. In construction it is like no other yet seen; the table top may be manipulated to full round, half round, or upright to fit in a corner. The lid when raised affords a deep well for storage. A New York card table, made with a triple top and a concealed storage well, is another example of an enclosed frame.*

In design, the bold, undulating shell and the triple-knuckled feet are similar to the chairs made for Robert and Margaret Beekman Livingston; the sprigs of foliage are like the carving on the Van Cortlandt chairs (Figure 26).

The interior lining is hard maple, white oak, and soft pine.

Colonial furniture was deemed an important bequest and was specified for each heir, as in the will dated 1768 of Caleb Pell, of Pelham Manor: ". . . to my dau. Ann Laurence a negro girl and a Mahogany Chest of Drawers and a dining table and a tea table to be made for her. To wife Mary a negro boy and woman & child . . . also my two best beds with furniture and a Mahogany tea table and one dozen best chairs . . . my silver plate, Looking glass and China."

Height 25″   Width (open) 35½″

305

306

307 · BREAKFAST TABLE
Mahogany

Newport 1760-1770

This table has features of John Goddard's documented work (Figure 373); namely, the cabriole legs which are sharp edged and square in section and the elongated sinuous claws grasping an oval ball. The swinging gates are made of white pine and sycamore. The double leaves when extended make a round top finished with a cyma or so-called thumb molding.

Height 28″   Width (open) 37¾″

308 · BREAKFAST TABLE
White Walnut, or Butternut

Massachusetts 1725-1745

Drop-leaf tables with round or oval tops and cabriole legs were turned out in a wide variety of sizes by New England cabinetmakers. The largest ones were dining tables; and the smallest, like this one, were for tea, breakfast, candlesticks, and other ready uses in rooms of limited dimensions. Their sovereign recommendation was apparent when the leaves folded to a foot or less in depth.

The legs of this table are distinguished by an extra shaping of the knees and the flattened ball under the pad foot. A dressing table, Figure 328, has the same outline of a raised knee.

The frame is soft pine.

Richard Williams, of Worcester, Massachusetts, owned in 1751 "one walnut Table £0.12/, one Side Table 2/, one Tea Table 3/, Two Pictures in Frames 8/, one walnut Table 16/, one Looking Glass 30/, one Silver Can 70/."

Height 26″   Width (open) 27½″

307

308

309 · BREAKFAST TABLE
Mahogany
Philadelphia 1750-1760

This unusual table fits neatly into a corner when the leaf is closed and the fourth leg is swung into the oak backframe. It is a variant of the square double drop-leaf tables which were widely popular in the colonies. The deep apron and heavy legs show the characteristic proportions of furniture of the middle and southern colonies.

Height 28½″   Width (open) 44½″   Depth 22¼″

310 · BREAKFAST TABLE
Mahogany
Massachusetts 1750-1760

A single drop leaf was rarely made on an American table where two leaves, if any, are customary. It had a dual purpose as a side table and, when extended, as a breakfast table. The absence of a leaf gave advantage to the profile of the frame. The claw feet are widespread, matching those on labeled Boston furniture by several makers.

This frame and the gates which swing out to support the drop leaf and make a square top are white pine.

Among many possessions left by John Ball, in Worcester, and listed on January 21, 1756, were:

1 Looking Glass £1:14:8 1 ovel Table 8/	£2: 2:8
1 Chamber Table 4/8 1 Low Chest of Drawers 8/	12:8
1 High Chest of Drawers 16/ 12 Slit Back Chairs 12/	1: 8:0
1 Bed & furniture with Red Curtins	5: 6:8
2 Lamps 2/ 3 Candlesticks 2/8 1 White Table 1/4	6:0
7 White Chairs 4/8 1 Iron Pot 7/ 1 Dish Kittle 1/	12:8
1 Table Cloath 4ᵈ 1 pair Scale & Weights 8ᵈ	1:0
1 Pigeon Net 10/ 1 meal Chest 8ᵈ	10:8

Height 28″   Width (closed) 14¼″   Depth 28½″

309

310

311 · BREAKFAST TABLE
Mahogany
Newport 1760-1780
Made by John Townsend

The Chinese Chippendale style was interpreted with peculiar grace by John Townsend, who labeled this breakfast table; it is one of a known pair. The rectangularity of the Chinese style is maintained by the square-edged, plain top and the straight, crossed stretchers. As a balance, the stop-fluted legs and symmetrically pierced braces are admirable light touches used by Townsend on several gaming and breakfast tables.

The use of maple for the drawer lining and curly maple in the frame, in addition to ash, is unusual; tulipwood and pine are customary there.

Inside the drawer, a printed paper (see Figure 399) states: *Made by John Townsend, Newport.* The date *1743* inscribed in ink is obviously not contemporary.

Height 26¼″   Width (closed) 20¾″   Depth 33½″

312 · BREAKFAST TABLE
Mahogany
Philadelphia 1760-1780

The name *Pembroke* was first used in Hepplewhite's *Guide* of 1788 to describe a drop-leaf table. But seventeen years earlier the following entry was made in the account book of Reuben Haines, cabinetmaker, as credit to Samuel Preston Moore, then building and furnishing his house in Philadelphia: "Reced May 9 1771 of Doctor Moore Six pounds for a pembroke Mahogany Table . . ." This is the first and earliest use of the name applied to a table known to the author. The identical piercing of this scalloped stretcher and the shaped leaves may be seen in Plate LIII of Chippendale's *Director* of 1762.

The underframing is of poplar. Unlike most tables of this form, no drawer is in the apron.

Height 28⅛″   Width (closed) 25½″   Depth 30″

311

312

313 · BREAKFAST TABLE
Mahogany
Philadelphia about 1790

This Pembroke table in the Chippendale style probably was made by Adam Hains at the end of the eighteenth century. The general form and many small details are like his signed table (Figure 314). Only the short spade feet give a clue to a date which coincides with Hains' first work. The son of Heinrich Hähns, a German immigrant tavern keeper in Philadelphia, Hains learned his craft well.* The felicity of the curved and straight members of this table, its fine moldings, no less than the rich surface pattern of Santo Domingo mahogany, produce a triumph of quiet elegance.

The underframing is made of ash and cedar. The latter is combined with poplar for the drawer lining.

Height 28″   Width (open) 42″   Depth 32⅛″

314 · BREAKFAST TABLE
Mahogany
Philadelphia 1790-1795
Made by Adam Hains

In 1775 ". . . a handsome Pembroke table" was offered for sale in Philadelphia. This is an early use of the name later adopted by Hepplewhite to describe a breakfast table in honor of his patroness, Lady Pembroke. This table, likewise of handsome design, was made belatedly by Adam Hains (born 1768) and is branded on the underside of the drawer by the inscription which is pictured in Figure 400.

Records indicate that Hains worked until 1815 as a cabinetmaker. The *Pennsylvania Journal* in 1792 stated: "An attempt was made one evening last week, to set fire to the house of Mr. Hains, Cabinet Maker, in Third near Vine street." Five years later "The Cabinet Manufactory of Adam Hains is removed from No. 135 North Third street to No. 261 South Market street."*

The sides and the wings of the frame of this table are made of oak; the drawer is framed with cedar and poplar.

Height 28½″   Width (open) 40½″   Depth 30″

Ex Coll. HOWARD REIFSNYDER

313

314

315 · CHINA TABLE
Mahogany
New York 1765-1775

The Gothic revival of the eighteenth century, epitomized by Horace Walpole's fabulous castle, Strawberry Hill, fan vaulted with lathe and plaster, echoed through all the decorative arts. In Chippendale's final edition of the *Director*, in 1762, Gothic pinnacles, cusped arcades, and traceried arches were smuggled into Chinese and rococo patterns then becoming outmoded. This rare table, with pointed arches forming its gallery, dates from that period of mingled tastes. Its lower structure is more robust than that shown in Plate LI of the third edition of the *Director*, although a solid rim is indicated there similar to those adopted by Philadelphia makers (Figure 316). Only one other matching New York table is known, but it has lost its pierced gallery.*

A heavy medial strip of white pine braces the underframe.

Height 28⅜″   Width 32″   Depth 17½″

Ex Coll. LUKE VINCENT LOCKWOOD

316 · CHINA TABLE
Mahogany
Philadelphia 1770-1785

Rectangular tables with a gallery edge were made to display precious china and to protect it from casualties. The shape of this one is taken from the first edition of Chippendale's *Director*, Plate XXXIIII — its serpentine top faithful to the engraving, its "stretching rail" and legs made somewhat more solid as supports. The carved rope edges and bead-and-reel vertical moldings on the legs are repeated on the armchairs made for the old United States Supreme Court Chamber by Thomas Affleck, in Philadelphia.*

Height 27″   Width 32½″   Depth 21½″

315

316

317 · DINING TABLE
Walnut
Probably Virginia 1725-1740

Few large dining tables for eight people or more dating from the early eighteenth century are seen. Unwieldy as mobile furniture, they have been mutilated or perhaps converted to other uses. For this important table a southern origin is suggested by the stout cabriole legs and the vertical molding which flanks the arched skirt. These features, in conjunction with the hard pine gates and inner frame, justify a Virginia attribution. The joint of the leaves fits into a shallow thumb molding later in date than the ruled joint (see Figure 303) and typical of early-eighteenth-century tables.

Height 28″	Width (open) 60″	Depth 50″

318 · DINING TABLE
Walnut
New York 1730-1750

New York furniture in the Queen Anne style often has a distinctive slipper foot not unlike a modern platform shoe. It was carved on case pieces, chairs, and tables. Its stout simplicity recommends it for hard usage, unlike the fragile waferlike feet often favored in New England. The thumb molding of the leaf joint is here extended to almost a circle.

The underframing is chestnut, and the drawer lining is tulipwood.

The inventory of Baltus Van Kleeck, of Flushing, in 1786 mentions:

1 Mahogany Dining Table	£3. 0.0
3 Mahogany sitting chairs	2. 5.0
3 black walnut do.	0. 8.0
10 China plates	0.10.0
Black walnut table	3. 0.0
6 Siting chairs	0. 6.0
1 large arm chair	0. 4.0
1 Windsor chair	0. 8.0
Chest and Draws	6. 0.0
1 Writing Desk	0.16.0

Height 28¾″	Width (open) 65″	Depth 54″

317

318

319 · DINING TABLE
Walnut

New York 1755-1765

The narrow, raised claws on the feet of this handsome table and the flat leaf carving recall the details of the signed furniture of Gilbert Ash, a New York joiner active from 1748 to 1770. The same details are repeated on the Johnson chair (Figure 149).

The frame is oak and cherry.

A similar table may have been in the estate of G. W. Leslie "late of Jamaica . . . April 23, 1784:

> 8 Mehogany chairs with damask seats
> 1 mehogany square Table
> 1 Tea D? 2 Tea boards
> 1 sett Red burnt China
> 1 Mehogany Scretore
> 8 pictures"

Height 26¾"   Width (open) 50¼"   Depth 36¼"

320 · DINING TABLE
Mahogany

Philadelphia 1750-1760

Dining tables of the mid-eighteenth century were usually the drop-leaf form, with swinging legs for support when opened. This form was an English design, and frequently several identical tables were extended end to end for greater accommodation. Similar tables were made in New England and New York. The Philadelphia features of this table are the indented corners of the top, the heavy, slow-curving cabriole legs, and the inset ends of the frame, flanked by a molded edge.

The frame and gates are ash and hard pine.

Height 28½"   Width (open) 60¼"   Depth 54"

319

320

321 · DRESSING TABLE
Walnut
New Jersey 1720-1735

The date and design of this dressing table, not much later than Figure 322, place it among the rarities of the period. The feet repeat an English variation of the Spanish foot not often followed by colonial cabinetmakers. The stamped brasses are contemporary.

The drawer sides are of unusual weight, five-eighths of an inch thick. The interior is made of hard pine; the back is oak.

Height 29¼″   Width 34½″   Depth 20½″

322 · DRESSING TABLE
Walnut
New Jersey 1720-1735

In construction and shape, the body of this dressing table follows the William and Mary period. It is dovetailed at the corners, to which the legs are pinned as the trumpet-shaped turnings always were about 1700. In construction this is the earliest of the Queen Anne dressing tables and shows the first use of the cabriole leg on case furniture, separated from the body by a molding. The fine Spanish feet with molded ankles are noteworthy.

The lining is made of hard pine.

Height 29¾″   Width 33½″   Depth 20⅝″

321

322

323 · DRESSING TABLE
Curly Maple
New Jersey or Philadelphia 1740-1750

The flat, chamfered corners of case pieces may be seen in northern-made furniture, but here the figured maple is combined with ash and tulipwood as secondary materials; moreover the high-arched skirting and widespread carved shells would place the origin of this example in the New Jersey or Philadelphia region.

Two of Jonathan Gostelowe's labeled chests of drawers have flat, fluted corners, but stand on ogee bracket feet which are a more nearly complete expression of the chamfered shape. The stools made for Charles Norris in 1756 (Figure 294) by John Elliott have shells similar to these. Maple was the choice for some of William Savery's labeled chairs in the Queen Anne style.

Height 27½″   Width 31¼″   Depth 20″

324 · DRESSING TABLE
Walnut
Probably Maryland 1745-1760

This dressing table is midway in style between two high chests of drawers, Figures 192 and 199, which are tentatively attributed to a Maryland origin, because it has some features of each of them. Another dressing table owned originally by the Barroll family of Baltimore is likewise allied to Figure 199. The pierced skirting is an innovation unknown on other dressing tables. A candle slide similar to those on contemporary bookcases is centered above the top drawer.

The drawer sides are tulipwood, and the bottoms are white cedar.

The *Maryland Gazette* for January 31, 1760, announced that "Henry Crouch, Carver, from London, Now living in Annapolis Makes any sort of Carv'd Work for Houses and ships."

Height 31″   Width 33½″   Depth 20″

323

324

325 · DRESSING TABLE
Walnut

Massachusetts 1740-1750

The baroque style that moved with whirlwind force from Italy to France and then to England and her colonies spent itself finally in the sober orderliness of the scrolled pediment, shell and leaf carving, and bombé and block-front shaped furniture. Seemingly that is far from the hand of a Bernini or a Vanbrugh, but it does epitomize the most individual and ambitious cabinetwork of the colonial period in New England.

This dressing table, with its front surface cut in several depths, recalls the famous three-pile Italian velvets that are world masterpieces; this table is relatively of that rank in American furniture. The effect of highlight and shadow is artfully contrived by the convexed and concaved surfaces of the block-front drawers and by the wide projecting pad feet that balance the deeply incurved legs.* The fanciful outline of the original brasses suggests a cockatoo in profile. The top is scalloped at each of the four corners. The interior is all of white pine.

Height 32¼″   Width 36¼″   Depth 21¼″

Ex Coll. Arthur W. Wellington

326 · DRESSING TABLE
Walnut

Probably Newport 1740-1750

The attribution of an unfamiliar piece of furniture is often made by the recognition of features which occur in better-known furniture. The principal clues here of the Newport school are the carved knees, the sharply tapering cabriole legs, and the use of chestnut and maple for interior construction. Less certain in origin are the center shell on the shallow skirting and the scalloped corners of the top, as they parallel the same procedure elsewhere, especially in New York. The pierced brass handles, imported from England, are more often seen on Chippendale furniture and find an early use here.

More than fifty cabinetmakers, chairmakers, and carvers were active in Newport before 1800, and the work of many of them is yet to be identified.

Height 32″   Width 40″   Depth 22″

325

326

327 · DRESSING TABLE
Cherry
Connecticut 1740-1760

The feature of especial interest in this dressing table is the scalloping of the top, seemingly to offset its severe frame and to parallel the curves of the skirt. This fanciful shaping of curves is a reminder of another Connecticut piece — Benjamin Burnham's signed and dated (1769) desk, made in Norwich, the interior drawers cascading in three successive banks of curved fronts. The drawers, lined with white pine, are unusually crude and heavy; the backs are three-quarters of an inch thick. The side of one drawer is inscribed: *Mary A Woodruff from Mother.*

Height 32″   Width 39″   Depth 24¼″

328 · DRESSING TABLE
Maple and Birch
Massachusetts 1740-1760

The ability and independence of the cabinetmaker are evident in the design of this dressing table, which incorporates several rare features; namely, the inset corners of the top, the concaved fan and skirting, and the broken curve of the cabriole legs. These innovations do not violate the conservative principles of New England cabinetwork, but add distinction to this unusual example. The ribbed fan often was carved on furniture in Connecticut* and New Hampshire, too, as well as in Massachusetts (see Figures 157 and 229).

The top is made of birch, and the frame is maple. The drawer linings are chestnut and soft pine.

The name *dressing table* was a variant of *low chest of drawers* and *low case of drawers*, as in the following inventories:

"Inventory attached of Wᵐ Myrick ᴴᵘˢᵇ· of Hardwick . . . December 22, 1758
a Looking Glass 4/   a Low Case Draws 21/ 4ᵈ   £ 1. 5.4.0
2 Common Chests 5/ 4ᵈ   a Comon Table 6/   1 small Dᵒ 4/   0.15.4.0"
"Inventory of Eleazer Reft ᴳᵉⁿᵗ· of Mendon
High chest, low chest of draws"

Height 32″   Width 35″   Depth 19¼″

327

328

329 · DRESSING TABLE
Walnut
Philadelphia 1740-1755

The first hint of the Chippendale style is given in the fluted quarter columns at the front corners of this well-proportioned table, introduced among the shells, scalloped outlines, and overhanging top of the earlier period. It is this combination of early and late details which gives infinite variety to colonial furniture.

The interior is made of tulipwood; the back is hard pine.

Height 29¼″   Width 35″   Depth 22¾″

330 · DRESSING TABLE
Walnut
Philadelphia 1760-1775

The unusual width of this dressing table is compensated by the airy disposition of the carved streamers on the drawer and skirting. The latter is similar to the easy chair Figure 94. The heavy solid shells on the knees are earlier than the other ornamental details, reminders of the Queen Anne period (see Figure 323).

The drawer linings are hard pine and white cedar.

A contemporary use of the name *dressing table* is found in the list of possessions left by Ann Yarnall, "Late of Springfield . . . the 1 day of the 8 Month 1780":

To a Walnut Chest and Dressing Table	£3. 0.0
To 12 Rush Bottom Chairs	2.10.0
To 6 Small and 2 Learge Windsor Chairs	3.18.0
To a Tea Chest, 5 sampler frames and Glasses	0.13.6
To a Tea Table, Cloths Press & a stand	3. 0.0
To a Box with knives & Forks, Watering Pott, looking Glass & 3 Whips	1.12.0

Height 29⅝″   Width 37″   Depth 19½″

329

330

331 · DRESSING TABLE
Walnut
Philadelphia 1765-1775

The shape of the scalloped skirting here recalls the simple curves of several looking glasses labeled by John Elliott, cabinetmaker. The squared knuckles of the claw feet are not typical of Philadelphia carving, but are more often associated with New York furniture (Figures 315, 340). The small size of this dressing table also sets it apart from other contemporaries.

The pierced fret brasses are exceptionally large and intricate.

The interior is made of tulipwood.

Height 29¼″   Width 33½″   Depth 21″

332 · DRESSING TABLE
Mahogany
Philadelphia 1765-1775

Here the Chippendale style is realized more fully in the consistently rich treatment of the skirting, drawer, and legs. The symmetrically carved shell from which the rocaille scalloping billows away is the last evidence of Queen Anne detail.

In two original bills in the Winterthur Collection George Claypoole, with whom the well-known cabinetmaker, Jonathan Gostelowe, learned his trade, charged "Mr. Greenberry Dorsy 1783 Octr 27 to a Mahogany Chamber table £10.1."; and three years earlier Mr. Dorsy purchased of Francis Trumble (who made the State House chairs at Independence Hall) "7 Round Top chairs at £6.2.6, 6 Fan back d° £3.6.0."

Height 30¼″   Width 34¾″   Depth 20¼″

331

332

333 · DRESSING TABLE
Mahogany
Philadelphia 1769

This dressing table is a pair with the high chest of drawers Figure 198 and, like it, is a spectacular achievement of expert carving and rococo ornament; although it does not show the pierced and undercut rocaille work of the larger chest because of limitation of size, the reduced scale faithfully carries a comparable lavishness. Sprays of foliation on the corners are a notable exception to the usual fluting there.

The original cast hardware is an exceptionally elaborate combination of Chinese and rococo Chippendale ornament, a happy complement to the rich woodwork.

In some instances the rear legs of prime Philadelphia chests are not carved; that is true of this pair, of the Van Pelt high chest (Figure 195), and of Figure 197. The well-known Pompadour high chest is carved on all four legs. *

The drawer linings are made of tulipwood and white cedar.

Height 28⅜″   Width 37″   Depth 18¾″

334 · DRESSING TABLE
Mahogany
Philadelphia 1765-1775

The carving here creates another rich example of the Philadelphia style. It is nearly a pair with the high chest Figure 197, varied only by a rearrangement of the ornament. Both probably were from the same shop. The inset top shows the adoption of the moldings from the contemporary high chests as an alternate for the single-board top.

Contemporary names for the so-called *lowboy* were *chamber table, dressing table,* and *low chest of drawers;* the last named is mentioned often with *high chest of drawers,* the present-day *highboy*.

Height 31″   Width 33¾″   Depth 21½″

333

334

335 · CARD TABLE
Walnut

Philadelphia 1740-1750

The simple dignity of this shapely table is enhanced by the carved trifid feet and the cast, gilded hardware on the drawer. The top, when open, has a plain surface.

The back of the frame is oak, and the drawer is lined with tulipwood and white cedar.

Height 29″   Width 36″   Depth (closed) 15½″

336 · CARD TABLE
Mahogany

Probably New Jersey 1725-1750

This very small card table has the wide overhanging top of maple "porringer-top" tables of the same period, rarely seen, however, except on New York tables. The top surface is flat, without depressions at the corners for candlesticks or ovals between them for coins. The original green baize covers the center.

The frame is hard pine. The drawer lining is chestnut.

An early mention of mahogany is made in the inventory of Richard Stillwell "of Shrewsbury in East New Jersey . . . Taken in New York as found in his house there . . . May 17, 1744 . . . In the Garrot":

1 Round Mahogany Tea Table	£2. 0.0
9 Old Cain Chairs	.18.0
1 Couch Bed Pillow & Rugg	2. 0.0
Old Iron & Sundry Old Trumpery in the Clock Loft	1.10.0
8 Chairs with Leather Bottoms	. . .
Window Curtains & Vallins	3.10.0
Sundry China in the Beaufett	7.15.0
38 oz. Old Plate	15. 4.0
Total Estate	£5732

Height 28″   Width 31″   Depth (open) 23″

337 · GAMING TABLE
Mahogany

New York 1740-1755

The crosshatched and leaf carving of the legs of this table is like that of a side chair, Figure 149, attributed to Gilbert Ash. The exaggerated overhang of the top may be seen again on other contemporary New York gaming tables (see Figure 339) with the same bold corners. The back frame is cherry, and the swinging gate of the supporting fifth leg is oak.

In Martin Van Bergen's account book, an entry under April 7, 1764, is made "To Gilbert Ash for Stuffing 8 Chair Seats £4.8.0." Gilbert Ash's name was listed among the Freemen of New York, September 13, 1748, as a joiner and carpenter.

Height 28½″   Width 32¾″   Depth (open) 32″

335

336

337

338 · GAMING TABLE
Mahogany
New York 1770-1780

The forceful curves of New York furniture are well displayed in this gaming table and are complemented by the strong, knuckled claw feet and florid carving on the front legs. A pair of tables which matched this one, except for the gadrooned edge along the skirt, was owned by Judge John Berrien at Rocky Hill, near Princeton, New Jersey, in the house where General Washington sat for his "most natural likeness" to Joseph Wright in 1784; the tables, by tradition, were presents from Washington to his host, Judge Berrien, at that time.

The top of this table is covered with old red baize except for the reserves for candlesticks and coins. It is square when open. A secret drawer, concealed by the swinging gate at the left, is customary in tables of this type and origin; here the original drawer is missing, but the runners remain.

The frame is made of tulipwood.

Height 28″   Width 34″   Depth (open) 33½″

339 · GAMING TABLE
Mahogany
New York 1765-1780

This table is unlike its more typical Manhattan contemporaries (Figures 338 and 340) because it lacks their serpentine form and is smaller in size. It presents an impression of strength in its stout proportions and squared feet; the forthright carving has a novel wheel motif incorporated in its rocaille ornament. The rear legs are uncarved.

The interior framing of cherry holds a secret drawer which is covered by a swinging gate of white oak.

This table is one of a pair. It was found in New Jersey.

In the inventory of Frederick Wolffse, on March 7, 1776, were:

    a Card Table Mahogany
    Corner Closet
    a Stand or small table of Boilstead
    a small painted Tea Table
    Two Windsor Chairs & 9 rush bottoms
    Four large painted Frame Pictures

Height 25¾″   Width 33¼″   Depth (open) 31″

338

339

340 and 341 · GAMING TABLE
Mahogany
New York 1760-1775

All through the eighteenth century gaming tables were popular forms of furniture and followed patterns of regional design and construction which now provide clues to their origin. The large scale of this Chippendale table, its bold curves, and its carved ornament are earmarks of the New York school. The secret drawer in the backframe was customary in New York tables, but has been observed only twice in Philadelphia ones.

Mahogany was lavishly used in colonial furniture, more often cut from the solid wood for deeply curved case pieces than in England. A rich bequest of imported wood is noted in a will probated January 19, 1769: "Thomas Jackson, late of Jamaica but now of New York. To my dau. Fanny Jackson of Jamaica 50,000 ft. of mahogany, part of 70,000 consigned to me by obligation of Richard Armstrong of Honduras."

Height 27″   Width 34⅜″   Depth (open) 33½″

340

341

342 · CARD TABLE
Mahogany
Philadelphia 1765-1780

This table has an extraordinary delicacy in outline and carving without loss of the vigorous spontaneity germane to the work of master craftsmen. It is an effortless triumph of the Philadelphia Chippendale style. A structural feature which is atypical of American card tables is the undulating edge imposed upon a straight frame, although it is occasionally seen on fine card tables in Philadelphia. More customary is the plain mahogany playing surface without covering of baize or inset gaming and candlestick sockets. Upon tables of this form made in New England and New York, the frame and top are parallel, as a rule.

The backframe is oak, and the inside structure is white cedar.

Height 27⅜″   Width 34″   Depth (open) 32¾″

343 · CARD TABLE
ONE OF A PAIR
Mahogany
Philadelphia 1760-1770

Observation of numerous pieces of Philadelphia Chippendale furniture reveals the insularity of cabinetmakers working in adjacent shops. Each one developed his own style that produced wide variations within one period and area. This card table is a sober English form in the round, buttressed corners and the carved volutes along the apron. The straight-lobed acanthus leaves down the knees are far from the fluttering leaves and broken curves on the Gratz high chest (Figure 198) or the *sample* side chair (Figure 138). The punched background and cut edges of the carving match the armchair Figure 51.

The top of the table is mahogany without pockets for coins or inset corners for candlesticks.

The wood of the backframing is hard pine, and the hinged gate is ash. The drawer is lined with tulipwood and cedar.

Height 31″   Width 32″   Depth (open) 31″

Ex Coll. HOWARD REIFSNYDER

342

343

344 · CARD TABLE
Mahogany
Philadelphia 1765-1780

The quiet elegance of this card table is identified with several side chairs and tables (see Figure 129) with similar carving on skirt and knee, but finished with hairy paw feet. They are in the finest tradition of Philadelphia Chippendale carving.

The framing and drawer lining are tulipwood. The original handles, probably imported from England, are in the Adam style then current abroad.

An original bill at Winterthur rendered to Mr. Samuel Meredith by George Claypoole, a well-established cabinetmaker, "1772 Dec. yᵉ 5ᵗʰ," lists:

	£	s	d
to 18 Mahogany Chairs	54	0	0
to two ditto dining tables	9	5	0
to two ditto card tables	12	0	0
to a ditto breakfast table	4	0	0
to a Walnut Cloaths press	11	0	0
to a Walnut Case of drawrs	9	0	0
to a bedstead, with two posts Mahogany	3	10	0
to a Cornish for ditto	1	15	0
to two window Cornishes	1	4	0
to a Mahogany Sopha	5	0	0
to a mahogany Easey Chair	2	5	0
to a Set of Casters for the Chair	0	4	6
to a Mahogany plate tray	1	0	0
to a frame for a Marble Slab	3	0	0

Height 29½″   Width 33½″   Depth (open) 32″

345 · CARD TABLE
Mahogany
Philadelphia 1760-1780

In Philadelphia carved paw feet are a hallmark of the finest Chippendale furniture. They appear on a firescreen (Figure 236), a set of four chairs (Figure 129), three of the *sample* chairs (Figure 138), the famous Cadwalader gaming table, and a sofa originally in President Washington's drawing room in High Street, but now in Independence Hall. Three known sets of ornate brass andirons, one of them at Winterthur, are cast with the same feet.

A concealed drawer behind the swinging rear leg is a rare feature in Philadelphia, although customary in New York tables. Among known tables, only the Cadwalader paw-foot card table has a similar secret drawer.

Oak and hard pine are used for the framing.

Height 28⅜″   Width 32″   Depth (closed) 15½″

Ex Coll. CADWALADER

344

345

346 · CARD TABLE
Mahogany
Philadelphia 1775-1785

The tapering legs of this table place it in the final years of the Chippendale period, when the classical revival, starting in England about 1760, belatedly reached American cities after the Revolution. Its fullest expression coincided with the appearance of furniture pattern books by Shearer, Hepplewhite, and Sheraton.

Here the gadrooned edge, cut with cameo sharpness, matches those on Adam Hains' signed breakfast table, Figure 314; and the carved corner brackets match those of the other breakfast table attributed to him, Figure 313. No baize or gaming pockets intrude on the playing surface of the top; the plain surface is typical of Philadelphia card tables.

The underframe is hard pine; the swinging gate is oak; and the drawer lining is tulipwood.

Height 29″	Width 36″	Depth (closed) 17¾″

347 · GAMING TABLE
Mahogany
Newport 1760-1770

Lacking the variety of entertainment available to all classes today, leisure hours in the eighteenth century provided problems not easily solved. Backgammon, chess, and cribbage were games for two; dicing and loo admitted more participants, and gaming tables, often made in pairs, furnished the means of indulging the sport.

The top, when open, shows square insets for candlesticks and oval pockets for coins surrounded by old red baize. The scrolled, or French, feet are rare examples in colonial furniture of an exact detail simpler than those on the Philadelphia *sample* chairs.

The carved shell and husk, flanked by scrolls, was a favorite device of English carvers in the George II era and appears on numerous walnut chairs and tables in the Percival D. Griffiths Collection.* In Newport and New York it was carved on tables and chairs (Figures 26, 106, 326, and 354).

The table is lined with white pine, and the back is maple, stained red.

A rare mention of an exact use of a gaming table occurs in the inventory "taken Septem' 1754 by Mess Ebenezar Storer, Samuel Grant and Samuel Adams":

House and Land at Boston the late Mansion house of	
Arthur Savage deceas'd	£4500——
a baggamon *[backgammon]* Table	1..10
a black Walnut framed Glass	18——
10 Cain Chairs wth yallow damask Cushings	
at 4.10/ 2 great D^o at 9£	63——
1 folding board 30; 2 Glass Sconces best Room 90/	6——
a tea Table and sett burnt China	18——
1 Prospect Town Boston	1..5
3 yallow China Window Curtains	2..10
5 black Walnut Chairs 30/	7..10
1 finiered black walnut Table	5——
a green Silk quilt 25£	25——
a black Walnut Table maple frame	2——
a Jappand Case for Maps	1——
a Chimney Glass	18——

Height 28¼″	Width 31¼″	Depth (closed) 15¼″

346

347

348 · CARD TABLE
Mahogany
Newport 1760-1770

On first sight, this card table matches in profile the tea table made by John Goddard in 1763 for Jabez Bowen (Figure 372). But the long claws do not stand clear of the oval ball foot, and the carved shells on the knees have more lobes. The combination of pad feet with claw feet is almost the rule for Newport furniture made to stand against the wall and may be seen on high chests, pier tables, dressing tables, and several gaming tables. No candlestick or money pockets were cut into the top surface. The square section of the legs is typical of Newport cabinetwork.

Under the top is inscribed: *For my daughter Catherine   A B Greene from A H Greene.*

The frame and gates are maple; strips of chestnut fasten the top to the sides of the table.

Height 27″	Width 33¾″	Depth (open) 33″

349 · CARD TABLE
Mahogany
Massachusetts 1770-1785
Made by Benjamin Frothingham

The leanness of this table and its delicate, widespread claw feet would suggest its origin was Massachusetts. Thus it is not surprising to read inside the drawer *Benjⁿ Frothingham Cabbinet Maker in Charlestown N E* upon a printed label, signed *N. H. Scp.* for Nathaniel Hurd, the well-known Boston engraver and silversmith, 1730 to 1777.

Charlestown, near Boston, is remembered for the Battle of Bunker Hill. Frothingham, the son of a Boston cabinetmaker, was active from 1756 to 1809. During the Revolution, when he served as a Major of Artillery, the British burned his house, shop, and barn in Walker Street. Well before 1789 he was re-established and received a visit from his friend and recent Commander, President Washington.*

Other labeled furniture by Frothingham includes a handsome block-front chest of drawers, a reverse-serpentine desk, and an inlaid Hepplewhite sideboard, all well made and conforming to the sober taste that Boston generally favored.

This card table is lined with white pine and maple.

Height 34⅛″	Width 34⅛″	Depth (open) 33½″

348

349

350 · MIXING TABLE
Maple, Painted Black, and Tile
Massachusetts 1720-1740

Tile or marble table tops were not marred by strong or hot liquids that have left wooden tops so grievously scarred. The Biblical subjects of the seventeenth-century Dutch tiles here may not have served to inculcate sacred lessons upon the gathered company, as Benjamin Franklin recommended similar tiles might do around a fire opening.

That the tiles were a part of the original top is certain by the construction of the table which has a cradle of white pine to support the weight of the top. The light scale and simplicity of the frame are typical of Massachusetts.

Height 27¼"   Width 29"   Depth 19"

Ex Coll. FREDERICK WHITWELL

351 · MIXING TABLE
Mahogany and Marble
New York 1735-1745

The dished top of gray marble suggests that its purpose was the service of spirits. The candle slides were useful to hold lights for meticulous concoctions. A drinking table might well describe this piece. A peg at each corner of the wooden top holds the marble firmly. This table is a rare and fine example of the Queen Anne period. It is related in design and construction to Figure 367.

Thin, vertical strips of white pine hold the inside corners.

Daniel Gautier, a Freeman in the New York lists of 1731, advertised his joiner's work frequently. In 1748 his will included:

    8 Black Wallnut Chairs
    1 Black Wallnut square Tea Table
    6 Black chairs
    1 Square Boylstead Tea Table
    1 Mahogany Tea Table   Round
    Two India Pictures
    4 Gilt frame Pictures
    6 small Pictures with Glass before them
    Two Silver Tankards, 7 silver Spoons, 1 Silver Pint Mug, 1 silver sugar tongs
    Two pair of Andirons 1 thereof with brass knobs
    2 pr. Mens Coffin Handles
    5 Doz. and 8 pair Childrens Coffin handles
    9 Doz. Mens Coffin handles
    1 Green Rugg
    2 old suits Curtains

Height 24"   Width 27"   Depth 15¼"

350

351

352 · TABLE
Curly Maple
Rhode Island 1720-1740

This table, with its top and apron scalloped on four sides, was planned to stand free of the wall, as earlier stretchered tables stood. The round-cornered top was used on so-called tavern tables of Newport origin. The strong cyma curves of the deep skirt, developed with especial skill in Newport, indicate the early talent of that school prior to the famous shell and block-front style.

In the long, straight-sided slipper feet there are subtle differences of shape from the slipper feet carved on New York, New Jersey, and Philadelphia Queen Anne furniture (Figures 97, 293, and 318).

Height 27″   Width 41½″   Depth 24″

353 · TABLE
Walnut and Marble
Massachusetts 1720-1740

In spite of the imposing size of this center table, the simple treatment of the frame, supported on light-scaled cabriole legs imparts a sense of restraint and delicacy which, by frequent repetition has become a tradition of Massachusetts design. Herein are some aspects of a tea table (Figure 365) from the same region, although the feet vary in shape and changes in the skirting prove the variety to be found in closely similar pieces.

The top of mottled red and gray Brescia marble is an example of the foreign marbles used in the American colonies. Other instances are the dark-yellow Siena marble framing the parlor fire opening at Marmion, in Virginia, and the top of the large side table which Thomas Affleck made for the Pennsylvania Hospital.*

Two medial braces under the top and the lining of the frame are soft pine. Stamped into the latter is *I. Hill,* probably the name of the maker. In the Boston *Gazette* for January 15-22, 1733, John Hill is mentioned in a different context: "There is newly erected in the Town of Boston, by Messieurs John and Thomas Hill, a Water-Engine at their Still-house, by the Advice and Direction of Mr. Rowland Houghton drawn by a Horse, which delivers a large quantity of Water twelve Feet above the Ground. This being the first of the kind in these Parts, we thought taking Notice of it might be of Publick Service, inasmuch as a great deal of Labour is saved thereby."

Height 30½″   Width 52½″   Depth 27½″

352

353

354 · SIDE TABLE
Walnut and Marble
New York 1740-1750

This table may be identified as of New York origin by a comparison with other furniture owned and used in Manhattan for two centuries. The deep cyma-molded frieze, chamfered at the corners, matches the side table from the Verplanck Mansion at 3 Wall Street, Manhattan. The legs are elongated versions of the Van Cortlandt chairs, the embellishment of cockleshells and husks and the heavily webbed claw feet being identical. An inside frame of cherry is braced with vertical blocks of white pine.

The gray marble top has a deeply molded and channeled edge, scalloped at the corners.

Height 29¼″   Width 53¾″   Depth 29″

Ex Coll. ROBERT WEIR, New York

355 · TABLE
Walnut and Marble
New York 1750-1760

On this center table, the ruffling of short cyma curves that trims the apron and the exaggerated knuckled feet are repeated on several New York tables either singly or together (Figures 306, 358, and 367). The effect of fine simple elements well assembled is an imposing one.

The marble "slab" so described on contemporary inventories and bills is of native gray and white marble.

The construction of the inside frame follows an English practice, often repeated in New York furniture, of diagonal corner strips set into the frame; in this case they are made of cherry, fixed to an ash lining.

Height 29″   Width 48″   Depth 25″

354

355

356 · SIDE TABLE
Mahogany and Marble
Massachusetts 1760-1775

Chippendale's *Director* furnished many ideas to the colonial craftsmen, and for this table the cabinetmaker referred to Plate CXCVI in the third edition, dated 1762, and used one of three "Gothick frets" illustrated there. In Philadelphia and New York, where a small-scale fret appears on the frieze of many high chests, they are always backed with mahogany. The open pattern on an enlarged scale provides a rare feature of this table. It serves to fulfill the promise of the author ". . . that every Design in the Book can be improved, both as to Beauty and Enrichment, in the Execution of it."

On several Massachusetts chairs (Figures 154 and 156) the same pattern of carving was used for the legs and feet.

The top is native white marble, its straight edge cut into quarter circles at the front corners. The backboard of the frame is cherry.

| Height 27¼″ | Width 32″ | Depth 19¼″ |

357 · SIDE TABLE
ONE OF A PAIR
Mahogany and Marble
Philadelphia 1760-1775

A few exotic shapes appear in colonial furniture which perhaps were made for a special position or purpose. This pair of tables is unique and probably flanked a sideboard table in a dining room. Inspired by Chippendale's Chinese designs, the interlaced frets at the corners are an ingratiating addition to the tables' severe outline.

The top is of gray Chester County marble. The inside framing is hard pine.

| Height 32¼″ | Width 21½″ | Depth 13¼″ |

Ex Coll. HOWARD REIFSNYDER

356

357

358 · SIDE TABLE
Walnut and Marble
New York 1760-1775

The rounded corners and undulating curves on the skirt of this table resemble several other tables with New York histories. The hairy paw feet, illustrated four times in Chippendale's *Director*, are observed more often on Philadelphia furniture (Figures 90, 138, 236, and 345) and less often in New England (Figure 55 and Figure 151). The underframing of cherry and the corner blocks cut in vertical strips of soft pine are typical woods in New York construction.

Mrs. James Alexander, the mother of the Earl of Sterling, lived in Broad Street, Manhattan, until her death in 1760. Her will lists some extraordinary furnishings: "To dau. Catharine Parker, one dozen and four crimson Damask chairs, and crimson Damask window curtains, the Looking Glass, the marble tables that now are in the Dining Room, the square table with the china thereon, in the Blue and Gold Leather room. Also ½ of all the china and glass in the closets, the Mahogany Dining Table, the next in size to the largest, the Mahogany Clothes Chest and also my wench called Venus and her two children, also my long silver salver; a silver Tea kettle in the large back room with the feather bed, Bolster and pillows bedstead and furniture belonging thereto, and my third best carpet and all my pictures not given to my other children, also £100 to buy furniture for a bed."

Height 29″	Length 48″	Depth 24″

359 · SIDE TABLE
Mahogany and Marble
Philadelphia 1760-1775

Side tables of this type were made as early as the Queen Anne period in the principal centers of cabinetmaking from Massachusetts to the Carolinas. The form was inspired by English and Irish tables of similar design. Marble tops were favored for the service of food and for mixing beverages. Few American side tables were so handsomely carved. The broad scale of the egg-and-dart and gadrooned moldings, the trefoil cartouche and leaf carving are admirably suited to the generous size of the frame. The carved leaves that fall nearly to the claw feet are turned over along the edges in a manner favored by Philadelphia carvers. The top is a slab of imported Brescia marble with a square-cut edge.

The back of the table is oak and yellow pine. The latter wood in vertical strips braces the inside corners.

The table was originally owned by the Norris family. Deborah Norris married George Logan, and in 1782 they took possession of Stenton, the house of his famous ancestor James Logan.*

Height 34″	Width 40½″	Depth 26⅞″

Ex Coll. CHARLES A. CURRAN

358

359

360 · SIDE TABLE
Mahogany and Marble
Philadelphia 1760-1770

It is difficult to establish concise dates for American period styles inasmuch as they often overlap. This table at first glance represents the fullest expression of Philadelphia Chippendale design. However, exactly the same ornament on the legs, as well as the central shell, appears on Queen Anne chairs (Figure 30 and Figure 116) and tables. The carved rocaille background of the frame and the tattered shells at the corners provide the later date for the table.

The underside, with three medial strips, is mahogany. The top is Chester County marble flecked in dark and light gray.

Height 30½"   Width 52"   Depth 25¾"

361 · SIDE TABLE
Mahogany and Marble
Probably Charleston 1760-1775

This "sweld front" table may well be one of the little-known masterpieces of Charleston origin. It was acquired at auction in South Carolina a gèneration ago and was owned there until lately. A torn paper under the top is inscribed: *Jn ——— Wyers*. The underframing wood appears to be pine or cypress and ash, woods which, together with cedar and mahogany, are often mentioned in the account book of Thomas Elfe, an important cabinetmaker in Charleston between 1748 and 1775.* In his shop numerous "handycraft" slaves were employed; and the list of his clients, and what they ordered, is an impressive one.

On February 3rd, 1772, he charged James Smith "for a Mohogany Bedstead Eagles, Claws, and knees, with Castors   £10

On May 6th to John Drayton	A Side Board Table	£10
	One p. Table	£26
May 30th to Benjamin Lewis	Double Chest of Draws	£80
December 23rd to Langford Nicholas	Library Book Case	£110
December 23rd to Alexander Chovin	a Scollop'd Tea Table	£24
	a China Tea Table	£30
February 8th 1773 to Jeremiah Theus	6 Mahogany picture frames	£30"

Other names in his book were Henry Laurens, president of the Continental Congress; Eliza Lucas, later Mrs. Charles Pinckney, who first introduced the culture of indigo into South Carolina; and two Signers, Arthur Middleton and Thomas Heyward.

Height 37⅛"   Width 48"   Depth 25"

360

361

362 · SIDE TABLE
Mahogany and Marble
Massachusetts 1760-1775

The angularity of the Chinese Chippendale style is relieved in this unique table by the reversed curves of the skirting, to which the gray marble top conforms in shape. Another, although inconspicuous, mark of distinction is the carved chain applied to the edge of the skirt. The legs are fluted, but not half-reeded as well, as was done on Townsend's work in Newport.

The top is mottled gray and white marble. The back of the frame is white pine.

Height 30½″   Width 56¾″   Depth 27½″

363 · SIDE TABLE
Mahogany and Marble
New York 1760-1775

A "Sideboard Table" of the same shape and with identical pierced frets as this was a popular and practical Chinese design that Chippendale published in all three editions of the *Director* from 1754 to 1762. The molded surface of the square legs and the gouge carving along the apron edge were the New York maker's inventions. The frame is veneered on the front and sides with branch mahogany for added richness and is a reminder that this ancient technique of cabinetmaking, although uncommon in the Chippendale period, continued sporadically until its widespread adoption during the classical revival.

The inset top is gray marble.

The underframe is cherry, braced at the corners with vertical strips of soft pine, like the side table seen in Figure 354.

Mrs. Alexander's will, quoted in part under Figure 358, also bequeathed "to my youngest daughter Susanah £1,500 being a sum equal to what has been advanced to her other sisters by my late husband and myself in his life time, also the two Large Looking Glasses, and the two marble tables which are placed and stand near them, and the 18 chairs with green bottoms, and the green window curtains, all which are in the Great Tappestry Room above stairs also the 3 Sconces suiting the above glasses, and the 12 chairs with green bottoms which are in the little front parlor below stairs, also the Looking glass and pictures that hang in the Old Parlor below, also the green Russell bed, and window curtains, and the green silk bed quilt."

Height 31¼″   Width 58″   Depth 28½″

Ex Coll. PHILIP FLAYDERMAN

362

363

364 · TEA TABLE
Cherry, Stained
New York 1730-1740

The deep frame, trimmed with an even scalloping of cyma curves, and the heavy knees upon which the elongated shell is mounted provide an interesting study of regional design when compared to Figure 365. The hock above the foot is a well-calculated mark of skillful work.

Height 26¼″   Width 27¾″   Depth 21″

365 · TEA TABLE
Walnut and Cherry
Massachusetts 1730-1740

In this table the restrained outlines and lightness of members are associated with New England and occur frequently in the early-eighteenth-century furniture made there. The frame has a straight, narrow frieze of curly-grained cherry; and the concaved rim of the top is indented at the corners as other tables of the period (see Figures 328 and 367).

Some idea of the types of tables in use in the homes of this period can be gotten from listings in inventories, wills, and other extant documents. In Boston, the inventory of Nathaniel Thomas' estate on December 10, 1745, mentioned:

1 Mahogany Table	£11.10
1 Tea Table	4.10
10 cane Chairs	15. 0
1 Round Table	1.10
One Silk Bed Quilt	12. 0
Chest of Drawers & Table	32. 0
One Looking Glass	8. 0
One Japan Box	.10
One Great Chair & Seven Small Ditto	4. 0
One Rount Table	4. 0
Trundle Bead Steed & Bottom	1. 0
one Easy Chair & Cushin	2. 0

Height 25″   Width 30″   Depth 20¼″

364

365

366 · TEA TABLE
Walnut
Massachusetts 1720-1740

The applied rim on the top of this table, not cut from the solid wood as in Figure 367, makes a strong profile for the wide, overhanging top. The latter balances the outcurving legs and lends stability to the composition of light, slender contours. The projecting apron, aligned to carry the sweeping curves of the legs, is a fortunate addition.

Height 25″   Width 27¼″   Depth 18½″

367 · TEA TABLE
Mahogany
New York 1750-1760

Rectangular tea tables and china tables with raised top rims were made before 1700 in the William and Mary style; they preceded round and square "turn-up" tables by half a century.

This table has some features of Figures 354 and 355 in the shaped skirting and flanking scrolls, but the carving shows an advance in date. The leafage on the legs and the heavy claws are repeated on other New York pieces of similar high quality.

The underframe has a medial brace and vertical corner blocks of soft pine.

Height 26½″   Width 31″   Depth 19⅜″

366

367

368 · TEA TABLE
Maple, Painted

New England 1720-1740

The independence of provincial cabinetmakers is shown in their interpretation of a style that departs from routine practice. This lively expression of the Queen Anne style is simplified to bare essentials, but achieves success in the bold rake of the legs, the inset skirt, and the applied cyma molding around the top, all calculated with a sense of proportion best suited to the purpose of the table.

The frame is held together with wooden pins, without blocks.

Old dark-green paint is worn to the maple surface along the edges.

Thomas Johnston (or Johnson) was an engraver and japanner in Boston, whose trade card is dated 1732. Evidence that he was still working five years before his death is found in a bill dated August 20, 1762, in which he charged Samuel P. Savage:

To Collouring & Varnishing a Table Son	£0..2——
To painting a Beadsteed green	0..8——
To fixing Roles on to Six large Mapps Collouring and	
Varnishing ditto	4..16..0

In May, 1763, he charged the same customer:

To painting y^r Silling Room Twice Over	£1..12——
To Gilt paper for a Screen	0..3..4

Height 25¼″   Width 24¼″   Depth 17¼″

369 · TEA OR DRESSING TABLE
Walnut, Inlaid

Massachusetts 1720-1740

In the Queen Anne period, small tables were made in great variety to serve for writing, gaming, reading, and dressing. This one might have been put to all of those uses, because of its mobility and fair size. The triple stringing of dark and light woods bordering the drawer front and top recalls several case pieces likewise inlaid with a star center (Figure 214). The drawer lining is white pine.

The brasses are a plain version of the bail form which preceded the intricately cut and pierced hardware after 1750.

Height 29″   Width 32¾″   Depth 20½″

368

369

370 · TEA TABLE
Mahogany
Massachusetts 1760-1780

A "tea bord," often noted on inventories and bills, was an essential piece of furniture for every fine colonial house. This table is one of three known examples having the frame and top scalloped in half-round bays, like miniature buttresses, as if to give special security to the tea service. No two of these three tables are alike. This one has the virtue of small size and carving in the advanced rococo style.* The construction of this form demanded the greatest skill of the joiner, whose light treatment of proportion and carved ornament suggest a Boston origin.

The concave, molded rim of the top is cut out of the solid board. Narrow strips of white pine fasten the top to the underframing.

In Wellfleet, on Cape Cod, February 26, 1783, Elisha Doane, Esq., left many unusual things, among them:

1 Mahog. Tea Table	£ 4. 4.0
1 carpett	10. 0.0
1 Mahogany Card Table	3. 0.0
1 large round Mahog. table	3.12.0
1 Large Japann'd Sarver	1. 4.0
4 qt. decanter	0.14.0
4 Doz wine Glasses 4/ a glass	2. 8.0
1 large looking Glass	8. 0.0
1 Mahog Desk & Book Case	12.15.0
1 Clock	7.10.0
6 Philadᵃ Round Green Chairs	2. 8.0
1 Carpet	10. 0.0
Bed & furniture of all Kinds	24. 0.0
Case Drawers	0. 7.0
Easy Chair	1.10.0
6 Chamber Chairs 36/. 3 Bed side Carpets 36/-	3.12.0

Height 27½″   Width 30″   Depth 19⅜″

371 · TEA TABLE
Mahogany
Newport 1765-1780

The conservative aspect of this table is markedly different from contemporary tea tables in other important colonial centers of furniture making; the absence in Newport of piecrust and pierced-gallery-top tables is remarkable in view of the superb card and dressing tables made there. Here the stop-reeded and fluted legs match John Townsend's labeled Pembroke table (Figure 311).

The apron is veneered mahogany on cherry.

Height 27″   Width 33¾″   Depth 23⅛″

370

371

372 · TEA TABLE

Mahogany

Newport 1760-1765

Probably Made by John Goddard

This table is made in every detail like another (Figure 373), the documented work of John Goddard. The tray top, from which the ogival curved edge is cut, is fixed to a frame of richly figured blister mahogany; the same rare wood, sometimes called plum-pudding mahogany, may be observed on the legs of a tripod tea table of Philadelphia origin (Figure 381). The legs are square in section, but soften somewhat at the ankles. Both tables have undercut claws, a tour de force of Goddard's carving, and identical carving on the knees.

Height 26⅝″   Width 32⅞″   Depth 19¾″

373 · TEA TABLE

Mahogany

Newport 1763

Made by John Goddard

To know the exact day and year, the maker, the place, and the first owner of a piece of colonial furniture is a rare circumstance indeed. And when that complete documentation can be attached to a triumph of cabinetmaking like the tea table here, the ultimate seems to be realized. A letter written by John Goddard, cabinetmaker, states that the table was finished on June 30, 1763, for Jabez Bowen in Newport.* Goddard and his brother-in-law John Townsend were the principal creators of the block-front and shell-carved furniture, so justly prized today.

Jabez Bowen was Colonel of the First Regiment of Militia of Providence County, 1776, and, as Justice of the Superior Court, was chosen to meet commissioners from other states in 1777. He was a member of the Council of War in 1781 and Deputy Governor of Rhode Island.

Height 27″   Width 32⅜″   Depth 19¼″

Ex Coll. PHILIP FLAYDERMAN

372

373

374 · TEA TABLE
Mahogany
New York 1760-1780

Among the rewards of studying American furniture is an appreciation of the infinite variations in each style. This table serves as an excellent example; for, aside from its rarity and elegance, it shows significant differences from the usual interpretation of the Chippendale style. The shape of the top and its extended edge, the gadrooned skirting carried around the corners without a break, and the elongated carving upon the legs are notable New York features.

The inside of the frame is cherry, three-fourths of an inch thick. The carving of the feet and legs is remarkably similar to Sir William Johnson's chairs (Figure 149), which are attributed to Gilbert Ash.

This table was originally owned by the Halstead family in Yonkers, New York.

In New York, Maria Farmer, widow, in her will dated March 3, 1788, bequeathed ". . . to Jacobus Lefferts my ebony tea table, to Gerard Walton my two eight square burned china bowls," and gave explicit directions for her funeral: "It is my desire to be buried in Trinity Church as near as possible to my late husband; also my funeral to be conducted by a genuine Dutch Minister; also by all the Ministers of the Church of England; also by the Reverend Doctor Rogers, and the assistant Minister of his Church; also by his Excellency the Minister of the United Netherlands; also by the Governor of this State and the Mayor of this City; also by Doctor Charlton, to all of whom I desire that scarves and gloves be given, as well as to my pall-bearers and in order that the procession may be conducted exactly conformable to the old Dutch custom I desire that the advice of Jeronymous Van Alstine be taken."

Height 27″   Width 34⅜″   Depth 21½″

375 · TEA TABLE
Mahogany
Philadelphia 1765-1780

The excellence of this table is evident in its perfect proportions, the skillful distribution of the carving, and the rich pattern of the mahogany. Although it is less spectacular than certain other Philadelphia tables, it would be difficult to match the several virtues which are its own. The deep "toad-back" skirting, as the carved gadrooning was described by cabinetmakers, is intercepted on the sides and ends by pierced shells and corners of fluid leaf carving. This is achieved with consummate grace.

Height 30″   Width 31⅜″   Depth 19⅝″

374

375

376 · TEA TABLE
Mahogany
Philadelphia 1765-1780

"Mahogany and walnut tea table columns" were advertised for sale to cabinetmakers in the *Pennsylvania Chronicle* in 1767 by Samuel Williams. This clarifies the purpose of the colonial table with a tripod base and circular revolving top, a form developed to perfection in Philadelphia.

This table, in the fully developed Chippendale style, is one of the handsomest of its kind. The pillar rises from a vase form rather than from the typical flattened ball seen on many Philadelphia tea tables; the encircling rocaille ornament, ruffled canopy above it, and guilloche band at the base are as expertly carved as the tripod.

Height 29½″   Diameter 29¾″

377 · TEA TABLE
Mahogany
Philadelphia 1765-1780

The emphatic character of this fine table is achieved by the stress given to its carved ornament, sharply cut with long, sure strokes, and isolated by plain surfaces. Emphasis is provided to the stability of the table by the oversize carved feet.

In the *Pennsylvania Chronicle* of June 26, 1769, William Crisp offered both carving and cabinetmaking "At his house in Arch-street, between Front and Second streets, Philadelphia, Choice MAHOGANY, Of all sorts, from the thickness of 5 inches to an half inch: The said CRISP follows the business of Carving in all its different branches, where Cabinetmakers, and others, may have their business done with care and dispatch, and have four months credit allowed them. Also follows the business of Cabinet-making, where town and country may be supplied, at the most reasonable rates."

Height 27½″   Diameter 33¼″

376

377

378 and 379 · TEA TABLE
Mahogany
Philadelphia 1765-1780

"A tea table upturned in the corner of the parlor" of Benjamin Franklin's house, mentioned in Watson's *Annals,* probably described a turn-up table of this shape. The rim or piecrust of the circular top is divided equally into ten straight and ten reversed cyma sections, instead of the customary eight, and is embellished with rosettes on the outside edge. The rarity of these innovations lends them an exceptional interest.

The thrust of the legs and the grip of the claws, so forcefully expressed by Philadelphia craftsmen, is particularly well shown here.

On every part of the table, in short — the top, the pillar, and the base — has been lavished the utmost care in shape and ornament, leaving nothing more to be desired.

Height 28⅛"   Diameter 34⅜"

378

379

380 · TEA TABLE
Mahogany
Philadelphia 1765-1775

A rare sense of quiet elegance in the ornament of this perfectly proportioned table places it in the first rank of quality. Even the small balusters of the bird cage are more slender than usual. The cartouche on the knees formed by two confronting C scrolls recalls the carved detail on Thomas Tufft's labeled lowboy.* The top is made of a single piece of superbly figured branch-grained wood.

Height 29"   Diameter 36¼"

Ex Coll. CHARLES A. CURRAN

381 · TEA TABLE
Mahogany
Philadelphia 1760-1775

Tripod-base tables with revolving, scallop-edged tops were among the most popular forms of the Chippendale period in Philadelphia. Varying from plain to the ultimate in rich carving, none ever seems to be without grace in its mass or line. This example, in development, stands between a simpler version Figure 380 and Figure 388. The well-planned and spaciously disposed carving of the base includes the *Garrya elliptica,* or pendant husk pattern, that became the signature of classical revival ornament in the years after the Revolution.

The piecrust edge, carved from the solid top, displays an unusual profile, its inner edge having a convex molding instead of a concave curve at its base.

Height 29¼"   Diameter 33⅛"

380

381

382 · TEA TABLE
Mahogany
New York 1765-1775

This table offers a valuable contrast to the more numerous Philadelphia tea tables. The differences are marked: The top does not turn, but tips up on a cherry block; the piecrust edge is incised with a pellet and diagonal line; the pillar has a vase-shaped base instead of a flattened ball; the panache of leaves and the ribbon-and-flower border may be seen on several New York pieces. The same border was carved on a set of chairs owned by Whitehead Hicks, a colonial mayor of Manhattan.

This table was found in Albany.*

In New York, mahogany and gumwood furniture were used together, to judge by the inventory of Cornelius Swartwout, taken July 10, 1787:

> 1 Mahogany stool
> 1 Bilestead [gumwood] Tea Table
> 1 do.   Stand
> 1 Mahogany dining table
> 1 Bilestead [gumwood] Chest
> 1 Mahogany tea chest
> Queens ware, Earthenware
> 1 Mahogany desk

Height 28½"   Diameter 32"

383 · TEA TABLE
Mahogany
Probably Massachusetts 1765-1780

This table and another one (Figure 382) are closely related in form to English tea tables; illustrations of them in well-known collections* follow the same outline of pillar and legs. The colonial interpretation gave it delicacy and regional character in the carving. The bird cage upon which the top revolves has been omitted, as is true in English tables occasionally. A curly-maple example with a bird cage and a similar vase shaft as these two is in the Franklin Collection, New York, and may have been made in New York.

The block on which the top tips up is mahogany.

Height 28¼"   Diameter 30"

382

383

384 · TEA TABLE
Mahogany
Newport 1760-1770

The especial interest of this rare table is the triangular shaft, with concave sides, flanked by fluted, engaged columns. A door on one side opens upon five wedge-shaped drawers which are lined with mahogany and cedar. The raised rim, cut from the solid wood, forms a dished top.

No piecrust edge tea table, the ultimate development in round-topped, pedestal tables, is known in Rhode Island furniture.

Height 28"   Diameter 32¾"

385 · TEA TABLE
Mahogany
Massachusetts 1765-1780

The carved pectin shells and rat-claw feet on this table, so often repeated on Boston-made furniture, serve to identify it. The revolving piecrust-top tea table, popular south of New England, was very seldom made in Massachusetts. In that state any revolving-top table with a pillared bird cage platform is a rare event. As in this case, the shape of the four, straight-sided balusters is universal in England, but almost unknown upon an American table; one New York example is in the Pendleton Collection, Rhode Island School of Design.

In the Boston inventory of Peter Minot dated 1757 a "Turn up Table" is listed, to describe a tilting top:

To a Mohogony Turn up Table	£10 . . ——
To 1. Coarded Bedstead & Coard	4 . . 10 .
To 3 Rugs & 1. Bed Quilt	20 . . ——
To 1. Mohogony Desk	30 . . ——
To 6. Leather Jack Chairs at £3.10.	21 . . ——
To 16. Pewter Plates at 10/	8 . . ——
To a pᵣ Brass Candlesticks	2 . . 5 .
To 1. Dozⁿ guilt glass fram'd Pictures	40 . . ——
To a Large Round Table	10 . . ——
To a Large Brass Coffee Pott	5 . . ——

Height 27½"   Diameter 35"

384

385

386 · TEA TABLE
Curly Maple
Pennsylvania 1765-1775

Maple is an uncommon vehicle for furniture in the Chippendale style. Here the molding of the top and deep turning of the pedestal utilize its best possibilities. The strapwork carving is no more than an incised outline. The extremely thin claws grasping the ball feet have raised joints which are repeated on another maple tea table (Figure 388).

This table may be the work of Jacob Bachman, a Swiss cabinetmaker who settled in Lancaster County in 1766.* A desk and bookcase lately acquired for the Winterthur Collection is a fine example of his carving.

Height 28½"   Diameter 37¼"

387 · TEA TABLE
Mahogany
New England 1775-1785

The stoutly shaped pillar of this table, fluted and reeded, at first sight recalls the work of Connecticut cabinetmakers. The small webbed claw feet and narrow scallop shells were often carved on Newport chairs; but like the block front which John Townsend introduced to Connecticut during the Revolution, they, too, may have been transplanted. No round-topped revolving tea tables made in Rhode Island are now known. A turn-up table on a triangular pedestal (Figure 384) is very rare.

Height 29"   Diameter 40½"

388 · TEA TABLE
Maple
Pennsylvania 1765-1775

This maple table, of curly grain on the legs and top, is probably of the same origin as Figure 386 and differs from it only in details. The sharply pronounced knuckles of the claw feet are exceptional, and the balusters of the bird cage are unusually thin. The turned pillar and deep curves of the cabriole legs are cut with rare judgment of line.

Height 27½"   Diameter 33¾"

386

387

388

389 · *(Label on chair, Figure 39)*

All Sorts of Chairs and
Joiners Work
Made and Sold by
William Savery,
At the Sign of the
Chair, a little be-
low the Market, in
Second Street.
PHILADELPHIA.

390 · *(Label on chair, Figure 134)*

Made and Sold by
THOMAS TUFFT
Cabinet and Chair Maker
Four Doors from the Corner of
Walnut Street in Second Street
Philadelphia

391 · *(Label on clock, Figure 207)*

MADE and SOLD, by
WILLIAM CONNELL,
CABINET-MAKER,
In *Third-Street,* the Corner of *Spruce-
Street,* PHILADELPHIA; where may be
had, all Sorts of Cabinet and Chair
Work, on the shortest Notice.

392 · *(Label on chest of drawers, Figure 173)*

KNEELAND and ADAMS
Cabinet and Chair Makers, Hartford;
Have constantly on hand, Mahogany Furniture, of the first quality; best warranted
Clocks and Time-Pieces; elegant Looking Glasses, of their own manufacturing; Cabinet
Work of every Kind may be had on very short notice, warranted equal to any made in
America.

393 · *(Inscription on double chest, Figure 181)*

Reuben Beman Junr

389

390

391

392

393

394 · *(Label on looking glass, Figure 267)*

JOSEPH WHITE
At the sign of the BOY and MORTAR,
A few doors above the upper Market House, on the
opposite side of the way, in Market Street,
WILMINGTON,
Has for sale, a complete assortment of
Looking-Glasses,
DRUGS, MEDICINES, PAINTERS COLOURS, &c
Which he is determined to sell at the lowest terms.

Printed by BONSAL *and* STARR, *Wilmington.*

395 · *(Label on looking glass, Figure 254)*

John Elliott

AT his Looking-Glass Store, the Sign of the Bell and
Looking-Glass, in *Walnut* Street, *Philadelphia*
Imports and sells all Sorts of English Looking-Glasses
at the lowest Rates.
He also new Quicksilvers and frames old Glasses
and supply's People with new Glass to their own Frames.

396 · *(Label on looking glass, Figure 264)*

JAMES & HENRY REYNOLDS,
CARVERS and GILDERS,
At their LOOKING-GLASS *Store, No. 56 Market Street,*
PHILADELPHIA,
EXECUTE all their various Branches in the newest and genteelest Taste
and likewise Sell all kinds of LOOKING-GLASSES in Carved and Gold, Cuya
and White or Carved Mahogany Frames, Ditto in Pediment, Mock Pediment,
Raffled or Ornamented Frames; Mahogany and Gold, Walnut and Gold, or
Plain ditto Swinging and Dressing Glasses: Also Bracketts for Patent Lamps
in Gold, White and Gold, or plain White of various Patterns.
PICTURE FRAMES, in Burnished or Oil Gold, White and Gold,
Black and Gold, or Plain Black, &c. in great variety
N. B.   Frames repaired, and old Looking Glasses new Silvered.

394

WILMINGTON,

Looking-Glasses,

395

This Looking Glass Store the Sign of the Bell
Looking-Glass, in _____ Street *Philadel*
imports and sells all Sorts of English Looking Gla
at the lowest Rates.

He also new Quickfilvers and frames, old Glasses
and supply's People with new Glass to their own Frame.

£8.12

Dichan Elliott

Wohnhaft zu Philadelphia in der _____ Straß,
_____ wo ein Schild heraus hängt
zur Belle und Spiegel, hat ein Stoor und großen Vor-
rath von allerley englischen Spiegeln, und verkauft sie
vor den niedrigsten Preiß.

Er macht auch neu Queckfilber und neue Rahmen
vor alte Spiegel, und machet neue Gläßer in der Leute
ihre Rahmen.

396

JAMES & HENRY REYNOLDS,
CARVERS AND GILDERS,
At their LOOKING GLASS Store, No. 50, Market-street,
PHILADELPHIA.

397 · *(Label on looking glass, Figure 266)*

John Elliott

AT his Looking glass Store, the Sign of the
Bell and Looking-glass, in Walnut-Street
in *Philadelphia,* imports and sells all Sorts of
English Looking-glasses at the lowest Rates.
He also new Quick silvers and frames old
Glasses, and supplies People with new Glass
to their own Frames.

398 · *(Inscription on sofa, Figure 276)*

Made by Adam S. Coe
Newport

399 · *(Label on breakfast table, Figure 311)*

MADE BY
JOHN TOWNSEND
NEWPORT

400 · *(Inscription on breakfast table, Figure 314)*

A. HAINS
PHIL^fecit

401 · *(Label on card table, Figure 349)*

Benjn Frothingham
Cabbinet Maker
in
CHARLESTOWN, N. E.

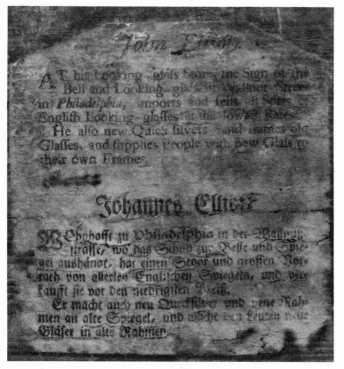

397

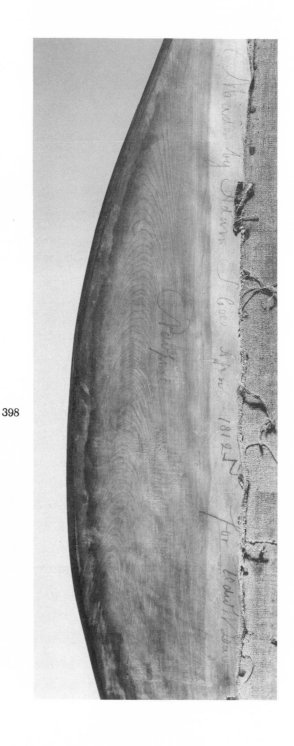

398

399

400

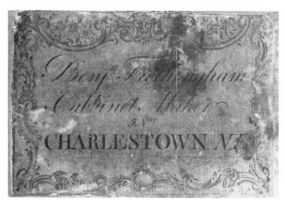

401

NOTES TO THE COLOR PLATES

II. (a) Described and illustrated in color, Plate XII, *Oriental Rugs and Carpets,* Arthur Urbane Dilley. New York: Charles Scribner's Sons, 1931.
(b) Bowen, Catherine Drinker, *John Adams and the American Revolution.* Boston: Little, Brown and Company, 1950.

III. Beverly, Robert, *History and Present State of Virginia.* London, 1705.

IV. (a) Walpole, Horace, *Anecdotes of Painting.* London: Bohn, 1849.
(b) Described and illustrated in color, Plate XIII, Dilley, *op. cit.*

V. Kimball, Fiske, "The Sources of the 'Philadelphia Chippendale,'" *Pennsylvania Museum Bulletin,* June, 1926.

NOTES TO THE ILLUSTRATIONS

1. Swan, Mabel M., "The Goddard and Townsend Joiners," *The Magazine Antiques,* April and May, 1946.

2. Downs, Joseph, and Ralston, Ruth, *New York State Furniture.* The Metropolitan Museum of Art, 1934. Illustrated, No. 76.

11. Bridenbaugh, Carl, *The Colonial Craftsman.* New York: New York University Press, 1950, p. 79. The cabriole leg is stated to have appeared in 1742.

18. In the collection of the Redwood Library, Newport, Rhode Island.

48. Hornor, W. M., Jr., *Blue Book Philadelphia Furniture.* Philadelphia, 1935. Plate 223.

50. See No. 89 in *Eighteenth-Century American Arts. The M. and M. Karolik Collection,* Edwin J. Hipkiss. Boston: Harvard University Press, 1941.

53. See Nos. 110 and 118 in *Baltimore Furniture,* The Baltimore Museum of Art, 1947.

55. Illustrated p. 58, *The Beck Family Genealogy.* Boston, 1900.
Also Figure 78, *The Colonial Furniture of New England,* Irving W. Lyon. Boston and New York: Houghton Mifflin and Company, 1891.

57. Hornor, *op. cit.,* p. 184.

58. Swan, Mabel M., "Joseph Short, Newburyport," *The Magazine Antiques,* April, 1945.

90. Illustrated Figure 11, *A Picture Book of Philadelphia Chippendale Furniture,* The Pennsylvania Museum of Art, 1931.

100. Sack, Albert, *Fine Points of Furniture.* New York: Crown Publishers, Inc., 1950.

102. Illustrated in *The Bulletin of the Metropolitan Museum of Art,* November, 1948, p. 82.

106. Illustrated in *The Bulletin of the Metropolitan Museum of Art,* March, 1935, p. 63.

121. Original drawings in the Collection of Ginsburg and Levy, New York.

134. Hornor, *op. cit.*, Plate 272.

138. Woodhouse, Samuel W., Jr., "Benjamin Randolph of Philadelphia," *The Magazine Antiques*, May, 1927.

153. Swan, Mabel M., "Joseph Short, Newburyport," *The Magazine Antiques*, April, 1945.

158. Lyon, Irving W., *The Colonial Furniture of New England*. Boston and New York: Houghton Mifflin and Company, 1891, p. 171.

159. *The New York Historical Society Quarterly*, Vol. XXXV, No. 4, October, 1951.

163. Hornor, *op. cit.*, Plate 262.

167. See p. 211, *The Magazine Antiques*, March, 1930, a block-front chest of drawers made by Benjamin Frothingham.

178. *A Picture Book of Philadelphia Chippendale Furniture*, Pennsylvania Museum of Art, 1931, Figure 8.

181. Manuscript records, The Connecticut State Library, Hartford, Connecticut.

188. Fraser, Esther Stevens, "A Pedigreed Lacquered Highboy," *The Magazine Antiques*, May, 1929.

189. Hawthorne, Nathaniel, *Mosses from an Old Manse*. New York: Wiley and Putnam, 1846.

191. Downs, Joseph, "The Furniture of Goddard and Townsend," *The Magazine Antiques*, December, 1947.

193. "The Dunlap Dilemma. Notes on Some New Hampshire Cabinetmakers," by the Editor, *The Magazine Antiques*, December, 1944.

202. George Richardson Manuscripts. Records of the Newport Historical Society, Newport, Rhode Island.

203. Palmer, Brooks, *The Book of American Clocks*. New York: The Macmillan Company, 1950, p. 256.

213. Rose, Jennie Haskell, "Thomas Elfe, Cabinetmaker. His Account Book 1768 to 1775," *The Magazine Antiques*, April, 1934.

219. See No. 38 in *Eighteenth-Century American Arts. The M. and M. Karolik Collection*, Edwin J. Hipkiss. Boston: Harvard University Press, 1941.

223. Hornor, *op. cit.*, pp. 76-77.

225. Illustrated in Figure 101, *Furniture of the Olden Time*, Frances Clary Morse. New York: The Macmillan Company, 1926.

259. Bigelow, John (Comp.), *The Complete Works of Benjamin Franklin*. New York: G. P. Putnam's Sons, The Knickerbocker Press, 1887, Vol. IV, p. 20.

273. Hornor, *op. cit.*, Plate 231.

276. Records of the Newport Historical Society, Newport, Rhode Island.

281. Hornor, *op. cit.*, Plate 441.

294. *Ibid.*, Plate 51.

301. No. 52, *Old and New England,* Catalogue of American Paintings in the Museum of Art of the Rhode Island School of Design, Providence, 1945.

302. Swan, Mabel M., "The Goddard and Townsend Joiners," *The Magazine Antiques,* April, 1946.

303. Bridenbaugh, *op. cit.*

305. Downs, Joseph, *American Chippendale Furniture. A Picture Book.* New York: Metropolitan Museum of Art, 1949, Figure 26.

313. Williams, Carl M., "Adam Hains of Philadelphia," *The Magazine Antiques,* May, 1947.

314. *Ibid.*

315. Formerly on loan in the Museum of the City of New York. Collection of Mrs. Henry Wilmerding Payne.

316. Hornor, *op. cit.,* Plates 298 and 299.

325. Sack, *op. cit.,* p. 193. One other known example illustrated.

328. Nos. 157 and 164 in *Three Centuries of Connecticut Furniture.* An Exhibition at the Morgan Memorial, Hartford, 1935.

333. Downs, Joseph, *American Chippendale Furniture. A Picture Book.* New York: The Metropolitan Museum of Art, 1949, Figure 4.

349. Nos. 417 and 418. *A Catalogue of the Collection of the Late Philip Flayderman.* New York: American Art Association, Anderson Galleries, Inc., 1930.

353. Illustrated in Figure 2, *Mount Pleasant, Fairmount Park, Philadelphia,* a Handbook. Philadelphia: The Pennsylvania Museum, 1927.

359. Hornor, *op. cit.,* Plate 209.

361. "Account Book of Thomas Elfe," published in the *South Carolina Historical and Genealogical Magazine,* Charleston, S. C.

370. Hipkiss, *op. cit.,* No. 60.

373. In the Collection of the Rhode Island School of Design, Providence.

380. Woodhouse, Samuel W., Jr., "Thomas Tufft," *The Magazine Antiques,* October, 1927.

383. See *The Dictionary of English Furniture,* Percy Macquoid and Ralph Edwards. New York: Charles Scribner's Sons, 1924, Vol. III.

386. Drepperd, Carl W., "Furniture Masterpieces by Jacob Bachman," *The American Collector,* October, 1945.

INDEX

Adams, Abigail, II
Adams, John, XIX, XXIV, II, 208, 226, 289
Adams, Lemuel, 173
Adams, Nehemiah, XXXIV
Advertisements
  back stool, 163
  bed curtains, 8
  cabinetwork, XXV, 224
  carving and cabinetmaking, 377
  deception bed, 10
  furniture, 30
  hair mattresses, 3
  imported fabrics, X
  japanned work, 187, 244
  lumber, XXV
  looking glasses, frames, repairs, 244, 255, 259, 264, 266
  looking glass store, 266
  runaway apprentice, XVIII, 35, 49
  stamped linen, 17
  tea table columns, 376
  upholstering, 5, 42, 73, 75, 274
Aesop's fables, 184
Affleck, Thomas, XXIV, 57, 163, 316, 353
Alexander, Mrs. James, XXIII, 358, 363
Allen, Priscilla, III
Anderson, John, XXV
Annapolis, Md., XXV
Apprentice system, XVII, XVIII
Artists
  André, Major John, 159
  Badger, Joseph, 271
  Copley, (John Singleton), V, 84, 162, 164, 275
  Durand, John, VII
  Earl, (Ralph), 164
  Greenwood, (John), 13, 19
  Hayman, (Francis), 164
  Hogarth, (William), XVII
  Johnston, William, X
  King, Samuel, 18
  Kühn, (Justus Englehart), 13
  Peale, Charles Willson, III, VII, 138
  Pine, Robert Edge, III
  Polk, Charles Peale, III
  Pratt, Matthew, 163
  Smibert, (John), XIV, 13, 19
  Smibert, Nathaniel, VIII
  Stuart, Gilbert, 301
  Sully, Thomas, 54
  Van Dyck, (Sir Anthony), II
  Verelst, (I.), XIX
  Verstille, William, X
  Williams, William, VIII
  Wollaston, John, II
  Wright, Joseph, 338
  Zoffany, (John), 164
Ash, Gilbert, XXIII, XXXII, 2, 105, 149, 319, 337, 374

Bachman, Jacob, XXXVIII, 386
Bachman, John, XXXVIII
Bacstowylls, 98
Bagnall, Samuel, XXIV

Baltimore, Md., XXV; (see also *regional characteristics*)
Barnard, Abner, XX
Barter by cabinetmakers, 302
Barton, Robert, 30
Bassett, Frederick, 34
Bathing facilities, 277
Beds, Queen Anne, 1; Chippendale, 2-10
  bed furniture, or hangings, XXIX, VIII, IX, X, 1-9; (see also *upholstery and textiles*)
  concealed, 10
  deception, 10
  hair mattresses for, 3
  high-post, 1-4, 6-9
  low-post, 5
  press, 10
  tall-post, 1-4, 6-9
Beman, Ebenezer, 181
Beman, Reuben, Jr., XXII, 181, 393
"Beuro," 228
Blott, John, XXVIII, 261
Boelen, Henricus, I
Bookcase, Chippendale, 223; (see also *desk and bookcase*)
Boston, Mass., XVIII, XIX; (see also *regional characteristics*)
Boudinot, Elias, V, 145
Bowdoin, James, 225
Brass, snuffer stand, standish, IX
Brincklé, Anna, (quoted) VI
Buckland, William, XV
Bulfinch, Charles, 173
Bulkley, Thomas, 173
Burgoyne, Major General John, 225
Burling, Edward, 161
Burling, Thomas, XXIII, 161, 174, 218
Burnap, Daniel, 209
Burnham, Benjamin, XXII, 55, 172, 327
"Buro," 219
Burr, Aaron, 277

Cabinetmakers
  Charleston, S. C., XXVII, XXVIII,
  Connecticut, XXII, X
  Maryland, XXV
  Massachusetts, XX
  New Hampshire, XXI
  Newport, R. I., XX, XXI
  New York, XXIII
  Philadelphia, Pa., XXIV
Cabinetmaking, schools of, XXX
Caldwell, John, XXXVIII
Cambridge, Mass., XIX
Candleslides, see *lighting*
Candlestands, see *stands*
Carne, Adam, XXVII
Carpets
  Asia Minor, I, IX
  English Wilton, VIII
  Feraghan, III, VI
  Ispahan, II
  Kuba, V
  Persian vase, IV
  Turkish, VII
  Ushak, IX, X

Chairs, Queen Anne, 11-32, 59-66, 71-80, 95-120; Chippendale, 33-58, 67-70, 81-94, 121-164
  armchairs, 11-58
  back stools, 98, 161-164
  "barber's," 67
  cane, 11, 12
  Chester County, 37
  commode form on, 13, 34, 36, 38, 41, 42, 44, 48, 49, 61, 65, 67, 70
  corner, XXIX, 59-70
  "drunkards'," 93
  easy, XXIX, 71-94
  elbow, XXIX
  folding, 93
  French, XXIX, 163
  ladder-back, 48
  lady's, 20, 22, 98, 159, 160
  pretzel-back, 48
  roundabout, XXIX, 67
  rush-bottom, 24, 25, 31, 32, 33, 59, 99, 109
  "sample," XXIV, V, 45, 90, 94, 129, 138, 345, 347
  side, 95-164
  slat-back, 48
  sleeping, 93
  slipper, 22, 95, 97, 98, 120, 159, 160
  stool back, 164
  tête-à-tête, 63
  "Washington," 53
  Washington, Martha, 19, 20, 58
  wing, XXIX; (see *easy chair*)
  writing, 67
Chapin, Aaron, XXII, 157, 158, 170, 181, 217, 230
Chapin, Eliphalet (Eliphelet), XXII, XXXII, 158, 170, 181, 230
Chapin, Laertes, XXII
Charleston, S. C., XXVI, XXVII, XLII; (see also *regional characteristics*)
Charlestown, Mass., 349
Cheney, Benjamin, XXII
Cheney, Benjamin, Jr., XXII
Cheney, Timothy, XXII
Chests, Queen Anne, 186-192, 200, 201; Chippendale, 165-185, 193-199
  block-front, 167-172, 175, 176, 183, 189
  bombé, 165, 166
  chest of drawers, 165-178
  chest-on-chest, XXIX; (see also *double chest*)
  double chest, XXIX, 179-185
  half, XXIX
  highboy, XXIX; (see also *high chest of drawers*)
  high chest of drawers, XXIX, 186-199
  kneehole chest of drawers, 175
  low chest of drawers, see *dressing table*
  Pompadour highboy, 184, 333
  serpentine, 173, 178
  simulated, 10, 219
  spice, 200, 201
  triple, XXIX

Chew, Chief Justice, xxiv
China, see *pottery and porcelain*
Chippendale furniture
  beds, 2-10
  bookcase, 223
  chairs, 33-58, 67-70, 81-94, 121-164
  chests, 165-185, 193-199
  clocks, 204-209
  desks, 217-222
  desk and bookcases, 224-233
  fire screens, 236-241
  looking glasses, 254-268
  settees, 270, 271
  sofas, 272-276
  stands, 277, 278, 281-290
  stools, 295-298
  tables, 305-316, 329-334, 338-349, 356-363, 370-388
Chippendale style
  source of, xvii
  end of in colonies, xviii
Claggett, William, 202
Clay, Daniel, xx
Claypoole, George, 332
Claypoole, James, xxiv
Claypoole, Josiah, xxvii
Clement, Moses, xxiii
Clocks, tall, Queen Anne, 202, 203; Chippendale, 204-209
  block-front, 202, 205
  English works in, 206
  grandfather, xxix, 208
  imported faces on, 207
  long case, xxiii
Clouston, R. S., (quoted) 282
Coe, Adam S., xxi, 276, 398
Cogswell, John, xxi, xxx, 169, 217, 227, 228
Cogswell, John, Jr., 228
Collections
  Barrett, R. R., 53
  Beck, Frederick, 55
  Blair, Mrs. J. Insley, 102, 186
  Bolles, (Eugene), 156, 179, 225
  Brooklyn Museum, 34
  Burnett, Mrs. Henry W., 183
  Cadwalader, (General John), 87, 131, 138, 204, 259, 345
  Carter, Gale, 179
  Cooke, Col. John, 288
  Curran, Charles A., 138, 281, 359, 380
  Fish, Mrs. Frederick S., 16, 57
  Flayderman, Philip, 58, 149, 169, 288, 363, 373
  Franklin, C. Ray, 55, 383
  Garvan, (Francis P.), 45, 129, 142, 149, 197
  Goodwin, William B., 102
  Graves, (George Coe), 270
  Green, Norvin H., 56
  Griffiths, Percival D., 347
  Harvey, Richard Wister, 177
  Independence Hall, 86, 273, 345
  Kane, Mrs. DeLancey, 137
  Karolik, (M. and M.), 50, 133
  Laurence, Hannah P., 39
  Lewis, Reginald W., 170
  Lockwood, Luke Vincent, 315
  Long, Breckinridge, 53
  Metropolitan Museum of Art, xxxix, 17, 102, 106, 129, 148, 156, 157, 178, 184, 186, 236, 237, 260, 270
  Museum of Fine Arts, Boston, 232

Myers, Louis G., 60, 260
Newport Historical Society, 191
Newport (R. I.) Library, 191
Palmer, George S., 63, 227
Parsons, Ella, 86
Pendleton, (Charles Leonard), 385
Philadelphia Museum of Art, 90, 177, 178
Reifsnyder, Howard, 41, 47, 94, 116, 119, 128, 195, 255, 314, 343, 357
Rhode Island School of Design, 183, 385
Rockefeller, (John D.), 129
Taradash, Mitchel, 139
Tiffany, 129
Van Cortlandt Museum, 120
Van Rensselear, Peyton, 52
Webb, Misses Anne R. and Caroline, 150
Weir, Robert, 354
Wellington, Arthur W., 325
White, Mrs. Miles, Jr., 53
Whitwell, Frederick, 350
Yale University, 34, 45, 171, 197
Colton, Elihu, 209
Commode
  forms on chairs, see *chairs*
  pewter, 34
Compagnée des Indes, X
Concord, Mass., xx
Connecticut, xxi; (see also *regional characteristics*)
Connell, William, 207, 391
Copeland, H., 259, 265
Cotton, John, (quoted) xviii
Couches, Queen Anne, xxix, 210-212
  chaise longue, 211
  daybed, 210-212
Covenhoven, John, xxiii
Crewelwork, 1, 2, 3, 9, 27, 29, 67, 73, 74, 101, 102, 116, 117, 118, 150, 152, 157, 212, 238, 241, 292; picture, III
Crips, John, xxvii
Crips, William, xxvii
Cushing, Thomas, X

Davis, Caleb, 227, 228
Deerfield, Mass., xix
DeGroot, Jacob, xxiii
Design books
  Anonymous, *Instructions in the Art of Japanning with the True India Varnish*, 187
  Chippendale, (Thomas), *The Gentleman and Cabinet-maker's Director*, xxiv, xxix, xxxiii, xxxiv, VI, 8, 41, 42, 44, 54, 55, 57, 131, 134, 135, 137, 139-142, 146, 163, 195, 238, 278, 312, 315, 316, 356-358, 363
  Edwards, (George), and Darly, (Mathias), *A New Book of Chinese Designs*, 187
  Gibbs, James, *A Book of Architecture Containing Designs of Buildings and Ornament*, 256
  Hepplewhite, A., *The Cabinet Maker and Upholsterers' Guide*, 8, 93, 164, 312, 314, 346
  Ince, (William), and Mayhew, (Thomas), *The Universal System of Household Furniture*, xxx, 163, 164

Johnson, Thomas, *One Hundred & Fifty New Designs, etc.*, xxx, IV, 265, 281, 282
———, *Twelve Gerandoles*, 281
Lock, (Mathias), and Copeland, (H.), *A New Book of Ornaments*, 259, 265
Manwaring, Robert, *The Cabinet and Chair Maker's Real Friend and Companion*, xxx, 46, 98, 141, 148
Salmon, William, *Polygraphice*, xxx, 187
Shearer, (Thomas), *Designs for Household Furniture*, 346
Sheraton, (Thomas), *The Cabinetmaker and Upholsterers' Drawing Book*, 346
Stalker, John, *A Treatise of Japanning and Varnishing*, 187, 246
Swan, Abraham, *Designs in Architecture*, xxx, V, VI
Vardy, John, *Selection from the Works of Mr. Inigo Jones and Mr. William Kent*, 258
Ware, Isaac, *A Complete Body of Architecture*, xxx, 256
Desk and bookcases, Chippendale, 224-233
  block-front, 225, 226, 232
  bombé, 227, 228
  name, xxix
Desks, Queen Anne, 213-216; Chippendale, 217-222
  block-front, 219
  fall-front, 219
  reverse-serpentine, 217
  scrutoir, xxix, 215
  simulating chest of drawers, 219
Dickinson, John, xxviii, 137, 177, 273
Downman, Rawleigh, VII
Drummond, James, xxviii
Duffield, Edward, xxiv, 204
Dunlap, Samuel, II, xxi, xxxi, 193
Dunlaps' work, 157, 193
du Pont, Admiral Samuel F., VI
Duyckinck, Evert, 244
Duyckinck, Gerardus, 244
Duyckinck, Gerrit, 244

East Windsor, Conn., xxii
Edge, Walter, xxi
Elfe, Thomas, xxvii, 213, 287, 361
  account book of, xxvii, xxviii, xlii
Elliott, John, III, 122, 254, 255, 264, 266, 294, 323, 331, 395, 397
Elliott, John, Jr., xxiv, xxxii, 266
Emerson, Ralph Waldo, 189
Evelyn, John, quotations from *Sylva*, xxxvii, xl
Exports
  British Customs reports on, xxxiv, xxxv
  types of consignments, xxxv
  wood, xxxvii, xl

Ferguson, Daniel, xxiv
Firebacks, III, VIII
Fire screens, Queen Anne, 234, 235; Chippendale, 236-241
  cheval, xxix, 234
  combined with candlestand, 235, 240
  folding, 234
  pole, xxix, 234

Fisher, John, xxvii
Fithian, Philip Vickers, (quoted) xxv, xxvi
Fleeson, Plunket, 75, 261
Flower Garden Display'd, The, (quoted) I
Flowerpots, VII
Folwell, John, xxiv, 223
Fowler, Richard, 163
Franklin, Benjamin, xxv, VII, 204, 208, 259, 350, 378
Franklin, B., and Hall, D., V
Freemen, xxiii
Freyers, John, 34
Frothingham, Benjamin, xx, xxx, 167, 169, 217, 349, 401
Furber, Robert, (quoted) II, V
Furniture, eighteenth-century contrasted with English, xviii
  qualities of, xviii
  terminology of, xxix

Gaines, George, xxi,
Gaines, John, xxi, 100
Galatian, Peter, xxiii
Games, 347
Garniture
  armorial mantel, VII
  Holland Delft, IX
Gautier, Daniel, 351
Gillingham, James, xxiv, VI, 41, 139
Girandole, xxix; (see also *looking glass*)
Gleaves, Thomas, xxiii
Goddard, John, xxi, 183, 191, 307, 348, 372, 373
Goddard, Stephen, 285
Goddard, Thomas, 285
Goddard, Townsend, 232, 285
Gostelowe, Jonathan, xxiv, 178, 185, 218, 323, 332
Gouverneur, Samuel and Experience, II
Gratz, Rebecca, 198
Greenfield, Mass., xx
Greenwood, Isaac, X
Guilford, Conn., xii

Hagerstown, Md., xx
Haines, Ephraim, xxiv, 48
Haines, Reuben, 312
Hains, Adam, xxiv, 313, 314, 346, 400
Hancock, John, xix, xx, VIII, 1, 226
Harland, Thomas, 209
Harrison, Peter, xx
Hartford, Conn., xxii; (see also *regional characteristics*)
Hatchment, VIII
Haugan, John, wife of, 17
Hawthorne, Nathaniel, 189
Hazard, Simeon, 276
Hewes, Thomas, 91
Hibbard, Joseph, xli, 78, 200
Highboy, xxix; (see *high chest of drawers*)
Hiller, Benjamin, VII
Holmes, (O. W.), (quoted) 215
Hopkins, Gerrard, xx, 199
Hoskins, Bartholomew, X
Hosmer, Joseph, xx, 169, 189
Houses and other colonial buildings
  Badminton, xvii
  Belle Isle, VII
  Blenheim, xvii
  Bohemia, xxv
  Brice, xxv
  Carters' Grove, xxv

Castle Howard, xvii
Cedar Grove, xxix
Cherry Hill, xxiii
Cliveden (Chew Mansion), xxiv, 163, 178
Cloverfields, xxv
Craigie-Longfellow, 165
Drayton Hall, xxvii
Fancy Hill, IX
Fort Crailo, xxiii
Governor's Palace (Williamsburg), xxv
Graeme Park, xxiv
Hammond-Harwood, xxv
Hampton Court, IX
Hasbrouck, xxxix
Houghton Hall, xvii
Johnson Hall, 149
Knole, 98
Lansdowne, xxiv, xxxv, 57
Lee Hall, xxv
Longfellow, Henry Wadsworth, xix
Lower Brandon, xxv
Manor House, xxiv
Marmion, 353
Mount Airy, xxvi
Mount Pleasant, xxvi, IV, IX, 57
Mount Vernon, xxv
Nomini Hall, xxv
Old State House (Newport), xx
Pastures, xxiii
Patuxent Manor, III
Port Royal, VIII
Powel House, 184
Readbourne, xxv, II
Redwood Library (Newport), xx
Saint James' Church, xxvii
Scott, Winfield, IX
Shirley, xxv
Sotterly, xxv
Springfield, VII
Stamper-Blackwell, xxiv, VI, IX
Stenton, xxiv, III, 85, 97, 137, 177, 222, 269, 294, 359
Stratford, xxv
Strawberry Hill, xvii
Synagogue (Newport), xx
Taylor, Zachary, 193
Trinity Church (Newport), xx
Upper Brandon, xxv
Vernon House, xx
Verplanck Mansion, 179, 354
Walnut Grove, 195
Warner, Jonathan, 182
Westover, xxv
Woodford, IX
Wye, VII
Hurd, Jacob, II
Hurd, Nathaniel, xx, 225, 349

Imports
  augmenting native arts, VII
  by way of Europe, IV, X
  English furniture, xxxv, xxxvi,
  see also *carpets, pottery and porcelain, upholstery and textiles*
Influences on colonial furniture
  English, xxx, VII, 18, 30, 46, 55, 69, 179, 226, 359, 383
  European, I
  French, IX
  migration, xxxiii
  prosperity, xix
  racial differences, xxx, xxxiii

spices, 200
style books xxx, xxxii; (see also *design books*)
tea and tea drinking, 200, 288, 289
see *imports, trade*
Inscriptions on furniture
  Beman, Reuben, Jr., 181, 393
  Brinley, Edward, 227
  Burnap, Daniel, 209
  Coe, Adam S., 276, 398
  Colton, Elihu, 209
  Duffield, Edward, 204
  Greene, A. H., 348
  Hains, A., 400
  Heale, John, Esq., 27
  Hill, I., 353
  Hunt, Samuel, 284
  Hurd, Nathaniel, 225
  Laurence, Elisha, 203
  Linton, John, 273
  Pearson, Isaac, 203
  Quincy, Josiah, 226
  Savery, William, 39
  Schumachers, 112
  Sparhawk, Col. Nathaniel, 243
  True, Daniel W., 214
  Wady, James, 202
  Wagstaffe, Thomas, 206, 207
  Wentworth, Elizabeth, 64
  Williams, David, 205
  Woodruff, Mary A., 327

James, Edward, 207
Japanned work, 187, 188, 244, 246, 247
  early methods, 187, 247
Jefferson, Thomas, xxii, 93, 178, 208
Johnson, Thomas, English engraved designs of, 265, 281, 282
Johnston (Johnson), Thomas, Boston japanner, xx, 187, 188, 207, 368
Johnston, Thomas, Jr., xx
Jones, John Paul, xxi

Kalm, Peter, 229, 233
Kas, I
Kingston, Joseph, I
Kneeland, Samuel, 173
Kneeland and Adams, xxii, 173, 392
Knight, Madam, (*Journal* quoted) 299

Labels
  Connell, William, 391
  Elliott, John, 254, 255, 264, 266, 395, 397
  Frothingham, Benjamin, 349, 401
  Kneeland and Adams, 173, 392
  Reynolds, James and Henry, 396
  Reynolds, James and sons, 264
  Savery, William, 389
  Townsend, John, 311, 399
  Tufft, Thomas, 134, 390
  White, Joseph, 267, 394
Lacquer, 187, 188
Lancret, Nicolas, V
Langley, Batty, xxx
Lawton, Edward W., 276
Ledell, Joseph, I
Lehman, Benjamin, *Catalogue of Cabinetware,* xxxvii
Letelier, John, V
Leverett, Knight, II
Lighting
  brass fixtures, VII

Lighting (Continued)
  candelabra, Chelsea porcelain, V
  candle slides, 225, 226, 324, 351
  candlesticks, Dutch, I
  chandeliers, cut-glass, V; English cut-
    glass, VI; English delft, I; Irish sil-
    ver, II; wood and gilded tin, III
  inset candlestick sockets, 337-341,
    347, 349
  quillwork sconces, silver candle
    branches, II
  standing lights, III
  wall arms, English brass, III
  wall branches, IV, VI
Linton, John, XXVIII, 273, 274
Logan, George, 359
Logan, James, 85, 97, 137, 222, 269,
  359
Looking glasses, Queen Anne, 242-253;
    Chippendale, 254-268
  chimney, 251
  girandole, XXIX
  mantel-tree, 251
  methods of making, 253
  mirror, XXIX
  pier glass, 252
  sconces, XXIX, II, IV
Lord, John, VII
Loring, Captain, I
Lowboy, XXIX; (see also dressing table)
Luyten, William, XXVIII

Macintire, Robert, XVIII
Mack, Elisha, X
Macphaedris, Archibald, XIX
Magrath, Richard, XXVIII
Marble
  fireplace frame, VIII
  imported, 353, 359
  kettle stand tops, 289
  table tops, IV, VI, 350, 351, 353-363
Marblehead, Mass., XIX
Marot, Daniel, III
Martin, William, 10, 42
Maryland, XXV; (see also regional char-
    acteristics)
Mason, John, 3
Mason, Captain John, XXI
Massachusetts, XVIII- XX, XXX, XXXI; (see
    also regional characteristics)
Mattresses, 3
Mayhew, Jonathan, IX
McGee, Samuel, XXIII
Medford, Mass., XX
Meschianza Ball, V, 195
Mezzotints
  Belcher, Jonathan, I
  Mather, Cotton, I
  Pitt, William, VII
  Prince, Thomas, I
  Whitefield, George, I
Mickle, Samuel, 121
Middletown, Conn., XXII
Mirror, XXIX; (see looking glasses)
Montieth, V
Moore, Robert, XXV, 53
Moore, Thomas, XXV
Moore, William, XXV
Morris, Lewis, 39
Morris, Robert, XXX, 143
Morris, Samuel, XXXV
Munday, Richard, XX
Myers, Myer, I

Newburyport, Mass., XX
New Hampshire, XXI. XXX; (see also re-
    gional characteristics)
Newport, R. I., XX, XXXI; (see also re-
    gional characteristics)
Newspapers, X
New York, XXII, XXXI, XXXII; (see also
    regional characteristics)
Northampton, Mass., XX
Norwich, Conn., XXII

Original owners of furniture
  Alexander, Mrs. James, XXIII
  Anderese, Nicholas, XXI
  Barroll family, 324
  Beekman, Dr. William, 106, 108
  Berrien, Judge John, 338
  Biddle family, 94
  Bleecker, Jon Johannes, 246
  Bleecker family, II
  Boudinot, Elias, 145
  Bowen, Jabez, XXI, 191, 348, 373
  Bowie, Governor, 37, 53
  Bromfield-Phillips family, 265
  Brown, Joseph, XXI, 183
  Cadwalader family, V
  Champion, Epaphroditus, IV
  Curtis family, 188
  Davenport family, 58
  Dawes, Col. Thomas, 182
  Derby, Elias Hasket, VI, 228
  Derby, Richard, 6
  Dickinson, John, XXVIII, 137, 177, 273
  Eddy family, 212
  Edwards, Elizabeth and Thomas, 130
  Emerson, Phoebe and William, 189
  Everson, Jacob, 263
  Faneuil, Peter, XXXI, 179
  Gratz family, 134, 198, 343
  Halsey, Col. Jeremiah, 230
  Halstead family, 374
  Hancock, John, XX, 1
  Hancock, Thomas, 1
  Harsen, Jacob, 52
  Hewlett family, 224
  Hicks, Whitehead, 52, 382
  Howe-Steel family, 177, 184
  Hunt, Samuel, 284
  James family, 17
  Johnson, Sir William, 149, 374
  Key, John Ross, 53
  Lambert family, 128
  Latourette family, 28
  Laurence, Elisha, 203
  Lawton, Edward W., 276
  Lewis family, 83
  Livingston, Robert and Margaret
    Beekman, 305
  Livingston-Parson family, 70
  Logan, James, 269
  Logan family, 134
  Loring, Commodore Joshua, 188
  Loring family, 148
  Luyster family, 245
  Norris, Charles, 122, 294, 323, 359
  Noyes family, 202
  Penn, Gov. John, 57, 163, 223, 271,
    272
  Pennsylvania Hospital, 353
  Post family, 218
  Prevoost family, 270
  Quincy, Josiah, 226, 265
  Quincy family, IV

Redwood, Mrs. Abraham, 191
Schuyler, Peter, 242
Scotton family, XXXIII
Shippen, Edward, 254, 255
Silsbee, Nathaniel, 154
Slocum family, 175
Smith, Robert and Abigail Griffiths, 29
Smith, Parson William, II
Sparhawk, Col. Nathaniel, 243
State Capitol at Hartford, 173
Ten Eyck, Hermanus, 149
Ten Eyck, Jacob, 247
Thomas-Wallace family, V
Tibbits family, 17
Trowlett, Michael, 188
True, Daniel W., 214
Turner, William and Mary, 195
United States Supreme Court Cham-
  ber (Philadelphia), 316
University of Pennsylvania, 208
Updyke family, 232
Van Alen, Mrs. John E., 256
Van Cortlandt, Stephanus, 26, 105,
  106, 305, 354
Van Cortlandt family, I
Van Pelt family, 194, 195, 333
Van Rensselaer, Mrs. Killian K., 267
Van Rensselaer family, 145
Verplanck, Judith and Samuel, 147
Ward, Samuel, XXI
Washington, George, 86, 273
Waters family, 225
Webb, Gen. Samuel Blachley, 150
Webb family, 70
Wentworth, Elizabeth, 64
Whittemore family, 4
Willard, Joseph, 159
Wister family, 178
Wright family, 65, 146
Original owners of houses
  Ashley, Rev. Jonathan, XIX
  Beekman, William, XXIII
  Bertrand, William, VII
  Bingham, William, XXIV
  Blackwell, Rev. (Robert), V
  Brewton, Miles, XXVII
  Byrd family, XXV
  Carter, Col. Robert, XXV
  Coleman, William, IX
  dePeyster, Abraham, XXIII
  Drayton, William, XXVII
  Grahame, Charles, III
  Hancock, Thomas, XIX
  Heyward, Thomas, XXVII
  Hollyday, Col. James, II
  Hooper, "King," XIX
  Howell, Samuel Ladd, IX
  Hutchinson, Governor Thomas, XIX
  Keith, Governor, XXIV
  Lee, Jeremiah, XIX
  Lee family, XXV
  Logan, James, XXIV
  Macphaedris, Archibald, XIX
  Macpherson, John, XXIV
  Nichols, Deputy Governor, XX
  Paschall family, XXIX
  Peirce, Jerathmeel, XIX
  Penn, Governor John, XXIV, XXXV
  Pepperell, Sir William, XIX
  Powel, Samuel, XXIV
  Ritchie family, X
  Roosevelt, Nicholas, XXIII
  Royall, Isaac, XX

Original owners of houses (Continued)
  Schuyler family, xxiii
  Sheldon family, xix
  Stamper, John, V
  Stiles, Edward, IV
  Tayloe, Col. John, xxvi
  Tryon, Governor, xxii
  Van Rensselaer family, xxiii
  Vassall, Henry, xix
  Verplanck, Samuel, xxiii
  Walton, William, xxiii
  Wentworth, Lieut. Gov. John, xix
  Williams, John, xix
Orne, Benjamin, Jr., xviii
Orrery, xxiv, 208, 223

Papier-mâché, 261
Parliament (see *Reports to Parliament*)
Partridge, Nehemiah, 187
Pearce, Abraham, xxviii
Pearson, Isaac, 203
Pelletreau, John, xxiii
Penn, Gov. John, xxiv, 10, 57, 163, 223, 271, 272
Penn, Hon. John, Jr., 10; (see *Penn, Gov. John*)
Penn, William, xxiii
Pewter, I, 34
Phelps, John, xxii
Phelps, Timothy, xxii
Phelps, Timothy, Jr., xxii
Philadelphia, xxiii, xxix, xxxii; (see also *regional characteristics*)
Pictures, see *crewelwork, mezzotints, portraits*
Pimm, John, xx, 188
Plumstead, Charles, xxxvi
Porcelain
  burnt image china, V
  Chelsea, V
  Chinese, V, VI; famille rose, IV; Ming, IV
  Worcester, transfer-printed, IX
Portraits at Winterthur
  Bennett, Richard Lloyd, III
  Brickerhoff, Catherine Herring, VIII
  Copley, self-portrait, V
  du Pont, Anne de Montchanin, III
  du Pont, Samuel, III
  du Pont de Nemours, Pierre Samuel, III
  Farmar, Hannah, VII
  Orne, Catherine Sewell, X
  Peck, Hannah Farmar, VII
  Stewart, General Walter, III
  Verstille, William, X
  Washington, General George, III
Portsmouth, N. H., xix, xxi; (see also *regional characteristics*)
Pottery
  Dutch delft, IX
  English delft, Brislington, III; Bristol, I, III; Lambeth, III; Wincanton, I
  enameled salt glaze, II
  Jackfield, VIII
Powel, Samuel, xxiv, xxxv
Pownall, Thomas, 226
Prince, Samuel, xxiii, 174, 218, 224

Queen Anne furniture
  beds, 1
  chairs, 11-32, 59-66, 71-80, 95-120
  chests, 186-192, 200, 201

clocks, 202, 203
couches, 210-212
fire screens, 234, 235
looking glasses, 242-253
sofa, 269
stands, 279, 280
stools, 291-294
tables, 299-304, 317-320, 335-337, 350-355, 364-369
Quillwork, II
Quincy, Josiah, 226
Quincy, Josiah, Jr., xxvi, xxvii, 226, 265

Randle, William, 187
Randolph, Benjamin, xxi, xxx, V, VI, 45, 49, 50, 122, 129, 133, 138, 142, 143, 236
receipt book of, xxiv, xli
Rea, Daniel, xx
Read, George, II
Read, Ruth, II
Redwood, Abraham, 18
Regional characteristics of furniture
  Baltimore, 53, 54, 144
  Boston, xxx, 52, 82, 84, 151, 155, 167, 227, 228, 239, 247, 370, 385
  Charleston, xxxiii, xxxvii, xlii, 287, 361
  Connecticut, xxxi, xxxii, xxxviii, X, 2, 7, 11, 12, 21, 22, 96, 102, 170-172, 179, 180, 182, 183, 217, 230, 231, 328, 387
  Dutch, xxxi, 24, 26
  Hartford, 218
  Hudson Valley, xxxix, 99
  Manhattan, 17, 145, 148, 218, 295, 339
  Maryland, xxxii, 51, 123, 199
  Massachusetts, xxx, xxxi, xxxviii, X, 21, 46, 56, 89, 103, 145, 151, 152, 154, 155, 156, 168, 176, 180, 182, 189, 217, 239, 284, 289, 304, 328, 350, 353
  Middle colonies, 309
  New England, xxx, xxxi, xxxii, xlii, 12, 24, 40, 48, 74, 80-83, 89, 110, 159, 165, 166, 169, 178, 214, 218, 229, 239, 270, 300, 308, 318, 325, 328, 342, 365
  New Hampshire, xxx, xxxviii, 193, 328
  New Jersey, xxxii, xli, 76, 323
  Newport, xxxi, xxxii, 2, 20, 21, 63, 64, 67, 79-81, 101, 103, 110, 125, 171, 172, 175, 205, 218, 285, 292, 326, 347, 348, 352, 371, 387
  New York, xxxi, xxxii, xxxviii, xl, VII, 2, 15-17, 21, 24, 40, 62, 64-69, 76, 80, 83, 89, 103, 108, 125, 145-148, 156, 174, 176, 218, 224, 241, 247, 286, 298, 318, 331, 336, 338, 340-342, 345, 347, 355, 356, 358, 363, 367, 382
  North Carolina, xxxiii, xli, xlii
  Northern states, xxxiii, 76, 82, 92, 167, 323
  Pennsylvania, xxxiii, xxxviii, xli, 66, 75, 109, 194, 199, 201
  Pennsylvania German, xxxviii, 14
  Philadelphia, xxxi, xxxii, xxxvii, xli, xlii, IV, V, 13, 15, 21, 27, 29, 30, 33, 36, 38-40, 42-51, 57, 60, 64, 76, 85, 86, 89, 90, 92, 94, 97, 113, 116, 123, 125, 129-131, 133, 135-137,

142, 145, 146, 148, 151, 153, 156, 158, 159, 174, 184, 185, 192, 194-196, 198, 208, 211, 228, 233, 236, 238, 249, 253, 254, 259, 269, 283, 286, 287, 291, 294, 320, 323, 333, 334, 342, 344-346, 356, 358-361, 375, 376, 378, 381, 382
  Portsmouth, N. H., 100
  Rhode Island, xxxviii, 171, 176, 304, 384, 387
  Salem, xxx, 4, 82, 151, 155, 239
  South Carolina, xli, xlii
  Southern colonies, xli, 192, 213, 287, 309
  Virginia, xxxiii, xli, xlii, 83, 213, 303, 317
Reports to Parliament
  on Connecticut, xxi, xxii
  on Maryland, xxxv
  on New York houses, xxiv
  on Virginia, xxxiv, xxxv
Reynolds, Henry, 264, 396
Reynolds, James, 259, 264
Reynolds, James, Jr., 264, 396
Rhoads, Mayor Samuel, xxv
Rittenhouse, David, 204, 208, 223
Roberts, Aaron, xxii, 181, 230
Roberts, B., xxvii
Rochambeau, (Count Jean), xx
Rooms at Winterthur
  bedrooms, VIII, IX, X
  dining, I
  entrance hall, IV
  sitting, II, III, V, VI, VII
Rosier, Robert, 189

Salem, Mass., xix, xx; (see also *regional characteristics*)
Sanderson, Elijah, xx
Sanderson, Jacob, 168
Savery, William, xxiv, III, 25, 33, 39, 60, 109, 323, 389
Schuyler, Col. Peter, 242
Sconces, xxix, II, IV, 242, 243, 250, 251, 261, 268
Screens
  black-and-gold lacquer, VI
  see also *fire screens*
Scrutoir, xxix, 215; (see also *desks*)
Secret drawers, 214, 215, 220, 231, 233, 338-341, 345, 384
See, Robert P., and Company, 276
Settees, Chippendale, 270, 271
Seymour, Thomas, 228
Shadow box, I
Shapes of furniture
  block-front, 167-172, 175, 176, 183, 189, 202, 205, 219, 225, 226, 232
  bombé, 165, 166, 227, 228
  reverse serpentine, 217
  serpentine, 165, 173, 178
  piecrust, 283, 287, 376-383
  oxbow, see *reverse serpentine*
Sheraton, Thomas, (quoted) xxxvi
Shoemaker, Jonathan, 121
Shoemaker, Thomas, xxiv
Short, Joseph, xx, xxx, 58, 153
Signatures
  Beman, Reuben, Jr., 393
  Coe, Adam S., 398
Silver
  Hiller, Benjamin, VII
  Hurd, Jacob, II

Silver (Continued)
  Letelier, John, V
  Leverett, Knight, II
  Myers, Myer, I
Skillin, John, xx
Skillin, Simeon, xx, 225
Skinner, George, I
Smith, Madam Elizabeth Quincy, II
Smith, Captain John, xxi
Smith, Parson William, II
Smither, I., 133
Soehnée, the Elder, X
Sofas, Queen Anne, 269; Chippendale, 272-276
  "sopha" in Independence Hall, 273
  Washington's, 86
Southern plantation houses, III
Southmayd, 102
Spar, Derbyshire, VI
Stands, Queen Anne, 279, 280; Chippendale, 277, 278, 281-290
  basin, 277, 278
  "bason," 278
  candlestands, 279-287
  piecrust shape, 283, 287
  portable washstands, 277
  wall bracket, 281, 282
  wigstands, 278
Sterling, Lord, xxiii
Stone and Alexander, xx
Stools, Queen Anne, 291-294; Chippendale, 295-298
  "ship and cabbin," 296

Tables, Queen Anne, 299-304, 317-328, 335-337, 350-355, 364-369; Chippendale, 305-316, 329-334, 338-349, 356-363, 370-388
  backgammon, xxix
  breakfast, 299-314
  chamber, 334
  china, xxix, 315, 316
  dining, 317-320
  dished top, 384
  dressing, xxix, 175, 321-334
  drinking, 351
  gaming and card, xxix, 335-349
  handkerchief, xxix
  lowboy, xxix; (see dressing table)
  mixing, 350, 351
  overhanging tops, 329, 337, 367
  Pembroke, 288, 312-314, 371
  piecrust, 283, 287, 376-383
  porringer-top, 301, 336, 352
  rectangular, early date of, 367
  revolving-top, 279, 280, 286, 287, 376-381, 385-388
  side or sideboard, xxix, 352-363
  square and round, history of, 367
  slab, xxix
  snap, xxix
  tea, 364-388
  "tea bord," 370
  tripod-base, 381
  turn-up, xxix, 299, 378, 382, 385, 387
  upright-top, 305, 306
  uses of, 300, 308, 310, 369
  with a flap, xxix
  with a fly foot, xxix
Taylor, Hyns, 8
Textiles, (see upholstery and textiles)
  manufacture of, X

Tiles
  Dutch, II, 350
  English delft, VII
  table tops, 350
  transfer-printed, Liverpool, xx
Toppan, Abner, xx, 168
Townsend, Christopher, xxi
Townsend, Edmund, xxi, 183, 219
Townsend, Job, xxi, 1, 20, 191, 202, 212
Townsend, Job, Jr., xxi, 302
Townsend, John, xxi, xxii, 55, 175, 176, 183, 205, 207, 232, 285, 288, 290, 311, 371, 373, 387, 399
Townsend-Goddard cabinetwork, xx, IX, 101, 232, 285
Trade
  basis of prosperity, xviii
  between colonies, xxxiv
  coastwise, xxxiv
  effect on American tastes, 166, 188
  products, xix, xx, xxvi, xxxiv
  through Europe, IV, X
  venture trading, xxxiv
  West Indies, xxxiv
  with Indians, xxii
Trade cards
  Burling, Thomas, xxiii
  Hurd, Nathaniel, xx
  Johnston (Johnson), Thomas, 187, 188
  Prince, Samuel, 224
  Randolph, Benjamin, 142, 143, 236
Transitional pieces of furniture, 11, 23, 31-36, 71, 72, 96, 100, 104, 115, 117-122, 126, 210, 220, 296, 329
Trotter, Benjamin, 48
Trumble, Francis, 332
Trumble, Joseph, xxiv
Trumble, William, xxiv
Trumbull, John, X
Tufft, Thomas, xxiv, 132, 134, 141, 273, 380, 390
Tutenag, IX

Upholstery and Textiles
  cotton, 46, 79, 107, 144, 147, 153, 154, 155, 212; English printed, 110, 156; French, 6, 22; quilted, 146
  leather, 13, 14, 18, 23, 26, 52, 60, 61, 68, 71, 78, 97, 103, 104, 106, 113, 114, 115, 140, 141, 163, 164, 211, 269, 294, 295
  linen, American resist-dyed, 2, 62, 108; embroidered in crewels, 1, 2, 3, 9, 152; English printed, IX, 36, 40, 159, 160; French, X, 82; linsey-woolsey, quilted, 34; resist-dyed, I, 17; toile de Jouy, 41, 134, 143
  moreen, VII, 15, 16, 66, 97; English, 19, 81, 145, 149, 297
  satin, quilted, 4
  satin lampas, French, 275
  silk, VI, 234, 293; Chinese painted, 236, 240, 298; French, V, 44, 89, 129, 135, 138, 272; Italian, 20, 90, 119
  silk brocade, English Spitalfields, 20; French, 5, 35, 45, 47, 49, 93, 98, 111, 123, 124, 125, 128, 133, 136, 139, 239, 270, 274, 291; Spanish, 76
  silk brocatelle, III; Italian, 39, 43, 70, 77, 83, 86, 105, 127, 142

silk damask, 7, 42, 151; English, 121, 122; French, 48, 50, 75, 126; Italian, 4, 21, 51, 53, 54, 57, 58, 63, 69, 84, 85, 88, 91, 92, 120, 130-132, 162, 273, 276, 296
silk lampas, French, 94, 161
taffeta silk, 8
velvet, 72; French, 64; Italian, II, 28, 38, 80, 87, 112, 271
wool, VIII, 6, 59, 95; damask, 148, 210; moquette, French, 100

Vanderspiegel, Jacobus, I
Van Gelder, Garrit, xxiii
Veneered pieces of furniture, 26, 28, 30, 106, 111, 184, 190, 224, 247-250, 252, 253, 256, 257, 262, 265, 268, 305, 363
Virginia, xxv; (see also regional characteristics)

Wady, James, 202
Wagstaffe, Thomas, IV, 206, 207
Wallpaper, Chinese painted, VI
Walpole, Horace, IV, 315
Walton, Samuel, xxiv
Warham, Charles, xxvii
Washington, George, xxvii, 338, 345, 349
Washington, Martha, 256
Watson, John F., (Annals quoted), 195, 378, 379
Weale, John, 282
Webb, Samuel Blachley, X, 150
Wenman, Richard, xxiii
Wentworth, Lieut.-Gov. John, xix
Weyman, Edward, 73
White, James, 5
White, Joseph, 267, 394
White paint, use of, 259
Willet, Marinus, xxiii
Williams, David, xxxix, 205
Williams, Samuel, 376
Williamsburg, Virginia, xxv, xxvi
Wilmerding, William, 263, 267
Winthrop, Governor John, xxviii
Wolsey, Cardinal, II
Wolz, George, xxv
Woods
  ash, xlii
  beech, xxxix, xl
  bilsted, xxxix
  birch, xxxix
  buttonwood, xl
  by-products of, xxxvii, xxxviii
  "canoewood," xxxix
  cedar, xl, xli
  cherry, xxxviii, xlii
  chestnut, xlii
  cottonwood, xxxix
  cypress, xli, xlii,
  "ghost tree," xl
  gum, xxxix
  mahogany, xxxvi, xxxvii
  maple, xxxviii
  oak, xli, xlii
  pine, xl, xli, xlii
  planewood, xl
  poplar, xxxix
  sycamore, xl
  tulipwood, xxxix, xlii
  walnut, xxxvii, xxxviii
  whitewood, xxxix
Wren, Christopher, 230